The T. E. Lawrence Puzzle

THE T·E·LAWRENCE P·U·Z·Z·L·E

EDITED BY
STEPHEN E·
TABACHNICK

THE UNIVERSITY OF
GEORGIA PRESS
ATHENS
1984

Copyright © 1984 by the University of Georgia Press
Athens, Georgia 30602
All rights reserved

Designed by Francisca Vassy
Set in 11 on 13 Goudy Old Style
Printed in the United States of America

The paper in this book meets the guidelines for permanence and
durability of the Committee on Production Guidelines for Book
Longevity of the Council on Library Resources.

Library of Congress Cataloging in Publication Data

Main entry under title:

The T. E. Lawrence puzzle.

Bibliography: p.
Includes index.
1. Lawrence, T. E. (Thomas Edward), 1888–1935—Addresses,
essays, lectures. 2. Lawrence, T. E. (Thomas Edward), 1888–
1935—Criticism and interpretation—Addresses, essays, lectures.
3. Scholars—England—Biography—Addresses, essays, lectures.
4. Soldiers—Great Britain—Biography—Addresses, essays, lectures. I. Tabachnick, Stephen Ely.

D568.4.L45T23 1983   941.083'092'4   83-1119
ISBN 0-8203-0669-x

C·O·N·T·E·N·T·S

Acknowledgments

I would take this opportunity to thank: all the contributors, association with whom became a personal, rather than a merely professional, pleasure; the editors at Georgia, particularly Iris Tillman Hill and her successor, Charles East, for encouraging this project; various colleagues here and abroad, most notably Paul Alkon and Dan Duman, for helpful suggestions; my wife, Sharona, for good advice; the reference librarians at the Ben-Gurion, Hebrew, and Tel Aviv Universities, for hard work; and the Ben-Gurion University Research Fund, for a small grant which aided in the preparation of the manuscript.

Permission to quote from Lawrence's works and letters and to reproduce illustrations is courtesy of the following publishers, institutions, and individuals, who are gratefully acknowledged: Doubleday and Co., Jonathan Cape, Ltd.; the T. E. Lawrence Trusts; the Bodleian Library; the British Library; the Henry E. Huntington Library; the Houghton Library; the University of Texas Humanities Research Center; Ms. Penelope Hughes-Stanton; Mr. C. J. Kennington; Mr. J. D. Roberts; and Ms. Sarah Roberts. Access to government documents was kindly provided by the Public Record Office, London, the Service Historiques de la Armée, Vincennes, and the Archives des Affaires Etrangères, Paris.

Abbreviations of Sources Frequently Cited

CC   T. E. Lawrence. *Crusader Castles.* London: Golden Cockerel Press, 1936. 2 vols.

HL   M. R. Lawrence, ed. *The Home Letters of T. E. Lawrence and His Brothers.* Oxford: Basil Blackwell, 1954.

L   David Garnett, ed. *The Letters of T. E. Lawrence.* London: Cape, 1938.

M   T. E. Lawrence. *The Mint.* New York: Norton, 1963.

SP   T. E. Lawrence. *Seven Pillars of Wisdom.* London: Cape, 1935. Where authors have found it necessary or desirable to refer to the 1920–22 Bodleian MS., the 1922 Oxford text, the 1926 Subscribers' Edition, or other editions, this has been clearly indicated in their essays. For descriptions of the various texts of *Seven Pillars*, see the "Preface by A. W. Lawrence" in the 1935 and later editions of the book.

CAB   Cabinet Papers

C.O.   Colonial Office Papers

F.O.   Foreign Office Papers

PRO   Public Record Office

W.O.   War Office Papers

Page or document numbers follow these abbreviations in the text and notes.

A Fragmentation Artist

STEPHEN E. TABACHNICK

When applied to the life and career of T. E. Lawrence (1888–1935), the clichéd adjective *fragmented* becomes, for once, genuinely meaningful. His career was multifaceted; his self-regard was deeply divided; and views of his personal, cultural, and political legacy have been spread across a spectrum running from hero worship to bitter condemnation. Archaeologist, intelligence agent, guerrilla leader, military theorist, diplomat, writer, translator, book designer, mechanic and guilt-scarred flagellant, lover and hater of publicity, and boyish leg puller, Lawrence's personality and roles in life are so various that it requires the combined effort of scholars in many fields to put together the pieces of the puzzle he represents. And, because Lawrence's often contradictory variety means that he will remain all things to all men to a large degree, the reader of this collection must, through agreement and disagreement with the varying views expressed in its essays, ultimately arrange its "pieces" for himself in order to form his own Lawrence.

The outline of Lawrence's life, at least, is clear. As the product of a bigamous relationship between an easygoing aristocratic father and a talented but religiously rigid lower-class mother, Lawrence began life with a felt social handicap, but also with the intellectual advantages arising from parental disparities of outlook and mild social alienation. An active and inquiring boyhood filled with sports and collecting pursuits led to a highly successful Oxford humanities career. In 1910 he received his B.A. with an unusual thesis on the military architecture of the Crusades, which was based on his own personal field research in France and the Middle East, then a dangerous place to travel alone.

Brought to an archaeological site at Carchemish, Syria, by D. G. Ho-garth and C. L. Woolley of the Ashmolean Museum after his gradua-tion, he proved himself skilled in dealing with local workers, adept at learning Arabic, and voraciously interested in the various peoples and topography of the area.

Lawrence was an obvious candidate for intelligence work when World War I began in 1914[1] and soon found himself making maps of Turkish army dispositions and gathering information on Beduin tribes for Brit-ish intelligence based in Cairo. Here he worked with Hogarth, Ger-trude Bell, Gilbert Clayton, and other brilliant minds on an equal intellectual basis. In 1916 Lawrence semireluctantly helped choose himself for actual fieldwork in the Arab Bureau's pet covert project: an uprising of Beduin tribes against the Turks in the Hejaz sector of Arabia under the leadership of the family of Sherif Hussein of Mecca. Always ready for a new experience, Lawrence found in this project an appeal to many levels of his personality and intellect. Riding and living like a Beduin tribal leader, Lawrence—with the support of Arab Bu-reau gold and a dedicated backup crew of British and French officers, soldiers, and sailors[2]—aided General Edmund Allenby's major offen-sive against the Turkish armies in Palestine and Syria. Using a varied group of Beduin fighters, Lawrence and Emir Feisal, one of Sherif Hussein's sons, succeeded in pinning down a substantial number of Turkish troops in the Eastern desert with a series of hit-and-run attacks against the Hejaz Railway and other isolated targets.[3] For this task, Lawrence had to develop the talents of intelligence field operative, political agent, strategist, and tough tactician, in unique circum-stances, and the strain of carrying through these demanding roles among a people with different mores, as well as the physical punishment that he received, frequently pushed him to the limits of his powers, and even beyond.

Lawrence had the satisfaction of watching the Eastern war culmi-nate successfully with the capture of Damascus by Allied forces in October 1918. But he turned his attention to high diplomacy with less success, serving as Feisal's adviser in pleading the Arabs' case for in-dependence in Syria at the Versailles Peace Conference of 1919 and trying to reconcile hostile elements such as Zionists and Arab nation-alists in the bargain. Failing to win the Syrian mandate for the British and Feisal, their chosen ruler, despite his eloquent gifts of persuasion in several languages, Lawrence watched Feisal evicted from Damascus by the French mandatory government in 1920. Then, as a member of Winston Churchill's Colonial Office and a participant in the Cairo Conference of 1921, Lawrence helped solve Feisal's dilemma with the creation of the states of Iraq and Transjordan, which were assigned, respectively, to Feisal and his brother Abdullah as rulers.

Now followed a period of intensive working of his notes on the campaign into literature—the composition and publication in 1926 of the first, limited, edition of *Seven Pillars of Wisdom* as a "book beautiful"—while he served as a private in the Tank Corps and Royal Air Force by his own choice. Lawrence's poetic autobiography was succeeded by a popular abridgment, *Revolt in the Desert* (1927), and the writing of an autobiographical sequel about life in the ranks, *The Mint*, published only in 1955. Despite severe bouts of depression during these early postwar years, Lawrence produced numerous political and literary letters and articles, and eventually translations from the French and, much later, Greek; and he also became a national hero owing to Lowell Thomas's image building and his own collaboration in it.

Lawrence had always displayed a moody, complex, self-critical, mocking, and somewhat mysterious personality. These tendencies were aggravated after the war by his wounds and experiences in Arabia, which festered in memory, by the strain of reliving these situations while writing his books, by the strain of writing itself, and by the pangs of conscience generated by knowledge of his own double Arab-British role as intelligence agent. The resulting depression involved him in requesting and receiving severe and secret beatings at the hands of service colleagues at least seven times during the last twelve years of his life, as a kind of masochistic expiation for felt sins; these beatings furthered his sense of failure rather than salving it. In view of Lawrence's oft-stated disdain for sexuality of all varieties, and the lack of normal sexual outlets that this disdain entailed, Lawrence's rarely employed flagellation need should perhaps not be taken much more seriously than another man's heterosexual activities, however embarrassed Lawrence may have been by it. The wide range of his intellectual and practical activities during this period as a whole reveals that he was able to be productive, even "happy," despite these occasional lapses. He became a skilled mechanic who has to his credit the development of a ram-jet prototype and the forerunner of the PT boat of World War

II, as well as the smooth running of his series of motorcycles, on one of which he met his death in 1935.

His cottage at Clouds Hill, to which he retired in 1934, testifies to his austere good taste in decoration, and its collection of books and records, as well as the vast number of letters he wrote there, show his wide intellectual interests and his friendship with a variety of leaders in the arts, including Thomas Hardy, Robert Graves, E. M. Forster, and G. B. Shaw. All these pursuits indicate that Lawrence's career may have been far from exhausted despite his reluctant retirement from the R.A.F. because of age, and that he might have proved himself of service to Britain in World War II. But this interpretative point, like so many raised by his personality and career roles, in contrast to the certain facts of his life, remains under dispute. Perhaps the least disputatious way to arrive at an appreciation of the quality of his total achievement is to see him not in magnificent isolation but against the background of his contemporaries' careers.

· II ·

Too often, studies of Lawrence focus so exclusively on him that we forget, paradoxically, how and why he transcends the background of his times and remains interesting to us today. Although he may have been excelled by individuals in given narrow fields of action, a comparison of Lawrence's personality and achievements with those of his contemporary near peers reveals why he remains internationally famous and they—despite their great gifts—are practically unknown outside their respective countries. Most of all, we will find that Lawrence did more things well than anyone else of his period, and led a more complex, fascinating, and controversial life as a result.

As Robert Asprey has noted, at the same time that Lawrence was applying his own guerrilla warfare strategy to the destruction of the Turkish army and its German and Austrian advisers, the German General Paul E. von Lettow-Vorbeck (1870–1964) was making fools of a vast number of British, Boer, and Portuguese generals and their troops in German East Africa.[4] Despite many differences in their campaigns, the strategies and goals of both leaders were remarkably similar: to divert from more important fronts and by means of indirect actions the maximum amounts of enemy men and equipment. Both were completely successful: Lawrence helped take Damascus; and Lettow-Vorbeck, although he surrendered when Germany's total capitulation forced him to do so, remained undefeated and the cause of enormous British expenditure in men and money.

If we consider the scope of the forces arrayed against him, and his own small resources, the facts revealed in Lettow-Vorbeck's concise summary of his campaign entitle him to consideration as one of the most resourceful guerrilla commanders of the century, and one of the first:

> In cold truth our small band, which at the most comprised some 300 Europeans and about 11,000 Askari, had occupied a very superior enemy force for the whole war. According to what English officers told me, 137 Generals had been in the field, and in all about 300,000 men had been employed against us. . . . Yet in spite of the enormously superior numbers at the disposal of the enemy, our small force, the rifle strength of which was only about 1,400 at the time of the armistice, had remained in the field always ready for action and possessed of the highest determination.[5]

Although precise figures are difficult to determine, it is clear that Lettow-Vorbeck was vastly outnumbered, and proved capable of leading his men in a three-thousand-mile trek over largely inhospitable territory during a four-year period without faltering. His brilliance, bravery, and gallantry toward captured and wounded enemy soldiers have been confirmed by English sources.[6]

Like Lawrence, Lettow-Vorbeck operated for a large part of the war among untrustworthy tribes, and was severely wounded several times, at one point becoming almost totally blind. Unlike Lawrence, he had no steady source of supply once he had been expelled from the major centers of the German colony, and had to survive on self-made and captured materiel and his knowledge of the plants and crops of the region. Yet outside Germany, where he was proclaimed a hero after World War I, very few people know his name, and fewer still have read his fascinating campaign memoir, *My Reminiscences of East Africa* (1920).

As an exciting, picaresque figure and wonderful raconteur of amazing adventures in the Red Sea area during the early twentieth century, the Frenchman Henri De Monfreid (1879–1974) is almost without parallel. He strikes us as a combination of a Rimbaud who has told us what actually happened to him after he disappeared from view in French Africa, and Baron Munchausen, except that De Monfreid's tales appear to be true. As Colin Wilson tells us in a generally excellent introduction to one of the two De Monfreid books (of the more than sixty that he wrote) to be published in English, this adventurer is all the more remarkable for having begun his life of adventure in Djibouti at the relatively advanced age of thirty, after having become bored with mundane life in France. Thereafter, from 1910 to 1930, he led a precarious and lone existence as a hashish- and gun-runner in the Red Sea, outwitting French, British, and Turkish authorities, international drug syndicates, and small-time local pirates and smugglers so successfully that he was able to retire to write in Abyssinia.

Having failed to assassinate his notorious guest resident, whose publicity disturbed him, Haile Selassie had De Monfreid deported, only to see him return, this time as a foreign correspondent, with Mussolini's army at the start of World War II. In 1941 De Monfreid was imprisoned in Abyssinia by a conquering British army, but was cleared of any complicity with Mussolini's forces. He served for a time as an estate manager near Mount Kenya, and then lived in the jungle with one of several mistresses, surviving by hunting for three years. Finally returning to France after the war to write, De Monfreid could not sit still. In search of facts about the pirate Levasseur, he took ship for the Indian Ocean in his seventies, was lost at sea, but managed to return to civilization unscathed. At the age of eighty-five, he recorded a disc of sea chanties, and until his death at ninety-five was still writing and painting vigorously and well at his (final) home at Ingrandes, France.

In his afterword to *Adventures of a Red Sea Smuggler* (1935; 1974), the sequel to his first book, *Secrets of the Red Sea* (London: Faber & Faber, 1932), De Monfreid at the age of ninety-four states his personal credo in the romantic terms that endeared him to his lifelong friend Teilhard de Chardin, among others:

> I have learned that, in this material world, life has sense and meaning only for those who draw their faith from the fountain-head of creation; and I isolated myself among primitive people—or, more accurately, men joined with Nature in an immutable and perfect equi-

librium—in order that I myself could consciously remain her creature.[7]

Wilson notes, during a brief introductory comparison of Lawrence and Monfreid, the similarity of their respective attraction to the freedom of desert and ocean, and then goes on to comment, rather to Lawrence's disadvantage, that

> Lawrence's love of the desert, however, sprang from rather neurotic personal motivations: the shame of his illegitimacy and his physical masochism. Moreover, for him, the need for adventure seemed to burn itself out after the Armistice of 1918. Monfreid continued to be a wanderer until he was almost seventy; and, in the late 1940s, finally settled down, it seems, only when modern communications had turned the Mediterranean, that wide ocean he had loved, into a duck-pond.[8]

Although Wilson's characterization of Lawrence's motivation owes rather too much to our period's single-minded and exaggerated emphasis on personal—rather than historical, religious, aesthetic, intellectual, and moral—causes of action, and although he fails to note that the Red Sea, the most important of De Monfreid's haunts, is not a "duck pond" even today, and that therefore De Monfreid must have had other reasons for settling down, it is clear from De Monfreid's books themselves that we are dealing with a rare individual who needs no exaggerated foil to point up his unusual qualities. Yet how many readers outside France know of De Monfreid? In *Contemporary Authors* a bare few sentences are devoted to his voluminous works, and the *New York Times* obituary[9] covers only a few column inches.

In seeking to explain De Monfreid's and Lettow-Vorbeck's relative lack of fame, we might cite De Monfreid's taint, however slight, of collaboration with Mussolini in World War II, and Lettow-Vorbeck's residence in Germany (although he was not a Nazi) during that period, as well as his forced capitulation in World War I. Both men are, then, somehow associated with the losing side during and/or after their period of adventures. What then of the three English personalities—Captain W. H. I. Shakespear, Colonel G. E. Leachman, and Gertrude Bell— who were exactly contemporaneous with Lawrence and performed their bravura deeds of exploration and intelligence work on the British side in the Middle East?

As H. V. F. Winstone's lucid biography,[10] the only one on Shakespear (1878–1915) to date, informs us, its subject was a great traveler and mapmaker, who accomplished many hazardous solo Middle Eastern journeys—especially the great trip from Kuwait to the Red Sea in 1914—by camel and motorcar, when to do so was extremely risky and a great novelty; and who died while witnessing a battle between the forces of Ibn Saud of Riyadh and Ibn Rashid of Hail for dominance in Arabia. As political agent in Mesopotamia and the Persian Gulf, and therefore connected to the India Office rather than to the dominant and rival Foreign Office and Arab Bureau of the British intelligence service in Cairo to which Lawrence belonged, Shakespear had early felt that Ibn Saud, and not the Hussein family favored by the Arab Bureau, should be supported by Britain because Ibn Saud would eventually be the dominant force in Arabia.

Shakespear is one (Bell is another) of the few contemporaries Lawrence mentions by name in his own *Seven Pillars of Wisdom*. And indeed H. St. John Philby has even claimed that if Shakespear had not died, Lawrence might not have had the chance to boost the Hussein family and act the part in history that he did.[11] But despite Shakespear's foresight, bravery, and earned respect as political officer who represented British policy to the Beduin tribes in the field under very difficult conditions, his story is unknown even in England to those outside a very restricted field of study. Winstone advances as a reason for this lack of fame Shakespear's status as one whose opinions were in advance of his contemporaries', and who is therefore conveniently forgotten by bureaucrats and organizations that made what are, in Winstone's opinion, the wrong decisions. To which we can add the fact that Shakespear left no book behind to state his case.

G. E. Leachman (died 1920) too never committed his fantastic adventures—which included the single-handed facing down of whole Beduin tribes and a Kim-like capacity for disguise and physical feats—to paper, and acted in the Mesopotamian, rather than Arabian and 'Syrian, theater. Only one biography, by Major N. N. E. Bray, an associate of both Leachman and Lawrence, records Leachman's bravery, resourcefulness, and death by assassination.[12]

In his biography Bray describes a meeting around May 1917 between the two British agents in Feisal's tent at Wejh, and leaves no doubt about whom he personally considers the greater intelligence practitioner, and why:

The contrast between the two Englishmen was patent: Lawrence, acting the Arab and maintaining his prestige through the medium of his magnificent clothes. His servility to Feisal and his seeming unreality form a picture which still lingers in my mind.

Leachman on the other hand was so obviously and unashamedly the Englishman, and a masterful one. His sufferings and hardships were mapped on his lean visage and pride showed behind the curtains of his eyes. He had endured five years of toil and danger, and three more still harsher years were in store for him. The other two had undergone a few months of rough campaigning, and their total experience was to last but another fifteen months.

All three are dead now, but while of the edifice the first two built not one vestige remains, the work the other accomplished endures to-day and will endure. Whereas all the world outside Arabia has heard of Lawrence; yet by a strange tick of fate, comparatively few Arabs have heard that name, yet the name of Leachman is still borne by countless sons of a warrior people and among them is still the synonym for gallantry and loyalty.[13]

Bray's last paragraph contains obvious inaccuracies. Both Jordan and Israel are reminders of the long-lasting effects of Lawrence's support of the family of King Hussein and of Zionism, and the work of George Antonious, Suleiman Mousa, Sari Nasir, and Anis Sayigh, as well as interviews conducted with Beduin chiefs by John Mack, show that Lawrence's name is scarcely unknown, even today, among the Arabs, however questionable his status among them might be.[14] One might in contrast ask what of Leachman's work in preserving British control by force over Mesopotamia (modern Iraq) remains? Even if we must answer this question negatively, we may still lament that such an "outstanding personality among the Arabic-speaking portions of Iraq,"[15] as Leachman was, does not merit even a brief article in any encyclopedia.

Gertrude Bell (1868–1926) was yet another of the amazing "Arabians" produced by Great Britain in the early years of our century. The winner of a Royal Geographical Society Gold Medal in 1912 for her solo travels in northern Arabia and a practitioner of intelligence and political skills for more than twenty years, Bell is all the more remarkable for having made her mark as a woman in the pro-masculine Middle East. It was Bell who recognized that the young Lawrence would "make a traveller," as she put it, and who worked with him in the Arab Bureau in Cairo at the beginning of World War I, during the 1921 Cairo

Conference that put Feisal on the throne of Iraq after the French ousted him from Syria, and by herself served as Feisal's adviser in Iraq after 1921, taking up where Lawrence had left off. She was already well known in the Near East and the author of the lasting travel book *The Desert and the Sown* (1907) as well as a respected archaeologist by the time Lawrence appeared on the scene in 1914, and her work in the area continued five years beyond Lawrence's final exit in 1921. She died in Iraq in 1926, after having helped establish it as an independent state.

With typical modesty, Bell—like Shakespear and Leachman—refused to place her intelligence role in the literary spotlight, and could compare herself to disadvantage with other Anglo-Arabians:

> There are two ways of profitable travel in Arabia. One is the *Arabia Deserta* way, to live with the people, and to live like them, for months and years. You can learn something thereby, as Doughty did; though you may not be able to tell it again as he could. It's clear *I* can't take that way; the fact of my being a woman bars me from it. And the other is Leachman's way, to ride swiftly through the country with your compass in your hand, for the map's sake and for nothing else. I might be able to do that over a limited space of time, but I am not sure.[16]

It should be noted that Bell wrote this before Lawrence was available for comparison, and that she held him in the highest respect, even coming around to his views on Iraq's need for independence after initial disagreement, and proving as staunch a supporter of the Sherifian as opposed to the Saudian cause as Lawrence and Hogarth. Few people did more than she to alter the shape of the future Middle East, and yet only two substantial biographies (one consisting largely of her own diaries), a collection of letters, and her own largely out-of-print books, remain to mark her role.[17]

In contrast to the treatment of these other figures, Lawrence's life has been told in at least nineteen full or partial biographies available in English—seven of which have appeared since 1969 alone—and innumerable shorter memoirs and full-length historical, military, and literary studies.[18] A closer look at our five figures in comparison with Lawrence reveals why.

Lettow-Vorbeck remains the classic example of the dedicated and precise Prussian officer, whose mental flexibility was limited to his brilliant adaptation of the rules of war he had been taught and to his marshaling of knowledge to suit the strange situation in which he found himself. Never once in his book does he question the idea of war or the world as it is or embark on larger philosophical or personal speculations. De Monfreid to his death remained the free spirit who appears in his picaresque books, with never a pessimistic or Dostoyevskian anguished glance backward at the world or his life. Perhaps for this reason his books are the object of a youth cult in France and ultimately rather thin matter for continuous adult reading. Furthermore, De Monfreid's eye is always on his own personal survival, and the larger world of his period remains vague and shadowy in his portrayal; his books lack the historical perspective, complexity, and interest that one finds in the very events in which Lawrence was involved. Captain Shakespear, for all his successes as explorer and as political agent, comes across in Winstone's biography and the picture given in A. T. Wilson's *Loyalties* rather like a bluff and limited sportsman and pillar of empire, interested most of all in polo, car trips, sailing, and the sport of Beduin battles, without much intellectual freight attached to his mind.

Colonel Leachman, although amazingly resourceful and brave, was the classic imperialist, who retained an almost fanatic belief in the rightness of England's colonial cause and England's right to dominate men of other nationalities and skin colors. His gross insensitivity on this point is demonstrated by a letter of 16 July 1910 in which he writes, about the Armenian holocaust perpetrated by the Turks, that there were in his area of travel "two great massacres, in the most recent of which, three years ago, many thousands of Armenians were killed; I rather feel for the Turks, for the Armenians are a nasty people."[19] In contrast, Lawrence writes in *Seven Pillars*, with open sympathy for the Armenians, that "They had been disarmed and destroyed piecemeal, the men by massacre, the women and children by being driven and over-driven along the wintry roads into the desert, naked and hungry, the common prey of any passer-by, until death took them."[20] Gertrude Bell testifies that Leachman was actually hated by many Arabs,[21] thus confirming Lawrence's (rather than Bray's) opinion of him: "I should call him a man too little sensitive to be aware of other points of view than his own: too little fine to see degrees of greatness, degrees of rightness in others. . . . I think he was first and foremost a bully. . . .

He was too shrill, too hot-tempered, too little generous."[22] Here, as in Bell's testimony that the Emir Feisal, for instance, was "Vain and feeble and timid, his fine ideals can never come to maturity,"[23] exactly as Lawrence portrays him near the end of *Seven Pillars* (p. 565)—"Feisal was a brave, weak, ignorant spirit. . . . I served him out of pity"—we find that Lawrence's view of his contemporaries is frequently precise, objective, and penetrating. Perhaps this is one reason he survived and Leachman did not.

As we see in our comparison with Leachman, Lawrence's anti-colonialism and sympathy for the oppressed are advanced opinions for his period. Even the liberal and similarly sympathetic Gertrude Bell, whose opinions are almost identical to Lawrence's on most Middle Eastern questions—except for the possible implementation of Zionism, which she thought a dream—and who was in many ways Lawrence's intellectual equal in archaeology, translation, and intelligence work, falls short of his breadth and stature. She could not have actual military experience, was in Mesopotamia out of the main theater of the Arab Revolt for much of the war, and strikes today's reader as a wonderfully lucid and sparkling rather than deeply engaged, searching, and complex writer.

In contrast to his contemporary "Arabians" and other adventurers, Lawrence, in his letters as in his books, gives us many glances backward at his roles and his own personality, most of them severely deprecating; many self-conscious doubts about his and Great Britain's wartime and postwar spiritual and moral honor; and most of all, the complex style, vision, and sympathy for others, often contradictory, of the true literary artist. The fact that we must turn to Lawrence's autobiographies themselves for much of our idea of him and of the historical events he experienced, and that we do so with obvious pleasure in the reading, gives us an important reason for Lawrence's fame and his contemporaries' lack of it. Lawrence is not merely a charming writer like De Monfreid or Gertrude Bell but a "writer of magnitude," as R. P. Blackmur puts it.[24]

By writing about himself and the events through which he passed so well, Lawrence crossed the boundary that separates the historical figure and memoir writer (such as Lettow-Vorbeck) from the immortal artist and living character in his own work. Lawrence transformed himself from an appendage of World War I, suitable for study only by scholars of political and military history, to our contemporary. We can open *Seven Pillars of Wisdom* in our or succeeding periods, and find Lawrence in all his contradiction, teasing, and "relevance" staring us in the face. He has made his struggles ours. And Lawrence's powerful recording of a historical struggle that remains as open to interpretation today as ever—namely, the framing and import of the Sykes-Picot Treaty, the Balfour Declaration, and the McMahon-Hussein correspondence dealing with the boundaries of post–World War I Arab dominions[25]—means that over and above the personal interest, his book as history will continue to arouse opposition and agreement. The question of how accurate it is as straight history is as important an element in its literary interest and value as a work of art as in the cases of the histories of Thucydides, Macaulay, Gibbon, Ranke, or Burckhardt, "literary" historians who have occasioned wide controversy because of the tension between drama and "objective" event in their work. We will consider Lawrence's historical accuracy later in this introduction; but now we will be able to get a reasonable perspective on this question if we remember that Lawrence's book is about one man, essentially, and presents that man's attempt to see himself as he was in the complex events in which he was involved. In short, we should always remember that Lawrence's book is autobiography rather than "objective" third-person history.

We soon come to realize that of all Lawrence's roles, his role as writer—as the organization of this collection is meant to indicate—is perhaps his most important, for one reason: if he had not written *Seven Pillars*, we would not be nearly so interested in Lawrence as we are; not much more interested, in fact, than we are in Shakespear, Leachman, Bell, or Lettow-Vorbeck, however unfortunate or unjust that might be. And we should recognize that, even as we blame or praise Lawrence for more or less accurate recording of the Arab Revolt's progress, and as fascinating as the historical aspects of the Arab Revolt remain in themselves, without the version given in Lawrence's book, the revolt itself would be considerably less interesting to us than it is. Whatever our political or historical judgment of Lawrence's book— and the most recent assessments are almost unanimously favorable— he is likely to be judged ultimately as an artist. As W. H. Auden wrote of W. B. Yeats's political involvement, "You were silly like us: your gift survived it all. . . . / Time that is intolerant / Of the brave and innocent, / And indifferent in a week / To a beautiful physique, / Worships language and forgives / Everyone by whom it lives; / Pardons cowardice, conceit, / Lays its honours at their feet."

What essentially happened in Lawrence's case is that he created such a fascinatingly ambiguous and powerful self-image in *Seven Pillars* and its coda, *The Mint*, as well as such a colorful and striking canvas of characters and events, that he has provoked biographers and historians to seek out the "real" or historical Lawrence—as well as the real or historical Feisal, Auda, Storrs, and Meinertzhagen, for instance—ever since. And the natural controversiality that arises from such investigations into historical personalities is yet another reason for his continuing interest and fame. Because of his sharp, and often sharply critical, portraits of his colleagues and his tendency toward ambiguous self-portraiture, as well as his multifacetedness, we may never arrive at a perfectly clear picture of Lawrence and his circumstances. In the face of all biographies and historical studies that will continue to be written about him, we may find that the closest we will ever come to the "real" man is the contradictory and teasing figure who comes across in *Seven Pillars* and *The Mint*. And of all Lawrence's contradictions, none is more important and typical of him than his concern with the problem of mind-body relations and relations between different parts of the mind. In examining this issue as it appears in his two books, we epitomize Lawrence as a man as well as his roles of thinker and artist.

· III ·

Where Lettow-Vorbeck, De Monfreid, Shakespear, Leachman, and Bell saw themselves in their statements, memoirs, and letters as effective and self-contained individuals, Lawrence gives the impression of always falling into pieces and of experiencing less than the full success he had anticipated and perhaps achieved in reality. He records his fragmentation rather than wholeness, and never managed to form a consistent intellectual synthesis of his experiences. In his life and work, Lawrence serves constantly to remind us of the gulf between desire and attainment, intellectuality and practicality, idealism and hardheadedness, heroism and absurdity, will and emotions, and—most of all—

body and mind, and of the difficult struggle to reconcile these felt opposites. And this struggle—more than any success of his—is likely to remain the essence of Lawrence's experience for us and the reason we most value him.

The question of the nature of the mind and its relationship to the body has exercised philosophers for centuries. Where does Lawrence stand on this problem? Although he speaks of this matter at many points in both *Seven Pillars of Wisdom* and *The Mint*, the answer is far from easy to derive. For Lawrence is deeply contradictory on this point, now holding that mind is one thing and that mind and body are one thing, and then asserting that mind consists of a bunch of warring elements lacking unity and that mind and body are separate and very different things.

In this contradiction Lawrence resembles the one philosopher whom he cites overtly on this issue, the Renaissance thinker Bernardino Telesio (1509–1588).[26] Lawrence writes of Telesio ("Telesius") in connection with his own experience of a profound mental division and division between mind and body after the beating at Deraa:

> The spent body toiled on doggedly and took no heed, quite rightly, for the divided selves said nothing which I was not capable of thinking in cold blood; they were all my natives. Telesius, taught by some such experience, split up the soul. Had he gone on, to the furthest limit of exhaustion, he would have seen his conceived regiment of thoughts and acts and feelings ranked around him as separate creatures; eyeing, like vultures, the passing in their midst of the common thing which gave them life. (SP, 452)

Telesio in fact posits—just as Lawrence says he does in the above quotation—the coexistence of two souls in man, one material, similar to the "spirit" in animals, which expands and contracts in pleasure and pain, and which is related to the care of the body and its needs, and another, totally immaterial and meditative, responsible only for the ability to contemplate abstract things, which is unique to man:

> Be it permitted to mention that even though the spirit in animals drawn from the sperms shall be considered the substance of the soul, it does not follow that one shall also take this spirit as the substance of the soul of man, because not only the Holy Script but even human reasons convince us that in man dwells another entirely divine sub-

stance placed there by God himself. We recognize in man, namely, actions, sufferings and strivings quite distinct from animals, which must be ascribed to a higher substance than the spirit drawn from the sperms; for man is not satisfied, as the rest of the animals are, with sensation, cognitions and enjoyments of the things that feed, conserve, and please him, but he also investigates with greatest zeal the substance and effects of such things as are of no use to him and cannot even be conceived by any sense, especially those concerning the divine essence and divinity. Nay, he even forgets, disdains and neglects, while persistently and blissfully contemplating them, even that which pertains to the well-being and enjoyment of his body.[27]

But, despite Telesio's two-soul doctrine, which establishes divisions in the mind itself and seems to set mind and body against one another, he is elsewhere in his *De Rerum Natura* a forerunner of "psychic atomism" who "tried to establish the compatibility of psychic and physical motions," as D. G. Runes informs us.[28]

Lawrence himself feels an intellectual tension between notions of unity and division, and, like Telesio, frequently contradicts his own assertions for or against mind-body and mind unity. Telesio's *De Rerum Natura* would indeed appeal to Lawrence's tastes in reading, because like his favorites *Moby Dick*, *Thus Spake Zarathustra*, and *The Brothers Karamazov*—and Lawrence's own books—it is "neither a scientific study nor a philosophical treatise, but a hybrid combination of science and philosophy not quite in agreement with the rigorous empirical method he [Telesio] professed to follow," as Bernardine Bonansea has commented.[29]

First we will consider the evidence that Lawrence developed the view that mind itself and mind and body are one thing, and then we will turn to the reasons for believing that this was not the only view he held on this matter. In an important passage that his friend Vyvyan Richards, himself a student of philosophy at Oxford, has written off as a "fine cataract of words—and nothing more,"[30] Lawrence clearly upholds a monistic viewpoint:

> The conception of antithetical mind and matter, which was basic in
> the Arab self-surrender, helped me not at all. I achieved surrender (so
> far as I did achieve it) by the very opposite road, through my notion
> that mental and physical were inseparably one: that our bodies, the

universe, our thoughts and tactilities were conceived in and of the molecular sludge of matter, the universal element through which form drifted as clots and patterns of varying density. It seemed to me unthinkable that assemblages of atoms should cogitate except in atomic terms. My perverse sense of values constrained me to assume that abstract and concrete, as badges, did not denote oppositions more serious than Liberal and Conservative. (*SP*, 468)

Lawrence, in contrast to the Arabs who, according to him, achieve feats of courage or endurance by subordinating either mind or body as the occasion demands, has as his goal the fusion of the two so that no difference between them is felt to exist, as happened to him, for instance, in the frenzied excitement of battle.

Richards charges that Lawrence had no interest in the academic philosophy of F. C. S. Schiller and Bertrand Russell or indeed in any academic philosophy,[31] but he has failed to notice that Lawrence in this quotation has espoused the position of "neutral monism" first outlined by William James in 1912 and then taken up by Bertrand Russell in 1921, precisely when Lawrence was rewriting *Seven Pillars of Wisdom*. In his *Essays in Radical Empiricism*, James writes that "thoughts in the concrete are made of the same stuff as things are,"[32] and Russell in his *Analysis of Mind* says that "The view that seems to me to reconcile the materialistic tendency of psychology with the anti-materialistic view of physics is the view of William James and the American new realists, according to which the 'stuff' of the world is neither mental nor material, but a 'neutral stuff,' out of which both are constructed."[33] We have here proof that Lawrence—whether through direct reading or hearsay[34]—has arrived at the most advanced (for his time) monistic view of the mind-body problem.

Nor is this the only evidence that Lawrence was seriously in the process of becoming a firm advocate of mind-body and mind unity during the last half of his life and career. *The Mint* gives us even stronger indications in that direction. Early in the book, in the "Chapel" chapter, Lawrence comes out with his strongest anti-Platonic statement of mind-body unity yet: "Our ranks were too healthy to catch this diseased Greek antithesis of flesh and spirit. Unquestioned life is a harmony, though then not in the least Christian."[35] Here dualism is a disease, to be brutally rejected as a possible philosophy. But what might the desirable "unquestioned life" that Lawrence sets against dualism be in concrete terms? He gives us a further hint later in the book, while indicating his own personal failure to achieve it yet:

> There it goes again: the conflict of mind and spirit. Whereas here are men so healthy that they don't chop their meat into mince for easy digestion by the mind: and who are therefore intact as we are thereby diseased. Man, who was born as one, breaks into little prisms when he thinks: but if he passes through thought into despair, or comprehension, he again achieves some momentary onenesses with himself. And not only that. He can achieve a oneness of himself with his fellows: and of them with the stocks and stones of his universe: and of all the universes with the illusory everything (if he be positive) or with the illusory nothing (if he be nihilist) according as the digestive complexion of his soul be dark or fair. (M, 179)

If we want to understand precisely what Lawrence is talking about here, rather than to dismiss this passage as another "fine cataract of words," we have only to turn to the philosophy of the Absolute of F. H. Bradley. Although Lawrence never mentions Bradley specifically in his books or letters, Bradley was the leading philosophical thinker at Oxford during Lawrence's studies there, and his influence was all-pervasive. Lawrence could have learned of Bradley's theories from his tutor L. C. Jane, the lecturers Ernest Barker and A. L. Smith, or his friend Vyvyan Richards himself. Whether Lawrence actually read Bradley or only heard of his theories is irrelevant; the important point is that Bradley's ideas explain things in *The Mint* otherwise inexplicable.

It is Bradley who believes, like Lawrence in the above quotation, that thinking is the enemy of wholeness, and that only in "felt thought" or "sentience" is it possible to transcend multiple-appearing, fragmented reality to a plane of transcendental wholeness that is capable of achievement in normal life. In such a state, introspection ceases, and mind, mind and body, and indeed the self and the universe become one. In such of Bradley's thoughts as "The self is no doubt the highest form of experience which we have, but, for all that, it is not a true form" (*Appearance and Reality*, p. 119); "reality is sentient experience" (p. 146); "The Absolute holds all possible content in an individual experience where no contradiction can remain" (p. 147); "Every element of the universe, sensation, feeling, thought and will, must be included within one comprehensive sentience" (p. 159); "Reality is one, and is a single experience" (p. 533); and "Absolute truth is corrected only by passing outside the intellect" (p. 545),[36] we find the impelling force behind Lawrence's final assertions in *The Mint*.

As Jewel Spears Brooker puts it in a discussion of T. S. Eliot, another Bradleian of Lawrence's period and one of whom Lawrence was well aware, Bradley offers a transcendental experience "which permits a return of sorts to the wholeness and unity of immediate experience. . . . The villain is the discursive intellect, and the transcendance of relations such as self and space and time becomes largely a matter of reforming the discursive intellect from a servant of division and fragmentation to a partner in the achievement of wholeness."[37] Frederick Copleston's summary of Bradley's thought, like Brooker's, explains abstractly not only Bradley's doctrines but what Lawrence is aiming for in *The Mint* as well:

> We must recall his theory of an immediate basic feeling-experience or sentient experience in which the distinction between subject and object, with the consequent sundering of ideal content from that which it is predicated, has not yet emerged. On the level of human reflection and thought this basic unity, a felt totality, breaks up and externality is introduced. . . . But we can conceive as a possibility an experience in which the immediacy of feeling, of primitive sentient experience, is recovered, as it were, at a higher level, a level at which the externality of related forms such as subject and object ceases utterly. The Absolute is such an experience in the highest degree.[38]

And in fact the final passages of *The Mint* assert Lawrence's attainment of precisely Bradley's Absolute as described by Brooker and Copleston, and in a form free of the negative possibilities ("if he be nihilist") of the earlier passage from *The Mint*:

> We were too utterly content to speak, drugged with an absorption fathoms deeper than physical contentment. Just we lay there spread-eagled in a mesh of bodies, pillowed on one another and sighing in happy excess of relaxation. The sunlight poured from the sky and melted our tissues. From the turf below our moist backs there came up a sister-heat which joined us to it. Our bones dissolved to become a part of this underlying indulgent earth, whose mysterious pulse throbbed in every tremor of our bodies. The scents of the thousand-acre drome mixed with the familiar oil-breath of our hangar, nature with art: while the pale sea of the grass bobbed in little waves before

the wind raising a green surf which hissed and flowed by the slats of our heat-lidded eyes. . . . Such moments of absorption resolve the mail and plate of our personality back into the carbo-hydrate elements of being. They come to service men very often. . . . (M, 249)

And airmen are cared for as little as they care. Their simple eyes, out-turned; their natural living; the penurious imaginations which neither harrow nor reap their lowlands of mind: all these expose them, like fallows, to the processes of air. In the summer we are easily the sun's. In winter we struggle undefended along the roadway, and the rain and wind chivy us, till soon we are wind and rain. We race over in the first dawn to the College's translucent swimming pool, and dive into the elastic water which fits our bodies as closely as a skin:—and we belong to that too. Everywhere a relationship: no loneliness any more. (M, 249–50)

Through rest after hard work, simple living, and physical exercise, joint activity with a unit of men, free of "thought," Lawrence, at least during these moments and others like them, becomes one with his body, other men, and nature itself, instead of divided, isolated, and overawed by nature. There are few more beautifully concrete realizations of Bradley's Absolute in literature; a comparison with the import, if not skill and complexity, of Eliot's later poetry is not wholly out of order here.

In these passages we have clear evidence that Lawrence gradually developed into a firm advocate of a monistic position on the mind/mind-body problem, and even into a believer in the unity of all things, animate and inanimate, in the universe. If we understand that Lawrence achieved the wholeness he claims for himself in the above passages during moments of unintellectual activity or rest, we will be able to credit his statements as true and genuine, even as they apply to his own life and not merely as an "idea" or a good ending for his book. He seemed to achieve such moments more often and in a quieter way in the R.A.F. than had been possible to him before, if we accept the testimony of both *The Mint* and his letters. In 1924 he writes to Mrs. Shaw that "I can't find comfort in your compartmenting up our personalities. Mind, spirit, soul, body, sense and consciousness—angles of one identity, seen from different points of the compass."[39]

So much for the drift toward monism in Lawrence's life and work. But in his books as in his life there is also a retrograde tendency toward divisions within the mind and mind-body separation, which contradicts his assertions of felt unity in these passages. For instance, he finds at Deraa that he could become the mental "spectator" of his body's degradation (*SP*, 445), and we have seen in the Telesio passage the results of this experience, the splitting up of his mind into separate selves and its division from his body. In *Seven Pillars* too, immediately after the "atomistic" passage asserting the unity of mind and mind and body, he states with some passion that "While we rode we were disembodied, unconscious of flesh or feeling: and when at an interval this excitement faded and we did see our bodies, it was with some hostility, with a contemptuous sense that they reached their highest purpose, not as vehicles of the spirit, but when, dissolved, their elements served to manure a field" (*SP*, 468). Even later in the book he can assert that Westerners are "monks in our bodies' cells" (509) and that "I so reverenced my wits and despised my body that I would not be beholden to the second for the life of the first" (532). In the chapter "Myself," he fails to describe himself physically at all, except to remark how ashamed of his "physical envelope" (562) he is, and concludes the chapter by claiming that "our possession of bodies was degradation enough" (566). And even in *The Mint* he deplores his own continued diligence in "restlessly cataloguing each aspect of my unity" (178) and speaks of sexuality—the body—of all varieties as something "dirty" (128). And finally there is the "flagellation disorder," which, though practiced only rarely over a space of twelve years, indicates the use of the mind—even at the end of Lawrence's life—to humiliate the body by destroying its sexuality, as John Mack has argued.[40]

Furthermore, the very multiplicity of terms Lawrence uses in his books to describe the parts of his mind—mind, intellect, soul, wits, spirit, senses, will, self, brain, character, to name only a few—indicates mental division, as does the primacy that he continuously assigns to one element in his mind, the Will, as is apparent below:

> True there lurked always that Will uneasily waiting to burst out. My brain was sudden and silent as a wild cat, my senses like mud clogging its feet, and my self (conscious always of itself and its shyness) telling the beast that it was bad form to spring and vulgar to feed upon the kill. So meshed in nerves and hesitation, it could not be a thing to be afraid of; yet it was a real beast, and this book its mangy skin, dried, stuffed and set up squarely for men to stare at. (*SP*, 564)

In fact, this muddy passage, which speaks vaguely of the will to dominate and its inhibition, may be more explicable on the basis of Kipling's story "The Mark of the Beast," in which the Englishman Fleete is possessed by the spirit of a wolf as a punishment for having desecrated native gods, or perhaps by reference to Henry James's "The Beast in the Jungle," in which John Marcher discovers that the "beast" he has been waiting for all his life is in his mind rather than outside it,[41] than by any coherent idea of the relations between Will, senses, brain, and self.

If we assess Lawrence as a philosopher, he will appear a very inconsistent one because of the major contradictions we have noted and because he never explains *how* he arrives at a given position or defines his terms precisely. The speculative passages in his books appear as suddenly as lone trees in the midst of Arabia, and are as quickly left behind, to tantalize our conscious minds and work quietly upon us in a deeper way. We may locate Lawrence along the general line of philosophers that runs from Telesio through Spinoza (who is mentioned in *Seven Pillars*, but in a negative context) to Bradley, with touches of William James, Russell, and Nietzsche and Schopenhauer (as J. Meyers and T. J. O'Donnell have shown) thrown in for good measure. We may also come to the salutary realization that, despite our contemporary desire to explain everything in terms of psychology, Lawrence himself—who was well aware of Freud by the time he began writing *Seven Pillars*—preferred more or less academic philosophy as a means of explaining his experiences to himself and others. But for all this, we are forced to conclude that, while a knowledge of Telesio's or Russell's or Bradley's philosophies may help throw light on Lawrence's meaning in isolated passages or on the general drift of his thought, he remains ultimately unique, inconsistent, contradictory, unsystematic, and finally understandable in terms of the *attempt* to explain himself intellectually rather than in any achievement of a universally applicable system of thought derived from his experiences. As his letter of 4 February 1935 to Robert Graves shows, Lawrence understood that he had failed in this respect in *Seven Pillars*: "What I was trying to do, I suppose, was to carry a superstructure of ideas upon or above anything I made. Well, I failed in that."[42]

But it would be a mistake for us to conclude that Lawrence's books are failures because of their lack of philosophical coherence. Here as elsewhere Lawrence is more than the sum of his parts. He fascinates and engages our sympathy precisely when he cannot seem to "pull it all together" in a comprehensive vision. Perhaps if he had dilated on his progress from Telesio's thought to Bradley's Absolute, he would have been a bore, merely a derivative second-rate thinker, besides being inaccurate; for he cannot be fit, as we have seen, into any convenient categories, even self-imposed ones. Instead, his use of shards of philosophies, some of them contradictory when seen whole, like William James's and Bradley's, and his manifold allusions to the works of literary artists—Henry James and Kipling, among many, many others—create a fascinating, unique artistic collage of ideas and feelings that sends the reader in search of a coherent pattern in them and ultimately in search of the writer who has stuck them all together in this intriguing way. In the end, then, the philosophical reader, like Lawrence's biographers, historians, and literary critics, is sent in search of—and never quite finds—the "real" Lawrence owing to this conscious or unconscious technique, and finds him interesting as a result.

Perhaps the personality most like Lawrence in our century is Malraux, who also was a complex mixture of intellectual, artist, and man of action, as has been noted by Malraux himself and numerous commentators.[43] But if we think again of the fragmentation revealed in Lawrence's books, the difficulty of summing him up, and the mystery of his personality for us, we see that Lawrence surpasses Malraux in interest, as he does all the other parallel contemporaries. There is, however, another reason that Lawrence is better known than even Malraux, and another dimension to Lawrence's experience that the others, including Malraux, did not pass through. For Lawrence remains one of the first subjects of the successful publicity campaign in our century, and this aspect of his fame and the difficulty it has created for scholars trying to understand Lawrence demand full attention.

· IV ·

Neil Van Deusen begins his *Telesio* by remarking: "Every man whose achievements are sufficient to raise him above the level of mediocrity tends to become the focal point for a legend which is constructed slowly by the pens of his biographers and commentators. As the legend grows, the man vanishes, and in his place we find the theories and sentiments of his friends and critics."[44] In Lawrence's case, this natural development was artificially exaggerated by an actual publicity campaign focusing on his exploits. Partially as a result, observers' opinions about him have been as deeply divided as his own view of himself. Only half a century after his death have researchers begun to see him more or less as he was instead of through a mythical or debunking vision.

Lowell Thomas, Lawrence's first biographer, painted a glorious portrait in his 1919 Covent Garden slide show and then five years later in his *With Lawrence in Arabia* (New York: Century, 1924). As someone who was in the Near East only a few weeks and knew nothing about it, and who talked to Lawrence for only a few hours and was forced to rely uncritically on Lawrence's own alternately semi-ironic, self-serving, self-mocking, and capricious self-description, Thomas produced a minimally creditable and inflated and inaccurate—but enormously popular—"image" of Lawrence.

The Thomas book is the work of an excellent public relations man who knew he had a good "scoop." It is therefore full of touristic clichés about the "mysterious East," and stresses the romantic and Christian Crusader connection, while lacking any deep or complex appreciation of the history and politics of the area and Lawrence's personality. This first view of Lawrence deliberately simplifies and heightens his psychological and physical appearance. Lawrence becomes a "modern Arabian knight" who took part in "the war in the Land of the Arabian Nights" in "the most romantic campaign in modern history" (p. viii). After this description of Lawrence, we are not surprised to find Auda Abu Tayi—despite his greed, rapacity, and acknowledged double dealing with Turks and British that we see in *Seven Pillars of Wisdom*—referred to as "the Bedouin Robin Hood" (p. 155), Feisal—a king rather than a president—as "the George Washington of Arabia" (p. 337), and Allenby—who was fighting a modern war against Germany's Turkish ally rather than a religious crusade—as "Britain's modern Coeur de Lion" who led his army "in the most brilliant cavalry campaign of all time" (pp. viii–ix).

Lawrence has been blamed for his unacknowledged part in creating Thomas's myth of him, since he never publicly corrected Thomas's distorted portrait. He did have a "craving to be famous" (*SP*, 563), as he admitted himself; and, as Stephen Spender has commented generally, "An important thing to remember is that most people who are famous have a kind of public relations side to their character; they are careful to hide certain things about themselves."[45] However, the picture of himself that Lawrence gives in *Seven Pillars*, which followed Thomas's biography by only two years, is far more contradictory and critical than that given in Thomas's book, including the admission of his liking glory as well as his "horror of being known to like being known" (*SP*, 563). Thus, even though Robert Graves and Liddell Hart, if somewhat less incautiously than Lowell Thomas, presented largely uncritical views of Lawrence in their biographies of 1927 and 1934, respectively, there was always an undercurrent of people like Herbert Read and D. H. Lawrence who could find Lawrence's own self-portrait far from heroic or even estimable,[46] and so there was always a countervailing force to Lawrence's fame. But this corrective undercurrent was the exception and limited to an intellectual audience.

Given the hagiographic nature of Thomas's book and the less vulgar but still uncritical biographies of Graves and Hart, it is amazing that the debunking of the Lawrence image that was carried out by Richard Aldington in 1955 did not come much earlier. Thomas's Lawrence is a hero too good to be true, and, be it noted, a hero lacking in interest for us today because of his simplicity; and Thomas's book is full of the exaggerations that invite puncturing. Thomas even claims that Lawrence was sent on a short expedition to Sumatra, where he escaped from headhunters, a capricious Lawrence-inspired tale that recalls Sherlock Holmes's adventure of the giant rat of Sumatra "for which the world is not yet prepared," in Watson's words!

Just as Thomas had the personal motive of ambition for promoting Lawrence, so Aldington had personal reasons for hating him. Lawrence did not think that Aldington was a very good novelist, a view recently upheld by Spender, who calls Aldington a "man of no talent."[47] Aldington had the personality of the born debunker, the man who makes his reputation at the expense of others who were more successful in life than he felt himself to be, and this personality quirk was complicated by his war injuries. Aldington seems to have felt that anyone who had not fought on the Western front must be a coward, as John Morris's perceptive sketch reveals:

For much of his life Richard Aldington (1892–1962) felt his country had forgotten him. Significantly, perhaps, "authorities" disagree on where he was born and where he lived. Nor is it entirely clear why he should have argued with, and become angry with, so many former associates like Pound and Eliot with whom in his youth he worked. . . . Certainly he came to feel a sense of betrayal by the British literary "Establishment" which—after the Great War "had been declared against him personally"—included the entire social spectrum: Government, church, class, family, the arts. For Aldington the war, in which he was gassed and shell-shocked, brought home unforgettably, as Burma did for Orwell, a sense of the hypocrisy upon which nation, Empire and class depended.[48]

Aldington's bitter dismissal of T. E. Lawrence as "the appropriate hero for his class and epoch"[49] is only Aldington's most famous hatchet job. In fact, he had performed similar decapitations of former friends in his novel *Death of a Hero*, in which D. H. Lawrence is viciously characterized as Bobbe, T. S. Eliot as Tubbe, and Harold Munro as Jeames.

Aldington's desire to unmask a hypocritical society lends an unobjective and obsessive quality to his "enquiry" into Lawrence's life. But precisely because of his obsessiveness, Aldington conducted deeper research than had anyone else to 1955, and managed to throw legitimate doubt on a great deal of Lawrence's assertions in *Seven Pillars* and in life and on the statements of his supporters. This passage from Aldington's book constitutes a fair summary of his view of Lawrence:

Behind his self-consciousness, the diffident Oxford manner and schoolboy behaviour was a watchful adventurer of intense ambition, a mind of versatility and skill, an unscrupulous will-to-power, a wilfulness impatient of control, a self-assertiveness which was allied with contempt. We must add to this that in his carefully calculated relationships which seemingly never became intimacies he kept each in a watertight compartment and presented himself in a certain predetermined role; and that he possessed what is called "Irish charm" or as he once put it "some quality that he could turn 'on or off like a tap'" which appealed to people.

But the most startling and disconcerting trait in Lawrence's character is the propensity which seemed uncontrollable in him to put out highly embellished stories of himself and his doings.[50]

A far cry from Lowell Thomas's "knight of the desert"! Or even from Jean Beraud Villars's more balanced Lawrence, also of 1955:

> In the gallery of great men T. E. Lawrence . . . is one of the rare
> men, perhaps the only man, to have been at once a war leader and
> an artist. . . . The artist and the fighting man are paradoxical
> entities. . . . To be an artist is to be egocentric, to be a soldier is to
> sacrifice and forget self. Two philosophies so contradictory within the
> same man can but produce anomalies and heartbreaks.[51]

Like Aldington, Beraud Villars cast doubt on Lawrence's sexual nature
and on his relationship to the French, whose defeat, it was charged,
was more important to Lawrence than the defeat of the Turks; and
Beraud Villars—perhaps influenced by the Franco-Algerian troubles
of his own times—also claimed that Lawrence had exaggerated the
military value of the Arab Revolt. Now Lawrence became controversial, more controversial than ever before, and—further encouraged by
the University of Texas's purchase of Lawrence manuscripts and the
increasing availability of important historical evidence—a few bold
academics began infiltrating a field of which they had been hitherto
very shy. It was not, however, until the publication of *The Secret Lives
of Lawrence of Arabia*, by Phillip Knightley and Colin Simpson in 1969,
that academics entered the field in force and what we may term the
academic Lawrence revival began. Knightley and Simpson were in-
vestigative reporters rather than academic researchers, but their book
contained much valuable new Public Record Office documentary evidence and interviews concerning Lawrence's public and private life,
and served, if in a somewhat sensationalist manner, to spark the interest in him that had been accumulating since the Robert Bolt–David
Lean film of 1962 and the 1967 Arab-Israeli war and the first hints of
the oil crisis that was to strike in 1973.

The resulting change in Lawrence studies was a great one. Before
the 1970s, there could scarcely be said to have been formal Lawrence
studies at all. There were a few pioneering works by academics, beginning with R. P. Blackmur's attempt to apply the New Criticism to
Lawrence's books in the 1940s, and continuing through works by Elie
Kedourie, Stanley Weintraub, and Irving Howe, among others, in the
1960s, as well as sporadic French interest in Lawrence. But as the
subject of *T. E. Lawrence by His Friends* (or T. E. Lawrence by his
enemies) he had been the object of his contemporaries' opinions. After
1969 a number of serious and disinterested academics, working in many
fields of history, literature, politics, psychology, and the arts, decided

that Lawrence was important enough to our cultural and political history to merit their full attention. Although the controversy around Lawrence is still far from over, the oft-repeated claim that Lawrence's interest for us today is owing only to Lowell Thomas has been shown to be false. A full half-century after Lawrence's death we find serious people more interested in him than ever before, and the result is a depth of research never imagined by Thomas. Trained historians have investigated the tangle of documents surrounding the rival British agencies in the Middle East in Lawrence's period; literary scholars have examined Lawrence's manuscripts and have arrived at a reasoned appraisal of the literary worth of his contribution; a psychiatrist has pronounced judgment on the complex relation between Lawrence's personality and his achievements; military historians have evaluated his role in the Arab Revolt.

The cynical may refer to a budding Lawrence industry propagated by academics eager for intellectual employment, but the solid benefits of only ten short years of scholarly study of Lawrence are already apparent. Scholarly distance has cooled the tone of the debate over Lawrence's worth, and the evidence brought to bear by manuscript, archival, and interview material has given the discussion a solidity and objectivity lacking in the appraisals of earlier periods. We no longer discuss whether Lawrence was the out-and-out liar that Aldington saw—he was not—but whether his undeniable influence on the politics of the Middle East should be seen positively or negatively in the long run; why he exaggerated when he did; and whether his literary contribution will be lasting. We no longer see Lawrence as *either* the chivalrous knight of the desert, unselfishly helping an alien nationality gain its independence with no second thoughts, *or* as the unscrupulous adventurer who wishes only to satisfy his own twisted personal needs and the interests of British colonialism. Thus, although we may still divide Lawrence scholars roughly into pro and con camps—and Aldington must be given his due for having generated this lasting schism—and the debate is lively as ever, the tone is more moderate, and a genuine desire for seeing Lawrence as he really was is now the object, whether or not this is always possible to achieve.

Most Lawrence scholars of the past ten or fifteen years—which means most Lawrence scholars, period—fall more or less into the "pro" camp. John Mack's comprehensive biography, the best to date, typifies, if in a heightened form, the view of the positive party. Mack, while admitting Lawrence's many foibles, such as a flair for self-advertisement and exaggeration and deep psychological divisions resulting in some strange behavior, sees Lawrence nonetheless as a man who contributed to the political health of the contemporary world:

> He retained on the one hand a childlike immaturity—like a gifted schoolboy—and a responsiveness to the child's world, while at the same time he assumed throughout his life extraordinary adult responsibilities. He possessed an unusual capacity for relationships with many different sorts of human beings, while retaining an essential isolation and aloofness. He was highly open to sensuous experience yet remained always an ascetic who rejected many of the pleasures of the flesh, especially sexual ones. Self-absorbed and egocentric, he was nevertheless unselfish in giving of himself. He suffered troubling forms of psychopathology and was "neurotic" in many ways. Yet out of his sufferings he found new solutions and values, and was often able to convert his personal pathology to creative public endeavors. . . . He was to a degree a hero fashioned along the lines of the Victorian revival of medieval romanticism. Yet he may contribute ultimately to the destruction of this form of heroism and help to replace it with a model of a hero more self-aware, responsible, and realistic.[52]

And this view is supported, somewhat more cautiously, by Uriel Dann's appraisal of Lawrence's place in history:

> If the argument of the foregoing presentation is accepted, "Lawrence of Arabia" emerges far smaller than the Lawrence Bureau of the nineteen-twenties and thirties would have him, and yet as of greater consequence than the backlash of the nineteen-fifties and sixties tends to allow. No Captain of History. But a man in the second rank who used his great gifts and self-made opportunities to leave an imprint on affairs which is of moment in the past and can be traced to the present. One may add, within the outlook and limitations of his own times a man who played his part with honour.[53]

In contrast to these positive views, we have the more jaundiced opinions of the smaller but nonetheless important "con" group of researchers. Elie Kedourie, in a critical review of Mack's biography, makes some points of undeniable importance:

> Lawrence's record, then, shows bravery in war, a great capacity for physical endurance, ingenuity as a guerrilla leader, and later some

literary talent. But it also shows that he was self-centered, mercurial, and violently unstable. . . . The cause of Arab nationalism which he embraced (and which he falsely claimed to have been double-crossed and betrayed by his country) was not more virtuous or worthy than any similar cause. Why a foreigner should so fervently embrace it, and what it has contributed to civilization, are both quite obscure. Lawrence, on the other hand, promoted a pernicious confusion between public and private, he looked to politics for a spiritual satisfaction which it cannot possibly provide, and he invested it with an impossibly transcendental significance. In doing so, he pandered to some of the most dangerous elements to be found in modern Western mentality. His influence and cult, here at their most extensive and enduring, we may judge to be not civilizing, but destructive.[54]

And the biographer Phillip Knightley, in a letter of 29 May 1980 to me, expresses a similarly negative summary evaluation of Lawrence:

I think much of the unhappiness in the Middle East in the past 50 years can be directly attributed to British policies that Lawrence had a hand in implementing. I think his fame was largely due to one man: Lowell Thomas, and all Lawrence's later difficulties were due to an overwhelming sense of guilt at the double game he had played—not an uncommon problem for spies and double agents, I'm told. He was only a minor cog in a bigger political wheel, but he found a place in history because Thomas made him a vulgar popular hero (at a time when heroes were scarce) and because he could write.

These conflicting positive and negative views, divergent as they are, are far more complex and less extreme than the earlier Thomas-Aldington divergence. Rather than a dispute about the facts of the case, they are a matter of interpretation and emphasis. They constitute the outer limits of the debate over Lawrence today, and show that he will continue to be controversial—and fascinating—but in a more solid and sophisticated way than previously.

But being controversial is not the same as being impossible to understand or substantiate. And some central issues concerning Lawrence's life and career appear to have been definitively cleared up by the scholarship of the past ten or fifteen years. For instance, Aldington had stressed Lawrence's alleged "hatred" of France as a prime motivating force in his career during the Arab Revolt and in the years immediately following it; and he was backed up in this by the biographies of Jean Beraud Villars and Knightley and Simpson. But in 1978 Maurice Larès's amazing 1,300-page doctorat d'etat (published in reduced form as a book in 1980)[55] on Lawrence and the French appeared. The first volume of this massive work is based on previously unpublished French (and other) Foreign Office archival documents and shows conclusively that Lawrence never, in fact, "hated" the French, but was instead deeply influenced by them in many ways. Larès points out, among other things, that Lawrence's criticism of the English role in Mesopotamia was more violent than his criticism of the French in Syria, and that "The pretended 'hatred' of T. E. Lawrence for France sometimes seems to be in fact the cover borrowed by mediocre French agents who thus justify themselves by it and transmit it to their superiors to make themselves look worthy."[56]

Aldington had also charged that Lawrence was a mediocre strategist and had exaggerated his military exploits; and Suleiman Mousa, an Arab writer, claimed that Lawrence had exaggerated his role within the Arab Revolt, failing to give full credit to Arab participation and leadership. But the most recent commentators on the military situation agree with Liddell Hart's early praise of Lawrence's skill rather than with Lawrence's detractors. Thus, Robert Asprey, in his comprehensive history of guerrilla warfare, *War in the Shadows*, calls Lawrence's actions "enormously" valuable to Allenby.[57] Douglas Orgill, author of the *Lawrence* volume in Ballantine's "War Leader" series, considers Lawrence a "classic guerrilla leader."[58] But the best answer to Aldington's and Mousa's charges of incompetence and exaggeration comes in Konrad Morsey's recent exhaustive study of the military aspects of the revolt. Morsey's work, like Mack's biography and Larès's study—all of which arrive at the same positive conclusions regarding Lawrence's activities—is especially valuable because it throws light of a most scrupulous and objective sort on the whole question of Lawrence's truth telling about the facts of the revolt, as well as on the more specialized military questions.

Morsey checks Lawrence's account in *Seven Pillars* point for point against all available government documents—including German sources—manuscript material, and primary and secondary accounts. He concludes that Lawrence's story is accurate apart from occasional and relatively unimportant literary heightenings. Lawrence, for instance, did not "choose" Feisal as the "prophet" of the Arab Revolt, as he asserts in his book, but simply acquiesced in the fact that Feisal was the only active and reliable son of Sherif Hussein; and their first meeting is romanticized. There are also deliberate ambiguities and silences admitted by Lawrence—such as the difficult Deraa chapter for which Morsey can find no outside confirmations or denials, and Lawrence's briefly mentioned secret solo trip to Syria (which he definitely *did* make, according to Morsey). The documents prove Lawrence's great importance in the Arab Revolt, although some points—such as precisely who was responsible for the planning of the Akaba attack in all its aspects—are difficult to clear up completely.

Probably Lawrence's main liberties as a historian, according to Morsey, are a tendency to present events in condensed or altered chronological order so as to heighten their literary impact and a tendency to present events in retrospect in *Seven Pillars* as more planned and less haphazard than they actually were. The attack on Akaba, for example, was decided upon tactically, when Lawrence and Auda were already on the road toward another goal, and not before, strategically, as *Seven Pillars* presents it—although Lawrence may well have had the Akaba idea in mind before leaving Wejh and did not tell anyone about it. Because of these tendencies, Lawrence's autobiography is not a strict, technically perfect history of the Arab Revolt, but "it is not justifiable to deny its importance as an historical source, despite the claims of Lawrence's detractors."[59] Lawrence's main worth, according to Morsey, a military historian, resides in his strategic theories. These have been studied in our time at various military colleges because they not only are suited to Lawrence's war but can serve as a model for all guerrilla warfare strategists. In assessing any history of Lawrence's career or any other historical event, we must remember that all histories must rely on documents and that they are therefore vulnerable to Lawrence's own criticism of modern histories, "the documents themselves are liars." But Morsey's work shows in the most objective and thorough manner possible that although Lawrence is really an autobiographer who wrote a necessarily subjective account of the revolt and his part in it, he told a true story that stands up well against *all* available evidence.

In addition to the issues of Lawrence and the French connection, Lawrence's worth as a military strategist, and the overall truth of Lawrence's historical record, his position as a writer has been considerably buttressed by the research of the recent Lawrence revival. No less than four books on Lawrence as a writer, each taking a different angle of investigation, and several important articles,[60] have argued convincingly on the basis of manuscript evidence, letters, and hardheaded literary analysis that Lawrence is a writer of importance in the history of English literature as a whole. Whether he is seen as a representative of the Anglo-Arabian writing tradition, the wider genres of the confession or the autobiography, or as the author of perhaps the only modern epic, the recent academic writers have strongly supported the conviction of such contemporaries as E. M. Forster, Robert Graves, and G. B. Shaw that Lawrence will be read not only in this century but in future centuries for the elegance of his prose and the interest of his characterization of himself and others, as well as for the wonderful tale he had to tell. These studies are all the more convincing because they are the first full-length criticism of the literary side of Lawrence's career ever undertaken, because of their reliance on modern critical and textual methods, and because of their unanimity—rare in Lawrence studies as in other scholarly fields—on the point of his worth as an artist. Be it noted that even such contemporary political or historical critics of Lawrence as Kedourie and Knightley admit in their quotations above that Lawrence, whatever else he was or was not, was a good writer. One reason that Lawrence's merit as a writer is less disputed now than, say, his political vision, is that his writing is available to us in full in the form of manuscripts as well as published works, while other aspects of his career depend upon the interpretation of incomplete and thorny archival documents and eyewitness testimony many years old, as well as on ideological positions regarding nationalism, colonialism, and the third world. We can analyze and assess Lawrence's writing in manuscript and book form as art with only minimal need for further confirmation or denial from sources outside the writings themselves.

Lawrence has suddenly become popular with literary critics because of the recent Northrop Frye–inspired emphasis on prose as opposed to fiction, among other things.[61] Burton Hatlen offers a possible and somewhat uncomplimentary (to Lawrence) alternate explanation for the sudden interest of literary critics in the course of a theoretical article in which Lawrence is not mentioned: "Any text which the philosophers, the scientists, or the social theorists have discarded can, it seems, 'become literature.' But as long as our colleagues are interested in a text, it is not 'literature' but something else: a 'philosophic essay,' or a 'sociological treatise,' etc."[62] In other words, when a text becomes discredited in another field, it becomes an object of interest to literary critics, so long as it is well written. But Lawrence here as elsewhere proves the exception to the rule, however well Hatlen's theory holds generally. For Lawrence seems to be increasing in importance to literary critics at the precise moment that his books are proving their accuracy as well as their worth to historians, psychologists, strategists, translators, and others.

For all the agreement about certain sides of Lawrence's career and production, there remains a good deal of disagreement, especially regarding his own personality. In many cases, documented revelations spur increased dissension rather than the certainty that had been anticipated. Scholarly disagreements continue to arise in the following main areas:

The autobiographical aspect. The truth of Lawrence's presentation of his own personality in *Seven Pillars* and *The Mint*. The Knightley and Simpson biography and, more conclusively, Mack's work have demonstrated that Lawrence's great life secret was his discovered masochism and continued "flagellation disorder," prompted by the beating and possible rape he experienced at Deraa, which he reveals only very circumspectly in his account of the Deraa incident and in *The Mint*, and from which he was not able to free himself in later life. This disorder would seem to be the—or one very important—cause of his frequent and otherwise unexplained depressions in the postwar years. It has also been shown, with some weight of evidence, that the "S.A." to whom the poem at the beginning of *Seven Pillars* is dedicated was— as was suspected earlier—Dahoum, or Salim Achmed, Lawrence's Arab servant. We no longer accuse Lawrence of "lying" on these points, but see them as the result of the very human right to preserve privacy and spare himself embarrassment while attempting, in a tortured way, to live up to the artistic demand of the autobiography to speak the whole truth, and the literary desire, augmented by the Anglo-Arabian travel tradition in which he wrote, to create an aura of mystery in the book. In fact, Lawrence has revealed more of himself publicly in *Seven Pillars* and *The Mint* than most other autobiographers ever do, and this candor has actually whetted our desire for total revelation and led us to blame him for holding back more than we would someone who had been less candid from the outset, as Mack has noted.

Despite this, the revelation of Lawrence's "secrets" by scholars has only increased rather than dispelled controversy. If "S.A." is known to be a man, then the question of homosexuality arises. John Mack has found absolutely no evidence of overt homosexuality after ten years of study of Lawrence's life; but the solid connection of Dahoum, Lawrence's "personal motive" for the Arab Revolt, and the very sensual poem dedicated to him, causes Jeffrey Meyers to think the opposite. If Lawrence was the victim of self-imposed flagellation at rare intervals during the last twelve years of his life, what light does this shed on the circumstances of his death in a motorcycle accident? Mack, a psychiatrist, speculates that Lawrence actually committed a kind of inadvertent suicide on his motorcycle, owing to a subconscious death wish caused by his inability to solve his flagellation problem. But Desmond Stewart, the most recent biographer, has replied that Lawrence's depression upon leaving the R.A.F. "could have heralded some new phase of action,"[63] and that Lawrence, far from being on the verge of suicide, probably would have gone on to another vigorous phase of his career as the 1930s moved toward World War II, as he had after other periods of personal stress.

Although he makes good sense on the point of Mack's alleged suicide theory, Stewart—on very thin evidence, it must be said—has claimed that the Deraa incident never occurred, but took place in modified form at Azrak, and that Sherif Ali, rather than Dahoum, is the "S.A." of the poem and the man who played the role of sadist to Lawrence's masochism; and that Lawrence was murdered by the British government. While the evidence we do have is against Stewart's claims on all these points, his two pages of questions about the accuracy of the account of Deraa in *Seven Pillars*[64] and arguments about the overall happiness or despair of the last phase of Lawrence's life indicate that there will be controversy about some parts of Lawrence's biography for some time to come. Even Lawrence's very death has the ambiguity necessary for dispute. Far from being merely academic or cultic points of disagreement, these personality questions bear on how we should read *Seven Pillars* and *The Mint* and interpret Lawrence's career as a whole.

The historical-cultural aspect. The Arab view of Lawrence and his view of them. Although Lawrence's view of the French and vice versa has been considerably clarified by the work of Larès, we lack a similar reference for his relation to the Arabs. The Arab view of Lawrence has shifted dramatically over the course of the century, as John Mack has pointed out. During the revolt, "Aurens" was regarded by the Arabs as a national hero. Then nationalistic Arab writers such as George Antonious and, later, Suleiman Mousa, downplay—but still acknowledge—his role, giving Auda rather than Lawrence credit for the Akaba plan, for instance. Finally, in our own time, ideological writers such as Edward Said and Sari Nasir denigrate Lawrence by accusing him of creating colonialist stereotypes of the Arabs.[65] At the same time, Western writers—Aldington, Beraud Villars, Kedourie, for instance—have been at pains to show that Lawrence in his book greatly underplayed the importance of the British contribution to the Arab Revolt in his desire to glorify Feisal and make the revolt appear a full national liberation movement.

In fact, almost all questions of historical accuracy seem to revolve around one central point: did Lawrence, and, if so, how much did Lawrence exaggerate the importance of the Arab Revolt in order to win more support for Feisal? Kedourie, for instance, has charged on good evidence that Lawrence in *Seven Pillars* concealed the fact that the Arabs were allowed to enter Damascus first by the British as a gesture of good will, rather than simply having arrived first owing to their own fighting ability.[66] Since both Western and Arab sides have a vested interest in debating such points, the precise value of the respective British (including Lawrence's) and Arab contributions to the Arab Revolt will remain in question for a long time to come. As John Mack has commented, "there remains a need for an objective analysis by a scholar familiar with both the Western and Arab cultures of Lawrence's part in the Arab revolt from both the political and military standpoint."[67] This is an almost impossible prescription, unfortunately, for it involves finding someone familiar with both cultures and partial to neither.

Until such time as such a person materializes, we are bound to state that the view that Lawrence presented a largely accurate, if occasionally exaggerated, picture of the course of the revolt and the Arabs' role in it—and, given his period, as "objective" a portrait of another people as a non-anthropologist and person from outside a given culture can manage—has been supported, for instance, by Mack's biography, Morsey's investigations, and the literary work of Tabachnick and Meyers.[68]

For the present, suffice it to say that the majority of recent full-length Lawrence studies present him as a cultural relativist, a troubled imperial agent who was able to sympathize deeply with an oppressed people, rather than as the racist and colonialist that extreme nationalists and other detractors see in him. If not as advanced a case as our contemporary Wilfred Thesiger, who feels himself corrupt compared to the Beduin he visits,[69] Lawrence is still far more culturally relativistic and farsightedly anti-colonialist than most of his contemporaries; and *Seven Pillars*, as a result, presents a largely favorable view of the Arab Revolt.

Another thorny issue arises in connection with Lawrence's ties to Zionism as well as to Arab nationalism. Some Arab historians try to show, for instance, that he was an all-out proponent of Zionism, who actually tricked Feisal into signing joint cooperative papers with Chaim Weizmann,[70] while some Zionists have claimed that he cared not at all for the Zionist movement and was interested only in securing Feisal's rule with the aid of assumed Jewish capital.[71] Instead, it appears, according to the most recent evidence in Mack, Stewart, Larès, and others, that Lawrence (unlike the pro-Arab Gertrude Bell or the pro-Zionist Richard Meinertzhagen) was one of the few and one of the last people in his own time and ours to achieve true sympathy for both national movements. His references to both movements in *Seven Pillars* are positive. He actually believed that they could be reconciled, and, although subsequent events have seemed to prove him wrong at least to date, this belief only redounds to his credit. But once again Lawrence's divided sensibility, his ability to see both sides of issues, has caused differing perspectives among his commentators, who find it hard to understand, from our present point of view, how someone might have held a double view on this as on other matters. The debate will go on, fueled by current Middle Eastern disagreements.

The political aspect. The validity of Lawrence's political vision in the long run. Was Lawrence right to support the Hussein family rather than Ibn Saud's Wahabi movement, which eventually triumphed over all rivals by consolidating Arabia in 1926, sending Sherif Hussein into exile in Cyprus? Were Lawrence's political solutions to the area's problems, as seen in his work in the 1921 Cairo Conference, for instance, of lasting value, or simply short-run expedients that have caused only trouble? Did Lawrence really believe that, as a result of this conference, the British "were quit of the war-time Eastern adventure, with clean hands" (*SP*, 276), or was he merely a cynical agent who did not really care about clean hands at all?

Philby, A. T. Wilson, H. Winstone, and David Howarth, among others, have charged that the choice of Hussein rather than Ibn Saud was a serious misjudgment. As Howarth writes in his *The Desert King* (New York: McGraw-Hill, 1964):

> The British in Cairo had no option but to choose the Sherif as the nominal leader of their Arab Revolt against the Turks, and once having made their choice, to offer him ever-increasing rewards in gold and arms and power. The misfortune of Arabia was that they believed that their choice of a man was right in Arab eyes. . . . with Lawrence's genius and Britain's wealth, the revolt went from strength to strength. Yet it was always hollow: it was always an expression of Lawrence's will and of British power, and never of any permanent Arab aspiration. (pp. 112–13)

In truth, Feisal was quickly expelled from Syria by the French mandatory power in 1920, and failed to establish a stable regime in Iraq, where the British placed him partially on Lawrence's recommendation in 1921, dying there in 1933 after losing his grip on power. His son and successor, Ghazi, was not an effective politician, and a long series of coups and countercoups have followed to this day. Abdullah—given control over Jordan by the British as a result of the same Cairo Conference in which Feisal received Iraq—was assassinated in 1951. And King Hussein of the Hejaz was exiled to Cyprus by a victorious Ibn Saud and died in exile in Amman in 1931. Of all Lawrence's work in this respect, there has been only one direct, lasting result: Jordan has remained in the hands of the Hussein family, for how long and to what value is not clear.

Perhaps this entire question of whether Britain should have supported Hussein rather than Ibn Saud is really a historical nonquestion, as Briton Cooper Busch points out in his *Britain, India, and the Arabs 1914–1921*, for the historian "is on dangerous ground if he raises such a wide-ranging hypothesis, the answer to which includes so many unknown quantities."[72] But some historians have tried to answer it. Thus, as Gary Troeller has pointed out in an article of 1971, "to assert that

Britain backed the wrong horse is to view the situation prevailing at the time in the light of Ibn Saud's subsequent career."[73] Hussein was the only logical choice of leader at the time for many reasons. This judgment was made not just by Lawrence but by Hogarth and the entire Arab Bureau, as well as by the Foreign Office, and was later seconded by the Colonial Office headed by Winston Churchill. The opposing view of the India Office and the British authorities in Mesopotamia was motivated largely by interoffice rivalry. And, as Hogarth himself admitted in 1925, "In adopting this policy we were not looking beyond the war."[74] In short, the British authorities made the best decision they could under the circumstances of war, and hindsight is not particularly relevant or valuable. What we can say for sure is that Lawrence maintained a commendable loyalty to Feisal and was not easy in his conscience until he saw both Feisal and Abdullah installed in positions of leadership as he had promised they would be, as his activities at the Versailles Conference and the Cairo Conference, and his postwar writings show.[75]

Even if we do the historically unthinkable and look at Lawrence's support of the Husseins with hindsight, this support does not seem reprehensible, either morally or politically, given the nature of politics in the Middle East. In his definitive work on the Cairo Conference, Aaron Klieman concludes: "The Cairo Conference, in short, was perhaps too ambitious, grafting monarchies and seeking to project the sharifians onto the entire Arab world, only to find that they were neither powerful nor respected enough to lead the Arabs. Leaders, like ideas, proved vulnerable and obsolete in the transitional Middle East."[76] However, he notes that, in contrast to the unrest facing the British in the form of uprisings in Mesopotamia in 1920 and in Palestine, the atmosphere among both British and Arab nationalists improved in the period immediately after the conference. And we must ask ourselves, in response to critics such as Philby and Howarth, if the subsequent rulers of Syria, Iraq, and for that matter Saudi Arabia were more particularly worthy or stable than Feisal or the present King Hussein. Lawrence's solutions would seem to be no worse—if no better—than any other in an area where leadership is of notoriously short duration. If he was not a prophet, he did have an accurate view of the area in his day, and it is possible to see his work as taking as its goal what he conceived to be the best path available to British and Arabs alike at the time—the choice of Feisal—although their paths would inevitably collide. His descriptions of Syria, for instance, as seen in his *Arab Bulletin* articles, are still regarded as masterpieces of precise description and political understanding that are relevant even today, as Gideon Gera points out. But this question, or nonquestion, of the long-range effect of his policies has the ambiguous elements that make for long-range argument.

If we take the sum total of all these disputed points, and attempt to see Lawrence as a whole in the light of all the scholarly views of the past ten or fifteen years, positive and negative, we come up with something like the following. Although Lawrence may have been less than a major historical figure because of the weakness of the Turks, the relatively small scale of the Arab Revolt, and the failure of the Lawrence-supported Hussein family to establish anything more than a precarious hold on Jordan as an old-style monarchy; although he may have resorted to a charismatic and willful power of manipulation to gain his ends (like most successful people in all fields); although he may have been a complex, guilt-scarred flagellant and even remotely possibly a homosexual; although *Seven Pillars of Wisdom* may contain oblique personal hints and artistic "epic" exaggerations rather than objective personal and political truths at all times; although he himself may have been confused about his profusion of roles—Lawrence *was* brilliant in not just one but many fields; Lawrence *did* help lead Arab forces in an unusual war bravely, effectively, imaginatively, and at considerable personal risk and hardship; Lawrence *was* extraordinarily sensitive to his personal, moral, philosophical, and artistic predicaments; Lawrence *was* consistently able to convince important and intelligent people such as Churchill, Feisal, Allenby, and Clayton to do what he wanted; and Lawrence *did* write brilliantly, powerfully, and truthfully of the events in which he was involved and of his own personality, as he saw them. In short, the Lawrence we have today is more human, more complex, more believable, and more realistically brilliant than he appears in the Thomas and Aldington portraits. And for the majority of Lawrence scholars, who are well aware of his failures as well as successes, Lawrence is considerably more positive than his detractors have portrayed him, and a man and writer of lasting interest.

· V ·

The present volume brings to the reader the most recent perspectives in Lawrence studies in the form of fourteen essays (including this introduction) written especially for it. It unites the efforts of pioneers of the Lawrence revival and the latest book and dissertation writers, thus announcing the establishment and development of a new academic subject cutting across many fields. It does not pretend to cover all facets of Lawrence's career and related subjects, but it does comprehend the major aspects, some of them for the first time in any seriousness and depth. Although pride of place has been accorded Lawrence's literary activities on the theory that *Seven Pillars of Wisdom* constitutes his most important and enduring contribution to culture, the reader receives a comprehensive view of a career astonishing in its range and brilliance and interesting even in its failures and near misses. Previously unstressed areas of Lawrence's endeavors—for instance, his "Twenty-seven Articles," a guide for political officers working among the Arabs, which is found worthy of analysis by several of the essay authors—are seen to deserve more attention than they have received in the past, and reveal that Lawrence's manifold career will continue to surprise and intrigue us as it is sifted and analyzed.

The literary section begins with M. D. Allen's exploration of Lawrence's medieval interests and their literary results. Allen shows for the first time the true depth of Lawrence's attachment to this period by examining his B.A. thesis *Crusader Castles*, and his knowledge of brasses, heraldry, and medieval literature. Allen is thus able to explicate the language and symbolism of many previously overlooked or misunderstood passages of *Seven Pillars*, as well as to provide a fresh perspective on Lawrence's entire career. Thomas O'Donnell's essay explains the influence of romantic philosophy and literary tradition on Lawrence, thus proving once again that Lawrence has something for everyone in the range of his interests. Further developing, refining, and modifying the theory at the heart of his book on Lawrence, O'Donnell shows how Lawrence is divided between asserting himself in the military sections of *Seven Pillars* and denying himself in the introspective sections of that book and in *The Mint*. For O'Donnell, Lawrence's attraction results from the tension between his willful self-assertion and the almost religious bareness, simplicity, and renunciation of the first two sections of *The Mint*—in Lawrence's attempt, however unsuccessful, to deny will.

Keith Hull's work challenges O'Donnell's (and others') view of Lawrence's divisions by emphasizing his wholeness as an artist. He amasses evidence to show that Lawrence was very much in conscious control of his combination of documentary and spiritual, fact and mystery, in *Seven Pillars*, and deliberately wished to create an atmosphere of contestability through it. Instead of presenting Lawrence's admitted divisions as signs of an artistic flaw, he sees their adroit management as a great success, and points out parallels in the work of modernist writers and beyond into our own period. Tabachnick's brief essay—a paper read in the British Travellers to the Near East session of the Modern Language Association meeting in December 1981—complements Hull's suggestion of modernist affinities and exploration of the subjective landscape of *Seven Pillars of Wisdom*. By comparing Lawrence's use of ruins with T. S. Eliot's in *The Waste Land*, Tabachnick shows how for Lawrence they symbolize the state of the Arab Revolt and the British Empire in his time, his actual personal situation, and his theory of the incompleteness and fragmentation of art and life: in both form and content, Lawrence's book may be seen as the equivalent of Eliot's *Waste Land* in twentieth-century autobiography, paradoxically combining control and disintegration.

Although Jeffrey Meyers has written much on *Seven Pillars*, this is his first look at *The Mint*. Meyers uses the book to sum up Lawrence's entire spiritual career. Emphasizing Lawrence's sexual nature as he sees it, he reveals the hidden autobiographical currents under the surface of *The Mint* in the course of a judicious and comprehensive literary evaluation that balances Lawrence's artistic strengths and failures.

The important neglected areas of Lawrence's writing—his thesis, letters, mechanics' manuals, archaeological reports, and technical passages of *Seven Pillars*—allow Rodelle Weintraub to show in more detail than ever before the extent of Lawrence's success as a technical writer. She points up Lawrence's skills as archaeologist, soldier, and mechanic while demonstrating his ability to bridge the gap between art and technology as a forerunner of currents found in Persig's *Zen and the Art of Motorcycle Maintenance*. Her essay concludes this section of the collection by impressing upon us an important perspective: instead of being blamed for lacking fictional imagination, Lawrence as a writer deserves praise for his power to create lively and lasting nonfiction.

The second part of this book—on the "Other Aspects" of Lawrence's achievement—opens with Charles Grosvenor's work on *Seven Pillars* as visual art. Grosvenor provides an in-depth view of the various artists Lawrence assembled for his project and their position in the spectrum of early twentieth-century art, and concludes that on this basis alone the 1926 edition of Lawrence's book is an important document in the artistic history of our century. He then examines in great detail the relationship between text, layout, and decoration, also producing previously unpublished portraits rejected by Lawrence. He establishes for the first time a serious and reasoned assessment of Lawrence's success and failure as book designer and visual artist, thus filling an important gap in Lawrence studies.

Lawrence's military career has been subject to at least as many questionings and doubts as all other aspects of his life and work. Using British archival documents as well as articles published after his own book appeared, Konrad Morsey marshals hard evidence to prove that Lawrence must be regarded as a major strategic thinker. Opposing the views of such critics as Walter Laqueur, Richard Aldington, and Suleiman Mousa, he demonstrates that Lawrence did evolve his theories—for the most part—at the time of the revolt and not retrospectively, and that, despite some propagandizing for the Sherifian cause and some artistic polishing, his *Seven Pillars* constitutes a highly accurate historical source for the revolt and his part in it. Since Lawrence's death, his theories have gained wide currency and are under constant study in military academies around the world even today.

As Gideon Gera reveals, one reason why Lawrence has appeared mysterious and therefore untrustworthy to many people is simply that he was not at liberty to reveal important events in his career—such as the details of his famous secret trip behind Turkish lines into northern Syria—which can now be shown definitely to have taken place. When we see Lawrence primarily as an intelligence officer committed to maintaining necessary secrecy, his whole career appears in a new light. Gera finds that Lawrence's intelligence experience—as far as we can assess it, even today—follows a pattern of unusual expertise in all areas that makes him one of the last outstanding generalist agents, a type rarely found in today's world of technological information gathering and analysis.

Lawrence's activities as go-between among English and Arabs, English and French, and Jews and Arabs have proved perhaps the most controversial aspect of his work. The essays by Larès and Klieman attempt to clarify these issues. Larès gives us the fruit of his massive investigations into Lawrence's relations with the French in concise form. Utilizing French documents and other unpublished sources, he relentlessly exposes the myth of Lawrence's alleged hatred of the French: Lawrence and France may not have been the best of friends, particularly with regard to Middle Eastern policy, but they were not enemies either, except for pockets of French officialdom that resented his comparative success with the Arabs, and even went so far as to concoct a hitherto unrevealed assassination plot.

Klieman carefully examines Lawrence's Colonial Office career in terms of his degree of originality, resourcefulness, and success as a policymaker. Using archival material and recent articles and studies, he concludes that Lawrence was a synthesizer of ideas rather than an original political thinker, but that he was able to realize his goals because of his drive and good working relationship with Churchill, and that the Kingdom of Jordan must be regarded as the measure of his success or failure.

Stanley Weintraub's essay presents not Lawrence as a writer, but rather the fascinating shifts in Lawrence's literary image that have taken place from his time to our own. Greatly expanding his earlier work on this subject, Weintraub gives us the most complete survey and evaluation available to date of poems, novels, films, and plays in which Lawrence figures as a character, thus revealing Lawrence's status as the mirror of the concerns of generations of writers (and readers).

In the hope that this volume may have stimulated the reader to further Lawrence pursuits, its final essay offers practical advice toward that end. Philip O'Brien, Lawrence collector, print expert, and librarian, supplies guidelines to those who would like to begin collecting Lawrence materials themselves. As O'Brien's account of available Lawrence bibliographies—the most complete assessment yet—progresses, it becomes apparent that, despite all that has been written about him during the past fifty years, those interested in the serious collection and documentation of Lawrence materials will find great scope for their endeavors even today.

And the same can be said about Lawrence studies as a whole. This volume attempts to mark not the end of the serious attempt to fit together Lawrence's pieces but only the beginning.

N·O·T·E·S

1. In a conversation in Beersheva during the filming of *Masada*, Peter O'Toole, a distant relative of Lawrence, told me that Lawrence's own father was involved in intelligence work and that he, and not D. G. Hogarth, as is generally assumed, first brought Lawrence into such work; O'Toole cited family gossip as the source of his information. This may or may not be another of the apocryphal stories surrounding Lawrence's entire biography (John Mack in a letter of 14 July 1980 to me calls the whole idea "loony"); I repeat it here because I have not seen this information in any biographical source.

2. For the non-British contingents involved in the revolt, see M. Larès, *T. E. Lawrence, la France et les Français* (Lille: Lille University Reproduction Service, 1978), vol. 1, chap. 7. For discussion of naval contingents used in the revolt, see Charles Parnell, "Lawrence of Arabia's Debt to Seapower," *United States Naval Institute Proceedings* 105/8/918 (August 1979): 75–83.

3. For military evaluations of the revolt and Lawrence's military ability, see Robert Asprey, *War in the Shadows: The Guerrilla in History* (Garden City, N.Y.: Doubleday, 1975), 278–85; M. Larès, "La science et l'art militaires de T. E. Lawrence," *Etudes de Litterature Étrangère et Comparée* 77 (1979): 143–55; Konrad Morsey, *T. E. Lawrence und der arabische Aufstand 1916/18* (Osnabrück: Biblio, 1976); Douglas Orgill, *Lawrence* (New York: Ballantine, 1973); and Konrad Morsey's essay in this volume.

4. Asprey, *War in the Shadows*, 279. There is no indication in their letters and memoirs that Lawrence and Lettow-Vorbeck ever met or knew of one another. However, Colonel Richard Meinertzhagen, who had taken part in the campaign against Lettow-Vorbeck before becoming Lawrence's associate in the Middle East, might possibly have mentioned the German general to Lawrence either during the war or after it. After the war, both Lettow-Vorbeck and Lawrence were guests in Meinertzhagen's home. See John Lord, *Duty, Honor, Empire* (New York: Random House, 1970), 386.

5. Paul E. von Lettow-Vorbeck, *My Reminiscences of East Africa* (London: Hurst and Blackett [1920]), 325.

6. For recent studies of this campaign, see Brian Gardner, *German East* (London: Cassell, 1963), and Leonard Mosley, *Duel for Kilimanjaro* (London: Weidenfeld and Nicolson, 1963).

7. Henri De Monfreid, *Adventures of a Red Sea Smuggler* (New York: Stonehill, 1974), translated by Helen Bell, introduction by Colin Wilson, 287.

8. Colin Wilson, introduction to *Adventures of a Red Sea Smuggler*, xiii–xiv.

9. "Henri De Monfreid, 95, Dies; Adventurer Wrote 60 Books," *New York Times*, 14 December 1974, 32.

10. H. V. F. Winstone, *Captain Shakespear* (London: Cape, 1976).

11. H. St. John Philby, *Arabia* (New York: Scribner's, 1930), 233–34, and *Arabian Days* (London: Hale, 1948), 157.

12. N. N. E. Bray, *A Paladin of Arabia* (London: John Heritage, 1936).

13. Ibid., 297–98.

14. George Antonious, *The Arab Awakening* (New York: Capricorn, 1965); John Mack, *A Prince of Our Disorder* (London: Weidenfeld and Nicolson, 1976), 206–8; Suleiman Mousa, *T. E. Lawrence: An Arab View* (Oxford: Oxford University Press, 1966); Sari Nasir, *The Arabs and the English* (London: Longmans, 1976); Anis Sayigh, "An Arabic Opinion of Lawrence," *Hiwar* 5 (July–August 1963): 15–23, in Arabic; Anis Sayigh, *The Hashemites and the Great Arabic Revolution* (Beirut: Dar al-Tali'ah, 1966), in Arabic.

15. A. T. Wilson, *Loyalties: Mesopotamia 1917–1920* (Oxford: Oxford University Press, 1936), 292.

16. Gertrude Bell, *Gertrude Bell: From Her Personal Papers 1889–1914*, ed. Elizabeth Burgoyne (London: Ernest Benn, 1958), 296–97.

17. See the above biography in two volumes (the second is *Gertrude Bell: From Her Personal Papers 1915–1926* [London: Ernest Benn, 1961]); H. V. F. Winstone, *Gertrude Bell* (London: Cape, 1978); and *The Letters of Gertrude Bell*, ed. Lady Bell, 2 vols. (Harmondsworth: Penguin, 1939). Bell's own works include *Poems from the Divan of Hafiz* (1897), *The Desert and the Sown* (1907), *The Thousand and One Churches* (1909), *The Palace and the Mosque at Ukhaidir* (1914), and *The Arab War* (1940).

18. See n. 14 of Philip O'Brien's article and the bibliography in this collection for a full listing of works in several languages.

19. Bray, *A Paladian of Arabia*, 194.

20. *SP*, 48. See John Mack, "Lawrence and the Armenians," *Ararat* 21, no. 3 (1980): 2–8, for a description of Lawrence's position on the Armenian question.

21. See *Gertrude Bell: From Her Personal Papers 1915–1926*, 163.

22. *L*, 490–91.

23. *Gertrude Bell: From Her Personal Papers 1915–1926*, 295.

24. R. P. Blackmur, "The Everlasting Effort: A Citation of T. E. Lawrence," in *The Lion and the Honeycomb* (New York: Harcourt, Brace, 1955), 108.

25. See, for instance, George Antonious, *The Arab Awakening*; Briton Cooper Busch, *Britain, India, and the Arabs, 1914–1921* (Berkeley and Los Angeles: University of California Press, 1971); C. Ernest Dawn, *From Ottomanism to Arabism* (Urbana: University of Illinois Press, 1973); Elie Kedourie, *England and the Middle East* (London: Bowes and Bowes, 1956) and *In the Anglo-Arab Labyrinth* (Cambridge: Cambridge University Press, 1976); Stephen H. King, "The British Successor States in the Post-War Middle East," Ph.D. dissertation, Claremont Graduate School, 1978; Aaron Klieman, *Foundations of British Policy in the Arab World* (Baltimore: Johns Hopkins University Press, 1970); Elizabeth Monroe, *Britain's Moment in the Middle East, 1914–*

1956 (Baltimore: Johns Hopkins University Press, 1963); and Zeine N. Zeine, *The Struggle for Arab Independence* (Beirut: Khayats, 1960). Isaiah Friedman's article, "The McMahon-Hussein Correspondence and the Question of Palestine," *Journal of Contemporary History* 5, no. 2 (1970): 83–122, and 5, no. 4 (1970): 185–200, the response to it, are also helpful.

26. Lawrence probably read Telesio during his study of Campanella—another Renaissance philosopher, deeply influenced by Telesio—while preparing for a political science examination at Oxford. See *L*, 110.

27. "Man Has a Divine Soul," excerpt from Bernardino Telesio, *De Rerum Natura*, in D. G. Runes, *A Treasury of Philosophy* (New York: Philosophical Library, 1955), 1161–62.

28. Ibid., 1161. See also Neil Van Deusen, *Telesio* (New York: Columbia University Press, 1932), 21, 23, 78.

29. Bernardine M. Bonansea, "Telesio, Bernardino," in *The Encyclopedia of Philosophy* (New York: Macmillan, 1967), 8:93.

30. Vyvyan Richards, *A Portrait of T. E. Lawrence* (London: Cape, 1936), 234.

31. Ibid., 23.

32. William James, *Essays in Radical Empiricism* (London: Longmans, 1912), 37.

33. Bertrand Russell, *Analysis of Mind* (London: Allen and Unwin, 1921), 6. I thank Dr. Richard Shusterman of my department for consultation on the similarity of Lawrence's and Russell's points.

34. In a letter of 1927—the only one of all his letters in which he cites Russell—Lawrence calls Russell "foolish," "silly" and a "fat-head" without telling us why. This shows at least that Lawrence was reading or had read Russell, if at a later date than the composition of *Seven Pillars* and *The Mint* (*L*, 756). He may have heard of Russell's philosophy from the philosophers at All Souls when he was resident there in 1919–1920.

35. *M*, 249–50.

36. F. H. Bradley, *Appearance and Reality* (1893; London: Swan Sonnenschein, 1908).

37. Jewel Spears Brooker, "F. H. Bradley's Doctrine of Experience in T. S. Eliot's *The Waste Land* and *Four Quartets*," *Modern Philology* 77 (November 1979): 152.

38. Frederick Copleston, *A History of Philosophy*, vol. 8, *Modern Philosophy Bentham to Russell* (Garden City, N.Y.: Image, 1967), 236.

39. Mack, *A Prince of Our Disorder*, 423.

40. Ibid., 438.

41. I thank Mrs. Noah Ben Porat of my spring 1980 "Neglected Literature" seminar for pointing out the relation between the passage from Lawrence and Henry James's story.

42. *L*, 853.

43. See André Malraux, "Lawrence and the Demon of the Absolute," *Hudson Review* 8 (Winter 1956): 519–32; and Denis Boak, "Malraux and T. E. Lawrence," *Modern Language Review* 61, no. 2 (1966): 218–24; John Friedman, "The Challenge of Destiny: A Comparison of T. E. Lawrence's and André Malraux's Adventure Tales"

(Ph.D. diss., New York University, 1974); and Larès, T. E. Lawrence, la France et les Français, 2:1067–72. Larès is now editing Malraux's recently discovered biography of Lawrence.

44. Van Deusen, Telesio, 1.

45. Stephen Spender, "Interview: The Art of Poetry XXV," Paris Review (Winter–Spring 1980): 127.

46. In Lady Chatterley's Lover there are disparaging remarks about a "Colonel C. E. Florence." See Stanley Weintraub's essay in this collection. For Read's comments, see "Lawrence of Arabia" in A Coat of Many Colours (London: Routledge, 1945), 19–26. This essay was originally published in The Bibliophile's Almanack (1928).

47. Spender, "Interview," 50.

48. John Morris, "Richard Aldington and Death of a Hero—or Life of an Anti-Hero," in The First World War in Fiction, ed. Holger Klein (London: Macmillan, 1978), 388.

49. Richard Aldington, T. E. Lawrence: A Biographical Enquiry (Chicago: Henry Regnery, 1955), 388.

50. Ibid., 106–7.

51. Jean Beraud Villars, T. E. Lawrence; or, The Search for the Absolute (London: Sidgwick and Jackson, 1958), xi.

52. Mack, A Prince of Our Disorder, 457–58.

53. Uriel Dann, "Lawrence 'of Arabia'—One More Appraisal," Middle Eastern Studies 15 (May 1979): 161.

54. Elie Kedourie, "The Real T. E. Lawrence," Commentary 64 (July 1977): 56.

55. Maurice Larès, T. E. Lawrence, la France et les Français (Paris: Imprimerie Nationale, 1980).

56. Larès's dissertation (Lille, 1978), 1:594. My translation.

57. Asprey's entire section on Lawrence (278–85) is very favorable.

58. Orgill, Lawrence, 31.

59. Morsey, T. E. Lawrence und der arabische Aufstand, 17. Translated by Shlomo Arbel.

60. Jeffrey Meyers, The Wounded Spirit (London: Martin, Brian and O'Keeffe, 1973); Stanley Weintraub and Rodelle Weintraub, Lawrence of Arabia: The Literary Impulse (Baton Rouge: Louisiana State University Press, 1975); Stephen E. Tabachnick, T. E. Lawrence (Boston: Twayne, 1978); Thomas J. O'Donnell, The Confessions of T. E. Lawrence (Athens: Ohio University Press, 1979). Keith Hull, "T. E. Lawrence's Perilous Parodies," Texas Quarterly 2 (Summer 1972): 56–61; "Lawrence of The Mint, Ross of the R.A.F.," South Atlantic Quarterly 74 (Summer 1975): 340–48; "Creed, History, Prophets, and Geography in Seven Pillars of Wisdom," Texas Quarterly 18 (Autumn 1975): 15–28. For Lawrence as a translator from the French, see the second volume of Larès's dissertation.

61. For a discussion and review of the recent work on Lawrence as a writer and the reasons for his revival as such, see Stephen E. Tabachnick, "The T. E. Lawrence Revival in English Studies," Research Studies 44 (September 1976): 190–98.

62. Burton Hatlen, "Why Is The Education of Henry Adams 'Literature,' While The Theory of the Leisure Class Is Not?" College English 40 (February 1979): 671.

63. Desmond Stewart, *T. E. Lawrence* (London: Hamish Hamilton, 1977), 293.

64. Ibid., 241–43.

65. See Mack, *A Prince of Our Disorder*, 206–8; Antonious, *The Arab Awakening*; Mousa, *T. E. Lawrence: An Arab View*; Nasir, *The Arabs and the English*; and Edward Said, *Orientalism* (New York: Pantheon, 1978).

66. Elie Kedourie, "The Capture of Damascus, 1 October 1918," in *The Chatham House Version* (London: Weidenfeld and Nicolson, 1970), 33–51.

67. Mack, *A Prince of Our Disorder*, 184.

68. See Mack, particularly chaps. 14 and 15; Morsey, passim; Meyers's review of Said's *Orientalism*, *Sewanee Review* 88 (Spring 1980): xlv–xlviii; Tabachnick, *T. E. Lawrence*, particularly chaps. 5 and 8. O'Donnell, however, supports a more critical view of Lawrence's activities. See his essay in this volume, especially n. 50.

69. See Tabachnick, *T. E. Lawrence*, chap. 8, for a comparison of Thesiger and Lawrence.

70. See, for instance, A. L. Tibawi, "T. E. Lawrence, Feisal, and Weizmann," in his *Arabic and Islamic Themes* (London: Luzac, 1976), 315–23.

71. In Renee Weingarten's review of Knightley and Simpson's biography, "T. E. Lawrence, the End of the Legend," *Midstream* 16 (May 1970): 57–65, she seems eager to accept uncritically their evidence that Lawrence was not pro-Zionist. See particularly p. 62. But John Friedman, in "Lawrence of Arabia and Zionism," *Jewish Spectator* 40 (1975): 43–46, adduces evidence to show that Lawrence was strongly pro-Zionist.

72. Busch, 481–82.

73. Gary Troeller, "Ibn Sa'ud and Sharif Husain: A Comparison in Importance in the Early Years of the First World War," *Historical Journal* 14 (September 1971): 633.

74. D. G. Hogarth, "Wahhabism and British Interests," *Journal of the British Institute of International Affairs* 4 (1925): 72.

75. For the postwar writings, see Stanley Weintraub and Rodelle Weintraub, eds., *Evolution of a Revolt* (University Park: Pennsylvania State University Press, 1968).

76. Klieman, *Foundations of British Policy in the Arab World*, 247.

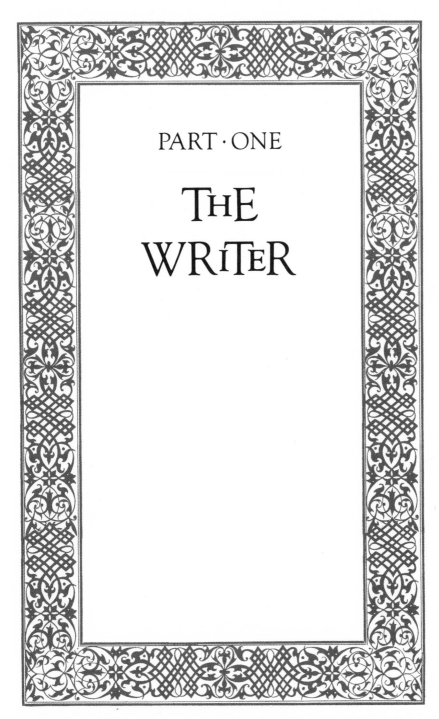

PART · ONE

THE
WRITER

Lawrence's Medievalism

M. D. ALLEN

As a schoolboy and young man, Lawrence threw himself into antiquarian pursuits with formidable thoroughness. Perhaps the first awakening of interest in the past occurred when he watched his father at his various hobbies, which included the study of the architecture of castles and cathedrals;[1] and any smoldering enthusiasm for the Middle Ages would have been fanned into flame by the reminders of the past to be found in many of Oxford's streets. Turn-of-the-century Oxford may have lost a little of its former glory, but only forty-three years before the Lawrences moved there, "Oxford was still in its outward aspect a medieval city, 'a vision of grey-roofed houses and a long winding street and the sound of many bells,' as William Morris later described it."[2] Morris's disciple Lawrence found himself in a more modern environment; even so, had he been offered the opportunity, he could hardly have chosen a place that would have better stimulated interest in the past.

With the publication in 1937 of *T. E. Lawrence by His Friends* and in 1938 of the *Letters*, the world first learned in some detail of Lawrence's interest in medieval literature and the authors of the nineteenth-century medieval revival; in castles, monumental brasses, armor, and heraldry. A. W. Lawrence, in his editorial postscript to the first book, considered his brother's "medieval researches [as] . . . a dream way of escape from bourgeois England [but] . . . I doubt whether he continued them when he lived in the East. I do not know whether he had read deeply about any aspect of the Middle Ages other than the military, the chivalrous and the social."[3] On the other hand, the editor of the *Letters*, David Garnett, wrote that "he had a passionate absorption in the [medieval] past. . . . This was not a boyish hobby but a lifelong interest."[4] Since then Richard Aldington has impugned Lawrence's medieval scholarship, and a more sympathetic biographer, John Mack, has written briefly but suggestively about the young Lawrence's reading in chivalric and courtly literature;[5] but the entire subject demands investigation in depth.

There exist testimonies to the thoroughness with which Lawrence the schoolboy knew the Oxford of his own day and its antecedents. "He was then best known, almost to notoriety, for his archaeological rummagings . . . in and about Oxford. Every excavation and rebuilding in the city was penetrated, and fragments of glass and stoneware zealously recovered . . . we became familiar with medieval names of the Oxford streets, Fish Street, Canditch, Horsemonger Street."[6] The celebrated exploration of subterranean Trill Mill stream was inspired by a reading of the seventeenth-century Oxford historian and antiquary Anthony Wood.[7] Lawrence studied Oxford's Gothic buildings, especially those of the Perpendicular, "late" Gothic period, such as Merton College and the Cloisters of New College. He frequented the Ashmolean and University museums and the Bodleian and Radcliffe libraries; he studied medieval pottery and made a collection of brass rubbings. One expert reports Mrs. Lawrence as informing him that "a few of her son's best efforts [at brass rubbing] were presented to the Ashmolean Museum, Oxford, as they were found to be of superior quality to some of the examples housed in the collection there."[8] The museum's manuscript catalog, prepared by the Oxford Architectural and Historical Society, was "largely amended and corrected by Lawrence himself, and the characteristic handwriting appears on many of its pages."[9] Obviously, this argues for a great deal of erudition on Lawrence's part.

A thorough knowledge of monumental brasses demands a knowledge of armor and heraldry, for it is impossible to understand a brass properly if one cannot date it roughly by any armor borne by the engraved figure, and "the heraldry of a brass can, to the discerning, be almost as informative about those commemorated as the inscriptions."[10] Lawrence made a friend of Charles J. ffoulkes, who lectured on armor at Oxford University in 1909–10. On ffoulkes's behalf he later looked in Syria for a man who still practiced the "mystery craft" of chain-mail making.[11] With a schoolboy friend he compiled heraldic rolls of arms, "painted in their proper tinctures. . . . A herald's jargon eventually enriched the vocabulary of the *Seven Pillars*."[12] By the time he was fifteen, Lawrence had traversed the southern and eastern counties on brass-rubbing expeditions; two years later he had exhausted most accessible British examples of Gothic architecture and in the summer of 1906 began a series of vacation trips to France.[13]

To read the letters to his family dating from these tours is to receive an impression of intellectual and physical vigor, of a rather precarious pride, and of a consciousness of latent capacities. Disbarred from smooth social ascent or even unquestioned acceptance in many "suitable" careers by his illegitimacy and personal eccentricity, Lawrence found comfort and involvement in exploration of another age, and, to a great extent, identification with its values. Lawrence's interests enabled him to distance himself, emotionally and physically, from the combination of town and time that made demands he could not or would not fulfill.

Lawrence's interests were also in tune with some of the artistic and literary preoccupations of the day. The Pre-Raphaelites praised medieval Italian painting. Ruskin claimed that the ugly was not a suitable subject for treatment in art: this seemed to exclude much of the contemporary world of an increasingly industrial England. (Lawrence closely read "The Nature of Gothic," the chapter of *Stones of Venice* in which the social implications of Ruskin's medievalism are made clear, and its influence in theme and phrase on *Seven Pillars* and *The Mint* is plain to see. Lawrence saw in Ruskin's distinction between "servile ornament" and "the mediaeval, or especially Christian, system of ornament" a parallel to—it was probably an inspiration for—his own differentiation between the natures and roles of regular armed forces and Arab guerrillas). Morris, whom Lawrence resembled so much and whose rebellion against late Victorian England and its values took a practical turn, as Lawrence's own was later to, made plans as a young man for an "Order" or "Brotherhood," and wrote to a friend that "We must enlist you in this crusade and holy warfare against the age."[14]

In the summer of 1906 Lawrence cycled vigorously and pursued his medieval interests with satisfying completeness. Technical terms pepper the loving and detailed letters sent back to Oxford, and Lawrence's capacity for imaginatively reconstructing his period in practical specifics is in evidence: "By the side of the large gate is a little postern about 2 feet wide, also with drawbridge: this saved moving the enormous pont-levis that the large door must have had, since the little one was large enough for ordinary purposes."[15] Next year Lawrence visited the castle of Richard I, Chateau Gaillard, which delighted him. "Richard I must have been a far greater man than we usually consider him: he must have been a great strategist and a great engineer, as well as a great man-at-arms."[16] A letter written five days later discusses Richard's final wound and where exactly the arrow came from; the crusading and chivalrous Richard occupied a central place in Lawrence's imagination.

What Garnett described as "the most beautiful and emotional of his early letters"[17] dealt with Chartres, which Lawrence considered glorious, but (owing to Ruskin's influence) "a gallery built by the sculptors to enclose a finer collection than the Elgin marbles" rather than a triumph of general form and size. However, the writing by which we should judge Lawrence's intellectual development as an adolescent and young man is the thesis that he presented in addition to his Finals papers in 1910, then entitled "The Influence of the Crusades on European Military Architecture to the End of the Twelfth Century" and now known as *Crusader Castles*, under which title it was published in 1936, the second of the two volumes consisting of letters written home while he was traveling in search of material. It is impossible for a layman to comment on the validity of the work, which, in direct opposition to the generally accepted view of the time, claimed that "the Crusading architects were for many years copyists of the Western builders."[18] In other words, according to Lawrence, the Crusaders did not take back to Europe from Byzantine examples their knowledge of engineering and fortification but brought it with them to the East from their home countries. The dispute has still not been finally settled, but it seems that Lawrence, with characteristic originality and self-consciousness, overstated his case. Modern experts believe that there was more mutual influence than earlier scholars had accepted or—in the other direction—than Lawrence admitted. Lawrence's work assisted in the modification of views, but he went too far.

As a definitive statement on the evolution of twelfth-century military architecture, *Crusader Castles* may not therefore be acceptable. As evidence of remarkable reading and traveling, consequent remarkable knowledge, and the ability to master ideas and handle them to suit a purpose, it is eminently so. Lawrence is sufficiently sure of his grasp of the topic to interpret, in a prose that is consistently fluid and self-confident, a mass of complex and technical detail in a way that supports his thesis (he had made up his mind before leaving Europe, of course).

Robin Fedden describes Chastel Pèlerin (Athlit),[19] a fortress flanked on three sides by the sea, as follows:

> On three sides the rocky promontory, wading deep into the waves, offered in itself a strong protection to a garrison who were also masters of the sea. On three sides therefore the Templars confined themselves to building a single massive wall rising almost from the water's edge, with one or two rectangular towers. . . . Wisely the main defences were piled up on the landward side of the promontory. They are still impressive, and this largely by reason of the cyclopean stones of which they are built.[20]

The complex defenses protecting the landward side, adds Fedden, "represent perhaps the fullest Crusader development of that conception of fortification associated with Byzance."

Lawrence, however, first explains that the two military orders into whose hands the ownership of almost all the large castles devolved—because the cost of their upkeep was too great for the vast majority of feudal lords—each added to or rebuilt its acquisitions in its own style. "The Templars, always suspected of a leaning towards mysterious Eastern arts and heresies, took up the mantle of Justinian, as represented by the degenerate fortresses in Northern Syria, and amplified it, in making it more simple." The Hospitallers, on the other hand, "drew their inspiration from the flourishing school of military architects in contemporary France."[21] He then goes on to criticize Chastel Pèlerin:

> [The Templars] held possession there of a narrow promontory of rock and sand, eminently defensible according to mediaeval ways. Yet here they . . . threw aside all the carefully arranged schemes of flanking fire, all the covering works, all the lines of multiple defence which were being thought out meanwhile in Europe. At Athlit they relied on the one line of defence—an enormously thick wall, of colossal blocks of stone, with two scarcely projecting rectangular towers upon it. . . . The strength of Athlit was brute strength, depending on the defence-less solidity of the inner wall, its impassable height, and the obstacle to mining of a deep sea-level ditch in the sand and rock before the towers. The design is simply unintelligent. . . . Given unlimited time

and labour, anyone can make a ditch so deep and a wall so high of stones so heavy as to be impregnable: but such a place is as much a prison for its defenders as a refuge: in fact a stupidity. Such is Athlit.[22]

Fedden, then, considers it "wise" that the weak—the landward—side of the castle should be heavily defended. But Lawrence is positively scathing about the Byzantine-inspired castle: Chastel Pèlerin is a "stupidity." He has to denigrate the Chastel. It is the burden of his song that the splendid erections still standing in the Middle East derive from Europe; that the military engineers of genius were Western; in particular that his admired Richard was in the forefront of intelligent castle building. "There is no evidence that Richard borrowed anything, great or small, from any fortress which he saw in the Holy Land: it is not likely that he would do so, since he would find better examples of everything in that South of France which he knew so well."[23]

The B.A. thesis is something of a triumph. Not only is it a precocious work of learning still treated with respect (although with caution too) by experts today, but it also represents the successful imposition of a view that its holder finds comfortable and heartening onto a large amount of technical detail of absorbing interest—and hence by extension onto chaotic life itself, which—challenges, threats, promises, and all—was just opening before Lawrence. This imposition does no violence to the understanding of author or reader.

There was a time too when Lawrence thought that he could see the Arabs as worthy successors to Richard or, perhaps more accurately, to his enemy the Kurdish Saladin, again without doing violence to the facts (a view he never entirely abandoned). "The Arabs made a chivalrous appeal to my young instinct, and when still at the High School in Oxford already I thought to re-make them into a nation, client and fellow of the British Empire."[24] Lawrence as a schoolboy, and later as student and archaeologist, was reading the literature of chivalry. He wrote lushly of the pleasure of reading Malory all night, projected a new edition of Froissart "illustrated only by contemporary art," bought and carried about with him in France in 1910 Antoine de la Sale's *Le Petit Jehan de Saintré*, "a xv Cent. novel of knightly manners—very good," and later claimed that "I also read nearly every manual of chivalry. Remember that my 'period' was the Middle Ages, always."[25] When, six years after writing his thesis, Lawrence began fighting with the

Arabs, he found a number of similarities between the societies depicted in his favorite reading and that society he was trying to influence to fight the Turks. At one point in *Seven Pillars* Lawrence refers to the "chivalrous semi-feudalism" of the Druses, but the phrase will do well to describe Beduin society too. The nomadic Beduin obviously did not (or do not) have a system that revolves around service in exchange for land tenure. But they are represented as having a flexible hierarchical society with hereditary privileges, the Sherif of Mecca and his sons, descendants of the Prophet, being at the summit. The revolt involves curiously anachronistic fighting. In great contrast to the battles taking place in Flanders, the outcome of Arab engagements can be visibly affected by the courage and prowess of an individual warrior; men fight under their territorial (i.e., tribal) leaders; a man can make a speech to his sword, by name, before beginning to fight (*SP*, 480). Arab society tends toward intertribal warfare, which is the means of obtaining honor and profit (Auda Abu Tayi, the possessor of an "immense chivalrous name" [*SP*, 175], is careful to have quarrels with all his neighbors), but rules are observed and the Arabs are horrified when they are broken:

> This bitter taste of the Turkish mode of war [i.e., the rape and slaughter in Awali] sent a shock across Arabia; for the first rule of Arab war was that women were inviolable: the second that the lives and honour of children too young to fight with men were to be spared: the third, that property impossible to carry off should be left undamaged. The Arabs with Feisal perceived that they were opposed to new customs. (*SP*, 93)

> Arab rules of war forbad to kill men in cold blood. [Oxford *Seven Pillars*; omitted from chapter 1 of later editions.[26]] The Howeitat were very fierce, for the slaughter of their women on the day before had been a new and horrible side of warfare suddenly revealed to them. In all their history were only two remembered instances of a woman intentionally harmed in life or body, and they had been brought up to execrate the authors of these outrages in passionate songs. (*SP*, 303. Second sentence in Oxford *Seven Pillars* only).

The Turks are not chivalrous enemies, and *Seven Pillars* contains more than one account of bloody massacre, Turk and reciprocal Arab. But the elements of medieval conflict at its best are present; and an eccentricity such as the "confirmed smoker" Feisal's sending pack animals loaded with cheap cigarettes to a tobaccoless enemy garrison is an incident from a war that is personal, individual, archaic, as is Abdullah's writing an exultant letter to a Turkish commander (Fakri Pasha), telling him of an important capture of Turkish booty and leaving it where it would be found and passed on.

The war is, moreover, fought upon historic ground, sometimes under "the old Crusader fort of Monreale . . . very noble against the night sky" (*SP*, 471, 495). Toward the end of the campaign, when uniformed Allied troops and their machines are more in evidence, Lawrence at first feels "guilty at introducing the throbbing car, and its trim crew of khaki-clad northerners, into the remoteness of this most hidden legendary ["mediaeval" in Oxford version] place [i.e., Azrak]" (*SP*, 559). For Azrak is "steeped in an unfathomable pool of silence and past history, instinct with strange knowledge of wandering poets, and champions, and lost kingdoms, all the crime and chivalry and dead magnificence of the legendary desert-courts of Hira and Ghassan, whose most sober story read like Arthur come again" (Oxford *Seven Pillars*; appears in slightly different form in later editions.)[27]

A medievalist's account of such a war, fought in such a region, will produce some interesting results. So far we have seen an idealistic and somewhat dreamy attitude toward the place and circumstances in which Lawrence, by extraordinary good luck (or, more portentously, fate), found himself. But he was not fighting in the heyday or even the decadence of chivalry, but in the twentieth century, and this fact must make itself evident.

Lawrence tries to link his war to the Crusades by his use of heraldic language in *Seven Pillars*. His study of heraldry had made its jargon part of his idiolect. Oxford is a happy hunting ground for one with an interest in the subject. The city, university, and college arms provide numerous examples—almost textbook examples—of the elements of heraldry; of fields, ordinaries, and charges; of canting arms and marshalings. The entrance gateway of Christ Church shows the arms of college benefactors, kings and commoners; other colleges could show other collections. Lawrence, furthermore, was growing up at a time when the study of heraldry was becoming intellectually respectable again. He read not only genuinely medieval works but also the poetry of Tennyson and the Pre-Raphaelites, who inherited something of the romantic attitude toward heraldry. Tennyson, whom Lawrence the schoolboy had selected for special study and quoted in letters, could incorporate more or less correctly heraldic terms into his poetry:

> [Merlin] found a fair young squire who sat alone,
> Had carved himself a knightly shield of wood,
> And then was painted on it fancied arms,
> Azure, an eagle rising or, the sun
> In dexter chief; the scroll, 'I follow fame.'
> Gawain saw
> Sir Lancelot's azure lions, crown'd with gold,
> Ramp in the field.[28]

The letter of 9 August 1906 (which should be read in this context) describing Léhon Abbey in northern France shows Lawrence to be a competent, if not omniscient, amateur herald.[29] He is familiar with the stylized depiction of an eagle when a charge on a coat of arms; he knows the heraldic use of *badge*, and what is meant by *billets or*. Heraldic terminology invaded his letters in nonheraldic contexts, precursors of his usages in *Seven Pillars*: "All the country is of one colour," he wrote home of Syria, "a murrey brown, but very subtly beautiful."[30] The *OED* reports "murrey" as historical or archaic, and gives no example of it in literary use after 1847. "[Indian] wall hangings are usually stamped with yellow figures of tigers ramping" he told a brother[31]— "ramping" almost certainly being inspired by "rampant." When he read *Le Petit Jehan de Saintré* in 1910, he would have learned about the duties of heralds and improved his knowledge of explicitly French heraldic language, for chapter fifty-eight consists largely of a list of the men who, la Sale claims, accompanied Saintré on crusade and their coats of arms, described in properly technical language. To take an example almost at random, "Le vidame de Chartres, d'or à trois faisses de sable, à ung orle de six merlectes de mesmes, et crye: Merlo."[32] In fact there are many heraldic references scattered throughout *Le Petit Jehan*.

How then does Lawrence apply this learning? The Arabs did bear before them the plain crimson flag ("crimson" is Lawrence's word, and nonheraldic) of the Hashemites, the family claiming descent from Mohammed. The flags are referred to as banners and the men who carry them called standard bearers, somewhat inconsistently. With that ex-

ception, heraldic terminology must be used in *Seven Pillars* in a transferred sense, not describing concisely and unambiguously lines and
shapes on a shield but lines and shapes in the writer's surroundings.
(But it may be noted here that a standard—a swallow-tailed flag bearing badges and motto, with the arms themselves perhaps in the hoist—
was last used in war in the Palestine campaign of 1917, by Commander
and Lt.-Col. H. Pirie-Gordon of Buthlaw.[33] Pirie-Gordon does not
appear in *Seven Pillars*, but he was a friend of Lawrence's.) It is characteristic of Lawrence's borrowings that not even the most unbending
purist could object to them as abusing heraldic language. They create
resonances for any reader of *Seven Pillars* who has even a tyro's knowledge of heraldry.

> [T]he Turks had dug trenches and stoned up an elaborate outpost of
> engrailed sangars [a sangar being a stone breastwork]. . . . (*SP*, 361)

Lawrence meant "engrailed" to indicate the shape of "curvilinear in-
dentations," referred to by the *OED* and denoted by the word in modern blazon. He may be remembering line 113 of Tennyson's "The Palace
of Art" ("Or over hills with peaky tops and engrail'd"), a poem he
thought "as good as good can be."[34]
His usage of "diaper" is in effect preheraldic:

> [H]e entered the station yard, carefully, for fear of the mines, whose
> trip and trigger wires diapered the ground. (*SP*, 523)

> I felt restless as the dusty sunlight which splashed a diaper over the
> paths, through chinks in the leaves. . . . (*SP*, 616)

"Diaper" originally referred to a textile of Byzantine or Levantine make,
so woven that light reflected a diamond pattern from its surface (*OED*).
In modern blazon, it denotes an accessory decoration of the shield.
The most ingenious heraldic borrowing is

> We lurched across plots of grass, between bars and fields of rough
> stone, in our two tenders and two armoured cars. (*SP*, 590)

The juxtaposition of "bars" and "fields" makes a heraldic reference
undeniable—for ordinaries (simple geometrical charges, a bar being a
horizontal band) do stand out in relief from the field (i.e., the background on which they are imposed). Lawrence would unite in the
reader's mind two wars, both fought in the same area, both in ideal-

istic endeavor, the one by men with shields, the other by men in armored cars.

He produces the same effect with "mural crown," which is a form of
crown or coronet, represented as consisting of stones such as those
used in the building of city or fortress walls. La Sale tells us that "Les
Romains, ainsi qu'ilz honnoroient de couronnes ceulx qui faisoient les
grans vaillances d'armes, si comme celui qui premier passoit le fossé ou
le palis de l'ost aux ennemis, estoit couronné de la couronne Valere,
et celui qui premier montoit sur l'eschielle et sur les murs, à l'assaut
d'une cité ou chastel ou ville, estoit couronné de la couronne Mu-
ralle."[35]

> Politically, [Aleppo] stood aside altogether, save in Arab quarters
> which, like overgrown half-nomad villages scattered over with priceless
> mosques, extended east and south of the mural crown of its great cita-
> del. (*SP*, 334–35)

> We went over the ridge and down to the base of the shapely cone,
> whose mural crown was the ring-wall of the old castle of Monreale,
> very noble against the night sky. (*SP*, 495)

The use of "crested" is probably suggested by a study of heraldry, a
crest being the device worn on top of the helm in jousts and tourna-
ments.

> We turned our camels to the right and advanced towards the rock,
> which reared its crested domes so high over us that the ropes of
> our head-cloths slipped back round our necks as we stared up. (*SP*,
> 375–76)

> Behind his tall figure the ruins were crested by a motley band, samples
> from every village and tribe in the Hauran. (*SP*, 611)

Finally, Lawrence's use of various forms of "rampant" should not be
ignored, although the word can make up part of the vocabulary of
those with no knowledge of heraldry. One Arab has been twice de-
moted in the Turkish army for "rampant nationalism" (*SP*, 92); fifty
wild mules were to be seen "ramping about the stalls" (*SP*, 146); a
certain type of Englishman becomes "the more rampantly English" the
longer he is away from England (*SP*, 346).

During the Arab Revolt, Lawrence was sustained by chivalric dreams,
and took refuge in them when reality was discouraging ("In my saddle-

bags was a *Morte d' Arthur*. It relieved my disgust" [SP, 485]). But even *Seven Pillars*, in which a high-minded antique campaign is high-mindedly recalled, is invested by some suspicions about the contingency of the chivalric ethos. In *The Mint*, as at the introduction of an armored car's "trim crew" to Azrak, Lawrence is wary of phlegmatic northerners:

> Perhaps, in days of Chivalry, even the north took the parade of arms lovingly, and throbbed at the feel of swords, the sight of banners. Perhaps: though I've chased through mediaeval literature after the days of chivalry, and found their revivals, and legends or reminiscences or ridicule of them, but never the real thing. Today these modes are right out of tune with the social system, whose firm-seatedness makes one doubt if an Englishman's blood can ever have flowed hotly enough for him to swallow a tomfoolery divorced from alcohol.[36]

The writing of *Seven Pillars* was an attempt to add a book to the shelf of "titanic" works Lawrence admired. One of these "big books" is *Don Quixote*,[37] which, by recounting the absurd adventures of the deluded would-be knight-errant (who is not quite as anachronistic as the "Arabian knight"), satirizes romances inspired by the chivalry Lawrence here fears never really existed, at least in the North. Heraldry, chivalry's daughter, does not escape Cervantes' attention. Don Quixote has mistaken two flocks of sheep for opposing armies, and now identifies the famous warriors he thinks he sees before him:

> But cast thy Eyes on this Side, *Sancho*, and at the Head of t'other Army see the ever victorious *Timonel* of *Carcaiona*, Prince of *New Biscay*, whose Armour is quarter'd *Azure*, *Vert*, *Or*, and *Argent*, and who bears in his shield a Cat *Or*, in a Field *Gules*, with these four letters, *MIAU*, for a Motto, being the beginning of his Mistress's Name, the beautiful *Miaulina*, Daughter to *Alpheniquen* Duke of *Algarva*. . . . He whom you see pricking that py'd Courser's Flanks with his arm'd Heels, is the mighty Duke of *Nervia*, *Espartafilado* of the Wood, bearing in his Shield a Field of pure *Azure*, powder'd with *Asparagus* (*Esparrago*) with this motto in Castilian, *Rastrea mi suerte*: *Thus trails, or drags my Fortune*.[38]

Cervantes' commentator sympathizes with the Spaniard's scorn, and glosses the word *Esparrago* thus:

> The Gingle between the Duke's Name *Espartafilado* and *Esparrago* (his Arms) is a Ridicule upon the foolish Quibbles so frequent in

Heraldry. . . . The *trailing* of his Fortune may allude to the Word Es-
parto, a sort of Rush they make Ropes with. Or perhaps he was without
a Mistress, to which the Sparagrass may illude: For, in Spain they have
a Proverb, *Solo comes el Esparrago*: As solitary as Sparagrass, because
every one of 'em springs up by itself.[39]

Canting arms—that is, arms that make a punning reference to a
name, usually the name of their bearer—are the object of Cervantes'
scorn here. (The motto, really an adjunct to the coat of arms itself,
may also cant.) Lawrence was familiar with the concept, having been
educated in a city the arms of which show an ox crossing a ford; and
having rubbed the brass of, to give only one example, Sir Roger de
Setvans (1306) at Chartham, Kent, whose surcoat and *ailettes*[40] show
seven winnowing fans—*sept vans*—and his shield three similar fans.
The young Lawrence's consistent misspelling, *Septvans*, with a medial
p, in the letter about Léhon, for example, is a forgetful product of his
knowledge of the knight's coat of arms and its inspiration.

Mockery of canting arms implies more than mere impatience with
recondite puns. This type of arms evolved in an age of general illit-
eracy, but it is easy to see how a knight could identify more readily
with a coat of arms that embodied his name than with one that did
not. (Heraldry's beginnings were purely utilitarian—based in the need
to make one's identity plain in the period of the closed helm—but the
honor accorded a knight and that accorded his coat of arms soon, again
by natural extension, became one and the same.) To attack canting
arms is implicitly to attack a whole series of correspondences. If canting arms are "foolish Quibbles," then individual acts of bravery may be
fortuitous, lacking significance, and not the product of awareness of a
transcendental code and the necessity of living up to it. Chivalry itself
(if it ever existed) may be the result of a method of waging war that
had its day and then became obsolete, not an earthly reflection of what
is forever pleasing to God. (That Lawrence knew that acts of bravery
or cowardice *are* sometimes fortuitous may be inferred from his correspondence with Ernest Thurtle, the M.P. who tried to have abolished
the death sentence for cowardice in the face of the enemy.)

Lawrence knew that he lived in an age of the relative outlook. He
contrasted himself with C. M. Doughty, who "had a fixed point in his
universe, and from one fixed point a moralist will . . . build up the
whole scheme of creation."[41] He contrasted himself with Herbert Read,

who, in reviewing *Seven Pillars*, said that "Great books are written in moods of spiritual light and intellectual certainty."[42] He knew that he was not the only twentieth-century medievalist to be aware of the conflict between relative and absolute. James Branch Cabell, the American author of a number of stories set in a fictional Poictesme of the Middle Ages, had a cynical explanation for chivalry's popularity. It appeals to man's pride "through an assumption of man's responsibility in his tiniest action." The chivalrous man considers himself God's representative on earth; he is supported by a "flattering notion of divine vicarship. . . . There is no cause for wonder that the appeal was irresistible, when to each man it thus admitted that he himself was the one thing seriously to be considered."[43]

Lawrence had read Cabell's *Jurgen* (1919), an ironic retelling of the solar myth of regained youth, and admired it.[44] The eponym of the "comedy of justice," possessor of a young body and an experienced heart, spends some time at the court of Glathion, where the chivalric ethos is highly regarded but imperfectly practiced. Jurgen spends his time not unpleasantly, seducing the Guenevere who will later marry Arthur (and finding her much like other women when the barriers are down, and before), but he is made uncomfortable by the inability to believe in the wisdom of an omnipotent creator and the doubts that flow from that inability. "And all the while he fretted because he could just dimly perceive that ideal which was served in Glathion, and the beauty of this ideal, but could not possibly believe in it. . . . Jurgen abode among these persons to whom life was a high-hearted journeying homeward. God the Father awaited you there, ready to punish at need, but eager to forgive, after the manner of all fathers: that one became a little soiled in traveling . . . was a matter which fathers understood."[45] Serving the king is an idea not to be taken seriously, for the king "was a person whom Jurgen simply could not imagine any intelligent Deity selecting as steward." The chivalric conception of courtly love cannot be taken seriously: "when it came to serving women, what sort of service did women most cordially appreciate? Jurgen had his answer pat enough, but it was an answer not suitable for utterance in mixed company."[46] Everywhere is self-deceit. In the week of tourneys and feasting preceding Guenevere's being taken to London for marriage, "dukes and earls and barons and many famous knights" contend for honor "and a trumpery chaplet of pearls."[47]

Cabell, Jurgen, and Lawrence believe they have asked for bread and have been given a stone. It is impossible not to fail one's vision and high-colored ambitions after adolescence, despite one's longing for a world in which they could be honored. Jurgen, second time round, kills the man who in reality married Dorothy la Désirée, the local lord's daughter, whom, for one idyllic youthful summer, he had loved and been loved by. Jurgen's words to his victim are "it is highly necessary you die tonight, in order that my soul may not perish too many years before my body."[48]

They are words that Lawrence remembered. Sherif Nasir is one version of the perfect warrior. The same romantic aura surrounds him that surrounds Auda Abu Tayi, whose first appearance is followed by a page and a half of almost infatuated description ("knight-errant . . . saga . . . heroic . . . poems of old raids and epic tales of fights" [*SP*, 222–23]); that surrounds the armed prophet Feisal, "black against the sun, whose light threw a queer haze about his slender figure, and suffused his head with gold, through the floss-silk of his head-cloth" (*SP*, 519). But Nasir, with his sophisticated Medina background, is the Arab most like Lawrence. He stands out in the glorious court and military life of Arab warriors and aristocrats. He lives in an alien world. "[H]e was body-weary after months of vanguard service, and mind-weary too, with the passing of youth's careless years. He feared his maturity as it grew upon him, with its ripe thought, its skill, its finished art; yet which lacked the poetry of boyhood to make living a full end of life. Physically he was young yet: but his changeful and mortal soul was ageing quicker than his body—going to die before it, like most of ours" (*SP*, 228). "[I]n most men," Lawrence later writes, "the soul grew aged long before the body" (*SP*, 412).

Lawrence always maintained a belief in the possibility of chivalric action, in the twentieth century and before. But after the horrors of the war, particularly the traumatic Deraa episode, he forsook honor for himself. Although Lawrence was able to lose himself in idealistic effort and ambition when writing *Seven Pillars* (and thus recalling earlier efforts), true heroism otherwise seemed often nebulous and far away. This pessimistic view is reflected in a letter written after a trip to Glastonbury in 1924 to see a musical version of Thomas Hardy's *The Famous Tragedy of the Queen of Cornwall*. Glastonbury is identified by Giraldus Cambrensis with Avalon; it is where the tomb of Arthur and Guenevere was found in the reign of Henry II. "[I]ts tremendous past makes one walk expectant in the streets, so that the smallest sign is a wonder: only why (except to try us) is all the wonder of the Abbey sunk to a perfectly-preserved kitchen?" The principal actors did not impress. Perhaps Tristram gave most offense. "[H]e was fat faced, & shiny-faced, with a long turned-up nose, & glittering lecherous eyes. His mouth slobbered, & when he hugged, or was hugged by the pair of Iseults the satisfaction on his face was too horrible for words. Of course it may have been true, & Tristram far from being heroic may have been just a stout greasy snarer of women."[49] That last sentence gives us some indication of Lawrence's final submission.

N·O·T·E·S

1. John E. Mack, A Prince of Our Disorder: The Life of T. E. Lawrence (London: Weidenfeld and Nicolson, 1976), 8.

2. Philip Henderson, William Morris: His Life, Work, and Friends (London: Thames and Hudson, 1967), 11.

3. A. W. Lawrence, ed., T. E. Lawrence by His Friends (London: Cape, 1937), 586; hereafter Friends.

4. L, 39.

5. E.g., Richard Aldington, Lawrence of Arabia: A Biographical Enquiry (London: Collins, 1955), 47, and Miriam J. Benkovitz, ed., A Passionate Prodigality: Letters to Alan Bird from Richard Aldington, 1949–1962 (New York: New York Public Library, 1975), 20, 41, 57, 59, 61. Mack, A Prince of Our Disorder, 41–47.

6. Friends, 41.

7. Friends, 47. Lawrence had probably been reading Anthony Wood and J. Peshall's Antient and Present State of the City of Oxford (London, 1773) or the later, and better, edition by A. Clark, Survey of the Antiquities of the City of Oxford, 3 vols. (Oxford: Oxford Historical Society, 1889, 1890, 1899).

8. H. T. Kirby, "Lawrence of Arabia—Brass Rubber," Apollo (July 1938): 18.

9. Ibid., 18. This catalog is no longer in existence. It was the property of the Oxford Architectural and Historical Society, and possibly was destroyed by an officer of that society unaware of the catalog's value.

10. Ashmolean Museum, Notes on Brass-Rubbing, rev. ed. (Oxford: Ashmolean Museum, 1973), 32. The front and back cover illustrations of the seventh edition are reproductions of two of Lawrence's rubbings—namely, that of Thomas, Lord Berkeley (1417), Wotton-under-Edge, Gloucestershire (front), and William, Viscount Beaumont and Lord Bardolf (1507), Wivenhoe, Essex (back).

11. Friends, 65.

12. *Friends*, 53.

13. *Friends*, 52, 54.

14. Henderson, *William Morris*, 22.

15. *HL*, 38.

16. *HL*, 55.

17. *L*, 86 (n. 1).

18. *CC*, 1:56.

19. Athlit is the name of the present-day village. The castle was called Chastel Pèlerin (Castrum Peregrinorum) because it was built, in 1218, with the aid of pilgrims.

20. Robin Fedden, *Crusader Castles* (London: Art and Technics, 1950), 57–59. A plan of Chastel Pèlerin may be found in Fedden, p. 58. Plan 49 of Lawrence's *Crusader Castles* is of Chastel Pèlerin.

21. *CC*, 1:42.

22. *CC*, 1:42–43.

23. *CC*, 1:56.

24. T. E. Lawrence, *Seven Pillars of Wisdom* (Oxford, 1922), 308. Omitted from epilogue to bk. 10 of later editions. All quotations from *Seven Pillars* will be made from *SP* (the 1935 Cape edition) unless otherwise specified.

25. *HL*, 110; *Friends*, 53; T. E. *Lawrence to His Biographers Robert Graves and Liddell Hart* (London: Cassell, 1963), 2:50.

26. *Seven Pillars of Wisdom* (Oxford, 1922), 124.

27. Ibid., 179; *SP*, 414.

28. "Merlin and Vivien," ll. 470–74; "Lancelot and Elaine," ll. 658–60 in Christopher Ricks, ed., *The Poems of Tennyson* (London: Longmans, 1969), 1608, 1639.

29. *HL*, 11–12.

30. *HL*, 238–39.

31. *HL*, 290.

32. Antoine de la Sale, *L'Hystoyre et Plaisante Cronicque du petit Jehan de Saintré*, ed., J.-Marie Guichard (Paris: Gosselin, 1843), 177. I am unable to examine the edition read by Lawrence, and found in his library at his death, but that too reproduces the text established by Guichard.

33. Robert Gayre of Gayre and Nigg, *Heraldic Standards and Other Ensigns* (Edinburgh and London: Oliver and Boyd, 1959), 67 (n. 1).

34. British Library Add. MS. 45904. Letter of 8 May 1928 to Charlotte F. Shaw.

35. La Sale, 5–6. "The Romans were wont to honour with crowns them that did great feats of arms; and that he who first passed the moat or the rampart of the enemy's host was crowned with the Crown Valerian, and he who first mounted upon the scaling ladder or upon the walls, at the assault of a city or a castle or a town was crowned with the Crown Mural." Antoine de la Sale, *Little John of Saintré*, trans. Irvine Gray (London: Routledge, 1931), 35.

36. *M*, 226–27.

37. *L*, 467, 548.

38. Miguel de Cervantes, *Don Quixote*, trans. Peter Motteux, rev. Ozell (London: John Lane, Bodley Head, 1934), 115.

39. Ibid.

40. *Ailettes* "were small shields fastened at right angles to the shoulders, to lessen the force of a sweeping blow." Muriel Clayton, *Victoria and Albert Museum—Catalogue of Rubbings of Brasses and Incised Slabs* (London: Board of Education, 1929), 13.

41. British Library Add. MS. 45903. Letter of 4 May 1927 to Charlotte F. Shaw.

42. Quoted and discussed *L*, 548.

43. Quoted in Carl Van Doren, *James Branch Cabell* (New York: Literary Guild, 1932), 15.

44. *L*, 423.

45. James Branch Cabell, *Jurgen: A Comedy of Justice* (New York: Robert M. McBride, 1919), 103.

46. Ibid., 102.

47. Ibid., 109.

48. Ibid., 54.

49. British Library Add. MS. 45903. Letter of 30 August 1924 to Charlotte F. Shaw.

The Assertion and Denial of the Romantic Will in *Seven Pillars of Wisdom* and *The Mint*

THOMAS J. O'DONNELL

He who humbles himself wills to be exalted.

FRIEDRICH NIETZSCHE

The literary works of T. E. Lawrence are sometimes thought difficult to read. *Seven Pillars of Wisdom* appears to lack unity of structure, style, and mood, and *The Mint* depends heavily on an understanding of the earlier work. Both works are said to be anomalies, to display unique literary forms. The difficulty of reading Lawrence is aggravated when we are told to compare him to nineteenth-century travel writers, to Richard Burton and Charles M. Doughty. These models are unsatisfactory; they seem limited, peculiar, below or irrelevant to the extravagant ambitions Lawrence professed, below what he called the titanic books, "*The Karamazovs, Zarathustra,* and *Moby Dick*."[1]

What initially seems problematic in Lawrence reflects his absorption and modification of romantic tradition. Lawrence's use of this tradition is best shown by his dramatization of will in *Seven Pillars* and *The Mint*. Lawrence explores two concepts of will in these works. His complex development of these concepts is characteristic of the traditional romantic hero's conflicting desires both to assert and to deny will, both to use will and to expiate for the excesses this use generates. In this essay I argue that both Nietzsche's concept of will and Schopenhauer's concept, strongly in conflict, are dramatized by Lawrence, that Lawrence moves from primary emphasis on Nietzsche's concept to primary emphasis on Schopenhauer's, and that this movement, central to both *Seven Pillars* and *The Mint*, is distinctly romantic.

I use the term romanticism in the larger sense common among such contemporary critics and theorists as M. H. Abrams, Harold Bloom, Robert Langbaum, and Morse Peckham, and among such popular writers about Western culture as Kenneth Clark. Like them, I extend the limits of romanticism well beyond a period of thirty or forty years at the beginning of the nineteenth century.[2] Romanticism is the tradition of philosophic, artistic, and literary thought first expressed fully in the work of Rousseau and subsequently developed in England by Blake, Wordsworth, Coleridge, Byron, and other late eighteenth- and early nineteenth-century writers. In England the romantic impulse carries through the Victorian period and is powerfully expressed even in such writers as Carlyle, who professedly react against it. In the twentieth century Yeats and D. H. Lawrence, contemporaries of T. E. Lawrence, embody romantic aspirations and attitudes in an intense, radical form and readily acknowledge the influence of early nineteenth-century writers. Certainly T. E. Lawrence read and was influenced by Rousseau, Blake, Coleridge, Byron, Carlyle, Melville, and D. H. Lawrence. He acknowledged and praised their work in correspondence, in reviews, and in his anthology *Minorities*; he had their works in his library at his death.

I want to look first at the apparently opposing concepts of will elaborated in the nineteenth century by Schopenhauer and Nietzsche. Schopenhauer's major work, *The World as Will and Idea*, was published in 1818. Schopenhauer argued that will and reality were one; will was the "thing-in-itself," the one real thing behind manifold appearance. In man "the whole series of actions, and consequently every individual act, and also its condition, the whole body which accomplishes it, and therefore also the process through which and in which it exists, are nothing but the manifestation of the will, the becoming visible, *the objectification of the will*."[3] But the scope of will is much greater than that observed in any individual man or in men. This will is not only in men and animals as their inmost nature but it is:

the force which germinates and vegetates in the plant, and indeed the force through which the crystal is formed, that by which the magnet turns to the north pole, the force whose shock he experiences from the contact of two different kinds of metals, the force which appears in the elective affinities of matter as repulsion and attraction, decomposition and combination, and, lastly, even gravitation . . . —all these, I say, he will recognize as different only in their phenomenal existence, but in their inner nature as identical, as that which is directly known to him so intimately and so much better than anything else, and what in its most distinct manifestation is called *will.*[4]

The will is the force symbolized by Shiva, the Hindu god whose image is hung with skulls and the lingam, the god of both death and generation.[5] Most strongly visible to man in reproduction, the will is in some of its manifestations an unconscious force. As many commentators have noted, Freud's concept of will strongly parallels Schopenhauer's at several points.

The most extraordinary aspect of Schopenhauer's philosophy is his conviction that will can and should be denied by man. Once a man can grasp intellectually and emotionally Schopenhauer's knowledge of will, his

will turns round, no longer asserts its own nature. . . . Essentially nothing else but a manifestation of will, he ceases to will anything, guards against attaching his will to anything, and seeks to confirm in himself the greatest indifference to everything. His body, healthy and strong, expresses through the genitals, the sexual impulse; but he denies the will and gives the lie to the body; he desires no sensual gratification under any condition. Voluntary and complete chastity is the first step in asceticism or the denial of the will to live.[6]

The artist also can momentarily deny the will during creation, can stand beside the will and contemplate it, though he himself is the will that he objectifies.[7]

Whether T. E. Lawrence read the works of Schopenhauer has not been established, though one can demonstrate that his indirect knowledge of Schopenhauer's philosophy was extensive. He read widely in the works of contemporary writers influenced by the philosopher. Both Thomas Hardy and D. H. Lawrence derived their concepts of will from Schopenhauer and dramatized them in their poems and novels.

Virtually the complete works of D. H. Lawrence and more than a dozen volumes of Hardy were in T.E.'s library. Schopenhauer's influence on late-nineteenth- and twentieth-century British writers has been greatly underestimated by literary critics.[8]

Lawrence certainly knew Schopenhauer through Nietzsche's works. In his library he had Nietzsche's *The Joyful Wisdom, Thus Spake Zarathustra, Twilight of the Idols,* and *The Antichrist.* In all of these works Nietzsche, writing more than a half century after Schopenhauer, presents and then attacks the earlier philosopher's concept of will. Nietzsche concisely states his objections to Schopenhauer in *The Will to Power:*

> Schopenhauer's basic misunderstanding of the *will* (as if craving, instinct, drive were the *essence* of will) is typical: lowering the value of the will to the point of making a real mistake. Also hatred against willing; attempt to see something higher, indeed that which is higher and valuable, in willing no more, in "being a subject *without* aim and purpose" (in the "pure subject free of will"). Great symptom of the *exhaustion* or the *weakness* of the *will:* for the will is precisely that which treats cravings as their master and appoints to them their way and measure.[9]

Nietzsche declares that willing is not "'desiring,' striving, demanding: it is distinguished from these by the affect of commanding. There is no such thing as 'willing,' but only a willing *something:* one must not remove the aim from the total condition. . . ."[10] Nietzsche clearly and precisely delineates his basic difference from Schopenhauer: will is command, not desire.

In *The Joyful Wisdom,* Nietzsche attacks romanticism and identifies Schopenhauer as the type of romantic who appalls him:

> What is Romanticism? Every art and every philosophy may be regarded as a healing and helping appliance in the service of growing, struggling life: they always presuppose suffering and sufferers. But there are two kinds of sufferers: on the one hand those that suffer from *overflowing vitality,* who need Dionysian art, and require a tragic view and insight into life; and on the other hand those who suffer from *reduced vitality,* who seek repose, quietness, calm seas, and deliverance of themselves through art or knowledge, or else intoxication, spasm, bewilderment and madness. All Romanticism in art and knowledge responds to the twofold craving of the *latter;* to them Schopenhauer . . . responded.[11]

Nietzsche does not see that "overflowing vitality" and "reduced vitality" are both stages that the romantic hero passes through (usually
sequentially). Both the stage of expansion of the self and its powers
and the stage of contraction of self to the point of annihilation are
present in *Seven Pillars* (though not sequentially), and I will explore
Lawrence's use of them later in this essay.

Nietzsche's hero, the man of overflowing vitality, is "beast and su-
perbeast; the higher man is inhuman and superhuman: these belong
together. With every increase of greatness and height in man, there is
also an increase in depth and terribleness: one ought not to desire the
one without the other."[12] A philosophy that teaches denial of the will
is "defamation and slander—*I assess the power of a will by how much
resistance, pain, torture it endures and knows how to turn to its advantage.*"[13]

This will and the Nietzschean hero are clearly in evidence throughout the war narrative of Lawrence's *Seven Pillars* (though not in chapters in which he engages in self-analysis). Both before and after the
flagellation and the attempted rape at Deraa, the Nietzschean will is
powerfully and prominently displayed. The opening lines of the dedicatory poem to *Seven Pillars* assert, "I . . . wrote my will across the sky
in stars."[14] In the book's opening chapters Lawrence compares himself to the prophets who had gone alone into the desert and emerged
from it with an idea, prophets driving forward a great wave "against
the coasts of flesh." Lawrence ends chapter 3 asserting, "One such
wave (and not the least) I raised and rolled before the breath of an
idea, till it reached its crest, and toppled over and fell at Damascus."
Lawrence's pride in his will is superbly expressed in the iambic dimeter
of the parentheses breaking through the three accented words with
which the sentence begins and determining the iambs that follow. The
prophets are Christ, Mohammed, and even, perhaps, Zarathustra.

Lawrence conceives of himself as a heroic redeemer and compares
himself to Christ in chapters 99–100 of *Seven Pillars*; here he analyzes
what he calls the revolt's ethics of sacrifice. Lawrence had felt that
"our endurance might win redemption, perhaps for all a race. . . . we
felt we had assumed another's pain or experience, his personality. It
was triumph, and a mood of enlargement; we had avoided our sultry
selves, conquered our geometrical completeness." He had taken pride
in the Arabs, "our creatures." The Arab response to his role as a re-

deemer, the "mounting together of the devoted hopes of years from near-sighted multitudes, might endow even an unwilling idol with Godhead, and strengthen It whenever men prayed silently to Him." Lawrence believes he absorbs others, usurps their wills. He finds that no "pride and few pleasures in the world were so joyful, so rich as this choosing voluntarily another's evil to perfect the self." In the Bodleian manuscript, he writes that the role of the redeemer gave "a sense of greatness, a super-humanity."[15]

The power of Lawrence's will is not in question in the war narrative, even in these late chapters: "I had found materials always apt to serve a purpose, and Will a sure guide to some one of the many roads leading from purpose to achievement. There was no flesh" (SP, 564). Lawrence displays supreme confidence in the campaigns he conducts. In the final march on Damascus,

> A shiver of self-assertion and self-confidence ran across the camp. I had made myself the magnet of their hidden longings, and knew that they were ready to do any service we asked of them. The whole country lay willing to our grasp, and I determined to . . . go through with it completely: . . . to do the unreal myself, and to drag the changed hopes and loves of a nation madly after my whim. (MS 396; cf. SP, 618)

In the published version of Seven Pillars, as opposed to the Bodleian manuscript, Lawrence's will is consistently muted, though by no means extinguished. In the manuscript he writes of the Damascus march that "we thought we had ordered all that fortuitously passed, and no more than passed" (MS, 377). After the capture of Damascus he boasts that the "lone hand had won against the world's odds" (SP, 659). Even the Epilogue emphasizes Lawrence's great ambition and his strength of will. He had dreamed of a new Asia. Damascus was to lead "to Anatolia, and afterwards to Bagdad; and then there was Yemen. Fantasies, these will seem, to such as are able to call my beginning an ordinary effort." Who, he implies, could call all *that* an ordinary effort? Who is so powerful that he would dare to do so? The reader submits before the romantic egoism of this assertion, the last words in the book. With every step Lawrence's advancing head knocks out a star from heaven.

The heroic redeemer, the being of "super-humanity," of overflowing vitality, who uses his will to turn resistance, pain, and torture to his advantage, resembles Nietzsche's superman. To use Lawrence's word in the Epilogue, there is an element of "fantasy" in these expressions of will, though the energy and conviction with which *Seven Pillars* is written carry us forward to the point that we suspend our disbelief.

Paradoxically, Lawrence uses his failure to complete his military and political plans for Arabia as a demonstration of the power of his will. Lawrence himself deliberately shatters the unfinished house of wisdom and freedom that he believed was within his power to create (*SP*, 5).

Lawrence's emphasis on the power of the will is characteristic not just of Nietzsche's hero but of the first stage in the development of many romantic heroes. Coleridge sees the strength and dangers of such an assertion of will quite early; he writes:

Will becomes Satanic pride and rebellious self-idolatry in the relations of the spirit to itself, and remorseless despotism relatively to others; the more hopeless as the more obdurate by its subjugation of sensual impulses, by its superiority to toil and pain and pleasure; in short, by the fearful resolve to find in itself alone the one absolute motive of action, under which all other motives from within and from without must be either subordinated or crushed.[16]

It is the will characterized by Kenneth Clark as the "insatiable urge to conquer and explore,"[17] the will of Melville's Ahab, of Nietzsche's Zarathustra. It is the will described by Wordsworth: "The mind is lord and master—outward sense / The obedient servant of her will."[18] The self absorbs others, dominates men and events, lends value and meaning to the world.[19]

Yet, alongside the well-developed sense of the romantic will as lord and master, Lawrence introduces another concept of will. On his thirtieth birthday and immediately before the final march on Damascus, Lawrence dissects his beliefs and motives. Shyness "held a mask, often a mask of indifference or flippancy, before my face, and puzzled me. My thoughts clawed, wondering, at this apparent peace, knowing that it was only a mask; because, despite my trying never to dwell on what was interesting, there were moments too strong for control when my appetite burst out and frightened me" (*SP*, 563). But will is allied to appetite, for Lawrence on the next page declares:

True there lurked always that Will uneasily waiting to burst out. My brain was sudden and silent as a wild cat, my senses like mud clogging its feet, and my self (conscious always of itself and its shyness) telling the beast it was bad form to spring and vulgar to feed upon the kill. So meshed in nerves and hesitation, it could not be a thing to be afraid of; yet it was a real beast, and this book its mangy skin, dried, stuffed and set up squarely for men to stare at. (*SP*, 564)

Will here is not lord and master but an animal within Lawrence which, despite the efforts of "my self" to restrain it, springs from its cage. In a 1924 letter to the critic and dramatist Harley Granville-Barker, he affirms the animal nature of will. Lawrence is now a common soldier in the Tank Corps, and in that unlikely atmosphere he finds that Granville-Barker's *The Secret Life* "couldn't be as witty as all that without cracking sometimes, and letting the roar and growling of the beast be heard. . . . at bottom we are carnal: . . . our appetites and tastes and hopes and ideals are beast-qualities, coloured or shaped somewhat fancifully, but material always" (*L*, 453). It is this concept of man's will as beast, a concept parallel to Schopenhauer's, that emboldens Lawrence to deny both the will of Nietzsche and the will of Schopenhauer (i.e., both the will to power and the will to live). Further, the writing of *Seven Pillars* itself, he implies, slays the will, turns the will, which both Lawrence and the reader stand beside and contemplate, into a stuffed, mangy beast.

Lawrence best describes his recognition of the bestial source of will in a 1927 letter to an airman: "Once I fancied I was very near the angels, and the coming so abruptly to earth was a jar—and a very wholesome jar. Angels, I think, we imagine. Beasts, I think, we are." Yet he likes the beasts "for their kindliness and honesty." Nonetheless this kindly beast, who embodies Schopenhauer's will, becomes in the next paragraph a creature to be restrained, mastered by the Nietzschean will: "the beast remains, sometimes supine, but sometimes rampant. You will find it taking charge of you, at some weak second of your will" (*L*, 554–55). Full use of Nietzschean will—Lawrence's expansion of self during the war, his assuming another's pain or experience—leads to the appearance of the beast: "When men take the governors off their spirits, the spirit seems to fly away, and the animal to creep out of its den, and come snarling into daylight."[20] Lawrence himself divides his two literary works between the Nietzschean sense of will, the angel, and the Schopenhauerian sense, the beast: "The

S.P. [*Seven Pillars*] was man on his tip-toes, trying very hard to fly. These notes [*The Mint*] are men on their very flat feet, stumbling over a sticky and noisome earth."[21]

Immediately after Deraa, Lawrence says that he dared not probe into the sources of his energy of will (*SP*, 468). Later he writes that he tries never to dwell on what is interesting (*SP*, 563). During his torture at Deraa and in his use of power during the war, Lawrence comes to recognize that the source of will is not reason but passion. There *is* flesh, he now acknowledges. Besides, there are always many things he cannot control by Nietzschean will, great areas that escape it. For example, he can never bear to touch or be touched: "This was an atomic repulsion, like the intact course of a snowflake. The opposite would have been my choice if my head had not been tyrannous" (*SP*, 563). Further, the image of the snowflake insinuates his feelings of fragility and his fear. He comes to perceive that both Nietzsche's will and Schopenhauer's have their sources in the beast and must be forgone.

Lawrence's attempt to deny his will after the war is a characteristic stage through which the romantics and their heroes pass. Kenneth Clark writes: "Few episodes in history are more depressing than the withdrawal of the great Romantics."[22] Schopenhauer sees such a withdrawal as exemplary; he argues that the values of assertion and denial are parallel to the values of damnation and salvation in Christianity: "Certainly the doctrine of original sin (assertion of the will) and of salvation (denial of the will) is the great truth which constitutes the essence of Christianity. . . . Therefore Jesus Christ ought always to be conceived in the universal, as the symbol or personification of the denial of the will to live."[23] Nietzsche's repeated attacks on Christ are based on a similar understanding of His role and a very different apprehension of His meaning.

Of course Lawrence does compare his role in Arabia to Christ's role, yet he sees assertion as well as denial in Christ and finds assertion of will even in His sacrifice:

> To each opportunity there could be only one vicar, and the snatching
> of it robbed the fellows of their due hurt. Their vicar rejoiced, while
> his brethren were wounded in their manhood. To accept humbly so rich
> a release was imperfection in them: their gladness at the saving of its
> cost was sinful in that it made them accessory, part-guilty of inflict-

ing it upon their mediator. . . . we seemed like the cells of a bee-comb, of which one might change, or swell itself, only at the cost of all. (*SP*, 550–51)[24]

Self-sacrifice "uplifted the redeemer and cast down the bought"; the only role left for others was copying and this was the "meanest of things" (*SP*, 551). Crucifixion benefits the saint only, not complex modern man.[25]

Assertion of the romantic will usurps the wills of others. In *Beyond the Tragic Vision*, Morse Peckham summarizes his analysis of the characteristic dilemma of what he calls the heroic redeemer:

> The imposition of the will upon reality, when given political and social instrumentality, meant the denial to others of their own moral responsibility. To redeem society could only mean to do for others what the nineteenth-century vision had made possible for the alienated individual to do for himself: the creation of a genuine moral responsibility in everyone. . . . to create the social conditions necessary for the assumption by all men of moral responsibility meant a temporary and perhaps permanent . . . denial of the very responsibility the imposition of the will was designed to create. . . . his actions, through the exercise of power, reinforced the egocentricity which his beliefs were designed to break down.[26]

In introspection in the last books of *Seven Pillars* Lawrence weighs at length the adverse effects of the romantic will and the deficiencies of the heroic redeemer. Nonetheless, Lawrence's analysis of himself as a redeemer is too metaphysical, detached, and derivative to provide an adequate explanation of his denial of will. Certainly the reasons for the denial are many, but the basic cause is a fantasy about the threat he is to others. The fantasy is clearest in a 1925 letter to Charlotte Shaw:

> Do you know what it is when you see, suddenly, that your life is all a ruin? . . . Thinking drives me mad, because of the invisible ties about me which limit my moving, my wishing, my imagining. All these bonds I have tied myself, deliberately, wishing to tie myself down beyond the hope or power of movement. And this deliberation, this intention, rests. It is stronger than anything else in me, than everything else put together. So long as there is breath in my body my

strength will be exerted to keep my soul in prison, since nowhere else can it exist in safety. The terror of being run away with, in the liberty of power, lies at the back of these many renunciations of my later life. I am afraid, of myself. Is this madness?[27]

The year before in a letter to Granville-Barker, Lawrence, speaking of a character in *The Secret Life*, emphasizes a fear "of being *pulled* back . . . the conviction that he'd have to sell the part of himself which he valued, for the privilege of giving rein to the part of himself which others valued, but which he despised or actually disliked" (*L*, 453). The language illustrates the ambivalence Lawrence has. How is it a "privilege" to give rein to the part he despises, and why does he qualify the word "despised" by the less pejorative "disliked"?

Lawrence fantasizes that he himself must rein in these impulses to power and that he would use power destructively. He alone can restrain himself; after all, society actually encourages his indulgence in these urges. He inveighs against the license society gives him: "Out upon joyless impunity!" (*SP*, 565). This fantasy is not simply a result of the war. Lawrence's fear of touch, of intimacy, which antedates the war, reflects a sense of himself as a danger to others, a fear of what he would do if touched. His fear of intimacy protects not just himself but others from a dangerous, corrupting force.[28] Of course Lawrence is neither so dangerous nor so powerful as he fantasizes, and his fantasy suppresses the constructive use of his "energy of will," which he in other moods acknowledges.

Lawrence intends to deny both the will of Nietzsche and the will of Schopenhauer. Lawrence's steps to annihilate the will are already delineated in *Seven Pillars*. To him there seems, in Schopenhauer's words, "no middle path between desiring and renouncing."[29] Unlike in *Seven Pillars*, the dramatization of this denial in *The Mint* relies more on action in character, inner drama, than on character in action, outer drama, though his enlistment in the Royal Air Force ostensibly makes external the force of denial. Lawrence is to seek the discipline of the peacetime army, to seek an absolute below, not above: "In peace-armies discipline meant the hunt, not of an average but of an absolute . . . the level of the weakest man on parade" (*SP*, 339). British soldiers wear a "death's livery which walled its bearers from ordinary life, was sign that they had sold their wills and bodies to the State: and contracted themselves into a service not the less abject for that its beginning was voluntary. . . . those only received satisfaction who had sought to degrade themselves, for to the peace-eye they were below humanity" (SP, 641). Lawrence will soon shed his Arab robes for this death's livery. *The Mint* vividly shows the burning out of free will and self-respect and delicacy from Lawrence's violent nature, as he well knows (L, 419). Lawrence hopes that someday he will really feel degraded, be degraded to the level of the soldiers and airmen among whom he lives. Some people do perceive his degradation and, he writes, "I long for people to look down upon me and despise me, and I'm too shy to take the filthy steps which would publicly shame me, and put me into their contempt. I want to dirty myself outwardly, so that my person may properly reflect the dirtiness which it conceals."[30] Such degradation will make him unfit to lead, protect him from the others whom he endangers and from those who endanger him.

The machine is the symbolic goal of Lawrence's denial of will. By the end of *Seven Pillars*, praise of the organic, cyclical pattern of the Arabs yields to praise of the mechanical, progressive pattern of the English and the West. As the Arab force joins the English, Lawrence's destruction of the locomotives that intrude upon the pastoral desert yields to his enthusiastic use of armored cars and airplanes as instruments of destruction. In *The Mint* the expressed ideal is thoroughly mechanical. Aircraft hangars become cathedrals (M, 214), airmen become blue cylinders (M, 225), male genitals are reduced to a bicycle pump and tool bag (M, 114), and a motorcycle with "a touch of blood in it is better than all the riding animals on earth" (M, 245). Lawrence is learning to be sterile (M, 190).

Like Carlyle a hundred years before, Lawrence declares that this is the "mechanical age." Yet unlike Carlyle, he now praises this age and seeks to become mechanical in head and heart. Three months before his death, Lawrence writes that he "went into the R.A.F. to serve a mechanical purpose, not as leader but as a cog of the machine. The key-word, I think, is machine. . . . one of the benefits of being part of the machine is that one learns that one doesn't matter!" His becoming a machine should end the pride and pain of romantic egoism, the romantic will. Further, there are "no women in the machines, in any machine" (L, 852–53). Woman, he implies, is the antithesis of the mechanical. The machine to which he submits is the symbol of the strong male, the mass will to power rather than the individual will. The submission, he imagines, also protects him from yielding to the woman in himself, to his emotional component. The machine embodies Lawrence's exaggerated sense of what it is to be male, a fantasy of exalted male power he shares with Nietzsche, though he himself is now reduced to a cog.

In *Sartor Resartus* Carlyle attacks the romantic egoism of writers such as Byron and sees the first preliminary moral act as an "Annihilation of Self."[31] Lawrence's process of learning that one doesn't matter is such an act: the denial of the will, the second stage in the romantic hero's development. The boundaries of the self contract. Lawrence's withdrawal into the R.A.F., "the nearest modern equivalent of going into a monastery in the Middle Ages" (L, 853), parallels the withdrawal of other romantic heroes. For example, the hero of Byron's poem *The Giaour*, after a violent assertion of his will, withdraws to a monastery; the poem ends with a long confession replete with the hero's desire for rest and death.[32]

Carlyle believes that there must be a third stage. The hero has rejected romantic egoism and will; he now returns to society, not absorbing it, but accepting his absorption by it, giving, not ordering or demanding. Lawrence delineates the third stage of the romantic hero in the following passage from *The Mint*:

> Man, who was born as one, breaks into little prisms when he thinks: but if he passes through thought into despair, or comprehension, he again achieves some momentary onenesses with himself. And not only that. He can achieve a oneness of himself with his fellows: and of them with the stocks and stones of his universe: and of all the universes with the illusory everything (if he be positive) or with the illusory nothing (if he be nihilist) according as the digestive complexion of his soul be dark or fair. Saint and sinner touch—as great saints and great sinners. (M, 179)

In Part Three of *The Mint*, Lawrence does attempt to describe the experience of absorption, the oneness of himself with his fellows and with the stocks and stones of the universe. In the book's final chapter, he lies among the airmen in the sun, "too utterly content to speak, drugged with an absorption fathoms deeper than physical contentment. . . . Our bones dissolved to become a part of this underlying indulgent earth" (M, 249).

But Lawrence's own statement that Part Three is "vamped up" (*L*, 620) is accurate; in this final section of *The Mint*, he still portrays his separation from the other airmen. Three representative incidents poignantly illustrate his isolation. He rides out alone from his R.A.F. barracks on the expensive motorcycle he has been given and finds himself racing a plane (*M*, 242–44). He listens to a funeral sermon on Queen Alexandra; while one airman hisses "Balls," Lawrence recalls in detail his audience with the aged queen (*M*, 220–22). And he retells the furtive sexual experience of another airman in a manner that makes the reader feel what Lawrence earlier in the book described as "the attraction of unlikeness" (*M*, 223–24, 35). In fact the attraction of unlikeness permeates the whole of *The Mint*. After he has completed the book he wonders if these notes "convey my isolation in their crowd: the chiel taking notes, using my feelings just as pegs to tune my strings. I pretended to be one of them."[33]

To summarize, Lawrence seeks to deny his will after Arabia, desires "mind-suicide" (*L*, 411; *SP*, 564), and chooses to dramatize the process of denial in *The Mint*. The pattern of assertion and denial is clear, and that pattern is characteristic of romanticism. Both the assertion of the will and the denial of the will parallel the stages of development undergone by romantic heroes: first, a stage of expansion of self; second, a stage of withdrawal from society (or what the hero previously considered society) and contraction of self to the point of annihilation. The movement from one stage to another is best seen in "The Everlasting No," "Centre of Indifference," and "The Everlasting Yea" chapters of Carlyle's *Sartor Resartus*. The contrast between Nietzsche's and Schopenhauer's concepts of will illustrates these two stages. The third stage—a oneness with himself, his fellows, and the natural world (*M*, 179)—is not achieved by Lawrence.

Nonetheless, the pattern is not so neat as this summary suggests (or so neat as Lawrence sometimes perceived it to be). Assertion of will does take precedence in *Seven Pillars*; denial, in *The Mint*. But denial of will penetrates assertion, assertion penetrates denial, like Yin and Yang.

Lawrence declares in *The Mint* that, after the willful life in which he seemed so set, "my will has apparently turned against self" (*M*, 105). How is this will that Lawrence turns against himself for the purpose of denying will different from the Nietzschean impulse of mastery and command? With Lawrence there is the same problem as with Schopenhauer. Isn't the principle that denies will also will? Schopenhauer says knowledge of the will driving him enables him to deny will when he perceives the pain it inevitably generates. In self-renunciation, according to Schopenhauer, there is "a contradiction of the phenomenon with itself."[34] However, as Frederick Copleston points out, the "self-renunciation of an ascetic is a free act, . . . but it is only self-contradiction in this sense, that the ascetic denies himself the satisfaction of certain impulses and desires, while at the same time he affirms himself according to other capacities and desires."[35] Schopenhauer's denial of will, according to Patrick Gardiner, is really analogous to a religious conversion, "a total reversal in the direction of a man's personality and will."[36]

Eventually Lawrence comes to understand that the force used to deny will is the same as the force of will. Both assertion and denial are irrational, and the motives for both are, in the end, unknown to him. From his point of view after the war, the irrational bestial principle of will somehow masters and controls another irrational principle, ultimately also seen as bestial, the so-called angel dominant during the war. The unknown motive of will seeks this inner control just as the unknown motive previously sought external power. The unknown motive of will now seeks to attack self, restrain self, even extirpate self. From Lawrence's perspective, both will and the denial of will contain a strong element of mastery: mastery over others in Nietzsche, mastery over self in Schopenhauer. The will is basically mastery, and what it seeks to master is the beast of others and the beast of self. Yet the will itself is really beast, emotion, an unconscious force that can, in the exceptional man, be made conscious.

The dynamics of Lawrence's developing concept of will are clear. At first the basic meaning of will is seen as mastery, a force that emerges from the self to create order and value, a shaping, creative force. Then the basic meaning comes to be the force that drives through all things, through body, hope, even ideals (*L*, 453), a force that controls, that takes charge. Once Lawrence understands that Nietzsche's will is not an angel, not an escape from material limits, from passion, and from flesh, then he must deny it, just as he has always sought to deny his body, his emotions, his sexuality. He must conquer the Nietzschean will. The ultimate denial is death. Immediately after speaking of turning his will against the self, he writes, "How welcome is death . . . to them that have nothing to do but to die" (M, 106). The uniformity and order of the R.A.F. is death: "Chaos breeds life: whereas by habit and regularity comes death, quickly" (L, 529).

In this mind-suicide and constraint of the body, there is also a triumph of will and there is conscious pleasure in this triumph. Lawrence scarcely disguises this pleasure.[37] Speaking of the Beduin, whom he created in his own image, Lawrence writes, "The desert Arab found no joy like the joy of voluntarily holding back. He found luxury in abnegation, renunciation, self restraint" (SP, 41). Speaking of himself, he declares that "voluntary slavery was the deep pride of a morbid spirit" (SP, 565). Lawrence illustrates this curious pleasure repeatedly in The Mint. When he serves food to other airmen in the R.A.F., he serves himself short: "No virtue there. Like the Lady of Shalott I prefer my world backwards in the mirror" (M, 160). In a 1923 letter he states the paradox with elegance and precision; comparing himself to other soldiers in the Tank Corps, he remarks, "I get in denial the gratification they get in indulgence" (L, 416).

There is control of self and freedom from the demands of others in Lawrence's so-called denial of will. Yet there is also a sense in which Lawrence controls others by his withdrawal and renunciation, gets and maintains even until this day the interest of a great number of people. Most readers see greatness, strength, and virtue in his denials and renunciations, not in his assertions of will. Lawrence recognizes the religious dimension and appeal of his denial and immodestly compares himself to Saint Anthony and Saint Teresa. He finds it "terrible to hold myself voluntarily here: and yet I want to stay here till it no longer hurts me: till the burnt child no longer feels the fire. Do you think there have been many lay monks of my persuasion?" (L, 416).[38]

In The Joyful Wisdom Nietzsche notes that romantics seek repose and deliverance from themselves. After the war Lawrence seeks to establish an "equilibrium between conditions and expectations . . . so fine that I shun all disturbances."[39] This search for deliverance from self, the subject of the first two sections of The Mint, is original, daring, and courageous in its bareness and simplicity. The Mint recalls the intensity and inwardness of Puritan narratives of conversion such as Bunyan's Grace Abounding. The Mint's tightness is Lawrence's "guard against the hysteria which is the prime instinct of my nature. I'd like to choke out everything."[40] In *The Mint* the important conflicts are all inside. Lawrence's struggle to fulfill his "self-denying ordinances" (*L*, 575) is fascinating, his complex contradictions of the simple task he sets himself inevitable.

Only Lawrence's will is powerful enough to pass these self-denying ordinances, to master himself, to save the world from the danger he fantasizes himself to be. Like a child, he would rather feel guilty and afraid of himself than innocent, vulnerable, and afraid of others. He fantasizes that no power in society, in religion, or in an institution can keep his will in check except his will. Lawrence, like other romantic heroes, becomes his own prosecutor, own jury, own judge, and own executioner. In these literary works he plays all the roles, roles that might be distributed among several characters in a novel. He blesses himself, condemns himself.[41] We are both relieved and appalled. It is as if Napoleon renounced his urge to conquer, banished himself to Saint Helena, and began to take a slow poison.

In *The Mint* Lawrence in fact does assert his will to mastery, asserts himself against authority, and leads from the ranks. In *Seven Pillars* Lawrence says that among the Beduin "no man could be their leader except he ate the ranks' food, wore their clothes, lived level with them, and yet appeared better in himself" (*SP*, 157). He lives this way in the R.A.F. and at times assumes de facto leadership. Lawrence displays in *The Mint* the same sense of his superiority over the common airmen (often spoken of as uncomplicated, unfallen, and childlike) as he had earlier displayed over the Arabs. And he constantly narrates minor triumphs over his immediate superiors in the R.A.F. Many incidents not documented in *The Mint* show Lawrence's power over the highest officials in the R.A.F. For example, Lawrence was feared by the marshal of the R.A.F., Hugh Trenchard. The use to which *The Mint* might be put terrified Trenchard, and Lawrence knew it.

Even Lawrence's withdrawal into the ranks is a form of control; like a child playing peekaboo, he hides in order to be noticed. In some respects Lawrence's withdrawal resembles Rousseau's, whose *Confessions* he knows; Lawrence too claims that he wishes to live unnoticed but sends out powerful messages establishing his presence. His constant contact with the most powerful politicians and artists in England, his private circulation of his manuscripts, his two private editions of *Seven Pillars*, his best-selling publication of *Revolt in the Desert*, his translation of *The Odyssey*—these kept the world well aware of his presence.

Schopenhauer portrays the creation of art as a quieter of will. The artist contemplates the objectification of will, copies it, and is delivered from it at moments until the knowledge of the nature of will becomes a path out of life. The greatest art can "become a *quieter* of all will . . . ; the surrender of all volition, conversion, and suppression of will, and with it of the whole inner being of this world, that is to say, salvation."[42] Lawrence does say *Seven Pillars* slays his will; the book does objectify his will, and its writer does contemplate will. While in part *Seven Pillars* and *The Mint* turn a savage, murderous eye on Lawrence himself, the books are an assertion of will, for it is primarily these books that keep him known, embody his complexities, and perpetuate his dramatization of self. And Lawrence knew as well as any man how to promote such a book. He was not made famous by accident or by the intervention of others. *Seven Pillars* and *The Mint* are acts of will that permanently and intentionally alter his relationships to others.[43]

These books are art, and they remain dynamic; no biography can supersede their view from inside. Lawrence's complex vacillation between assertion and denial of will is the center of their strength. In July 1918, near the end of the war, he writes, "I hate being in front, and I hate being back and I don't like responsibility, and I don't obey orders" (*L*, 246). This vacillation is not resolved, even after Lawrence grasps that "things are done in answer to a private urge" (*L*, 419). His irresolution is like his reader's personal irresolution, though grander; to use one of Aristotle's categories of character in *The Poetics*, Lawrence is "better than we are"—better in both assertion and denial.

The attraction to Lawrence illustrates something deep in the grain, something unadmitted in our character.[44] Our interest is in the putative sequence; if the denial came first, the assertion last, we would not be so fond of these books and this life. Most of us can understand and identify with his denial more fully than his assertion. The denial makes him human.[45]

The reader admires such renunciations of self, admires the imitation of Christ in which the fantasy of renunciation is embodied. Lawrence remarks, "Christians often forget how many thousands of people have been crucified."[46] As I have noted, Schopenhauer well expresses the

West's and the Christian's admiration for denial of will and annihilation of self. Shaping one's life or the lives of one's heroes to imitate
Christ's life is common among late nineteenth-century writers, even
among the most unlikely ones. For example, Oscar Wilde's confession
De Profundis overtly makes Christ into a romantic hero, a Christ whose
aesthetic beliefs and rebellion turn out to resemble the beliefs and the
rebellion of Wilde, the promiscuously homosexual perjurer.[47]

Though Lawrence's great assertion of will is necessary to get the
reader's attention, it is after all not very interesting unless it serves as
a contrast to the strength required to deny will, as Byron and other
romantics knew (e.g., the hero of *The Giaour* or of Mary Shelley's
Frankenstein). World War I provides many examples of men who displayed powerful Nietzschean wills, though we now find most of these
historical figures at best moderately interesting. Even Lawrence himself cares little about men of will such as big, simple Allenby, whom
he seems to patronize.[48]

Lawrence's assertion of will, his rebellion, is made more appealing
to the reader, safer, because he does not rebel against his own society.
Lawrence is a rebel away, a conformist at home.[49] From the English
point of view, he conducts, as the subtitle of the Bodleian manuscript
of *Seven Pillars* suggests, only a "personal essay in Rebellion." Lawrence
affects, even determines, some arrangements in the Mideast, but not
in Dorset or Bedford Square. He did not dream, as the Marquis de
Sade did, of a real crime such as putting out the sun, just the Turks,
and that in a faraway land. And the changes he makes in political
arrangements easily became part of Britain's long-established imperial
pattern. In his essay "The Changing East," Lawrence implies that he,
among others, has brought the "civilisation-disease" to Asia, and that
he promulgates the Western creed of nationalism. The stage is set now,
and he declares that the politician not the Galilean will conquer.[50]
Lawrence breaks the cyclical, migratory pattern of the Beduin and sub-
stitutes the Western ideal of historical progress. Lawrence's interest
in and encouragement of what he calls European Jewish colonists, who
will carry to Palestine "samples of all the knowledge and technique of
Europe," reflect his devotion to Western values, technology, and attitudes.[51]

Lawrence was engaged throughout his life in a struggle against his
own romantic impulses. The real interest of Lawrence is not in the

external world but in the internal. His real excitement is in the study of himself and his conflicting impulses. On the one hand, Lawrence must struggle against his "overflowing vitality," against his imperious will to mastery, against his urge to conquer and explore, against his desire to quicken history in the East, against an impulse to exclaim with Marlowe's Tamburlaine, "And shall I die, and this unconquered?" He must gain control of his romantic individualism, reject the godlike role he has given himself, end his usurpation of the wills of others, and etiolate his psychological imperialism which recreates the Arabs in his own image. On the other hand, Lawrence must also struggle against his "reduced vitality," against his isolation, against his abnegation of self, against his masochistic sexual perversion, against his self-destructive urges. He must struggle against his intention to fix and slay himself in books and in the mind-suicide of the R.A.F. He must seek some way to affirm the life left to him, and he tries to do so in the last section of *The Mint*. Needless to say, Lawrence can vanquish neither romantic impulse.

Lawrence's attack on the romantic expansion of self and on the Nietzschean will that generates it is as characteristic of romanticism as that masterful expansion. The greatness of *Seven Pillars* and *The Mint* is in the opposition of and the unresolved tension between the assertion of will in the war and the professed denial of it after the war.

Lawrence's life viewed from outside does not fully reflect the pattern of assertion and denial he establishes in these books. Lawrence did a great deal of productive political and creative work after the war. He participated in establishing political arrangements in the Mideast and was proud of these arrangements. He translated several books, wrote his major literary works, worked on the development of flying boats, and generously encouraged the political and artistic works of others. Yet in the barracks he cried in bed at night, though he declared that the only grief he knew was his own insufficiency.[52] A few months before his death he wrote, with the deep pessimism of Schopenhauer, "I have learned only the word 'No' in 46 years."[53]

N·O·T·E·S

1. *L*, 360. For an opposing view about the similarity of Lawrence's book to works of travel literature, see Stephen E. Tabachnick, *T. E. Lawrence* (Boston: Twayne, 1978), chaps. 2 and 8.

2. See, for example, M. H. Abrams, *Natural Supernaturalism: Tradition and Revolution in Romantic Literature* (New York: Norton, 1973); Harold Bloom, *Yeats* (New York: Oxford University Press, 1970); Robert Langbaum, "Romanticism as a Modern Tradition," in *The Poetry of Experience* (New York: Norton, 1963), 9–37; Morse Peckham, *Beyond the Tragic Vision: The Quest for Identity in the Nineteenth Century* (New York: George Braziller, 1962); Kenneth Clark, *Civilisation: A Personal View* (New York: Harper and Row, 1970). See also Robert Harbison, *Deliberate Regression* (New York: Knopf, 1980), a book that verges on hysteria in its attack on romanticism and on its strong present influence.

3. Arthur Schopenhauer, *The World as Will and Idea*, trans. R. B. Haldane and J. Kemp, 3 vols. (London: Routledge and Kegan Paul, 1883), 1: 140. The emphasis is the author's. For general discussions of the concept of will, see Hannah Arendt, *Willing* (New York: Harcourt Brace Jovanovich, 1978), and Vernon J. Bourke, *Will in Western Thought: A Historico-Critical Survey* (New York: Sheed and Ward, 1964).

4. Schopenhauer, *The World as Will and Idea*, 1:142.

5. Ibid., 355.

6. Ibid., 490–91.

7. Ibid., 345–46.

8. A list of books in Lawrence's library at his death is provided in *T. E. Lawrence by His Friends*, ed. A. W. Lawrence (London: Cape, 1937), 476–510. Schopenhauer's influence on D. H. Lawrence is briefly discussed in Emile Delavenay, *D. H. Lawrence: The Man and His Work; The Formative Years: 1885–1919* (London: Heinemann, 1972); his influence on Hardy, in Helen Garwood, *Thomas Hardy: An Illustration of the Philosophy of Schopenhauer* (Folcroft, Pa.: Folcroft Press, 1969). Lawrence's use of Schopenhauer's will is best seen in the novel *The Rainbow* and in his series of poems on the tortoise in *Birds, Beasts, and Flowers*. Among contemporary writers, the British poet Ted Hughes acknowledges the significant influence of Schopenhauer on his work. See the interview with Hughes in Ekbert Faas, *Ted Hughes: The Unaccommodated Universe* (Santa Barbara, Calif.: Black Sparrow Press, 1980), 205.

9. Friedrich Nietzsche, *The Will to Power*, ed. Walter Kaufmann, trans. Walter Kaufmann and R. J. Hollingdale (New York: Vintage, 1968), 52. The emphasis here and in other passages from this book is Nietzsche's. Another important influence on Lawrence's concept of will is Epictetus. Lawrence initialed a copy of Epictetus' *Enchiridion* "T.E.L., Paris," presumably in 1919, the year he began writing *Seven Pillars* (see *T. E. Lawrence by His Friends*, 486). Epictetus, a Greek stoic of the first century A.D., strongly emphasizes the control of will over the body and desire. Both Schopenhauer and Nietzsche refer to Epictetus occasionally. The following passage from Epictetus suggests the tone of Lawrence's comments on will while narrating his conduct of the Arab Revolt. Epictetus writes, "Disease is an impediment to the body, but

not to the will, unless the will itself chooses. Lameness is an impediment to the leg, but not to the will." The quotation is from *Marcus Aurelius: Meditations; Epictetus: Enchiridion*, trans. George Long (Chicago: Henry Regnery, 1956), 174

10. *The Will to Power*, 353. In *The Other Victorians* (New York: Bantam, 1967), 23–24, Steven Marcus brilliantly discusses the power of the mind over outer circumstances, what is commonly called a "strong will." Marcus asserts that, "although the will is a form of consciousness and is consciously employed, its energies have historically been directed against consciousness itself—against intellect, introspection, self-examination, curiosity. Will is . . . a controlled consciousness which often contains within itself a fear of consciousness." In Lawrence the Nietzschean will is opposed to introspection and self-examination.

11. Friedrich Nietzsche, *The Joyful Wisdom*, trans. Thomas Common, in *The Complete Works of Friedrich Nietzsche*, ed. Oscar Levy (New York: Russell and Russell, 1964), 10: 332–35. Common's translation was in Lawrence's library. Levy's edition of Nietzsche was first published in 1909–11.

12. *The Will to Power*, 531.

13. Ibid., 206. For a discussion of the importance of pain and of overcoming resistance in both Nietzsche's and Lawrence's concepts of will, see Jeffrey Meyers, *The Wounded Spirit: A Study of "Seven Pillars of Wisdom"* (London: Martin Brian and O'Keeffe, 1973), 105–9.

14. *SP*, 5.

15. T. E. Lawrence, "The Seven Pillars of Wisdom," Bodleian MS. Reserve d.33., p. 356. Subsequent references to this manuscript will be given in parentheses after the passage referred to and preceded by MS. The Bodleian manuscript, written from 1920 to 1922, is the third and only complete manuscript of the book that survives. It is approximately 400,000 words, about 40 percent longer than both the text published privately in 1926 and the public edition of 1935.

16. Coleridge, *The Statesman's Manual*, in *The Complete Works of Samuel Taylor Coleridge*, ed. W. G. T. Shedd (New York: Harper, 1878), 1: 458. *The Statesman's Manual* was first published in 1816.

17. Clark, *Civilisation*, 300.

18. Wordsworth, *The Prelude*, XII, ll. 222–23, in *Poetical Works*, eds. Thomas Hutchinson and Ernest de Selincourt (London: Oxford University Press, 1969).

19. See Frederick Garber, "Self, Society, Value, and the Romantic Hero," in *The Hero in Literature*, ed. Victor Brombert (Greenwich, Conn.: Fawcett, 1969), 213–27, and Peckham, *Beyond the Tragic Vision*, particularly chap. 4.

20. *Shaw-Ede: T. E. Lawrence's Letters to H. S. Ede, 1927–1935*, ed. H. S. Ede (London: Golden Cockerel Press, 1942), 26.

21. Letter to Charlotte Shaw, 16 February 1928, British Museum Additional MSS. 45903–04. Subsequent references to Lawrence's correspondence with Mrs. Shaw are to this collection. His description of the sticky and noisome earth inhabited by the men in *The Mint* recalls his reference to himself in the ranks as Nebuchadnezzar (*L*, 364, 410). One of the plates in Blake's *The Marriage of Heaven and Hell*, his finest poem according to Lawrence, is of Nebuchadnezzar. Lawrence refers to Blake's poem in his letter to Charlotte Shaw, 14 April 1927.

22. Clark, *Civilisation*, 304. Clark names Wordsworth and Goethe as those who withdrew out of fear of the political consequences of their earlier views.

23. Schopenhauer, *The World as Will and Idea*, 1:524.

24. In *The Mint* Lawrence also uses the bee-comb image; he declares that in the Royal Air Force the "ideal of troops is to be as like and close-fitting as bee cells" (M, 239).

25. Letter to Charlotte Shaw, 31 December 1928. In *Twilight of the Idols*, Nietzsche condemns Thomas a Kempis's *The Imitation of Christ*. Lawrence had both *Twilight* and *Imitation* in his library. The latter was initialed "T.E.L. 1919," the year Lawrence wrote the first draft of *Seven Pillars*. See *The Portable Nietzsche*, ed. and trans. Walter Kaufmann (New York: Viking, 1968), 515, and *T. E. Lawrence by His Friends*, 494.

26. Peckham, *Beyond the Tragic Vision*, 236. Peckham does not mention Lawrence, but his concept of the heroic redeemer is based in great part on the works of Carlyle, Schopenhauer, and Nietzsche.

27. Letter to Charlotte Shaw, 28 September 1925. I do not know the origin of this fear, but I believe the fear antedates the war. In a letter to the same correspondent, 14 April 1927, Lawrence expresses with great clarity his adult terror of his mother. I speculate that what he fantasizes he would do in power parallels the fantasy of what he would do to that terrifying mother before whom he is still helpless and to whom, he admits, he is still bound.

28. On this fear, see R. D. Laing, *The Divided Self: An Existential Study in Sanity and Madness* (Baltimore: Penguin, 1965), 93

29. Schopenhauer, *The World as Will and Idea*, 2:354.

30. Letter to Charlotte Shaw, 28 September 1925.

31. Thomas Carlyle, *Sartor Resartus and Selected Prose*, ed. Herbert L. Sussman (New York: Holt, Rinehart and Winston, 1970), 180.

32. In many respects Lawrence resembles the Byronic hero, an important model for the heroes of such twentieth-century works as Joseph Conrad's *Lord Jim*, James Joyce's *A Portrait of the Artist as a Young Man*, and even for Birkin in D. H. Lawrence's *Women in Love*. On the sources and the influence of this hero, see Peter L. Thorslev, *The Byronic Hero: Types and Prototypes* (Minneapolis: University of Minnesota Press, 1962).

33. Letter to Charlotte Shaw, 20 March 1928.

34. Schopenhauer, *The World as Will and Idea*, 1:371.

35. Frederick Copleston, *Arthur Schopenhauer: Philosopher of Pessimism* (New York: Barnes and Noble, 1975), 155.

36. Patrick Gardiner, *Schopenhauer* (Harmondsworth: Penguin, 1971), 286–87.

37. In 1914 D. H. Lawrence declares that "the Egoist as a divine figure on the Cross, held up to tears and love and veneration, is to me a bit nauseating now." Such egoism ends in "the passion for the extinction of yourself and the knowledge of the triumph of *your own will* in your body's extinction." The emphasis is the author's. See *The Collected Letters of D. H. Lawrence*, ed. Harry T. Moore (New York: Viking, 1962), 1:300–304.

38. In a series of letters to Lionel Curtis written in 1923, Lawrence uses the term "masochism" to describe his denial of self and "sadism" to describe the attack his own

conscience makes on him: "Conscience in healthy men is a balanced sadism, the bitter sauce which makes more tasteful the ordinary sweets of life: and in sick stomachs the desire of condiment becomes a craving. . . . So because my senses hate it, my will forces me to it" (L, 416–18). For further discussion of Lawrence's sadomasochism, see my book, *The Confessions of T. E. Lawrence* (Athens: Ohio University Press, 1979), chap. 5.

39. Letter to Charlotte Shaw, 17 June 1926.

40. Letter to Charlotte Shaw, 20 March 1928.

41. The role of the romantic hero as godlike determiner of his own state of grace or of damnation is beautifully expressed in the final stanza of Yeats's "A Dialogue of Self and Soul":

> I am content to follow to its source
> Every event in action or in thought;
> Measure the lot; forgive myself the lot!
> When such as I cast out remorse
> So great a sweetness flows into the breast
> We must laugh and we must sing,
> We are blest by everything,
> Everything we look upon is blest.

42. Schopenhauer, *The World as Will and Idea*, 1:301; see also 1:345–46.

43. On the confession as an act which transforms the life of the writer, see the brilliant essay by Michel Leiris, the afterword to his confession *Manhood: A Journey from Childhood into the Fierce Order of Virility*, trans. Richard Howard (New York: Grossman, 1963), 151–62.

44. See Joan Didion's essay, "7000 Romaine, Los Angeles 38," in *Slouching towards Bethlehem* (New York: Simon and Schuster, 1979), 67–72. The essay is on Howard Hughes.

45. Garber, in "Self, Society, Value, and the Romantic Hero," 227, discusses the way the hero is made human.

46. Letter to Charlotte Shaw, 31 December 1928. This statement was inspired by H. M. Tomlinson's comment in a letter to Lawrence asserting that no critic of *Seven Pillars* "got near his formidable job, which might have been about a crucifixion, with himself [the critic] as the sinner, for whom this was done." Tomlinson's letter is in *Letters to T. E. Lawrence*, ed. Arnold W. Lawrence (London: Cape, 1962), 189–92.

47. On Christ as a nineteenth-century cultural model, see Peckham, *Beyond the Tragic Vision*, p. 198.

48. Lawrence on 3 May 1925 wrote to Charlotte Shaw that "To be very great a man must be pretty stupid." Allenby is of course not stupid, but he is portrayed without the interest and complexity of, say, Ronald Storrs, a man who does not possess Allenby's single-mindedness. Lawrence presents an interesting sketch of Storrs in *Seven Pillars*.

49. In *Tristes Tropiques*, trans. John and Doreen Weightman (New York: Atheneum, 1974), 383–84, Claude Lévi-Strauss discusses this principle as it applies to his

own experience as a French anthropologist in remote areas of Brazil and argues that he and most anthropologists are rebels in their own society, conformists in the one they study.

50. T. E. Lawrence, "The Changing East," in *Oriental Assembly*, ed. A. W. Lawrence (New York: Dutton, 1940), 71–97. This superb essay, first published in *The Round Table* in September 1920, discusses Lawrence's concept of the "new Imperialism." Though little known, the best book on the subtleties of colonialism and imperialism is Dominique O. Mannoni's *Prospero and Caliban: The Psychology of Colonization*, trans. Pamela Powesland (London: Methuen, 1956). Mannoni's book helps one understand how representative of imperialists Lawrence's characterization of the Arabs is. See also Edward W. Said, *Orientalism* (New York: Pantheon Books, 1978).

51. Lawrence, "The Changing East," 92–93.

52. Letter to Charlotte Shaw, 21 December 1927.

53. Letter to Charlotte Shaw, 31 December 1934.

Seven Pillars of Wisdom: The Secret, Contestable Documentary

KEITH N. HULL

Since T. E. Lawrence completed the earliest versions of *Seven Pillars of Wisdom*, perceptive, authoritative critics have seen a fundamental difficulty in the book. Writing to Lawrence in February 1924, E. M. Forster noted that *Seven Pillars* was "granular," that it presented life as "a succession of items which . . . have some sort of intervals between them." Later in the same letter Forster noted that some of the granules were reflective rather than narrative or descriptive, and that some of these in turn comprised "pseudo-reflection." Apparently sensing an inconsistency between some reflective passages and the principal structure of *Seven Pillars*, Forster advised Lawrence, "Don't let the reflective apparatus function unless it has something to reflect about."[1]

In 1940 R. P. Blackmur similarly faulted *Seven Pillars*. In his essay "The Everlasting Effort," he wrote of Lawrence: "The ungrounded idealism that was fatal to him as a man comes out in his writing as compositional weakness, and is indeed the rough counterpart to what we feel as the lack of an abiding conviction. What is meant here by composition is the sum of those inner modes and outward manners by which the materials of experience are set together so that they make a whole."[2]

What, Forster and Blackmur essentially ask, is the relationship between documentary information and the mystifying—"gummy," to use

Forster's phrase—introspective passages that lay bare Lawrence's soul? In 1960 American critic Albert Cook echoed the earlier critics' doubts about *Seven Pillars*. Agreeing particularly with Blackmur, Cook wrote in *The Meaning of Fiction* that "Lawrence's failure of action is the breach between his purpose and his act due to the shifting of the purpose itself. . . . The corresponding breach in his writings is the failure to integrate, to 'compose' as Blackmur says. . . . A breach exists between two sides. These two sides . . . are the closely observed natural detail and the moral generalization. . . . Detail never becomes analogy, moralization never points toward plot."[3]

Recently Thomas J. O'Donnell has brought this line of criticism full circle. In his book *The Confessions of T. E. Lawrence*, published in 1979, O'Donnell writes that *Seven Pillars* "fails to link the introspective to the epic, the unconscious self to the social self, the subjective to the objective, emotion and intellect to act." Then, with poetic symmetry, O'Donnell quotes Forster's 1955 comment from *Abinger Harvest*: "something has gone wrong here."[4]

All these critics and most others agree, however, that not too much has gone wrong, that *Seven Pillars* is a masterpiece. In defending this judgment, commentators historically have turned to two undeniably attractive aspects of the book: its documentary treatment of fierce action and intrigue in an exotic setting, and its mystifying delineation of Lawrence's spiritual journey. The success of *Revolt in the Desert*—an abridgment of *Seven Pillars* with the personal material excised—is testimony to the popular appeal of the documentary material; it sold 150,000 copies in Britain and the United States within four months of its 1927 publication.

In their book-length studies of Lawrence's works, Jeffrey Meyers and Stephen Tabachnick acknowledge and analyze the virtues that probably led to *Revolt's* popularity and to the continuing success of its parent volume. In individual chapters, Meyers treats *Seven Pillars* as military history, while Tabachnick discusses it as an "autobiography of travel." Neither Meyers nor Tabachnick, however, is lured into the position that the documentary side of *Seven Pillars* is its greatest asset. Instead both see equivalent or greater virtue in its personal, reflective aspects, stating finally that the presence of both elements creates the masterpiece. Tabachnick writes that the split between the two is a "fault" that *Seven Pillars* overcomes, while Meyers states that "Its greatness lies not in Lawrence's military history, as in *Revolt in the Desert*, but in his exposure of himself."[5]

O'Donnell essentially takes Meyers's contention to its extreme, focusing on *Seven Pillars* as a work in the confessional tradition encompassing Augustine, Abelard, Bunyan, Rousseau, and especially Schopenhauer, Carlyle, Mill, and other nineteenth-century narrators of "spiritual growth." Thus O'Donnell concludes, "It is Lawrence's unsystematic translation of the optimistic Romantic myth of self into the pessimistic psychological myth of our century that gives his confessions power, universality, and complexity" (p. 181).

These critics I have mentioned—and others—agree that *Seven Pillars* is a great book. Notably absent in Lawrence studies, however, is the view that *Seven Pillars* owes its greatness to its integration of documentary and personal material, that Lawrence had his book well under control, and that he was not torn irreparably between producing a history of some sort on one hand and a confession on the other. Lawrence himself was the worst enemy of such a view. O'Donnell quotes Lawrence's letters at length to demonstrate how they "separate introspection and history" (p. 31). Tabachnick reprints Lawrence's own estimation of how the separation of the two turned out: "What I was trying to do, I suppose, was to carry a superstructure of ideas upon or above anything I made. Well, I failed in that" (p. 75).

Lawrence, however, was one of England's great letter writers; his interests, reading, and experiences were broad and deep, his friends many, intelligent, and talented. Given the extremes of his psychological states, it is not surprising that his letters can be invoked to demonstrate his ambivalence and sense of failure. Both were real and thoughtful. Still, Lawrence's letters demonstrate with equal validity that he had mastered the aesthetic, generic idea that governed *Seven Pillars'* composition: the relationship between the book's documentary and reflective aspects creates a sense of mystery that is *Seven Pillars'* greatest strength.

In 1920 Lawrence wrote to F. N. Doubleday that Conrad was "absolutely the most haunting thing in prose that ever was." The reason was that each of Conrad's sentences "goes on sounding in waves . . . after it stops. It's not," Lawrence continued, "built on the rhythm of ordinary prose, but on something existing only in his head, and as he can never say what it is he wants to say, all his things end in a kind of hunger, a suggestion of something he can't say or do or think. . . . He's as much a giant of the subjective as Kipling is of the objective."[6]

This letter is from 20 March 1920, by which time Lawrence had finished and allegedly lost the first draft of *Seven Pillars* and had nearly finished a second draft after thirty days' intense work in January and February 1920. That he was writing under the influence of an idea similar to the one he saw behind Conrad's work is indicated by a letter to Lionel Curtis, asking of *Seven Pillars*, "Isn't it just faintly possible that part of the virtue apparent in the book lies in its secrecy, its novelty, and its contestability?" (*L*, 417). This letter is dated 30 May 1923, by which time Lawrence had completed a third draft of *Seven Pillars*, having destroyed that mentioned above; this third version had been printed privately by the *Oxford Times*, and Lawrence had begun revisions that were to result in the 1926 Subscribers' Edition. *Seven Pillars'* virtues of secrecy and contestability in this finished version remain consistent with Conrad's virtues Lawrence had outlined earlier to Doubleday.

Meyers, O'Donnell, and Tabachnick all point out similarities between Lawrence's work and Conrad's; so too do Stanley and Rodelle Weintraub in their largely biographical book-length study, *Lawrence of Arabia: The Literary Impulse*.[7] Each of these critics contributes to a reader's understanding of *Seven Pillars*, but their comments deal with thematic similarities; isolation, imperalism, guilt, and retribution are among the common themes. As Lawrence's letters indicate, however, if he saw any resemblance between his own and Conrad's books, they were technical, concerned with manner rather than matter. That thematic similarities are so strong, however, supports the idea that Conrad was on Lawrence's mind as he wrote and revised *Seven Pillars*.

The concept of contestability—that a book's meaning should be open to various interpretations—appears in other letters written during or shortly after *Seven Pillars'* composition and revision period. In October 1922, Lawrence wrote to Edward Garnett that "the personal revelations should be the key of the thing: and the personal chapter actually is the key, I fancy: only it's written in cypher." The "story" he describes in the same letter as "all spiritually true" (*L*, 366). To D. G. Hogarth, Lawrence wrote in September 1927, after the publication of the Subscribers' Edition, that C. M. Doughty's *Arabia Deserta* is "one of the mystery-masterpieces of the world," suitable and especially interesting for close critical analysis (*L*, 534).

Lawrence's lists of great books and his comments on them are also useful indicators of his literary thinking and lend additional support to the contention that secrecy and contestability were consistent principles in his thinking about literature. In December 1927 he wrote to Edward Garnett, replying to Herbert Read's review of *Seven Pillars*, contending that "the world's big books" grew out of ideas such as his own notion of contestability, not out of Read's contention that "Great books are written in moods of spiritual light and intellectual certainty."[8] The list of "big books" Lawrence offered Garnett is composed of *War and Peace*, *The Brothers Karamazov*, *Moby Dick*, Rabelais, *Don Quixote*. Then he added, "There's a fine set of cores of darkness!" (*L*, 548). Since Read had said that *Seven Pillars'* "core of darkness . . . puts one in doubt as to the essential greatness of the book," we find here Lawrence flushed out of hiding in his ambivalence and again crediting his book with a virtue truly great books possess. A core of darkness was in fact his conscious goal in writing *Seven Pillars* and his defense of its greatness.

Lawrence was also inadvertently defending himself against the critics who came to see *Seven Pillars* as a book flawed by the documentary-personal split. Read's review traced the cause of "darkness" to its source in "the author's mind . . . obscured by divided aims. . . . Who is the hero of the story: Colonel Lawrence or the Arabian Army?" We can conclude from Lawrence's defense against this charge that he saw Forster's "something wrong" as something right, that the split the critics above mention was to Lawrence a virtue.

One of the notable qualities of Lawrence's lists of titanic books is the consistent inclusion of *Moby Dick*. This fact has not escaped critical notice because it tells us much about Lawrence and *Seven Pillars*. Meyers, Tabachnick, and the Weintraubs leave little doubt that Melville's influence on Lawrence was profound; yet, as with Conrad, they see principally a thematic relationship. In his review of the Weintraubs' book, for instance, Meyers sums up some of the similarities between the two books: "Both . . . combine disparate genres and styles, contain an encyclopedic amount of technical information, are strongly influenced by biblical language and themes and engage in metaphysical speculation. Both works are primitivistic epics of masculine action that emphasize the idea of male friendship and divided loyalties, and end in a negative and destructive climax. And both works are studies of monomania and perverse psychology."[9]

Tabachnick pursues most of these parallels in greater detail, mentioning also that Lawrence was attracted to *Moby Dick* and *Clarel*, "combinations of fact and fiction that alternate lyric arias of meditation and expositions of technical fact, for the same reason that he loved Doughty's *Travels in Arabia Deserta* and *Dawn in Britain*: as a modern speculative pilgrim in the oceanic deserts of the Near East, Lawrence walks in the psychological, cultural, and literary footsteps of his most brilliant and powerful predecessors."[10]

Here again we see awareness of the division that so many commentators see in *Seven Pillars*; technical fact and technical information set against perverse psychology still reflect the split between the documentary and personal, reflective aspects of *Seven Pillars*. Interestingly, neither critic here sees the division as a flaw, and comparison with *Moby Dick*, an acknowledged masterpiece, indicates that Lawrence may have been right, that the documentary-personal split creates a core of darkness that is the heart of *Seven Pillars'* greatness.

In their book Stanley and Rodelle Weintraub's comments about the relationship between *Seven Pillars* and *Moby Dick* point the way to an understanding of how Lawrence sought literary greatness, creating a core of darkness: "When Lawrence repeatedly praised *Moby Dick*, he may have been suggesting . . . the structure for which he aimed." This structure they see as "the quest of the protagonist . . . interleaved with documentary chapters." The purposes of such interleaving were to give "background and dimension to [Lawrence's] own first-person narrative," and, second, to provide "form for Melville's treatises on cetology as for Lawrence's on Near Eastern history and sociology" (pp. 48–99).

Though the Weintraubs are dealing with technique rather than theme here, they do not press their ideas far enough. The analogy between cetology in *Moby Dick* and history and sociology in *Seven Pillars* is the key to understanding how "interleaving" works to create *Seven Pillars'* core of darkness, hence its greatness. Though the meaning of the cetology chapters will probably never be interpreted to every reader's satisfaction, critics have offered fruitful suggestions. Among these, one by J. A. Ward bears as much on Lawrence's work as on Melville's.

Ward contends that Melville did unify his novel in spite of the fact that early readers found "formal exposition and traditional narration" to be "incongruous." Defending Melville, Ward states that the novelist believed that "in the monistic universe that [he] implicitly accepts but cannot ultimately comprehend, all things are vitally related to all other things. . . . Thus the incredibly intense study of the whale is a search for total knowledge. There is hardly a detail in the cetological chapters that does not have meaning that extends beyond itself."[11] A reader substituting *Seven Pillars'* documentary passages for the cetological chapters could say the same thing about Lawrence's masterpiece.

Lawrence's personal reflections give meaning to *Seven Pillars'* documentary details, making the Arab Revolt a spiritual as well as literal journey. To clarify this idea we can look back briefly to *Moby Dick.* The pursuit of the white whale is patently a spiritual event, one suggesting many meanings, some inexpressible. These allegorical, symbolic qualities of the chase suggest that the cetology chapters must have allegorical, symbolic meaning as well; generally the presence of a strongly suggestive element makes the literalness of even the most literal elements suspect. What is the meaning of any whale chase when it is interleaved with one that is clearly a spiritual quest of some sort? Similarly, the principal contribution of the personal, introspective passages to *Seven Pillars* is the sense they give of great drama being played out under the surface of the Arab Revolt. The core of darkness is the result of Lawrence's confused, confusing spiritual wanderings interleaved throughout the documentary, political, military circumstances, making them seem even more profound.

Seven Pillars is a drama in which forces more fundamental and more powerful than politics clash. Some of these are natural, some are human, and some are supernatural. They all have in common, though, the suggestion that they lurk beneath surfaces, operating inexorably, forcing humanity into constant conflict with them. These forces are as vague as they are in other works that deal with similar themes. We see them in Melville's whale and Captain Ahab, in Conrad's seas and jungles, in the Greeks' gods, furies, and fate, in Joyce's subconscious currents, and in Pynchon's military-industrial combines. Ultimately these forces are unknowable and take many names—history, God, good, evil, nature, the cosmos, the unconscious, and so on, but always they test humanity by their own standards.

The personal passages in *Seven Pillars* are the most evident, compelling indicators of this drama and define its two most important aspects: Lawrence's struggle with outside forces and his corresponding struggle with forces within himself. Chapters 100 and 103 are probably the most widely cited examples from Lawrence's introspective undercurrent; both cross and recross the line between discussing documentary facets of the revolt and the deeper issues that power *Seven Pillars*.

Partly with these chapters in mind, Stephen Tabachnick writes that Lawrence always resorts to "a difficult, opaque prose . . . when describing his thoughts" (p. 57). This is an exact description; Tabachnick understands the reason for opaqueness when he writes of the difference between the final *Seven Pillars* and the Oxford text that the later version is "more symbolic and mysterious" (p. 73). The thought-filled chapters exemplified by chapters 100 and 103 deal with the dark and unknowable, with what Yeats said we can embody but cannot know.

Chapter 100 discusses the relationship between the revolt's leaders and their followers. The general theme is that Lawrence and other leaders—unnamed since he principally means himself when he says "we"—have taken advantage of Arab tribesmen by enrolling them in the revolt on the pretext of nationalism, only to embroil them in issues beyond their understanding. Addressing such issues, the chapter ends clearly: "How was it right to let men die because they did not understand? . . . There seemed no straight walking for us leaders in this crooked lane of conduct, ring within ring of unknown, shamefaced motives cancelling or double-charging their precedents. . . . Suffice it that since the march to Akaba I bitterly repented my entanglement in the movement" (SP, 551–52).

These sentences are from the chapter's end, however; they are the reader's opportunity to surface from deeper water. Greater forces are at play in Arabia, as the chapter's opening paragraph hints: "It might have been heroic to have offered up my own life for a cause in which I could not believe: but it was a theft of souls to make others die in sincerity for my graven image" (SP, 550). The diabolical metaphor here overstates the case. *Seven Pillars* makes abundantly clear the fact that Lawrence funneled enormous sums of British gold into Arab purses, while Auda's defection and the holding back from the revolt of Arab officers in the Turkish army scarcely indicate anything like Arab innocence.

Yet Lawrence writes, apparently of all the revolt's participants, that "our endurance might win redemption, perhaps for all a race. . . . The self-immolated victim took for his own the rare gift of sacrifice; and no pride and few pleasures in the world were so joyful, so rich as this choosing voluntarily another's evil to perfect the self" (SP, 550). The language here may sound biblical; the sentiment is not. The passage sets up resonances with the Bible—a common occurrence in *Seven Pillars*—to give a sense of something deeper going on, then creates a rich irony by reversing ordinary Christian sentiment: "There was nothing loftier than a cross, from which to emulate the world. The pride and exhilaration of it were beyond conceit" (*SP*, 551). In political terms, those upon the cross are the revolt's leaders or its early adherents who set the example of sacrifice, gaining pride—hardly a Christian virtue—by doing so.

Thus we see biblical language and parallels set up to hint at a drama deeper than political intrigue, then reversed to gain a deep sense of irony. We are dealing here not with a Christ-like sacrifice but with its perversion through pride, righteousness, and the willful spreading of sin; the situation suggests Satan's ironic perversions in *Paradise Lost* when he makes his antiheroic plunge into Chaos and the new, unexplored Universe. The forces at work are familiar: Good manifested in the desire for perfection and redemption; Evil, in the sinful inversion of noble motives; and perhaps even Ego, seen in the willful service of Evil.

Chapter 103 takes up forces within Lawrence. Again beginning from the circumstances of the revolt, Lawrence moves into deeper waters where we meet an assortment of fundamental human characteristics described as "bundled powers and entities" whose "character . . . hid" (SP, 563). Initially we see Lawrence as "actor" because he is not a "man of action"; acting is simply an adaptation he makes in order to lead. Similarly, his complaint about liking the recognition his leadership brings addresses his immediate circumstances. His modest self, at odds with his immodest self, feels a baroque "horror of being known to like being known" (SP, 563).

Shortly, however, the reader moves on to more nearly universal characteristics, old friends: "Always feelings and illusion were at war within me, reason strong enough to win, but not strong enough to annihilate the vanquished, or refrain from liking them better" (SP,

563–64). This sentence characterizes a mind split between reality and "illusion," and between emotions and reason. Feelings apparently favor illusions; reason condemns them, liking but not destroying illusions because it likes them. The relationships among these "entities" is vague. Clearly, however, these are powers in conflict within a single mind, with an "I"—a separate entity?—looking nervously on.

Then "Will" enters the fray—capitalized. Turning once again to Milton, we can see the parallels with Satan, who, in defiance of his reason, obeys his emotions to construct the illusions that hell is heaven, and that destruction is as great as creation. Will is the engine, the energy source, for Satan's transgressions. Lawrence's will is slightly more complicated, and seems able to operate on its own: "I had found materials always apt to serve a purpose, and Will a sure guide to some one of the many roads leading from purpose to achievement" (*SP*, 564). Though "Will" remains vague, we again confront universal human powers. The fact that Lawrence's descriptions of their conflicts evoke earlier writers and a long tradition suggests that he is writing not just about Lawrence in Arabia but about man in the cosmos as well.

The chapter dismisses Lawrence's physical being out of hand. Having mentioned that Will is "a sure guide . . . to achievement," Lawrence adds, "There was no flesh," a statement that flicks the physical flies off the metaphysical desk; the flesh does not count in the final analysis. That Lawrence was all his life contemptuous of his body is a persistent theme in his biographies, *Seven Pillars*, and *The Mint*. That he should dismiss it so effectively in a passage devoted to intangibles supports the proposition that feeling, reason, and Will are the true contenders in the inner battle as other intangible forces are the true contenders in Arabia.

At the other extreme from these intensely subjective passages are those that deal with relentlessly objective material, Arabian geography. Mountains, gorges, rock types, the angles of sedimentary strata, crops, the appearances of towns, the social classes and racial mixtures of populations—all come in for extensive description. A few minutes with a detailed atlas or encyclopedia can establish for any reader how verifiable and therefore objective *Seven Pillars* is on such matters. Characters and events of the revolt are to some extent open to interpretation; geography is truly documentary material.

If we concede that the reflective passages invite readers to see *Seven*

Pillars as allegorical and symbolic, then it is an easy step to interpreting geography as having allegorical, symbolic meanings. In fact Lawrence's treatment of it would invite such interpretation even if the reflective, personal passages did not show the way. The simple fact that *Seven Pillars* is set in biblical lands led Lawrence to such suggestive comments as these: "Allenby rode across Armageddon" (*SP*, 46) and "Palestine became a land of milk and honey to those who had spent forty years in Sinai: Damascus had the name of an earthly paradise to the tribes which could enter it only after weeks and weeks of painful marching" (*SP*, 256).

More important and finally more compelling, however, is the treatment Lawrence gives the mass of landscape descriptions. This most completely documentary part of *Seven Pillars* has its own quality that indicates the presence of forces as intangible and universal as those that dominate the reflective passages. These in turn suggest and magnify the two general groups of forces apparent in chapters 100 and 103. On the one hand, some landscapes seem to be the products of unknown cosmic forces; on the other, they are shaped by Lawrence's own state of mind.

Typical of the first type of description is this one, from early in the book: "The lava here was not the blue-black cinder-stone of the fields about Rabegh: it was rust-colored, and piled in huge crags of flowing surface and bent and twisted texture" (*SP*, 107). This much is typical of the vivid, concrete descriptions that give readers a complete sense of the scene. As the passage continues, however, a new aspect of the landscape emerges. It is the product of something sentient and powerful with a strange kink to its personality: "it was rust-colored, and piled in huge crags of flowing surface and bent and twisted texture as though played with oddly while yet soft." This unknown force is given an even more sinister twist by its looking forward to the Deraa rape scene in which the Turkish soldiers, holding their victim down, would "ease themselves and play unspeakably" with him (*SP*, 444).

On some occasions desert features have a divine, fruitful, benign air about them: "[Then] came the ride . . . over the breast-like curves of Imran . . . till we passed through the gap before the rock Khuzail, and into the inner shrine of the springs, with its worship-compelling coolness. There the landscape refused to be accessory, but took the skies, and we chattering humans became dust at its feet" (*SP*, 543). These two unlike passages create mysteries. What being or force or spirit is present in the desert? Is it one thing? Several? What is it (or they) like? Above all, what are its relationships to T. E. Lawrence and mankind?

Complicating these questions is the fact that many descriptive scenes reflect, as Jeffrey Meyers writes, "Lawrence's seared soul" (p. 100). A particularly brilliant passage illustrates how resonant such scenes can be. We have already seen in chapter 100 how Lawrence dates his "acquiescence in the Arab fraud" from the march to Akaba. About that time, June 1917, Lawrence became aware of the Sykes-Picot Treaty. In *Seven Pillars* this awareness is the beginning of the divided self that dominates Lawrence's self-characterization.

The landscape of Wadi Sirhan, through which the Akaba expedition must pass, becomes in the circumstances a powerful expression of Lawrence's spiritual, emotional state on the journey: "The landscape was of a hopelessness and sadness deeper than all the open deserts we had crossed. Sand, or flint, or a desert of bare rocks was exciting sometimes, and in certain lights had the monstrous beauty of sterile desolation: but there was something sinister, something actively evil in this snake-devoted Sirhan, proliferant of salt water, barren palms, and bushes which served neither for grazing nor for firewood" (SP, 271). Sirhan's barrenness suggests the futility of further labors on the Arabs' behalf that haunts Lawrence for the rest of the book. The snakes—dealt with at length—have biblical symbolic value, suggesting the sinfulness of Lawrence's willfully deceiving the Arabs after he himself had been deceived. The labored conscience of chapter 100 is the product of this sin—and "sinful" is precisely Lawrence's word for his relationship with the Arabs.

Interestingly, however, Sirhan has qualities independent of Lawrence's state. The place is hopeless, sad, monstrous, sinister, and "actively evil" in its own right. This description hearkens back to those earlier questions about the identity, nature, and relationships of the forces in the landscape. The same scene emphasizes forces outside Lawrence as well as those within; Sirhan is at once an independent, active agent and a mirror of Lawrence's spiritual state. What, again, is the tangled relationship between Lawrence and Arabia?

Lawrence constructs a Sirhan that is an image of his inner state; by assigning it an independent spirit as well, he confronts readers with a paradox. Whose energy in what proportions prevails in *Seven Pillars*, those forces outside Lawrence or those within—however they resolve their differences? This question cannot be answered directly. The external forces in the landscape are themselves paradoxical; sometimes they are sinister, sometimes benign, sometimes beautiful, sometimes monstrous. If these qualities describe one being, it is a complex one. If they describe several, they are contrary to each other, just as Lawrence is filled with contrary entities—and as the Arab Revolt in its documentary, political, military, historical aspects is the sum of contrary entities. Albert Cook is wrong. Detail does become analogy; moralization does point toward plot.

In an earlier essay, I discussed in detail the relationship between the course of the Arab Revolt and the historical forces that propelled and directed it.[12] Basically the argument is this. As outlined in the first seven chapters of *Seven Pillars*, the historical pattern of Beduin migration is northward from Yemen to Mesopotamia and Syria. Population pressures in the south force tribes into the desert and northward until, centuries later, they are broken up in the northern cities. The revolt follows this itinerary, losing its cohesiveness in Damascus, where its military leaders cannot produce the political, administrative abilities to govern peacefully. The correspondence suggests that the revolt was linked to this migration pattern. Additionally, *Seven Pillars* says the Semites show a propensity for begetting city-born prophets who seek revelation in the desert then return to their people with new religions, most of which fail for lack of converts. Lawrence sums up the Semites as people who "since the dawn of life . . . had been dashing themselves against the coasts of flesh. Each wave was broken" (*SP*, 43).

Feisal and Lawrence are treated in *Seven Pillars* as prophets of the quasi-religious Arab Revolt. Both are citified but find their creeds in the desert: Feisal preaches nationalism; Lawrence, guerrilla warfare based on foggy principles of rejecting the world and seeking out pain, failure, and abnegation. Lawrence describes Feisal as "sitting there iconically, drained of desires, ambitions, weaknesses, faults, . . . enslaved by an abstraction," while Lawrence's most prophetic moment occurs when he preaches a "Midnight Sermon" to the Serahin, a tribe reluctant to join the revolt for fear its failure would bring Turkish reprisals.

Lawrence's sermon is derived directly from *Seven Pillars'* early chapters where he describes the Arabs as people shaped by the desert: "His sterile experience robbed him of compassion and perverted his human kindness to the image of the waste in which he hid. Accordingly he hurt himself, not merely to be free, but to please himself" (*SP*, 41). To the Serahin he preaches that, "To be of the desert was, as they knew, a doom to wage unending battle with an enemy who was not of the world, nor life, nor anything, but hope itself; and failure seemed God's freedom to mankind" (*SP*, 412).

The message here is that risking the revolt's failure is a religious duty born of the desert's influence. Paradox lurks everywhere in this speech and its antecedent. How is success bred out of deliberately seeking failure? This paradox derives from a larger one. If this view of failure is "of the desert," isn't the job of the prophet simply to remind the Arabs of what they are like rather than to shape them? This question leads to an even larger paradox. Is the Arab Revolt the result of its prophets or of Arabian geography?

Essentially, Lawrence says, both are true. At the end of chapter 3, he says, "One such [Semitic] wave . . . I raised and rolled before the breath of an idea, till it reached its crest, and toppled over and fell at Damascus" (*SP*, 43). Lawrence here is responsible for the Arab Revolt; yet the wave idea makes the revolt another in the series of Semitic religious surges that may in turn be related to Beduin migration and destruction on the desert's fringes. In other words, history—for lack of a better term—provides the impetus and general semi-religious shape of the revolt, and its prophets are simply its tools. Feisal, in fact, is described in such terms, "in reality he was nationality's best servant, its tool" (*SP*, 547).

Here is a perpetually vexing question. What is the relationship of individuals to their circumstances? Do we shape history, or are we shaped by it? If both, in what proportions? Jeffrey Meyers treats *Seven Pillars* partly in such terms in *The Wounded Spirit*. In chapters on the relationships between Tolstoy and Nietzsche and Lawrence, Meyers finally comes down on the side of the great man: "Whereas random fate determines history in Tolstoy, in Lawrence the individual Nietzschean will is supreme" (p. 96).

Seven Pillars is not that simple, however. The influences of history and the desert on the revolt and on Lawrence himself are too great.

The book may emphasize will over circumstances, but the real question is the proportion of one influence to another. This question takes us back to Lawrence's comment on "contestability." He did not intend for *Seven Pillars'* puzzles to be solved; on the contrary, for him they were the book's strongest virtues, and he made a lifelong effort to keep them intact.

Lawrence was correct. *Seven Pillars'* greatness hinges on its mysteries. These in turn gain their effectiveness from their complexity and interdependence. The relationship of the great man to his circumstances is only one mystery. As we have seen, the Arabian landscape suggests that it is a bundle of self-willed separate entities or a single being with wide-ranging moods and whims; or it seems the reflection of Lawrence's own multiple entities. Thus *Seven Pillars* becomes a mystifying three-way struggle. The desert shapes men and politics; men shape the desert and politics; politics shape men and the desert. Each element of the struggle is itself composed of struggling, often contradictory parts. Lawrence never intended that this tangle should be resolved. Rather, he saw *Seven Pillars* as a "mystery masterpiece," an allegorical, symbolic suggestion of fundamental forces struggling under the guise of documentary fact.

Frederic Manning, a war novelist whose work Lawrence admired, and whom he personally liked and respected, saw the book in this light. In May 1930 he wrote Lawrence,

> The book is magnificent. . . . The difficulties of the subject are enormous: the background is continually dissolving and changing. There is the background of the desert; the background of the war; the political background, of the English in Egypt . . . and of the Arab revolt (in itself so ambiguous, a racial movement striving to assume a national character . . .). . . . Job, of course, was an Arab, and his present day progeny stand in the same relation to Allah as he stood in relation to Jahveh, so passionately asserting his own individuality against the engulfing one-ness. How far "the eternal illusion" as I might call it took hold of your own mind, I can guess, and yet in all your overt acts you are only harnessing its power to serve some temporal and even momentary end, in which you do not altogether believe, at least not with the spirit of worship which you feel towards the power it was your business to subjugate and canalise. That's the whole moral problem:

one not very different in kind from that confronting Paul on his road to Damascus. As I read your book, and it is a riddle, that is the conflict which subsists at least implicitly under the material action of the book. Or is it some bent in my own mind which forces me to consider you sub specie aeternitatis?

You don't simplify any of these problems by your method of treatment.[13]

To this astute criticism Lawrence replied a few days later: "As for my harnessing to my go-cart the eternal force—well, no: I pushed my go-cart into the eternal stream, and so it went faster than the ones that are pushed cross-stream or up-stream. . . . I am still puzzled as to how far the individual counts: a lot, I fancy, if he pushes the right way" (*L*, 693).

Using Manning's idea that *Seven Pillars* is a "riddle," we can posit answers to some persistent problems in understanding Lawrence's masterpiece. One of the book's most discussed aspects is the identity of S.A. Recent investigations by Colin Simpson, Phillip Knightley, and John Mack have established with reasonable certainty that S.A. was Lawrence's Carchemish companion Dahoum. This identification tells us something about Lawrence's motives, but it actually leads us away from the meaning of the poem. "To S.A." should be read in light of its contribution to the meaning of *Seven Pillars*. The poem is deliberately mysterious in order to establish the symbolic nature of the book the reader is about to encounter. S.A. is not a person; he—or it—is a symbol, a suggestion of one or some of the mysterious forces operating beneath the documentary surface. Reading Dahoum into the poem puts *Seven Pillars* too squarely in the realm of mundane experience— Lawrence sought to liberate the Arabs as a worthy gift to a loved one. Instead, S.A. is a symbol, an evocation of bundled entities within Lawrence and without, whose precise nature we can never know as certainly as we can know deep friendship or love.

Similarly, the excised first chapter should be seen in its literary rather than its historical, biographical context if we are to understand *Seven Pillars*' nature. The first sentence of the original opening chapter puts the book directly into a documentary context—repeating in essence the mistake of identifying S.A. too literally: "The story which follows was first written out in Paris during the Peace Conference, from notes jotted daily on the march, strengthened by some reports sent to my chiefs in Cairo."[14] By contrast, the first sentence of the present chapter 1 is a perfect signpost for the mysteries ahead: "Some of the evil of my tale may have been inherent in our circumstances" (SP, 29). The tentativeness of "some" and "may" forecasts the spirit of unsolvable questions, "some" even raising the question of proportion of influence between the individual and his circumstances. "Circumstances" itself is an open-ended term that, in tandem with "evil," suggests a cosmic issue may be at stake in what follows.

The style—or styles—of Seven Pillars is another aspect that has received wide attention yet one that is put into clearer perspective by seeing the book as deliberately contestable. Irving Howe has made the most penetrating general comment on Lawrence's style. In his 1962 essay "T. E. Lawrence: The Problem of Heroism," Howe writes, "He often uses words with a deliberate obliqueness or off-meaning, so as to charge them with strangeness and potential life. . . . All of this followed from conscious planning." Howe then quotes Lawrence: "I find that my fifth writing . . . of a sentence makes it more shapely, pithier, stranger than it was. Without that twist of strangeness no one would feel an individuality, a differentness, behind the phrase."[15]

Lawrence was after more than these qualities though. Seven Pillars' style is a deliberate effort to give readers a sense of deeper meanings—though contestable ones—lurking beneath the surface, and so he used not just oblique meanings but odd, archaic, or poetic words and constructions, sometimes even unacknowledged quotations. Jeffrey Meyers lists some of these, citing Lawrence's justification for using "words . . . which much-loved men have stooped to, and charged with rich meaning." "Everywhere," Lawrence writes, "there are such borrowed phrases and ideas." Identifying these passages is a highly subjective matter, but Meyers's selection is convincing and suggests, as he notes, the "range of borrowings" (p. 86). Seven Pillars' tenor and themes can be inferred from Meyers's list of quoted works—Macbeth, Hamlet, "Dover Beach," The Waste Land, and A Portrait of the Artist as a Young Man sketch out one strong thematic line.

The echo of "Dover Beach" is a fine example of how strong an undercurrent of meaning Lawrence can stir up. Early in Seven Pillars, before his personal crisis over Sykes-Picot, Lawrence describes himself and an Arab companion "[wandering] out across the darkling plain till we found a pleasant gun position" (*SP*, 201). "Darkling plain" echoes Matthew Arnold's plain where "ignorant armies clash by night," an appropriate comment on the situation that arises later when Lawrence realizes his culpability in the "Arab fraud." "Dover Beach" also suggests loss of faith, futility, and isolation, which are clear, strong themes in Lawrence's work. Yet the precious phrase "pleasant gun position" stirs an ironic countercurrent that also runs through *Seven Pillars*. The Arab Revolt as seen in the book has an exciting, romantic quality to which Lawrence responds consistently between bouts of guilty introspection. The ironic resonance between "Dover Beach" and the Oxford undergraduate aesthete's "pleasant gun position" is a compelling miniature of the whole book.

Finally, understanding *Seven Pillars* as a deliberate puzzle—to use Manning's word—can help us place Lawrence's work in the context of English-language literary history, so that eventually we can understand and evaluate it more fully. Again we should make a distinction between thematic and technical approaches. Jeffrey Meyers, Thomas O'Donnell, and Stephen Tabachnick do readers the valuable service of placing *Seven Pillars* in the traditions of military history, confessional, and "Anglo-Arabian travel writing," distinctions based largely on subject matter.

Another fruitful approach is to see *Seven Pillars* in its technical context. I have already pointed out Lawrence's kinship with Melville and Conrad, whose techniques involved the deliberate suggestion of undefinable meaning beneath a novelistic documentary surface. Poetry also provides illuminating parallels. Whitman, Yeats, and Eliot worked the same vein, dealing in documentary fashion with carefully constructed surfaces, then, by means that parallel Lawrence's, forcing the reader beneath the surface. Whitman's cosmic "myself," Yeats's historical forces, and Eliot's undercurrents of tradition set in motion by literary allusions, all find their parallels in *Seven Pillars*. Lawrence, incidentally, admired all these poets.

Joyce's *Ulysses*, in many ways a work that encompasses the novel and poetry, is *Seven Pillars*' cousin. Though Lawrence had extremely mixed feelings about the novel, its painstaking attention to detail, level on level of consciousness, puzzling suggestions of historical forces at work, all link *Ulysses* to its close contemporary. *Ulysses*' descendants comprise a tradition of which *Seven Pillars* is a part. In our own time the novels of Thomas Pynchon blend detailed, accurate renderings of historical events and places into symbolic representations of nebulous power. In *Ulysses* and *Gravity's Rainbow*, as in *Seven Pillars*, vast intangible forces are at work, suggesting an equally intangible network of influences that ends who knows where. The same basic question emerges from these novels. What are the connections? What links the documentary surface of Dublin with Odysseus' world? The technicalities of the V-2 with the Santa Monica Freeway? Arabian rock strata with the massacre at Tafas? The books suggest that the connections are there; their delightfulness lies in our not quite knowing where.

N·O·T·E·S

1. A. W. Lawrence, ed., *Letters to T. E. Lawrence*, (London: Cape, 1962), 58–61.

2. "The Everlasting Effort," in *The Expense of Greatness* (New York: Arrow Editions), 35.

3. "Romance as Allegory," in *The Meaning of Fiction* (Detroit: Wayne State University Press, 1960), 277–78.

4. (Athens: Ohio University Press), 26–27. Future references to this book will be in parentheses following the quotations.

5. Stephen E. Tabachnick, *T. E. Lawrence* (Boston: Twayne, 1978), 29. Jeffrey Meyers, *The Wounded Spirit* (London: Martin Brian and O'Keeffe, 1973), 74. Future references to these books will be in parentheses following the quotations.

6. *L*, 301–2.

7. (Baton Rouge: Louisiana State University Press, 1975). Future references to this book will be in parentheses following the quotations.

8. Reprinted in Herbert Read, *A Coat of Many Colors* (New York: Horizon Press, 1956), 24.

9. *Sewanee Review* 84 (Summer 1976): lxxxviii.

10. "T. E. Lawrence and *Moby Dick*," *Research Studies* 44 (March 1976):2. See also Stephen E. Tabachnick, *Charles Doughty* (Boston: Twayne Publishers, 1981) for further comparison of Lawrence and Doughty.

11. "The Function of the Cetological Chapters in *Moby Dick*," *American Literature* 28 (May 1956):172–73.

12. "Creeds, History, Prophets, and Geography in *Seven Pillars of Wisdom*," *Texas Quarterly* 18 (Autumn 1975): 15–28.

13. *Letters to T. E. Lawrence*, 134–35.

14. (Harmondsworth: Penguin Books, 1969), 21.

15. *Hudson Review* 15 (Autumn 1962): 358.

The Waste Land in
Seven Pillars of Wisdom

STEPHEN E. TABACHNICK

In 1925, when he was correcting the proofs of the Subscribers' Edition of *Seven Pillars of Wisdom*, T. E. Lawrence wrote of T. S. Eliot's poetry: "It's odd, you know, to be reading these poems, so full of the future, so far ahead of our time; and then to turn back to my book, whose prose stinks of coffins and ancestors and armorial hatchments" (*L*, 488). Despite this disclaimer, Lawrence's insistent literary use of "falling towers" to telescope the past and present remains an outstanding point of his contact not with medieval art but with Eliot's *Waste Land*, another 1920s document of spiritual quest. In contrast to the precise scientific analysis of old architecture that we find in his B.A. thesis *Crusader Castles* and his coauthored archaeological report *The Wilderness of Zin*,[1] Lawrence in *Seven Pillars* gives us a poetic archaeology of ruins which indicates subtly his attitudes toward life and art.

Like Eliot in the *Waste Land*, Lawrence in his poetic autobiography has little use for the present. Outside of the anachronistic aspect of his special war, including the romance of Beduin tents and heroic single combat[2] and his personal taste for fast motorcar and airplane rides, Lawrence rejects the trappings of modern warfare and the culture it represents, be it practiced by British, Turks, or Arabs. We see this revulsion subtly in the fact that the contemporary Near Eastern cities and their buildings—both contemporary and ancient—in and around which the Arab Revolt took place, play a largely negative role in *Seven Pillars of Wisdom*. This is surprising in view of Lawrence's overt narrative protestations of the military, political, and historical value of these cities, but such is the case. The great metropolis of Cairo, in which he worked for two years, is not described at all. The port of Jidda, in which the "foundations" (*SP*, 28) of the Arab Revolt against the Turks are laid, is ruinlike and redolent of a tasteless and fatal clash of cultures: "The style of architecture was like crazy Elizabethan half-timber work, in the elaborate Cheshire fashion, but gone gimcrack to an incredible degree. . . . The atmosphere was oppressive, deadly" (*SP*, 72–73).

Lawrence indicates his true feeling of letdown after the outwardly triumphant taking of Akaba most clearly through the architectural description that begins the Akaba chapter: "Through the whirling dust we perceived that Akaba was all a ruin. Repeated bombardments by French and English warships had degraded the place to its original rubbish. The poor houses stood about in a litter, dirty and contemptible, lacking entirely that dignity which the durability of their time-challenging bones conferred on ancient remains" (*SP*, 314). We should note that *Seven Pillars*' poetically selective, wartime vision of Akaba above is a much-degraded version of the description of the city that Lawrence recorded in his prewar *Wilderness of Zin*. In that report, Akaba, in addition to its modern and aesthetically uninteresting mud brick huts, also contains some interesting ruins, including a late fifteenth- or early sixteenth-century fort "built in stripes of pink and white," a ruin-mound covered with fragments of medieval Arab glass and glazed pottery, an enormous earthwork, and a Byzantine column capital "bearing on it a running ornament of an uncertain leaf."[3]

Lawrence has purposely selected the less beautiful side of Akaba— as of other war cities—for *Seven Pillars of Wisdom*. His poetic point is that modern war and the cities in and for which it takes place are in effect a waste land that produces no romantic ruins to compare with remnants of Hellenistic cities and Crusader castles in the deserts and mountains of Syria. Even Jerusalem, whose capture Lawrence terms "for me . . . the supreme moment of the war" (*SP*, 453), is apparently not worth any description at all in the chapter relating its capture; and a previous description in *Seven Pillars* is even less positive, calling it "a squalid town" (*SP*, 333), fanatic and dirty, with no almost obligatory mention of the Via Dolorosa, Mosque of Omar, or the Wailing Wall.

When these contemporary goals and places of war are not nondescript, dirty, fanatic, miserable, sinister, or not worth any comment at all—in contrast to the "clean" desert (*SP*, 317)—they are used in *Seven Pillars* as horrifying symbols of total spiritual and political disorder. Thus, Lawrence is tortured and possibly raped in the Bey's headquarters at Deraa, after having been moved through a military compound containing a seemingly vast series of nondescript places and rooms—a mud room, a guard room, across six railway tracks down a street, past a square, to a detached house with a bedroom and guard room, and then to a detached wooden room and separate dispensary—very suggestive of the breakdown of his self into parts that he describes in that chapter as a result of his experiences, the loss of the "citadel" (*SP*, 447) of his integrity mentioned at the end of the chapter. We notice Lawrence's use of architectural metaphor to characterize himself, and the fact that the Bey's compound—although complete in itself and full of complete, imprisoning rooms—appears a divided ruin as a result of Lawrence's description, which emphasizes its parts. Here—as at Jidda and Akaba—Lawrence uses ruins to symbolize a very unbeautiful degradation and disintegration of self and civilization.

Even Damascus, toward which the whole revolt has been striving since its inception, is a deliberate anticlimax in terms of its architectural description in *Seven Pillars*. As Lawrence approaches the city in triumph at the end of the book, it looks from afar like a "pearl in the . . . sun" (*SP*, 644). But the only buildings described in depth in the Damascus chapters prove to be the Town Hall, which contains a "gaudy salon" and "gold chairs, which writhed, about a gold table whose legs also writhed obscenely" (*SP*, 648), symbolic of serpentine treachery and corruption; and the terrible Turkish military hospital, whose court is "squalid with rubbish" and whose human war rubbish of dying and decomposing men contaminates Lawrence's white robes (*SP*, 655). Although Lawrence attempts to clean these sites of their filth, he feels "stained in estimation" (*SP*, 659) at the end of his work, and the reader retains these decadent views rather than any more inspiring image of the city of Damascus at the end of the book.

Lawrence's spiritual and aesthetic heart is clearly not in the urban war prizes of his book. Like Eliot, he feels that whatever human glory there is lies behind him, in his case in the ruined architectural monuments in the desert, far from the centers of the present. Artificial ruins had of course been a popular European garden prop since the mid-eighteenth century. And many other travelers of Lawrence's own and previous centuries—among them Lamartine, whom Lawrence admired—had transformed sometimes temporary passions for desert ruins into a literary cliché of Near Eastern travel. But, in contrast to such fleeting affinities, Lawrence's love of the past and the beautiful ruins that represent it for him is authentic: he spent years professionally excavating Hittite Carchemish, was one of the first to write authoritatively of Crusader castles and the Negev Nabataean wonder cities, and was the first to inspect and confirm the correct location of the biblical Kadesh Barnea in the Sinai desert.[4]

Lawrence becomes enthusiastic not when dealing with the rubble and squalor of the contemporary but when recalling the Hellenistic town of Gadara, "very precious with its memories of Menippus and Meleager, the immoral Greek-Syrian whose self-expression marked the highest point of Syrian letters" (SP, 388); or when describing the "shapely cone, whose mural crown was the ring-wall of the old castle of Monreale, very noble against the night sky" (SP, 495); or when observing the "rich green pasture of the ruins" at Ghassanid Bair (SP, 292). Only at these places—rather than in the Sinai Hotel's hot baths in British Egypt (SP, 318), which he indirectly contrasts with them in a subtle application of literary spatial form—can Lawrence find water—that is, beauty and cleanliness—in the waste land of modern war, politics, and tastelessness. At the forty-foot-deep wells of Bair on his thirtieth birthday, he explores his own "depth" (SP, 562). He tells us that the hot springs of Gadara "yet gushed out to the advantage of the local sick" (SP, 388). And near a broken Nabataean well-house in the Wadi Rumm, he washes his "soiled body" (SP, 355) and hears the only sermon of love in the book.

The Arab fort of the Saladin period built on Roman foundations and the beautiful pools of Azrak remain probably the best examples in the book of Lawrence's use of archaeological setting to underscore a positive mood. The fact that this inspiring backdrop is placed just before the chapter relating the tortures at Deraa, where all is ugliness, architecturally and otherwise, provides another example of Lawrence's modernistic use of spatial form, since he does not announce this contrast in any way; and makes Azrak especially poignant in the reader's memory. Here we find in abundance the three combined elements essential to Lawrence's personal aesthetic: art, nature (especially water), and history. Art is present in the skill of the fort's builders: "The door was a poised slab of dressed basalt, a foot thick, turning on pivots of itself, socketed into threshold and lintel" (*SP*, 436). Nature appears in the fact that the fort is far from any city, in its beautiful pools, and in its lack of any roof but the sky. Of history, Azrak's charmed citadel has an abundance: "We dreamed ourselves into the spirit of the place; sieges and feasting, raids, murders, love-singing in the night" (*SP*, 439). Although he is not described in architectural terms, Sherif Ali, Lawrence's companion in this favored place, combines the elements of art ("studied gesture"), nature ("unusual grace"), and history ("a two-thousand-year old" war-cry) in his person (*SP*, 437); and Lawrence even adds a touch of ruin to this characterization for good measure: "Yet, despite this richness, there was a constant depression with him, the unknown longing of simple, restless people for abstract thought beyond their minds' supply" (*SP*, 438). Instead of a series of limiting, imprisoning Turkish rooms symbolic of self-division and frustration, as at Deraa, the ruined fort at Azrak becomes a place of complementary intimacy and imaginative freedom, in which Lawrence and his men each have separate rooms but in one beautiful building under a limitless sky.

In this fine location, Lawrence plays the role of Arab potentate in the present, receiving great chiefs, horsemen, and merchants. Later, in another citation of Azrak, even Lawrence's British sensibilities are historically satisfied by the setting, when he thinks of adding King George V's name to those of Diocletian and Maximian, which are inscribed in the Roman altar there (*SP*, 574). In such a favored site, akin to Eliot's Saint Magnus Martyr but on a secular level, the past can bring out the noble aspects of an otherwise sordid present; for a few moments, Lawrence becomes a Grail knight or Moslem prince as he superimposes a myth of the past on his war.

For all this, Lawrence is no sighing follower of the romantic, La-martinesque cult of moonlit ruins: as he tells us about the discomforts of the Azrak fort, "In loneliness we learned the full disadvantages of imprisonment within such gloomy ancient unmortared places. The rains guttered down within the walls' thickness and spouted into the rooms from their chinks" (*SP*, 439). And just as Eliot uses the flirtation of Elizabeth and Leicester in *The Waste Land* to underline his appreciation that the past is not inevitably spiritually superior to the present, so Lawrence is capable of an objective vision. Christ's Galilee, for instance, was not only an architecturally sophisticated place of "polished streets among fora and pillared houses and rococo baths," but also "provincial and corrupt" and "tawdry" (*SP*, 356), much like the gaudy interior of the contemporary Damascus Town Hall.

For Lawrence, architectural beauty equals truth, but this beauty exists for him only where he finds the abrasive and yet complementary combination of authentic art, unspoiled nature, and long history in equal proportions, as at Azrak. Where one or more of these elements is lacking or flawed in a place or person, the result is ambiguous at best, negative at worst. Christ's Galilee lacks true art, substituting cheap luxury instead. The "tall and pillar-like" Feisal practices a manipulatory art of leadership without the natural ability and force necessary in a true ruler. His pillars ultimately convey a negative connotation as Lawrence shows him to be weak and ineffectual if not actually broken; and his rule in effect amounts to a "facade rather than a fitted building" (*SP*, 651).

We have now seen some of the metaphorical dimensions of *Seven Pillars*' architectural/archaeological descriptions. We have also noted some examples of an Eliot-like spatial form, which uses ruins to criticize or ennoble the present by instantaneously juxtaposing past myth and present reality, and by contrasting sites, sometimes hundreds of pages apart, sometimes close together in the book, without any direct notice that this is what is going on. But what are the full thematic and structural implications of Lawrence's choice of ruins to express both the positive and negative feelings in the book?

Seen in the light of the ruin motif, the title *Seven Pillars of Wisdom* suddenly becomes contradictory. Instead of indicating a complete structure—as Lawrence once claimed it did, correctly stating that "The figure 'seven' implies completeness in the Semitic languages" (*L*, 514)—this title now conjures up a broken temple or palace without walls or roof lying somewhere in the East. This second meaning is the more deeply appropriate one. For Lawrence's book impresses upon us the fact that the Arab Revolt he helped lead as well as King George V's empire were already becoming ruins in the desert by the time (1919–26) that the book was being written, revised, and published: Lawrence tells us openly in the final chapters that Feisal's rule in Damascus lasted only two years (*SP*, 651), and the suppressed introductory chapter's bitter attack on British colonialism in Mesopotamia reminds us, albeit indirectly, that King George's empire will soon go the way of Maximian's and Diocletian's, as Eliot too implies in his poem. Both British and Arab World War I aspirations are beautiful, like ruins, in the memory of their attempted execution, rather than for their political longevity or achievement.

Further, like the revolt he guided, and like Hieronymo in Eliot's *Waste Land, Seven Pillars'* author and main character, Lawrence himself, is a ruin.[5] He was approaching a nervous breakdown—much like Eliot—even as he was writing his masterpiece, at least partially as a result of his war experiences. *Seven Pillars* gives ample evidence of Lawrence's personal wartime and postwar fragmentation in his use of the metaphor of the lost citadel of his integrity and in the striking intellectual and emotional contradictions that occur throughout the book. Does Lawrence favor the British or the Arabs? Does he see himself as a heroic knight or a cynical intelligence agent? Is he a dreamy arts graduate forced to participate in a brutal war that destroys him or a willing sadomasochist who loves war too much? *Seven Pillars* has occasioned great biographical and critical controversy because of the impossibility of reconciling these and other ever-present clashing opposites.

But to make all of this personal and political ruin positive on an aesthetic level, the ruins in *Seven Pillars* stand for Lawrence's conception of the incompleteness of life and art. As he tells us in the book itself, "Always my soul hungered for less than it had" (*SP*, 277) and "When a thing was in my reach, I no longer wanted it; my delight lay in the desire" (*SP*, 566). In 1920 he wrote with admiration about Conrad that "all his things end in a kind of hunger, a suggestion of something he can't say or do or think" (*L*, 302). Ruin allows the imagination freer rein than completeness and perfection. In his artistic embrace of incompleteness and extreme exemplification of fragmentation, Lawrence, like Eliot in *The Waste Land* and elsewhere, can be seen as one of the very last romantics or, as we sometimes call such artists, a modernist or romantic modernist.

Perception of the prevalence of the ruin motif throughout the book leads us finally to see *Seven Pillars* itself as a beautiful ruin. Lawrence subscribed to William Morris's idea of the book as an architectural artifact, and the last section of *Seven Pillars*, referring to both Lawrence's book and the revolt, is entitled "The House Is Perfected." But all commentators—Thomas O'Donnell, Jeffrey Meyers, Stanley and Rodelle Weintraub, and I, among others—have noticed that Lawrence's book-house, far from being "perfected," is strangely divided and incomplete. They have seen this incompleteness in the contradictory meanings of the title and subtitles themselves; in the discordance between the well-ordered military history of the revolt and the wild disorder of the plot line containing the story of Lawrence's personal disintegration; in the disparities between what Lawrence says and what he does; in the profusion of greatly differing styles; in the fragmented allusions to other literary works; in the internal uncertainties of the Deraa torture chapter; and, as Charles Grosvenor has noted, even in the jarringly different styles of portraiture Lawrence approved for the limited 1926 Subscribers' Edition.[6]

Lawrence has sometimes been called out of control of his art because of these disparities, and his book has frequently been assessed as flawed as a result. But in the introductory "S.A." poem, which we can read as a comment on Lawrence's book as well as on the revolt and the secret and incomplete friendship the poem commemorates, we find the line: "But for fit monument I shattered it, unfinished." Has Lawrence deliberately shattered his *Seven Pillars of Wisdom*, as the only fit artistic monument to a shattered personality, friendship, and political movement, and in doing so made it artistically beautiful? During seven years of writing and revision, could he have been as unaware of the book's thematic and structural contradictions as all of his subsequent critics have been aware of them? Or, as Keith Hull has suggested, was Lawrence in more conscious and successful control of his ambiguities than has been hitherto thought?[7] Has Lawrence, like Eliot, left it to the reader's imagination to complete his book, just as Lawrence's own imagination was stimulated by the task of filling in the outlines of desert ruins? These questions, like so many others about Lawrence, defy a definitive answer. But even more than Eliot's poem, Lawrence's autobiography—his memory of a previous self and a political movement which were in the process of falling apart even as he was penning their story—is perhaps best seen as fragments shored against its author's ruins, and as his own beautiful ever-eroding and ever-remaining rampart against the buffets of time.

N·O·T·E·S

1. For Lawrence as technical writer, see the essay by Rodelle Weintraub in this volume.

2. For medieval aspects of Lawrence's art and experience, see the essay by M. D. Allen in this volume.

3. C. L. Woolley and T. E. Lawrence, *The Wilderness of Zin* (London: Palestine Exploration Society, 1915), 143–44. The sections on Akaba and the southern Negev and northern Sinai were written by Lawrence following his explorations there.

4. On ruins in European art, see Roland Mortier, *La Poetique des Ruines en France* (Geneva: Droz, 1974), and Rose Macaulay, *Pleasure of Ruins* (London: Weidenfeld and Nicolson, 1953). For the important ruins of empire motif, see Laurence Goldstein, *Ruins and Empire: The Evolution of a Theme in Augustan and Romantic Literature* (Pittsburgh: University of Pittsburgh Press, 1977), and W. C. Brown, "English Travel Books and Minor Poetry about the Near East, 1775–1825," *Philological Quarterly* 16 (July 1937): 249–71. About Lawrence's archaeological contributions, see Rudolph Cohen, "Did I Excavate Kadesh Barnea?" *Biblical Archaeology Review* 7 (May/June 1981): 23; Rudolph Cohen, "The Iron Age Fortresses in the Central Negev," *Bulletin of the American Schools of Oriental Research* 236 (Fall 1979): 61; and Nelson Glueck, *Rivers in the Desert* (New York: Grove, 1960), 33–35, 73–74, 261–64.

5. In a letter (British Museum Additional MSS) of 28 September 1925 to Charlotte Shaw, Lawrence actually writes, "Do you know what it is when you see, suddenly, that your life is all a ruin?" Here, as in his genuine interest in archaeology and his immediate application of the ruin theme to the British Empire's actual state in his time, Lawrence's life and art display a real fragmentation going beyond a romantic literary pose.

6. See the books by O'Donnell, Meyers, the Weintraubs, and Tabachnick listed in the bibliography; and the article by Charles Grosvenor in this volume.

7. See the article by Keith N. Hull in this volume.

T. E. Lawrence: The Mechanical Monk

JEFFREY MEYERS

They carry back bright to the coiner the mintage of man,
The lads that will die in their glory and never be old.
                              A. E. HOUSMAN, A Shropshire Lad

I understand that one of the most trying things about the
army is the lack of privacy.
                              W. H. AUDEN

Just as every aspect of Lawrence's early life seemed to prepare for and lead up to his crisis in Arabia, so everything that happened after it (his renunciation, enlistment, flagellation, suicidal rides) seemed to be a direct result of those two years in the desert that synthesized the experience of a lifetime. Lawrence began *The Mint* just after completing *Seven Pillars of Wisdom*, when he was transformed from the glamorous leader in Arab robes to the forlorn figure in tight military tunic. These two books, though apparently different—one is Arabian, exotic, romantic, triumphant; the other English, squalid, realistic, vanquished—actually have a great deal in common.

Both are idealistic and didactic accounts of self-betrayal and psychological martyrdom, in an alien setting that is at once hierarchic and democratic. In both works Lawrence simultaneously exposes and disguises his own character, and writes in a highly allusive and contorted style that mixes precise and often disgusting details (the Turkish hospital and the shit-cart) with moral and philosophical speculation.

Both reveal Lawrence's peculiar and paradoxical combination of affectation and honesty, exhibitionism and reserve, arrogance and humility, megalomania and self-abasement. In both works, the divided, pathological, guilt-ridden, death-driven hero—who hates the flesh and women—is torn between antitheses and drawn to homosexuality.

In the two military books Lawrence, "a standing court martial" on himself, opposes the ideal and the real, spirit and body, comradeship and solitude, freedom and authority, courage and fear, integrity and dissolution, honesty and deception, cleanliness and pollution. *The Mint* also contrasts refuge and torment, worship and blasphemy, training and service.

The Mint deals with training rather than combat (as in *Seven Pillars*), maintenance rather than aviation (as in *Night Flight*). And Lawrence's account of his self-imposed seven-year penance—of his brutal, humiliating, tyrannous, terrifying life among animals—has more in common with prison than with war books. It belongs with *The House of the Dead*, *Days of Wrath*, *Darkness at Noon*, and *One Day in the Life of Ivan Denisovich* rather than with the memoirs of Graves, Sassoon, and Blunden, and the novels of Hemingway, Ford, and Remarque. *The Mint* describes a passive military hero: not one who fights but one who endures.

Though Lawrence's book, like his situation, is unique, it shares significant characteristics with another odd "photographic" documentary that was written after, but published before, *The Mint*: Orwell's *Down and Out in Paris and London* (1933). In *Seven Pillars* Lawrence confesses: "I liked the things underneath me and took my pleasures and adventures downward. There seemed a certainty in degradation, a final safety. Man could rise to any height, but there was an animal level beneath which he could not fall. It was a satisfaction on which to rest."[1] And in *The Mint* he lists the reasons for his enlistment in the R.A.F.—imaginative exhaustion, need for manual labor, compulsion to relearn poverty—and emphasizes "my urge downwards, in pursuit of the safety which can't fall further" (M, 135).

Similarly, in the autobiographical ninth chapter of *The Road to Wigan Pier*, Orwell explains how the overpowering guilt that came from his years as a policeman in Burma forced him to seek expiation among the down and outs. Though Orwell knows he cannot really belong to this harsh world, he is desperate to be accepted and to shed his guilt:

"I wanted to submerge myself, to get right down among the oppressed, to be one of them and on their side against their tyrants. . . . I could go among these people, see what their lives were like and feel myself temporarily part of their world. Once I had been among them and accepted by them, I should have touched bottom and—this is what I felt: I was aware even then that it was irrational—part of my guilt would drop from me."[2] Like Lawrence, Orwell wants to encounter immediate and actual experience; to become part of an alien group; to extinguish, among outcasts, the sense of social class; to feel the pleasurable relief in sinking to the bottom and knowing he can stand it; to undergo the excitement of a sortie to the lower depths; to expiate his guilt.

In *Down and Out*, which also provides revolting descriptions of filthy kitchens and foul food ("earwigged, maggoty and worm-full"), Orwell praises the eccentric freedom from the normal and the decent, the mindless acceptance when he reaches destitution, the animal contentment of the simple rhythm of work and sleep. And, like Lawrence, he gives a social-realist account of the insulted and injured, and describes the disastrous physical and psychological effects—poverty, hunger, sexual deprivation—of sinking among the stigmatized outcasts, defeated by life.[3]

In May–June 1923, ten months after he joined the R.A.F., Lawrence, still torn between ambition and renunciation, explained to Lionel Curtis that his enlistment was based on a series of negative decisions that drove him into a corner and left no other alternative: "The burning out of freewill and self-respect and delicacy from a nature as violent as mine is bound to hurt a bit. . . . Free-will I've tried, and rejected: authority I've rejected . . . action I've rejected: and the intellectual life: and the receptive senses: and the battle of wits. They were all failures" (L, 419).

These rejections led the broken and exhausted Lawrence to present himself at the recruiting office at 4 Henrietta Street, Covent Garden, at 10:30 A.M. on 30 August 1922. As an ex-army officer, he knew precisely the kind of ordeal he would have to suffer: nothing less than the reshaping and stamping of a human body and soul into the uniform pattern of a soldier.[4] Lawrence deliberately chose a rigorous "rest-cure" that was calculated to provide the maximum discomfort and degradation; and he soon compounded his masochistic monasticism with therapeutic flagellations, provided by the accommodating John Bruce, which wounded his pride as well as his body.

We first confront the sensitive, introspective intellectual in a state of extreme vulnerability. *The Mint* opens abruptly and colloquially ("God, this is awful") as Lawrence narrates the anxious thoughts that pass through his mind as he screws himself up to enlist. He is impoverished, starved, weak, nervous, hesitating, fearful, out of control, betrayed by his bowels—a sharp contrast to the heroic figure of *Seven Pillars*. On the opening page, Lawrence characteristically combines apparent directness with an oblique reference to Sir Herbert Baker's story about the cornice; alludes to fear through a nursery rhyme: "Won't you walk into my parlour? / Said the spider to the fly," and to exposure through Job 1:21: "Naked came I out of my mother's womb, and naked shall I return thither."[5]

The examining doctor observes that Lawrence is five feet and six inches tall, has been short of food for six months, has nerves like a rabbit, and has deep scars on his ribs: " 'Punishment?' 'No Sir, more like persuasion. . . . A barbed-wire tear, over a fence.' "[6] It is obvious that Lawrence is lying about the beating he received at Deraa, which, more than any other factor, accounted for his breakdown and eventual enlistment, for a red flush of embarrassment lights up his naked body. It is equally clear that his dubious history and suspicious behavior would normally lead to Lawrence's rejection; and this is precisely what happened—in life but not in art—until the Air Ministry intervened on Lawrence's behalf and his identity was inevitably revealed.[7] So the first chapter, which strives for realism, undermines our confidence in the veracity of the first-person narrator.

As with *Seven Pillars*, the elusive Lawrence, forever "backing into the limelight," gave contradictory accounts (sometimes to the same friend) of his tantalizing technique of concealed self-revelation. He categorically told Edward Garnett, his literary midwife for this book: "*The Mint* gives nothing of myself away: personally, I shouldn't mind its appearing to-morrow"; yet an earlier letter to Garnett about *Seven Pillars* might describe the "Odd Man Out" chapter of *The Mint* as well: "The personal revelations should be the key of the thing: and the personal chapter actually is the key, I fancy: only it's written in cypher. . . . on no account is it possible for me to think of giving myself quite away" (L, 608, 366). He identified the central focus of the book in a defensive letter to Bernard Shaw: "*The Mint* is a private diary, interesting the world only in so far as the world might desire to dissect my personality. And, like my betters [i.e., Shaw], I disapprove of vivisection"; but he also told John Buchan, another member of the privy council who read the book in manuscript, that he had deliberately dropped his veil: "I have a fear that in it I have given away my limitations more bluntly than I would wish" (*L*, 605, 858).

Lawrence stresses that he fears mental breakdown and animal spirits "more than anything else in this world"; profoundly hates noise and finds physical contact repugnant. He portrays himself as a shy, constrained, tense, trembling, tearful insomniac; a humiliated, disgusted, nauseated, bruised, feverish, pitiful, exiled, guilt-ridden remnant of his former self. His only weapons are intellectual: silence, stoicism, cunning. But he exposes his weakening will (in the manner of *Seven Pillars*) to the full force of the seething carnality of the "libertine, brutal, loud-voiced, unwashed" men; the cursing, farting, pissing, shitting, vomiting, ejaculating beasts of the barracks. They strip off his "caddis-shell" and "natal caul," and cannibalize his nerves in their sensual cauldron.

Lawrence frequently expresses a desire for comrades, solidarity, squadronship; and shifts from "I" to "We" when he feels he belongs to a group. But he also devises shrewd ways of escape: anonymity, pain, exhaustion, moon-gazing, motor bikes, illegal excursions, warm baths, male bodies—and writing. He craves obscurity, but attracts attention to himself by his odd behavior, clever remarks, assumption of authority, famous friends, and direct connection to the chief of the air force.

Lawrence takes great pains to distinguish himself from the mass of men by covertly suggesting: "I'm not like them." He does this first by emphasizing his obvious difference from the brutes, and then by constantly evoking his hidden past. Lawrence is most obviously separated from the others by his education, and makes much of his book knowledge: his select library and reading of Laforgue, Goethe, and Jacobsen—in the original Danish. He spots a mistake when an officer confuses incidence with dihedral; thrice gives cheeky answers to his superiors, but always evades the charge of insubordination; is deferred to as "posh" and addressed by his respectful mates as "Mister." One confused airman says that Lawrence "was a deep fucker, whom he couldn't sort of size up." Lawrence also exerts considerable influence through his friendship with the Chief of the Air Staff, Sir Hugh Trenchard (who first enabled him to enter the service), and continues to exploit this connection for egoistic ends. He is released from the last weeks of depot drudgery by a ukase from the Air Ministry; sent from Uxbridge, after two and a half months, to the cushy photography school at Farnborough, Hampshire; and banqueted by the boys when he leaves.

Though Lawrence wants to hide his identity and reputation, and lies about his education, military career, and pull at headquarters, the force of his confession depends on our knowledge of his past and ability to interpret the obscure clues scattered through his pages. For he alludes to "the birth-place which I'd not seen since six weeks old!" (Tremadoc, Wales, August 1888); his fears at school (due to family pressures, 1896–1906); his seventeen years direct experience with the army (the escape from home to Cornwall to enlist in the Royal Artillery, 1905); his interest in the Middle Ages (the honors thesis on Crusader castles, 1910); his war wounds, beatings, and mental breakdown (Deraa, November 1917); his Handley-Page air crash in Rome (en route to Cairo, April 1919); his sitting for artists (John, Kennington, and others); his picture on the wall of the barracks (due to Lowell Thomas's publicity, 1919); his research fellowship in political theory (All Souls, 1919–20); the composition of *Seven Pillars* (in Barton Street, Westminster, 1920–22); his powers in war and diplomacy (at the Cairo Conference and as adviser to Churchill in the Colonial Office, 1921–22); his Ministerial parchment (to Transjordan, October 1921); the offer of an important political appointment (High Commission of Egypt, 1922); the offer to edit the highbrow *Belles-Lettres* (from Jonathan Cape, via Edward Garnett, September 1922); his illustrious friendships (with Garnett, Forster, Hogarth); his dismissal from Farnborough (due to adverse publicity, January 1923); reenlistment in the R.A.F. (after two years in the Tank Corps and threats of suicide, August 1925); and self-appointed exile (to Miranshah, to avoid the publicity of *Revolt in the Desert*, December 1926). *The Mint* is not merely an account of Lawrence in the air force but a paradigmatic history of his entire life.

Lawrence's allusive autobiography and contorted confessions explain his excruciating difficulties and eccentric behavior; emphasize that he was a strange sloth who had strayed into barracks where a "huge beast was stabled in the blackness." Lawrence understood that

he did not belong at Uxbridge, in Arabia, at All Souls, or in an Officer's Mess: "It's like having a unicorn in a racing stable. Beast doesn't
fit" (L, 351).

Just as Lawrence's past life explained his present condition, so the
writing of The Mint connected him to the solitude from which he had
recently escaped. Though he insisted: "Prose is bad when people stop
to look at it";[8] he also said: "Wherever choice offered between a poor
and a rich word richness had it, to raise the colour"[9]—and called the
camp "part bagnio, part ergastulum." His self-conscious, highly wrought,
unnatural prose, which mixes mandarin elegance with crude obsceni-
ties, draws attention to his thematic antitheses and his peculiar position in the ranks. Lawrence felt that his style—"A slow painful mosaic
of hard words stiffly cemented together . . . well fitted its subject: our
dull clothed selves; our humdrum, slightly oppressed lives; our tight
uniforms: the constriction, the limits, the artificial conduct, of our
bodies and minds and spirits, in the great machine which the R.A.F.
is becoming" (L, 697, 596). He mistakenly thought "The Mint was my
purest achievement, though still-born [unpublishable]. . . . For its restraint, & dignity, and form, & craftsmanship, The Mint may well be
better" than Seven Pillars (L, 775, 623).

Lawrence's uneven style is at its worst in the attempt at comedy in
"Rail Journey" and the mannered description of the moon in "My
Hours." This passage, like the rural idyll "In the Park," is awkwardly
introduced to provide escape from the camp:

> So the appellant moon easily conjures me outside, into its view. Dress-
> ing is the affair of a moment: gym shoes and trousers, with my shirt
> already on. Sharply the keen air refreshes the stubbled roundness of my
> head. If only the powers would realise how they dull their men's sensi-
> tiveness of reception, by having our hair clipped too short for the wind
> to play with. I slouch meditatively, my head ever forward, eyes on the
> ground, to give my negligent feet unconscious warning of obstacles.
> Wits inwardly turned cannot watch a man's path. (M, 137)

This passage fails because Lawrence too obviously strains for poetic
effects by reversing normal word order and forcing adjectives into unnatural conjunction with nouns. The contorted "Appellant moon . . .
conjures me outside" jars with the straightforward description of the
second sentence. The adverbial opening of "Sharply the keen" is a

tedious residue of *Seven Pillars*. The next sentence places Lawrence in characteristic opposition to "the powers" as he foolishly suggests that military barbers should attempt to increase, rather than decrease, "sensitiveness of reception" (rather than "sensitivity"). If Lawrence's eyes are focused on the moonlit ground, the warning to his "negligent feet" would be quite conscious. The last sentence picks up the moon of "meditatively" and concludes with an apothegm both obvious and banal.

The three best-written chapters—described with clinical asperity and particularity of sensory detail—provide a striking contrast to the falsity of "My Hours." Lawrence's Swiftian response to the miasmic "Shit-Cart" (which has some fascinating similarities with "Leaves in the Wind"),[10] and his cruel reaction to his mutilated "Commanding Officer" and the "Funeral" of Queen Alexandra, show how he dealt with his painful circumstances. Lawrence takes masochistic pleasure in the excremental vision of "Shit-Cart." When four garbage "bins refused to tip out, we had to spoon their contents forth with our hands. It was not so bad to the touch, but a shivery sight to see a clean arm go with it: and hard to know how to hold the polluted limb afterwards"—since it could not be comfortably detached from the body. But he has not yet experienced the worst of it. For the reek of the lorry cuts short his breath at the root; his trousers are "stuffed from the bottom with ordures of sorts. Something bubbly and soft is working up into my crotch"; the bins erupt over him in great gouts when the truck hits a pothole; and as he drops exhausted into bed, "the smell of swill and refuse oozed slowly from my soiled things and stagnated into a pool over me." This fecal duty allowed Lawrence to experience the "certainty of degradation," to evoke pity, to wallow in nauseous sensual details, and to prove—despite his sensitive touch and hatred of offal—that he could endure anything.

Lawrence shows no sympathy for his once-heroic wing commander Ian Bonham-Carter, and repays his superior's sadism (which he later links to sexual excitement) with his own kind of cruelty: "He is only the shards of a man—left leg gone, a damaged eye and brain (as we charitably suppose), one crippled arm, silver plates and corsets about his ribs." Lawrence represses his urge to strike the commander, a "public cad" who enjoys inflicting misery; and the caustic style of his apologue reveals the demonic will that accounts for the cripple's survival as well as for his sadism. One day, in full view of the squadron, the commander "started to walk across [the road] with a leashed dog in each hand. The excited beasts sprang forward after a cat. Down went the cripple, fairly pulled over on his face. He would not let go the dogs. Nor could he raise his blaspheming self." According to Lawrence's rough justice, the commander, who had forfeited his right to human consideration, is publicly degraded for humiliating his men.

The "Funeral" of Queen Alexandra, who died on 10 November 1925, is—with the retreat of the Greek army in Thrace and the fall of Lloyd George's coalition with the Conservatives, both October 1922—one of three historical events that places Lawrence's private agonies in a public context. Bernard Shaw mistakenly counseled Lawrence to excise this brilliant chapter, which he felt revealed an appalling lack of sympathy. As the hypocritical chaplain expounds upon the domestic "example which the Prince and Princess of Wales set their adoring people," before the great fornicator ascended the throne in 1901, Lawrence creates a cinematic montage of past and present. His thoughts flash back to a postwar audience with the once-beautiful Struldbrug queen and her palsied attendants, Miss Knollys and Sir Dighton Probyn, who won the first Victoria Cross in the Crimea: "When we reached the presence, and I saw the mummified thing, the bird-like head cocked on one side, not artfully but by disease, the red-rimmed eyes, the enamelled face, which the famous smile scissored across all angular and heart-rending: —then I nearly ran away in pity. The body should not be kept alive after the lamp of sense has gone out." The queen, a notable memento mori, was a painful reminder of the ravages of the flesh that Lawrence, who denied his body and risked his life until he lost it, was determined to avoid. (If he had survived his motorcycle accident, he would have been even more of a vegetable than the aged queen.) In "Shit-Cart," "Our Commanding Officer," and "Funeral," Lawrence confronts his three greatest fears—the revulsion of the flesh, the sadistic exercise of power, and the decay of the mind—and suggests his motives for enlistment.

In his review of The Mint, E. M. Forster (who had read the manuscript in the twenties) generously claimed: "It is soundly constructed: three sections which connect with one another to make a coherent whole."[11] But even the adoring Liddell Hart, who makes the best of a bad lot, reports: "Artistically, T. E. considers that the addition tends to spoil the effect, but it is characteristic of his fairness that he should have made it."[12] Lawrence tried to convince Forster (who did nothing more dangerous than feed his cat): "The Air Force is not a man-crushing humiliating slavery, all its days. There is the sun & decent treatment, and a very real measure of happiness, to those who do not look forward or back."[13] But the three-year gap between parts 1 and 2 (1922) and part 3 (1925), the awkward opening "Explanation" of the last part, and the radical shift in tone and temper from the Uxbridge depot to the Cranwell air base, all make the book incoherent.

Lawrence attempts to convey contentment and even happiness when his idealistic motive for enlistment (to "aid those who strove against the air") finally merges with his aeronautical duties. But the forced happy ending, which does not evolve from the structure of the book, nearly destroys the effect of his heroic resistance to the prolonged torture of his training. The mechanic's mystique about "those who have understanding of the souls of engines, and find their poetry in the smooth tick-over" is entirely unconvincing. For the Cranwell section is dominated not by his absorption in maintaining machines but by his escape from the base on his motorcycle for high-speed grocery shopping.

Lawrence would have agreed with Aldous Huxley's observation that speed was "the only *new* sensation this wretched century has produced."[14] His adolescent description of the 108-mile-an-hour motorcycle race against the Bristol fighter plane expresses both Lawrence's desire to rival and surpass the pilots he supposedly served and his suicidal impulse that could lead only to death.

Apart from sating his futuristic infatuation with velocity, the monasticism of the air force also provided the consolations of homosexuality—a pervasive theme in both *Seven Pillars* and *The Mint*. Both books contain blatant misogyny and a covert plea for male love. The ascetic boasts he has never had heterosexual relations, denies the accusation of barrack-room buggery, and satirizes the show-fag Gaby. He illogically equates sexual intercourse with speedy onanism, and argues, with clinical detachment: "if the perfect partnership, indulgence with a living body, is as brief as the solitary act [it isn't], then the climax is indeed no more than a convulsion, a razor-edge of time, which palls so on return that the temptation flickers out into the indifference of tired disgust." But he also mentions the wet dreams of the lusty celibates, refers to the playful "'ballock-hold' of our impolite wrestling code," and compares the kindness of the men to "hot fingers stroking my shame." He concludes his sexual confessions with a contented description of a Whitmanesque heap of male flesh—"Just we lay there spread-eagled in a mesh of bodies, pillowed on one another and sighing in happy excess of relaxation"—and a naked swimming scene.[15] He reveals his sexual feelings in The Mint, but must hide them from his comrades.

André Malraux, who had many affinities with Lawrence, provides an "existential" explanation that glorifies his hero's self-abasement. Lawrence had a "taste for self-humiliation, now by discipline and now by veneration; a horror of respectability; a disgust for possessions . . . a thoroughgoing sense of his guilt, pursued by his angels or his minor demons, a sense of evil, and of the nothingness of almost everything men cling to; a need for the absolute, an instinctive taste for asceticism."[16] Yet the effect of Lawrence's self-destructive career in the R.A.F., which was not redeemed by The Mint as the Arabian campaign was by Seven Pillars, remains deeply disturbing.

Noel Coward poked fun at Lawrence's tragic affectation by writing: "Dear 338171, (May I call you 338?)." Bernard Shaw was irritated by Lawrence's absurd position and urged him to abandon "this maddening masquerade that makes us all ridiculous."[17] But Wyndham Lewis, who often saw Lawrence in the twenties and defended him, while blind, against Aldington's attacks in the fifties, was the most serious and perceptive observer: "This metaphysical boy-scout . . . was saying farewell to ambition, in an act of social suicide. . . . The spectacle of this stupid waste of so much ability always depressed me. . . . It was a sort of hari-kiri he was indulging in, this self-immolation."[18]

N·O·T·E·S

1. SP, 564. For a thorough discussion of Lawrence's masterpiece, and his reasons for enlistment, see Jeffrey Meyers, The Wounded Spirit (London: Martin, Brian and O'Keeffe, 1973), especially p. 138.

2. George Orwell, The Road to Wigan Pier (London: Gollancz, 1937), 180, 182.

3. See Jeffrey Meyers, *A Reader's Guide to George Orwell* (London: Thames and Hudson, 1975), 74–79.

4. See E. M. Forster, "'The Mint' by T. E. Lawrence," *Listener* 53 (17 February 1955): 280: "Before the metal could be minted it had to be melted. If you want an extreme example of such breaking down and building up, read Orwell's *1984*: there you get *The Mint* in excelsis."

5. Lawrence also alludes on p. 106 to *Romeo and Juliet*, 3.5.24: "Come, death, and welcome! Juliet wills it so"; on p. 113 to Matthew 6:28: "Consider the lilies of the field, how they grow; they toil not, neither do they spin"; on p. 116 to Genesis 1:27: "So God created man in His own image"; on p. 170 to Psalm 121:8: "The Lord shall preserve thy going out and thy coming in from this time forth, and even for ever-more"; on p. 174 to William Morris's *Sigurd the Volsung*; on p. 179 to Milton's "On the Late Massacre in Piedmont": "When all our fathers worshiped stocks and stones"; and on p. 244 to Exodus 20:5: "for I the Lord thy God am a jealous God."

6. Colonel Richard Meinertzhagen, who shared a hotel room with Lawrence at the Paris Peace Conference in 1919, reports in *Middle East Diary* (London: Cresset, 1959), 32–33: "I was shocked to see red weals on his ribs, standing out like tattoo marks. 'Good God' I said 'whatever are those?' He said 'A camel accident at Azraq; dragged across barbed wire.'"

7. See W. E. Johns, "How Lawrence Joined R.A.F.," *Sunday Times* (London), 8 April 1951, 5.

8. T. E. Lawrence, *Men in Print* (London: Golden Cockerel Press, 1940), 44. See Orwell's statement: "One can write nothing readable unless one constantly struggles to efface one's personality. Good prose is like a window pane." "Why I Write," *Collected Essays, Journalism and Letters* (New York: Harcourt, Brace and World, 1968), 1:7.

9. [T. E. Lawrence], "Translator's Note" to *The Odyssey* (New York: Oxford University Press, 1965).

10. See *L*, 503, and the analysis of this passage in *The Wounded Spirit*, 125–26.

11. Forster, "The Mint," *Listener*, 279.

12. *T. E. Lawrence to His Biographers Robert Graves and Liddell Hart* (New York: Doubleday, 1963), 2:179.

13. *L*, 620. See W. H. Auden and Louis MacNeice, *Letters from Iceland* (London: Faber and Faber, 1937), 21: "Shaw of the Air Force said that happiness / Comes in absorption: he was right, I know it."

14. Quoted by Sybille Bedford in *Aldous Huxley, 1894–1963*, ed. Julian Huxley (London: Chatto and Windus, 1965), 139.

15. See Whitman's "Song of Myself," section 5, *Leaves of Grass*: "I mind how once we lay such a transparent summer morning, / How you settled your head athwart my hips and gently turn'd over upon me." For a discussion of Lawrence's inversion, and the tradition of boys bathing, see Jeffrey Meyers, *Homosexuality and Literature, 1890–1930* (London: Athlone Press, 1977), 114–30, 176.

16. André Malraux, "Lawrence and the Demon of the Absolute," *Hudson Review* 8 (1956): 531. For a discussion of Lawrence and Malraux, see Jeffrey Meyers, *A Fever at the Core* (London: London Magazine Editions, 1976), 143–46.

17. *Letters to T. E. Lawrence*, ed. A. W. Lawrence (London: Cape, 1962), 27; *L*, 351.

18. Wyndham Lewis, "Perspectives on Lawrence," *Hudson Review* 8 (1956): 606; Wyndham Lewis, *Blasting and Bombardiering* (1937; reprint, London: Calder and Boyars, 1967), 239. For Lewis's friendship with Lawrence, see Jeffrey Meyers, *The Enemy: A Biography of Wyndham Lewis* (London: Routledge and Kegan Paul, 1980), 128–30.

T. E. Lawrence:
Technical Writer

RODELLE WEINTRAUB

Throughout his lifetime Lawrence played many roles. From boyhood on, however, one remained constant. Whether youthful archaeologist, the exotic "El Aurens," or the enigmatic Private Shaw, Lawrence was, first and foremost, without artifice and with consummate skill, a technical writer. After the Arabian experience, he could have had a flamboyant career in politics or in the military, in government, or in society, in industry, banking, or education. He wanted none of them. Instead, having rejected honors and commissions, he sought anonymity as "Private Shaw" while perversely seeking fame in an area in which he felt he could not achieve success. Lawrence wanted not only to write some of the best prose in the language but recognition for doing so. He wanted to add a fourth book to those he considered "distinguished by greatness of spirit, . . . The Karamazovs, Zarathustra, and Moby Dick" (L, 360). In his epic Seven Pillars of Wisdom, he may have done so. Still he despaired that he had failed. In some respects he had—at least when he sought to achieve effects in imaginative prose. His strengths, and much of his writing, fit into another genre, technical writing.

Throughout his literary career, from his letters home as a teenager, through his thesis on medieval Crusaders' castles, to the last work published during his lifetime, The 200 Class Royal Air Force Seaplane Tender, his work fell into and was precursor of a newly burgeoning genre. His technical writing style was so uniquely his own that Bernard Shaw is quoted as recognizing an unsigned report used by a board of inquiry investigating a seaplane crash as Lawrence's. "Now, did you notice the jury's rider on that Air Force crash? . . . Well, when I read that, I saw at once [that] it was 'Shaw.' No one else at Portsmouth could write like that . . . whenever a specially difficult order has to be issued, they always call in 'Shaw' to draft it."[1] Shaw may have recognized the vivid language (the evocative imagery where it would convey information more accurately or more persuasively than would objective language) and the precise, confident presentation that gave Lawrence's writings a distinctiveness and a grace and readability that less skillful technical writing frequently lacks.

That Lawrence found satisfaction in his technical writing is well documented. Near the end of his service in the air force, he wrote, referring to the seaplane manual, "I pride myself that every sentence in it is understandable, to a fitter" (L, 760). Had he, as well as literary critics, recognized technical writing as a legitimate, respectable writing form, he might have found more contentment in his work instead of feeling frustrated by, and unable to satisfy, his gnawing literary impulse.

By what criteria can one judge a writer in order to determine whether his or her prose writings fall within the genre of technical writing rather than the broader category of expository prose? Standards do exist by which one can determine whether a piece of writing is intended as technical writing and whether the writer is indeed a technical writer. Analytical reports, experiment results, instructions, and business letters discussing technical matters can be considered technical writing—as can manuals, project proposals, progress reports, and other reports that concern themselves with how and why something should be done. (Business writing, in contrast, would concern itself with the costs of the project rather than with the technical implementation of it. An essay might discuss the philosophical or ethical merits of the same project. As differentiated from scientific writing, technical writing is often intended for the lay reader as well as for another professional.) Nonverbal illustrative material such as diagrams, charts, and maps usually supplement the text. The approach is primarily (although not exclusively) objective and quantifiable. Terms are defined; objects and processes described. Since technical writing may be intended for a lay audience, the writer will use any and all rhetorical devices, such as metaphor and simile, to enable the reader to grasp the technical data. Although technical writing can make up part of a fictional or poetic work, technical writing itself is verifiable nonfiction prose written for a specific audience and for a specific purpose. Fiction such as Herman Melville's *Moby Dick* and Robert Pirsig's *Zen and the Art of Motorcycle Maintenance* use technical description for the purpose of furthering the narrative or as a vehicle for philosophical rumination. While one does find technical information on whaling and information on the maintenance and operation of a motorcycle, one would not use either book as a manual on how to whale or how to repair, maintain, operate, or build a motorcycle. In contrast, Lawrence's "Evolution of a Revolt" and "Demolitions under Fire" can be valuable resource materials for persons planning guerrilla warfare. A technical document always intends in some way to further technical goals. Technical writing is practical and instructive. The author wants the reader to understand the information communicated and to apply that information to achieve the author's and the reader's goals. The reader needs the information conveyed.

Lawrence's education prepared him to understand and to communicate technical material. He earned a degree in history from Oxford and, as part of the degree requirements, journeyed to the Middle East, where he studied, measured, sketched, photographed, and wrote about the ruins of Crusaders' castles and their relationship to architecture in the later Middle Ages. Even before he was involved in individualized archaeological research, however, he had learned to employ the scientific and rhetorical tools of his profession.

While still only a student at the City of Oxford High School for Boys, T.E. had learned enough about archaeology, and enough about technical writing, to be able to provide concise instructions on how to go about conducting a simple archaeological dig. Writing to his younger brother Will in August 1906, Lawrence shared the boy's excitement while trying to help him better understand what he had discovered.

> Your letter has put me in a fever heat of expectation: but:—what is it you are going to dig up? Your letter bristles with inconsistencies. You think it is a Roman or Celtic camp (the two things are absolutely opposed to each other) and then you proceed to say that it is a

mound on some rising ground. If it includes a mound, say 40 feet high, it is a Saxon or Danish fortification, with probably an interment or two on the top; if the mound is 10 feet high or less, and is about 30 feet in diameter, then it is a barrow, as you said in the former parts of your description, which has a lamentable lack of exact figures. You next say that you cannot see traces of vallum or fossa, which are both terms to be applied to a Roman camp, and not to a Celtic, Saxon, British, or Danish erection. . . . If the mound is British it will be closely encircled by its fortifications, (if it ever had any). If the mound is Saxon, the encircling lines of fortification may be half a mile away. . . . So far all that you have told me which stands is that the mound is round. (L, 45)

He tried to help Will decide if the find was worth excavating, and, if so, he offered advice on how to go about doing so.

. . . a camp would not be worth excavating:—you might dig over half a mile of ground and only find a spear head: a burial, if a low mound, should have a trench cut through it, from S.W. to N.E., on the level of the ground. Keep all flints, [unless] the whole mound is flint and gravel, and by all means keep all bones; if you find human bones, do not disturb them, but dig around them . . . to recover the whole skeleton if possible: the skull is the most important part to determine the date. Any bronze implements found should not be disturbed at first, but try to trace the haft, which will have shrunk to the thinness of a pencil. . . . If the mound is small sift the earth you throw out. . . . Work very carefully, so as not to break any tender article. . . . If the mound is large, you should begin in the same way from the top, and work down until you are sure the strata have not been disturbed: i.e. if you find pure clay with no admixture of earth, you may be certain that it has not been moved. (L, 45–46)

The older brother also provided the younger with professional definitions and more precise terminology than the sixteen-year-old had used.

You may discover the whole mound to be natural (you say it is "unnatural," most archaeologists use "artificial") in which case only the upper three feet need be dug supposing it is a large mound. . . . In a small barrow 4–8 feet high, the articles would probably not be more than two feet from the body on each side: to search further out is an energetic course which occasionally repays itself, but not as a rule. . . . Let me know how the matter progresses, and unless it is very light soil, use small spades. (*L*, 46)

T.E. also reminded Will to prepare a report—technical writing—on his work and told him how to go about doing it: "Keep an accurate account of your progress, and mark on a plan where each important article is found." Already sensitive to the needs of his audience, Lawrence did not confuse Will by using obtuse technical jargon. Nor did his instructions provide more information than Will needed for this project.

In August 1907, writing to his mother, T.E. described the castle at Fougères, providing enough technical detail that she could understand what he wished to share, yet not overburdening her with data she did not need.

> The castle [Fougères] is quite above and beyond words. . . . The Tour des Gobelins is six stories in height, and circular. It stands on a granite cliff 80 feet high, and in the moonlight had a marvellous effect. It set off the strength of the Mélusine, a tower near, with an enormous expanded base. The talus shoots right out like the keep of Ch. Gaillard. Beyond the Mélusine, after a hundred yards of machicolated curtain come Raoul and Yrienne, two wonderful chefs-d'oeuvre of the military architect. They are semicircular bastions, projecting some 70 feet from the wall, are over 80 feet in diameter, and more than that in height; neither has a window or projection in the face and over against them leans the spire of St. Sulpice, the most crooked and the thinnest in Bretagne. (*L*, 52)

FIGURE I

He does not say that objects are merely large or small, near or far, but gives precise measurements where obtainable.

The letters written to his mother during this trip include maps (see figure 1), descriptions supplemented by drawings, and other technical writing techniques.

The machicoulis are still quite perfect & are each formed of 7 stones arranged thus. ⊓ ⊓ ⊓ They are all mathematically precise. The tower is ⊓ ⊐ ascended by a newel staircase, has most of its mouldings ⊐ renaissance, and bears the remains of a latrine on the face. ⊓ . . . This tower has a beautiful latrine of whose interior Scroggs made a sketch at my request. I enclose it, numbered 2. It projects from the wall as in that on the keep numbered 1. and looks like a sentry box. It has a little window and is fitted with a seat with large hole. The debris fell into the moat. The keep had three, one for each living room story. They were placed diagonally like this Scroggs made a sketch of the outside of the best pre- served. They are most interesting as improvements of the Norman variety which was just a little crude. The keep was the most interesting piece of work I have seen. It was a perfect circle and was hexagonal inside, and pierced by 15 openings; four of which were fireplaces. (CC, 2:14–15)

Lawrence would employ these devices in later letters in which he would record data for use in more formal writings. The practice of first re- cording his impressions and technical details to support them in letters that could then become the raw material for his later writings was one that he continued throughout his writing career. Much of the descrip- tive material in *Crusader Castles*, for example, was first included in letters to his mother. In some instances the letters contained more specific detail than did the later thesis.

Written in 1910, after Lawrence had visited most of the important castles in England, Wales, France, Syria, and northern Palestine, tracking down, measuring, and comparing the ruins in the Middle East with those of European castles of the same period, the thesis and an accompanying volume of letters were published posthumously in 1936. Although the text has only forty-four pages, the volume contains ninety- six illustrations in addition to three maps. The illustrative material includes Lawrence's drawings of site plans, floor plans, and details.

There are photographs of castle ruins, restorations, and details. Many of the drawings have scale and direction indicated. This illustrative matter is not included as ornamental or appendix material but is essential to the understanding of the text. The text includes references to the illustrations.

> The castle is entered (58) at D by means of a plain gate, and then a vaulted passage, almost dark, as far as the tower J, where is a large trap-machicoulis in the roof and other defences. To reach the inner ward one must go further, to the tower L, also in a dark vaulted passage, ascending steeply. . . . Through [the upper gate] one enters a small courtyard, opposite the great hall of the castle N. Another flight of stairs gives on the upper court K still unencumbered with houses (56). From it lead up more steps to G (59), the platform uniting the three great towers that together form the donjon. (CC, 1:46)

When Lawrence later went through the *Crusader Castles* manuscript to prepare it for possible publication,[2] he wrote criticisms and comments in the margins, faulting this early attempt for lack of specific information and for unfounded judgments:

Why?	It fills up nearly all the space within the containing wall and therefore to this extent looks like an afterthought . . . (CC, 1:35)
"Quality" not much of a word.	. . . of less size, and weaker quality. Their efficiency. . . . (CC, 1:25)
Much too abrupt.	Chateau Gaillard is no exotic growth, but a development of the multiple castle of the style of Taillebourg and Hautefort, in the hands of an engineer of genius. . . . (CC, 1:56)

The thesis included footnotes, some of which added color and some definition:

Also cows & fleas etc.	[1]It is not easy even to-day to stumble up the uneven steps, in a litter of pariah dogs and goats. (CC, 1:46)
	[2]'Machicoulis' are always used in two senses, the stone substitute for boards, on a wall top, and the square traps pierced in the floor of the room above an entry. (CC, 1:35)

It is of course not surprising that an archaeology thesis would employ technical writing techniques. What is surprising is the lightness of tone, the personal comments, the sarcasm, and the subjective language: "The design is simply unintelligent, a reworking of the old ideas of Procopius, only half understood. . . . Given unlimited time and labour, anyone can make a ditch so deep and a wall so high of stones so heavy as to be impregnable; but such a place is as much a prison for its defenders as a refuge: in fact a stupidity. Such is Athlit" (CC, 1:43). The style he developed for *Crusader Castles* combined dramatic description and subjective language with the concise technological detail more typical of technical writing. It is a strategy that he employed throughout the remainder of his writings and that gives his technical writing its uniqueness.

After taking first-class honors in history in 1910, Lawrence several times returned to the Middle East. In 1914, after digs at Carchemish in Syria, he accompanied Leonard Woolley on an ostensible archaeological expedition into the Sinai which really camouflaged a map-making reconnaissance from Gaza to Akaba. Whether the trip were archaeological or cartographical, it demanded communication of evidence gathered—technical writing—for it to have value. The report of the expedition, *The Wilderness of Zin*, was published under the names of both Woolley and Lawrence in 1915 by the Palestine Exploration Fund. Although it is not always possible to separate precisely the contributions of the collaborators, parts seem similar to the dramatic descriptive prose of Lawrence's letters home and of his earlier thesis.

> The way down is very splendid. In the hill-sides all sorts of rocks
> are mingled in confusion; grey-green limestone cliffs run down sheer
> for hundreds of feet, in tremendous ravines whose faces are a medley of
> colours wherever crags of black porphyry and diorite jut out, or where
> soft sandstone, washed down, has left long pink and red smudges on
> the lighter colours. The confusion of materials makes the road-laying
> curiously uneven.[3]

Although the language seems too subjective for technical writing, the details Lawrence recorded during this trip proved essential to the planning of the Arab campaign and to Lawrence himself when he became part of the Arab guerrilla forces.

Shortly after Lawrence returned to England from the Woolley ex-

pedition, World War I began. He quickly shifted from civilian em-
ployee of the War Office, charged with preparing a militarily useful
map of the Sinai, to new lieutenant, with duties at first little changed
from his civilian ones. The ministry's requirements tested Lawrence's
abilities to amalgamate demonstrable fact with colorful imagination.
He was expected to document all roads and wells, and outline the
hills. "As Sinai is in manuscript in 68 [grid] sheets," he wrote a friend,
"it meant a little trouble, for the sheets . . . were not numbered or
labelled, and so nobody could put them together. I came up like St.
George in shining armour . . . and by night behold there was a map
of Sinai eighteen feet each way in three colours. Some of it was accurate, and the rest I invented" (*L*, 187).

"Experts" on Arab affairs, especially those who had actually traveled
in Turkish-held Arab lands, were rare. Those who knew not only the
terrain but the habits and mores of the inhabitants were even rarer.
Assigned in December 1914 to the Intelligence Department of Army
Headquarters in Cairo, Lawrence began the dreary work of "adding
together scraps of information & writing geographies from memory of
little details" (*L*, 191). (It would prove useful experience.) Before long,
although technically still a map officer, he was interviewing prisoners,
producing a handbook on the Turkish army, receiving data from agents
behind the lines, planning small campaigns and dreaming of grandiose
ones, and contributing to the *Arab Bulletin*, a secret intelligence periodical meant to keep British diplomats and military commands all
over the Middle East informed about developments within the Arab
lands controlled by the Germans and the Turks. Even after he became
actively involved in the Arab uprising, abetting the revolt he had
sketched out in March 1915, he continued writing—in his usual style,
combining subjective commentary with technical detail—for the *Arab
Bulletin*.

> Rode at 5.30 a.m. and at 6.15 a.m. crossed the level bed of Wadi Tu-
> raa, and Wadi Hamdh at 6.45 a.m. The Hamdh was as full of *aslam*
> wood as at Abu Zereibat and had the same hummocky bed, with sandy
> blisters over it—but it was only about 200 yards wide, and shallow.
> We halted at 8 a.m. in W. Tubja, which was a sort of wilderness garden,
> with a profusion of grass and shrubs in which the camels rejoiced. The
> weather was very hot, with a burning sun that made the sandy ground
> impossible for me to walk on barefoot. The Arabs had soles like asbes-

tos, and made little complaint, except of the warmth of the air. There had been thunder all yesterday, and half a dozen showers of rain last night and today.

Using metaphoric elements, he described, for a general audience that would not have understood meteorological terminology, the storms that wrapped the nearby hills "in shapes and sheets of a dark blue and yellow vapour that seemed motionless and solid," and that approached their forces raising "scores of dust devils before its feet. It also produced two dust-spouts, tight and symmetrical—stationary columns, like chimneys—one to the right and one to the left of its advance." He then returned to his less subjective account of the railway demolition, employing technical jargon (such as "trigger central") with which his military audience would be familiar.

> We had some delay in finding a machine-gun position, for the railway runs everywhere near the eastern hills of the valley, and the valley is about 3,000 yards broad. However, eventually, we found a place opposite kilometre 1121, and I laid a mine (trigger central, with rail-cutting charges 15 yards north and south of it respectively) with some difficulty owing to the rain, at 12 p.m. It took till 1.45 a.m. to cover up the traces of the digging, and we left the whole bank, and the sandy plain each side . . . covered with huge footmarks. . . . I wiped out most of those on the embankment itself, however, by walking up and down in shoes over it. Such prints are indistinguishable from the daily footmarks of the patrol inspecting the line.[4]

These reports furnished military intelligence with information essential to the planning of the continuation of the campaign and to the planning of similar campaigns if needed. The *Arab Bulletin* would later provide much of the raw material for *Seven Pillars of Wisdom*.

During this period he also kept a journal and produced several lengthy political and military essays meant for official eyes. In August 1917 he prepared his "Twenty-seven Articles," a manual for political officers, explaining how to manipulate Arabs. Along with the objective writing essential to such documents, Lawrence added wit and wryness. Technical instructions should describe each step separately and lucidly, and each discrete step should include an explanation as to why it should be done and/or what will occur as a result of that action. "Twenty-seven Articles" conforms to these principles.

If you wear Arab things at all, go the whole way. . . . Fall back on Arab habits entirely. It is possible, starting thus level with them, for the European to beat the Arabs at their own game, for we have stronger motives for our action, and put more heart into it than they. If you can surpass them, you have taken an immense stride towards complete success, but the strain of living and thinking in a foreign and half-understood language, the savage food, strange clothes, and still stranger ways, with the complete loss of privacy and quiet, and the impossibility of ever relaxing your watchful imitation of the others for months on end, provide such an added stress to the ordinary difficulties of dealing with the Bedu, the climate, and the Turks, that this road should not be chosen without serious thought. . . .

The beginning and ending of the secret of handling Arabs is unremitting study of them. . . . Bury yourself in Arab circles, have no interests and no ideas except the work in hand, so that your brain shall be saturated with one thing only, and you realise your part deeply enough to avoid the little slips that would undo the work of weeks. Your success will be proportioned to the amount of mental effort you devote to it.[5]

The "Twenty-seven Articles" was written for use by military intelligence. Lawrence's technical article "Demolitions under Fire," which was published in the *Royal Engineers' Journal,* was intended for engineers familiar with explosives and possibly interested in the most effective way to carry out demolition of railroad track in wartime conditions. The article describes the types of explosives Lawrence had used, their preparation for use, and the relative efficacy of each. Although couched in more technical terminology than his intelligence reports, the article still maintains Lawrence's unique style and wit.

Our explosives were mainly blasting gelatin and guncotton. . . . [The former] is rather more powerful in open charges in direct contact, far better for indirect work, has a value of 5 to 1 in super-tamped charges, is quicker to use, and more compact. . . . Guncotton is a good explosive, but inferior . . . to gelatin, and in addition, we used to receive it packed 16 slabs (of 15 oz. each) in a wooden box of such massive construction that it was nearly impossible to open peacefully. . . . I have opened boxes by detonating a primer on one corner, but regard this way as unnecessarily noisy, wasteful, and dangerous for daily use.

Rail Demolition.—Guncotton in 15-ounce slabs is convenient for rail cutting. The usual method of putting a fused and detonated and primed slab against the web is quick and easy, but ineffective. . . . The slab cuts a six-in. section out of the line, leaving two clean fractured surfaces (Hejaz rails are of a mild Maryland or Cockerill steel). . . .

The best demolition we discovered was to dig down in the ballast beside a mid-rail sleeper between the tracks, until the inside of the sleeper (iron of course) could be cleared of ballast, and to lay two slabs in the bottom of the hole, under the sleeper, but not in contact with it. The excavated ballast should then be returned and the end of the fuse left visible over the sleeper for the lighting party. The expansion of air raises the middle of the sleeper 18 in. from the ground, humps the two rails 3 in. from the horizontal, draws them 6 in. nearer together, and warps them from the vertical inwards by the twisting pull of the chairs on the bottom outer flange. A trough is also driven a foot or more deep across the formation. This gives two rails destroyed, one sleeper or two, and the grading, for two slabs and one fuse. . . . The appearance of a piece of rail treated by this method is most beautiful, for the sleepers rise up in all manner of varied forms, like the early buds of tulips.[6]

With the exception of the reference to "tulips" and the beauty of the exploded rail, even the most pedantic of critics would recognize this passage as conforming to technical writing techniques. Dr. Hartwig Kummer, an engineer, upon reading the "tulip" description in 1967, immediately recognized the type and amount of explosive used to produce such an effect (just as "mushroom cloud" would now precisely identify a nuclear explosion).

A vital aspect of technical writing is its sense of purpose—its recording of data so that it becomes available for the use of others. Writing to Bernard Shaw to ask him to read the manuscript of *Seven Pillars*, Lawrence explained his reason for writing it and for asking Shaw to read it: "It's because it is history, and I'm shamed for ever if I am the sole chronicler of an event, and fail to chronicle it" (L, 357). Lawrence had already documented it in letters, journals, and secret *Arab Bulletin* articles and technical articles such as "Demolitions under Fire." In *Seven Pillars* he wanted to go beyond writing technical reports that would be seen only by a limited audience. He wanted to create an epic on the order of *Moby Dick*, and he attempted to use Melville's epic as the model for his own.[7] Interweaving chapters of documentary with chapters of narrative, he made a deliberate effort to use emotive language and create vivid imagery. Yet he did so without forsaking the precise methods compatible with technical writing. The enumeration of data and the cataloging of explicit detail, while in the tradition of the classical epic, are also essentials of technical writing. *Seven Pillars'* description of the Beduins' "savage food" demonstrates this combination of heightened language, enumeration of data, and cataloging of explicit detail.

> The bowl was now brim-full, ringed round its edge by white rice in an embankment a foot wide and six inches deep, filled with large legs and ribs of mutton till they toppled over. . . . The centre-pieces were the boiled, upturned heads, propped on their severed stumps of necks, so that the ears, brown like old leaves, flapped out on the rice surface. The jaws gaped emptily upward, pulled open to show the hollow throat with the tongue, still pink, clinging to the lower teeth. . . .
>
> This load was set down on the soil of the cleared space between us, where it steamed hotly, while a procession of minor helpers bore small cauldrons and copper vats in which the cooking had been done. From them, with much-bruised bowls of enamelled iron, they ladled out over the main dish all the inside and outside of the sheep; little bits of yellow intestine, the white tail-cushion of fat, brown muscles and meat and bristly skin, all swimming in the liquid butter and grease. . . .
>
> The fat was scalding . . . but they persevered till at last their scooping rang loudly on the bottoms of the pots; and, with a gesture of triumph, they fished out the intact livers from their hiding place in the gravy and topped the yawning jaws with them. (*SP*, 266)

By the time *Seven Pillars* was completed, Lawrence had exhausted the Arabian technical material on which he had drawn, and had joined the air force. Shunning a commission, he hid his background as well as his name and enlisted as "Ross." He would spend most of the remainder of his life in the armed forces, as Ross in the air force and then as Shaw in the Tank Corps and again in the air force. Writing from the Tank Corps to D. G. Hogarth in 1923, recalling his first enlistment, Lawrence claimed that his purpose in joining the air force had been to produce a book about it.

> When I joined the R.A.F. it was in the hope that some day I'd write a book about the very excellent subject that it was. At that time I thought my Arab Revolt book very bad. Since then [Bernard] Shaw has

turned my mind slowly to consider it good: and there's another ambition gone, for it was always in my hope to write a decent book: and
if I've done it there seems little reason to do another. A pity, for my
Uxbridge notes were good, & there was the making of a very good
thing out of the life of a squadron. (L, 425)

The Mint, the book based upon his Uxbridge notes and later impressions, would not be published until after his death. Using black humor
and barracks language, he captured with scalpel-like precision and
communicated, through description interspersed with dialogue, the
sights and sounds and smells of the recruits' day-to-day existence.

> Kit inspection in fifteen minutes. We broke into a mad rush.
> In rehearsal, kit-laying had taken an hour. First we rolled down our
> mattresses, and covered them with our brownest and least-torn blan-
> ket. The other bedding made a chocolate sandwich at the bed-head.
> On it we laid our great-coats, pressed as square as a box, with polished
> buttons winking down the front. On top of that our blue caps. We
> stood back in the alley-way, and trued the pile upright.
> Now the tunic, so folded that the belt made it a straight edge. Cov-
> ering it, the breeches, squared to the exact area of the tunic, with four
> concertina-folds facing forward. Towels were doubled once, twice,
> thrice, and flanked the blue tower. In front of the blue sat a rectangular
> cardigan. To each side a rolled puttee. Shirts were packed and laid in
> pairs like flannel bricks. Before them, pants. Between them, neat balls
> of socks, wedged in. Our holdalls were stretched wide, with knife,
> fork, spoon, razor, comb, toothbrush, lather brush, button-stick, in
> that order, ranged across them. Into the displayed housewives were
> stuck needles ready threaded with khaki cotton. Our spare boots were
> turned soles-up, each side of the holdall. The soles had been polished
> black and the steel tips and five rows of hobnails rubbed with emery-
> paper, to shine. Our five polishing brushes, washed and with glass-
> papered white backs, were lined across the foot of the bed.
> All our official effects were so on view, mathematically spaced,
> folded, measured and weighed: also largely numbered with our official
> numbers. That gave the game away. Airmen . . . will not wear
> garments which are visibly numbered. This stuff was just kit-inspection
> stuff, and our real dirty brushes, our really worn clothes were hidden
> in our boxes. "Proper bull-shit," grumbled Lofty when made to Silvo his
> boot-blacking tin till it simulated silver. Bull-shit it was. (M, 102–3)

Undisguised autobiography, *The Mint* relies upon the recording of precise detail and the rendering of that detail into effective, ordered description.

Without a technological or autobiographical base, Lawrence was frustrated as a writer. He wanted to write but, unless the military assigned him a report or a manual, he was without subject matter. Translation afforded him the opportunity to write without having to rely upon the imaginative process. The most ambitious of his translations[8] was his prose rendering of *The Odyssey*. From his own experience in warfare, he felt comfortable with the material. He considered Homer

> . . . adrift when it comes to fighting, and [as not having] seen deaths in battle. He had sailed upon and watched the sea with a palpitant concern, seafaring being not his trade. . . .
>
> Few men can be sailors, soldiers and naturalists. Yet this Homer was neither land-lubber nor stay-at-home nor ninny. . . . That famous doubled line where Cyclops narrowly misses the ship with his stones only shows how much better a seaman he was than his copyist. Scholiasts have tried to riddle his technical knowledge. . . . It is the penalty for being a pre-archeological.[9]

From his own experience Lawrence knew what it was like to be a sailor, soldier, and scientist, for he was absorbed in his work with R.A.F. watercraft, and could apply his own knowledge of shipbuilding to his translation of Odysseus' building a ship to leave Calypso's shores.

> First she gave him a great axe of cutting copper, well-suited to his reach. It was ground on both edges and into the socketed head firmly edged the well-rounded handle of olive-wood. Then she gave him a finished smoothing-adze and led the way to the end of the island where the trees grew tall, the alders and the poplars with heaven-scaling pines, withered long since and sapless and very dry, which would float high for him. She showed him where the loftiest trees had grown, did Calypso that fair goddess: then she returned to her cavern while he busily cut out his beams, working with despatch. Twenty trees in all he threw and axed into shape with the sharp copper, trimming them adeptly and trueing them against his straight-edge.[10]

Although Lawrence had started the translation eagerly, he quickly lost his enthusiasm for what he considered "manufactured writing." The manuscript was not delivered until a year after it hàd been promised. By then he was more interested in preparing his manuals for the R.A.F. than bothering with "Homer's namby-pamby men and women" (L, 708).

He also enjoyed responding to friends' requests for technical information. When Robert Graves, while working with Laura Riding on a novel under the joint pseudonym "Barbara Rich," asked for a description of a futuristic aircraft, Lawrence responded with several paragraphs of description.

All structural members were drop-forgings of cellular colloidal infra-steel, rubber-faced. The monocoque hull was proofed against sound and temperatures by panels of translucent three-ply crodex, between whose films were managed the ducts and condenser areas of the evaporative-cooling system for the eleven Jenny-Ruras picric-electric motors in the under-body.

Their power units were universally coupled by oil transmission and magnetic clutches alternatively to the lifting vanes (for hover or direct ascent) or to the propulsive rotor for horizontal travel. The vanes were geared into centrifugal governors which automatically varied their lifting angle according to load and air resistance.

In the rotor, the blade-pitch was adjustable at will, for speed and air density. The blades were set (with a clearance at maximum protrusion of .05m.) in the internal drum of a rotor-turbine of (tractor) Townend type, revolving about the nose of the fuselage which was paired for lead-in and baffled for internal turbulence. The slip-stream was deflected by scoops at the exit upwards against the bearing surfaces of the vanes, to increase lift in rare atmospheres or from salt water. A syphon-regulated ballast tank was fitted, to trim by the tail when taxying in rough water. The aircraft's landing springs were castored for ease of garaging and retractable for marine use. Landing speeds as low as 4 k.p.h. (downward) and 2 k.p.h. (forward) were attained. The maximum speed at 22,000 m. was—k.p.h.

All controls were of course directional operated, at will, and gyroscopically stabilised. Baehlen beam-antennae (of our-cycle frequency) were energised by the rotor-brushes. These were set to indicate by sound-signal to the pilot the presence of any body of more than atmospheric density within 300 metres. At 200 metres they began to induce deflection in the controls, and absolutely refused nearer approach than 18 metres until the motors were throttled back to landing speed. Antaeus indicators recorded height and earth-direction

continuously and nitro-generators supplemented the power-units at
great elevations. [11]

Concerned that this colorless description might be too technical for
their needs, he recommended that they could "cut the technical terms
. . . and delete the antennae . . . and the rotor propulsion." Only
mildly altered, the paragraphs appeared in "Barbara Rich's" novel *No
Decency Left.* Unlike most of Lawrence's writings, which had a factual
basis, his parody—a fiction—seems more "technical" than his real
technical writing. It lacks his wit, his subjectivity, and his personality,
and closely follows the basic outline for a description of an object.

His last publication while still in the air force was a manual on the
construction and handling of the 200 class R.A.F. seaplane tender.
The manual was issued to the coxswains and mechanics employed as
crew or responsible for servicing this craft. The format follows technical report style, each paragraph being numbered for easy access and
references. At all times he remembered his audience, their education
and experience, and to what use they would put the information.

> 213. The design is a compromise. . . . The boats are not much wind-
> driven and yet draw so little as to escape tide effect. . . . In good trim
> of engines and hull they can be made to do anything their coxswain
> wants. They will run on one engine alone and steer against it, though
> difficulty will be experienced with a hard beam wind on the same side
> as the working engine. These handling notes are only provided because
> few R.A.F. coxswains have had much experience of handling hard-
> chined fast boats in a sea-way; and because such boats behave rather
> unlike the previous round-bottomed craft.

> 214. The primary purpose of the class is to save life or Service equip-
> ment from a crash at sea. Between emergencies . . . they must always
> be kept in trim for high-speed work. Their coxswain's constant duty
> is to save the engines, by intelligent reading of the dashboard instru-
> ments and by moderation in use of the throttle. The engines are built
> to give 3000 revolutions at maximum; and to hold that speed through-
> out the boat's fuel endurance; but like all high-efficiency engines, they
> lose tune after much running at full throttle. [12]

Lawrence's final professional work, a seventy-nine-page manuscript
entitled "Power Boat Hull Reconditioning," remains unpublished. It

describes the work done on the overhaul of R.A.F. marine craft at Bridlington during 1934 and 1935. The last entry in the journal was made on 23 February 1935, three days before his discharge.[13]

With his discharge, Lawrence lost his sources for writing. While he still provided technical information in letters in response to queries, he felt frustrated at no longer being involved in ongoing research, as a letter to the manufacturer of his motorcycle reveals.

> About your fan. Our propeller experiments were all marine, and they showed how little was known yet, even in that much exercised branch. Air propellers (of the suction type) have been, I am sure, very little studied. Large diameter of course means noise, as do broad tips. Four blades are quieter than three and as efficient. You can push an air-prop pitch up to great steepness, so long as the revs are not extrava-gant. But frankly I cannot help you. Our props have so different an intention. The water is so solid an element. Have you considered Eth-ylene glycol for cooling? Or is the engine getting too hot for its oil? In the desert I ran a tiny condenser for our old Fords, and so boiled all day without using a pint of water, and with great thermal advantage. Later they doubled the Leader-tank, increased the pump output, and carried on without boiling. Petrol consumption then increased.
>
> I have wondered of late how the new engine was shaping. You were going to make a new angle of inlet for the mixture. Now you are working on the timing gears! Please tell Mr J.A.P. for me that if I had his sized firm and couldn't get an aircooled twin right in 18 months, I'd eat my test-bench and wash it down with my flow meter! (L, 867)

Otherwise, he drifted. He refused to translate *The Iliad* because it is a poem and "no great poem has ever been translated—yet."[14] Asked to comment upon the Douglas Credit Scheme, he found he could not, and returned Maurice Colbourne's *Economic Nationalism* claiming he could not "settle to it" (L, 866). He had been too long immersed in the air force and its technology to return to the interests of his pre-service years. To an air force officer and acquaintance he wrote, "My time passes between swearing at [the birds], cutting brush-wood, and inventing odd jobs. No letter-writing anymore, except under extreme need, and no duty. A queer lapse into uselessness . . ." (L, 868). To Eric Kennington, who had done some of the paintings for *Seven Pillars*, he wrote, "What I have done, what I am going to do, puzzle me and bewilder me. Have you ever been a leaf and fallen from your tree in autumn and been really puzzled about it? That's the feeling."[15] Like the leaf fallen from the tree, the technical writer, separated from his source of nourishment, had withered.

N·O·T·E·S

1. Edwin Samuel, *A Lifetime in Jerusalem* (New York: Random House, 1970), 113–14.

2. Lawrence apparently returned to and completed his revisions of his thesis after 1929. John Mack, in his biography *A Prince of Our Disorder*, quotes Lawrence as writing in 1929 that his thesis had been destroyed or left behind somewhere. A. W. Lawrence, in his preface to the posthumously published *Crusader Castles*, wrote that "In later years the author added further notes in pencil . . . he also placed a few more photos and plans inside [his] copy" (1:4). "Later years" might refer to the early 1930s.

3. C. Leonard Woolley and T. E. Lawrence, *The Wilderness of Zin* as quoted in *The Essential T. E. Lawrence*, ed. David Garnett (Baltimore: Penguin, 1956), 46.

4. *Arab Bulletin*, 4 April [1916], in *The Essential T. E. Lawrence*, 105–6.

5. "Twenty-seven Articles," *Arab Bulletin*, 20 August 1917, in *The Essential T. E. Lawrence*, 138–44.

6. "Demolitions under Fire," *Royal Engineers' Journal* 29 (January 1919), as quoted in Stanley and Rodelle Weintraub, eds., *Evolution of a Revolt* (University Park: Pennsylvania State University Press, 1967), 57–58.

7. See Stanley and Rodelle Weintraub, *Lawrence of Arabia: The Literary Impulse* (Baton Rouge: Louisiana State University Press, 1975), pp. 48–51, and Keith Hull's essay in the present volume for a discussion of Lawrence's debt to Melville.

8. For Lawrence as translator, see chaps. 4 and 6 of *Lawrence of Arabia: The Literary Impulse*.

9. "Translator's Note," *The Odyssey of Homer* (Oxford: Oxford University Press, 1959), [ii–iii].

10. *The Odyssey of Homer*, bk. 5, p. 76.

11. Reprinted in *T. E. Lawrence to His Biographers Robert Graves and Liddell Hart* (New York: Doubleday, 1963), 1:168–69.

12. Extracts from *The 200 Class Royal Air Force Seaplane Tender* are in *The Essential T. E. Lawrence*, 307–12.

13. The autograph manuscript of "Power Boat Hull Reconditioning," 79 pp., covering the period from 13 November 1934 to 23 February 1935, is in the Humanities Research Center, University of Texas at Austin.

14. Lawrence to H. G. Andrews, 6 March 1935, quoted in Charles Hamilton's auction catalog, no. 8, 20 May 1965, p. 27.

15. *L*, 871. Like the autumn leaf consigned to the bonfire, Lawrence died too soon after writing this letter for anyone to judge how permanent his ennui might have been.

PART · TWO

OTHER ASPECTS

The Subscribers' *Seven Pillars of Wisdom*: The Visual Aspect

CHARLES GROSVENOR

In Paris in January 1919, amidst the chaos and confusion of the opening of the Peace Conference, T. E. Lawrence began writing his memoir of the Arabian campaign. He began with an attitude of high ambition. The book was intended to be "Titanic," an "English fourth"[1] to place next to *The Brothers Karamazov*, *Thus Spake Zarathustra*, and *Moby Dick*. The success with which *Seven Pillars of Wisdom* attained that goal has recently been analyzed in writings by Jeffrey Meyers, Stephen Tabachnick, and Thomas O'Donnell. But for Lawrence the ambition he held for *Seven Pillars* had another aspect: beauty of production— the book must reach for visual as well as literary perfection. This aspect of what became the Subscribers' Edition of *Seven Pillars* (privately printed in London in 1926) has been greatly overlooked. The prime focus here will be the decorative aspect; the typography and binding will be mentioned only in regard to the overall impression the edition creates. In order to evaluate the success of Lawrence's decorative ambitions, it will first be necessary to examine his motivations and methods, the time period in which the book was produced, and of course the results themselves.

Lawrence's youthful interest in fine printing is well documented.[2] Growing up in the scholarly atmosphere of Oxford, Lawrence had this interest crystallize around the Kelmscott Press. In this he was not alone, for, as Philip O'Brien has pointed out, "along with many others of his generation, he was strongly influenced by William Morris."[3] The interest increased and became the focus of vocational schemes that

Lawrence developed with friends such as Vyvyan Richards. The plans, however tentative, were thrown into disarray with the coming of war. Yet for all the chaos and suffering the war brought Lawrence and his generation, it also provided a vehicle for literary expression; and in Lawrence's case the writing could lead to fine book production. His planned book on the Arabian campaign Lawrence came to consider "the-book-to-build-the-house":[4] the profits from its sales, which promised to be great, might help build and equip the Chingford hall in which Lawrence and Richards could print. Later determining that profiting from the book would constitute a further impropriety on his war role, Lawrence abandoned the idea and eventually settled on a scheme of issuing his memoir in a lavish limited edition. To produce the book lavishly, Lawrence needed an artist to decorate the book properly: a Burne-Jones to his William Morris. While serving on the British delegation to the Peace Conference he had come into contact with a number of prominent British artists. There to record on canvas the personalities of the conference, at least two of these artists, Augustus John and Sir William Orpen, found Lawrence a worthy subject and an individual obviously interested in the arts. Access to other prominent artists would become possible as Lawrence's public notoriety increased. Certainly a proper art editor could be found among them.

An avid frequenter of art galleries, Lawrence was impressed with several works by a young artist named Eric Kennington. He sought out Kennington and rapidly hammered out an arrangement for him to execute a number of portraits for his unfinished book. But portraits drawn from Lawrence's collection of war photographs, Kennington argued, "would be no good. The artist must see the person."[5] Kennington's trip to Arabia and his strikingly beautiful Arab pastels were the result.

Original plans called for *Seven Pillars* to be decorated primarily by Kennington. This soon changed. Other artists were sought out and given portrait commissions:[6] William Rothenstein and his student Colin Gill, William Nicholson, the brothers Gilbert and Stanley Spencer, Frank Dobson, and Henry Lamb. Wyndham Lewis and William Roberts accepted commissions. Blair Hughes-Stanton and his wife Gertrude Hermes agreed to produce a number of decorative woodcuts, and several students at the Royal College of Art would speculatively submit work for later judgment. J. Cosmo Clark and Paul Nash would produce decorative drawings of Arabian settings, but unlike Kennington they would work from photographs: a "dishonourable" and "damnable" proposition, as Lawrence noted, but not one that could not be rectified. The artists were given "complete freedom" of expression to "translate the photographs into life" however they saw fit.[7] The only stipulation given to all artists was to produce decorations and not illustrations. The works were to serve as ornaments, pictorial devices that would complement the page of type with which they were to be merged. Ideas embodied in the text could serve as springboards for designs, but pure depictions of events in the book were not desired. For, as Lawrence wrote years later to Bruce Rogers, "while I like decorated books, I do not like illustrated books."[8]

Lawrence must certainly have relished the fact that he and his book were the focal point of such artistic energies. These energies and abilities he deeply and enviously admired. "I can salve the regret of not being an artist," he wrote to Robert Graves, "by watching artists work."[9] Yet in gathering the artists to work on the *Seven Pillars* project, Lawrence went beyond salving his regrets: he in essence had created a loose form of medieval guild, what he himself referred to as his "team of artists."[10] Since childhood Lawrence had been deeply interested in the medieval, and we may hypothesize that the image of his being the patron of such a guild occurred to him, and pleasantly. The pleasure was mutual, though, as one "guildsman," Paul Nash, observed: "I think it's going to be great fun. . . . O what a dream! Lawrence is of the salt of the earth and I know he's doing much of this simply to help painters who find a difficulty in *affording* to paint."[11]

If Lawrence had indeed assembled a twentieth-century guild, what was the nature of the guildsmen? All of the artists commissioned for *Seven Pillars* were English, and most were regarded as stylistic independents. The most noticeable collective characteristic of the artists, however, was their youthfulness. The overwhelming majority were Lawrence's age or younger and consequently shared a bond with him. Lawrence recognized the strength of the generational bond and perhaps sought to exploit it in commissioning youthful artists.[12] *Seven Pillars*, despite its exotic setting and special circumstances, was a distinctly generational narrative: it presented "innocence, followed by betrayal and defeat at the hands of the older generation."[13] In this respect it was a narrative theme to which young Englishmen could relate.

The common experience of the war served as an important binding element for English youth, but, as Robert Wohl has pointed out, the bond went deeper:

> What bound the generation of 1914 together was not just their experiences during the war, as many of them later came to believe, but the fact that they grew up and formulated their first ideas in the world from which the war issued. . . . The primary fact of this world—and the first thing that young people noticed about it—was that it was being rapidly transformed by technology.[14]

It was the age of machinery. Since art is intimately associated with the character of its era, it would be expected that the generation of 1914 should produce a machine art. This it did, as evidenced in Italy by the futurists and in England by the vorticists.

Vorticism was a style for which Lawrence showed a "clearly marked preference,"[15] and a style that he wished represented in *Seven Pillars*. Wyndham Lewis and William Roberts, closely associated with vorticism, and Frank Dobson, whose work at times reflected vorticist leanings, were highly valued members of the artistic team. Roberts's work in fact eventually became Lawrence's favorite of all the *Seven Pillars'* art.[16] The decorative initials Lawrence selected for his book were also machine-inspired, being executed by Edward Wadsworth, another vorticist.

The *Seven Pillars* artists also reflected a stylistic tendency shared by other early twentieth-century visual art groups.[17] This was the attraction for the literary. In the case of the vorticists, this was an important aspect of their art. They attempted "to create spatial forms in literature and discover common aesthetic ground for all the arts."[18] Other literary tendencies were common to Lawrence's artistic guild as well. Paul Nash has been described by Dennis Farr as "a literary painter in that his imagination was caught by evocative phrases and poetical symbolism,"[19] and Eric Kennington had a keen power of literary insight. That Lawrence could have been unaware of this literary tendency in the artists he selected seems unlikely. In conversations with men such as

Edward Marsh and John Rothenstein, he probed deeply into the nature of the emerging generation of English artists. It seems likely that in commissioning the artists Lawrence consciously recruited youthful Englishmen whose literary tendencies would serve to enhance their decorations for *Seven Pillars*.

Lawrence's retinue of artists continued work on the decorations until just a few months before the book was issued. Kennington worked with the platemakers Whittingham and Griggs, overseeing the proofs of the color reproductions, and maintained a critical standard of excellence: one plate had to be proofed as many as seventeen times.[20] Other artists were also given judgmental powers over the quality of their works' reproductions.

The book finally appeared in December 1926, sumptuously and variously bound by some of London's foremost bookbinders: Sangorski and Sutcliffe, Macleish, Wood, Harrison, and Best. A brief description of the arrangement and nature of the decorations here seems in order.[21] The opening leaf of the book contains Kennington's woodcut "The Eternal Itch" (plate 1), a Boschian landscape of human torment and folly. It is the result, along with the rear endpaper, of Lawrence's offering Kennington the opportunity to "do something very lusty. . . . Here is a rare chance of publishing the censorable: of doing, without restraint, exactly what you feel like."[22] A flyleaf map by Bartholomew follows, and then several pages hence appears the frontispiece: John's Peace Conference portrait of Feisal, bordered by a thin black edge that Lawrence deemed a stroke of genius.[23] A small Kennington watercolor, "False Quiet," appears a number of pages later and completes the pre-text decorations.

The text follows, with its mass of chapter tailpieces and line-cut plates. The tailpieces in the early pages are primarily by William Roberts and, as the book progresses, the works of Kennington, Blair Hughes-Stanton, and Paul Nash are gradually infused. At the ends of three books are special full-leaf plates with color: "The Camel March" by Roberts after Book IV; "At a Well" by Cosmo Clark after Book V; and "Irish Troops Being Shelled" by Henry Lamb after Book VII. These were placed between books, as decorational islands, for aesthetic reasons, as Lawrence observed to Bruce Rogers: "To combine representational drawings (above all in colour) with the formality of type seemed

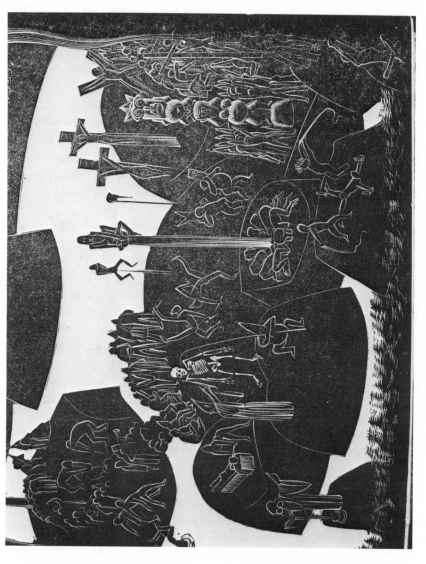

PLATE 1. Eric H. Kennington, "The Eternal Itch" (detail).
By permission of C. J. Kennington and the Henry E. Huntington Library and Art Gallery.

to me an impossible achievement."[24] A Royal Flying Corps aerial photograph of Mudowwara also appears within the text, at the close of Book VIII.

After the text and another map follows the great collection of color plates that were intended as "appendices or précis justificatives, rather than illustrations."[25] The plates were arranged differently in each volume to hinder, and perhaps intrigue, the bibliophiles, but a pattern still remains: Lawrence's photographs of Jidda; portraits of Englishmen, primarily by Kennington; a "buffer";[26] the Kennington Arab pastels; another buffer; the remaining English portraits; the "imaginative drawings" reflecting states of mind, Paul Nash's Cézannesque landscapes and Sydney Carline's "Bombing in Wadi Fara"; and Lawrence's photograph of Damascus. The book is then closed out decoratively with the rear endpaper "The World, the Flesh, the Devil," a woodcut by Kennington that Lawrence greatly admired.

Partially because of the literary nature of the artists who created these works, it might be expected that the visual art in *Seven Pillars* would serve more than just a decorative function. This indeed is the case. To varying degrees it represents a complement to the literary aspect of the book. First, on the book's overall, structural level, a correlation may be found. In a manuscript notebook at the Houghton Library, Lawrence delineates his initial plans for the book's structure in architectural terms.[27] In the published text itself, the revolt is likened to the building of a "seven pillared worthy house"[28] of freedom for the Arabs. This architectural metaphor is also present in the visual aspect of the book. The text closes with Book X, which is entitled "The House Is Perfected." A map follows, and then immediately the Appendix of illustrations begins, with Lawrence's five photographs of architecture-dominated street scenes in Jidda.[29] The photographs are so placed at Lawrence's insistence,[30] and may reflect an effort to reinforce the concept of the "house" of the revolt being perfected.

The book's basic page structure is also significant. William Morris once stated, and his admirer Lawrence may have agreed, that "the only work of art which surpasses a complete Medieval book is a complete Medieval building."[31] Morris went on to develop an analogy between books and architecture that became one of his most important design postulates: that books should become "architectural." Opposing pages of an open book must be regarded as a unit; the margins must increase in size from binding edge, to head, to fore, to tail; and decorations and "ornament must form as much a part of the page as the type itself."[32] While Lawrence did not adhere to all of Morris's principles in the production of *Seven Pillars*, he did follow this one.

Another structural principle of the literary *Seven Pillars*, and perhaps the most important, is its dramatic approach. In *The Confessions of T. E. Lawrence*, T. J. O'Donnell elaborates on this idea, interpreting the text in terms of Gustav Freytag's structure for a five-act play.[33] A dramatic function is also provided by the book's decorations. As Herbert Baker questioned when regarding some of the tailpieces at the ends of chapters: "Were they meant to relieve the tension of the drama, as the Fool's grim and gay humour in Shakespeare's tragedies? Or to express [Lawrence's] own sublime smile at the actors in the war-drama, whom he calls 'sentient puppets on God's stage?'"[34] A firm yes might be offered to both questions. The Kennington cartoons satisfy the first purpose, while the woodcuts of Blair Hughes-Stanton fulfill the second. Of the Kenningtons, "Wind" (*SP*, 320) and "A Miscarriage" (*SP*, 429) seem to be more obvious efforts at comic relief. In the Stanton works, the metaphysical element is pervasive in terms of general atmosphere, but in "The Sport of Kings" (*Seven Pillars*, 1926, p. 539) a "sentient puppet" is plainly depicted (plate 2).[35]

The Kennington comic drawings also reflect part of the wave/trough rhythm of the book's drama. Just as Lawrence interposed "flats" in the text before embarking on sections of relative excitement, so he inserted these drawings. For as Lawrence wrote to Kennington, "like the book itself, the pictures mustn't all be mountain peaks: it would be a better book if it had more soft and smooth places in it, where people could rest their minds before a new march: and the comic drawings will provide what I didn't."[36]

Just as these textual decorations serve a dramatic purpose, so does the collection of portraits gathered in the Appendix. If the book may be regarded, as Lawrence himself did, as "partly theatre,"[37] it is natural to expect a curtain call for the performers at drama's end. This is what the Appendix provides, as well as a complement to Lawrence's "summary descriptions"[38] of his performers.

Besides reflecting the overall structure and ebb and flow of *Seven Pillars*, the decorations also reflect more specific literary elements: themes, writing styles, motifs, and images.

PLATE 2. Blair Hughes-Stanton, "The Sport of Kings."
By permission of Blair Hughes-Stanton, Penelope Hughes-Stanton, and the Henry E. Huntington Library and Art Gallery.

Thematically, the idea of Lawrence straddling two cultures is central to *Seven Pillars*. He is represented as a "man who could see things through the veils at once of two customs, two educations, two environments."[39] This concept and its significance are delineated at length in Stephen Tabachnick's *T. E. Lawrence*. It is also reflected in the nature of two portraits of Lawrence. The first, a Kennington pastel (*SP*, facing p. 654), shows Lawrence the Westerner, the English colonial officer. The second, an Augustus John sketch from the Paris Peace Conference (*SP*, facing p. 610), shows the Arab sympathizer and leader of the revolt.

Stylistically, there are a number of variations in the literary *Seven Pillars*.[40] One is Lawrence's use of "self-deprecating humor."[41] In the decorative aspect of the book, this style is represented by Kennington's comic drawings. For besides providing comic relief or rest stops in the drama, they serve, as does Lawrence's irony, to help him, in Tabachnick's words, "keep a sense of who he is and what his position really amounts to."[42] Or, as Lawrence himself wrote about the drawings: "It's Kennington, pricking the vast bladder of my conceit. Hip, hip, hip,

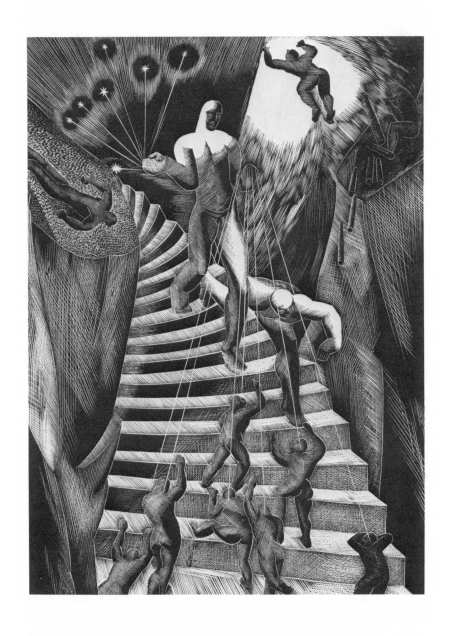

PLATE 3. Blair Hughes-Stanton, "Dedicatory Poem."
By permission of Blair Hughes-Stanton, Penelope Hughes-Stanton, and the Houghton Library,
Harvard University.

you see, & then a long fizz of escaping air before the poor frog could burst!"[43]

Another style of the written *Seven Pillars* is the reflective—embodied in Lawrence's reflections on metaphysical, theological, and psychological aspects of the revolt. It is perhaps this style that is most prominently displayed in the decorations of the book. On the obvious side stand the watercolor and pencil drawings by Kennington, tucked near the end of the Appendix. They are, as Lawrence wrote, "wonderful imaginative things in colour—drawings, Blake-like, of states of mind. One, illustrating dysentery, is as powerful a thing as I have ever set eyes on: & there is a lightning-coloured picture of the night over Tafas which is almost painful, in spite of its beauty."[44] These were meant to directly, though symbolically, represent Lawrence's introspection. Other reflections appear less blatant and are at times ciphered in pairs of drawings.

Lawrence's introspection regarding good and evil often takes the form of a conflict of angel versus beast in himself, as O'Donnell has pointed out. Lawrence's good side is depicted in Augustus John's sketch, which has been termed the "angelic" drawing. In contrast to this stands Kennington's "Cheshire Cat" sketch (reproduced in *T. E. Lawrence by His Friends*, facing p. 266), drawn during the Cairo Conference of 1921. Juxtaposed, the two works form a strikingly different pair. One is dominated by lightness, the other by darkness. The John is done with a few wisps of line on white paper, while the Kennington is bold white chalk on a black ground—the latter a distressing fact to the Arabs, who considered "the faces of the damned in hell [to be] black."[45] Together the works form a strong visual representation of the angel-versus-beast dichotomy in Lawrence. Yet, though it was drawn for *Seven Pillars*, the "Cheshire Cat" was eventually not included. "Reason: it was too obviously the spider in the web of its own spinning."[46] Lawrence's personal revelations could not be so obviously represented in visual terms when their literary counterparts were "written in cypher."[47] Thus, though the "Cheshire Cat" was rejected, a representation of the beast would be included in the book, but disguised in a cipher. It is most probable that the beast instead appears in Kennington's comic drawing "A Forced Landing" (*SP*, 304–5). As Lawrence wrote to Dick Knowles in 1927, "Once I fancied I was very near the

PLATE 4. William Roberts, "Appeasing a Tumult."
*By permission of J. D. Roberts, Sarah Roberts, and the Houghton Library,
Harvard University.*

angels, and the coming so abruptly to earth was a jar."[48] Several months earlier he had written to Charlotte Shaw that at the end of the revolt he "felt like Lucifer just after his *forced landing*."[49] When it is revealed that in a number of cases the titling of the drawings was done by Lawrence,[50] the idea that the comic "Forced Landing" is Lawrence's ciphered beast becomes plausible.

Closely related to the angelic personification is the literary image of Lawrence as Christ and the motif of crucifixion. Parallels in the visual also exist. William Roberts's stylized tailpiece "Appeasing a Tumult" (*Seven Pillars*, 1926, p. 347) shows a robed Lawrence bringing calm to several Arabs who kneel in reverential poses (plate 4). Yet these worshipers would be damned for their worship: "it was a theft of souls," Lawrence wrote, "to make others die in sincerity for my graven image."[51] Another drawing, by Kennington, pushes the Christ parallel further. Entitled "Strata" (plate 5) it appears near the end of the Appendix of illustrations. Referred to by Lawrence in his letters as the "snow-storm,"[52] it derives from the incident in chapters 88 and 89 where Lawrence brings gold to Zeid's troops through the force of an Edomite blizzard. While Lawrence's physical element struggles through the blizzard in immediate and the revolt in general terms, the spiritual element, godlike, takes it all in from the calm heights of a nearby

PLATE 5. Eric H. Kennington, "Strata."
By permission of C. J. Kennington and the Henry E. Huntington Library and Art Gallery.

mountain. In the act of physical sacrifice for the Arab cause, Lawrence emulates Christ, while emulating him also, as O'Donnell has observed, "in the parallels to Christ he establishes in his analysis of act."[53] As Lawrence wrote in *Seven Pillars*: "To endure for another in simplicity gave a sense of greatness. There was nothing loftier than a cross, from which to contemplate the world."[54] The drawing touched Lawrence deeply and, as Anthony Nutting has observed, he "was utterly amazed" by it "and kept repeating that he could not believe that anyone could have captured so completely what at times he had felt about himself during the desert campaign."[55]

Beyond the overall physical strain Lawrence suffered during the revolt, there stands the single incident of his night in Deraa. If we expand the Christ analogy, Lawrence's torture in Deraa represents his Passion. The only direct visual evidence of flagellation in the Subscribers' Edition appears on the book's front endpaper, where two small figures undergo beatings in the lower-right corner of the image. However, a more specific depiction of flagellation was in fact created for the book, one relating directly to Lawrence. Entitled "Torture" (plate 6), it is a pen-and-ink drawing by William Roberts which the artist intended as a chapter tailpiece for page 416 of the Subscribers' Edition. The work graphically depicts Lawrence's torture at Deraa, here by five Turks who obviously enjoy their work; it was rejected by either Lawrence or Kennington as inappropriate.[56] If indeed the drawing had been included on page 416, it would have preceded the Deraa chapter (80), which ends on page 429, and thus would have served as an undesirable warning to the reader of the event that would soon take place. Or, if it had been placed on page 429, the power of the chapter's closing would have been compromised. Rather the blank space that occurs—one of the largest such blanks in the book—is a much more successful solution. For chapter 80, no decoration would have been acceptable.

The culmination of the Christ parallel appears in the motif of crucifixion, a literary element of *Seven Pillars* that Lawrence readily acknowledged: "I did have that crucifixion motif in the back of my head. Christians often forget how many thousands of people have been crucified."[57] If the reader had forgotten, his memory is soundly jogged by the book's front endpaper, mentioned above. Entitled "The Eternal

PLATE 6. William Roberts, "Torture."
By permission of J. D. Roberts, Sarah Roberts, and the Houghton Library, Harvard University.

Itch," this woodcut by Kennington in one section depicts a number of figures in various stages of being crucified. Meanwhile, the link between Lawrence and crucifixion may perhaps be found in one of Kennington's drawings. Entitled "A Literary Method" (*SP*, 535), the drawing shows the entomologist author pinning characters to a literary collection board. All figures' limbs are arranged in the pose of crucifixion, and the central figure is Lawrence himself. The scene also thus presents a touch of irony in having Lawrence both the victim and the executor of the crucifixion.

With respect to smaller-scale literary elements—images and leitmotifs—visual parallels can also be found. The number seven, prominent of course in the title, is echoed in the front endpaper, which represents the "seven follies of man."[58] The image of the sword, which Meyers has deemed "a major leitmotif in the book,"[59] and which Lawrence himself expounded on in a letter to Eric Kennington,[60] appears

PLATE 7. William Roberts, "The Flashing Sword."
By permission of J. D. Roberts, Sarah Roberts, and the Houghton Library,
Harvard University.

as the first chapter tailpiece: "The Flashing Sword" by William Roberts (plate 7). Here the use of the sword takes on a phallic connotation, with the women who appear to the lower left in the drawing functioning as "machine[s] for muscular exercise."[61] The representation of human forms—both male and female—as machines in this drawing is typical of the art of Roberts, as it is of vorticist art in general. Roberts's art takes on an added significance when analyzed with respect to an important literary symbol in *Seven Pillars*: the machine.

Thomas O'Donnell has written that "The machine in the desert is the most extreme symbol of the triumph of Western values in Arabia."[62] And indeed the image of the machine thoroughly permeates *Seven Pillars* in one form or another: the British army is a machine; Arab heroism, as Stephen Tabachnick has observed, is "nothing more than a tool for winning the war for the British";[63] and Lawrence seeks to make the Arab Revolt "the engine of its own success."[64] Certainly the use of Roberts to do the lion's share of the tailpieces—almost precisely half of the total and twice that of any other artist—is appropriate. Kennington, who had a profound insight into many of the literary aspects of *Seven Pillars*, recognized the idea of the machine's encroachment on the desert. However, a comic drawing of his depicting that encroachment was rejected by Lawrence: "The picture of a tank pursuing an Arab wouldn't fit," he wrote the artist. "The exercise would be very beneficial for the Arab, & not dangerous at all."[65] Rather, the theme would be adumbrated by Roberts's vorticist style in the tailpieces.

O'Donnell rightly points out the compatibility of Lawrence's regard for the machine and the futurist manifesto of F. T. Marinetti.[66] But futurism was basically an Italian movement, and an English book devoted to a nationalistic theme would be, in a literary sense, inappropriately decorated by Italians. There was a smattering of English futurists, led by Nevinson, but their work was not as significant as that of Marinetti and his followers. The more prominent English equivalent of a "machine art" was, as mentioned earlier, vorticism. This coterie of English artists espoused the glorification of the mechanical with hard, geometrical abstractions, and represented the human body in mechanical forms. Their art followed the spirit of an Orick Johns poem:

> For behold the muscles of man—
> They are piston-rods; they are cranes,
> hydraulic presses, powder magazines.[67]

Roberts was intimately associated with vorticism, and his art reflected its precepts. His work for *Seven Pillars* is representative of his style. In a plate for the Appendix, "Night Bombing," the figures of the British soldiers are constructed from metallic-surfaced cylinders, while their conical tents are directly reminiscent of the geometric symbol that Ezra Pound used to name the style—the vortex. Similarly, the style was applied to the Arab army in "Camel March" (*SP*, facing p. 308), a lightly pigmented wash drawing that appears, in the Subscribers' Edition, as a plate at the end of Book IV. And in "Mucking In" (plate 8) (*Seven Pillars*, 1926, p. 280), the Arabs around the feast tray are analyzed into abstract geometrical forms whose patterns of piston-rod limbs are woven into a typical "mechanized ballet."[68] Man and his groupings have become machines.

As mentioned earlier, Lawrence greatly admired the machine-inspired art of the vorticists. By choosing Roberts to do the bulk of the tailpieces, he seems to be directly carrying out an aesthetic dictate put

PLATE 8. William Roberts, "Mucking In."
By permission of J. D. Roberts, Sarah Roberts, and the Houghton Library, Harvard University.

forth by Wyndham Lewis in "A Review of Contemporary Art": "In any heroic, that is energetic representation of men to-day the immense power of machines will be reflected."[69] And by doing so, Lawrence linked the visual aspect of his book with both its literary counterpart and the time period in which it was produced.

The gain of contemporaneity through the use of machine art underscores the concept of the generation of 1914 and the relation of *Seven Pillars* to it. Further reminders may be found in some of the more obscure chapter tailpieces, such as the last textual decoration in the book, Kennington's woodcut entitled "A Rabbit." In *T. E. Lawrence by His Friends*, Herbert Baker relates an explanatory incident.

> [Lawrence's] state of mind in relation to much post-war art can best be explained, perhaps, by his own comments on some of the illustrations in the *Seven Pillars of Wisdom*. As we turned over its pages he would explain their meanings; but of some of the stranger wood-cuts at the ends of chapters he would say, "I don't know what they mean; they're mad; the war was mad."[70]

It is the disorientation of the war generation visually presented, a goal that Lawrence may well have had in mind when initially offering the artistic commissions for his guild years before. And it further cements the bond between the literary and visual aspects of *Seven Pillars*.

A letter from Lawrence to Edward Garnett crystallizes the conception of the decorations, though not mentioning them at all. The letter discusses the text of *Seven Pillars*, and focuses on the author's use of literary style. His likening of it to "ornament" was prophetic, as the style's purposes seem reflective of the function that the book's visual ornament would later serve. Lawrence wrote:

> So far for the architecture of the book:—and now for the ornament: the style of it. As you, a critic, have seen, the thing is intensely sophisticated: built up of hints from other books, full of these echoes to enrich or side-track or repeat my motives. It's too elaborate and conscious a construction to admit simplicity—or rather, if I were limpid or direct anywhere people would (should) feel it a false stillness.[71]

The decorations are sophisticated, eclectic, supplementary to motives, and in being decorations rather than illustrations, indirect in presenting their messages. In sum, the visual aspect of *Seven Pillars* is intimately entwined with its literary inspiration.

The success of the visual design of the book will be examined later. However, it must be stressed at this point that regardless of the extent of that success the Subscribers' Edition of *Seven Pillars of Wisdom* is an important visual document. In it is preserved a partial cross section of English art of the 1920s, a period, as Dennis Farr has written, of "uncertainty"[72] in the arts resulting from the tumult of the previous decade. The work from the older, more classical draftsmen is represented in the portraits by William Rothenstein and William Nicholson. Augustus John's three portraits show his position in art as William Gaunt saw it: "a sort of interim between a world of tradition and the world of change."[73] Eric Kennington's independent modernity is preserved in his brilliant series of pastel portraits. The vorticist art of William Roberts and Edward Wadsworth stands as representative of London's avant-garde artists and their move toward the glorification of the machine. Also, there are the constructivist landscapes of Paul Nash; the rhythmic figure groupings of Cosmo Clark; the metaphysical woodcuts of Blair Hughes-Stanton; and the independent styles of Henry Lamb and the remainder of the young artists who contributed. Not all of the artists represented in *Seven Pillars* came to be regarded as masters, but it is precisely that fact that secures the importance of the Subscribers' Edition as an art historical document.

In evaluating the overall visual success of the Subscribers' *Seven*

Pillars, it is necessary to consider two factors: the quality of craftsmanship involved in the production and the strength of the overall design. Certainly the level of craftsmanship of the printers and platemakers was very high in *Seven Pillars*. Manning Pike's presswork on the text was quite admirable, as Lawrence recognized, terming it "glorious work" and "as good presswork as has ever been done."[74] On rare occasions, chapter tailpieces tend to muddy in certain areas, but this is usually the fault of the artwork itself. William Roberts used an overly fine hatching technique on some of his drawings, particularly in some that required significant reduction to fit their allotted spaces, and this resulted in blotting. Also, an examination of the original drawings in the Houghton Library reveals that some of the pencil underdrawing was done too darkly and consequently picked up when printed. But in general Pike's presswork was excellent. Similarly, Whittingham and Griggs's platemaking showed a high degree of craftsmanship. The Kennington pastels are nothing short of spectacular in their presentation. A great deal of their success was undoubtedly due to Kennington's stringently critical eye in evaluating the proofs, but this does not detract from their beauty.

While the craftsmanship of production in *Seven Pillars* is excellent, the strength of the design is not always of equal caliber. The typographical structure of the pages and the Caslon type that composes it are pleasing to the eye, as are the decorative initials. For the most part, the illustrations within the text are well placed and "architectural," a result aided by the fact that Roberts at least was given page proofs on which to fit his decorations. Also, some innovative concepts—such as Lawrence's idea to have no margins on most of the portraits—appear to have been successful. Yet others were not. Lawrence took particular delight in the awkwardness of the Kennington comic drawings: "Of course they don't fit the page, or the style of print: why they wouldn't be screamingly funny if they did."[75] This evaluation may be overly personalized, with the gulf between drawing and page design seemingly being too great to be effective. Also, the variety of artistic styles in the decorations hinders the book's overall visual impression. Lawrence consciously sought this variety, with at least part of his intention being revealed in a letter to Kennington regarding several works of which he believed Kennington would disapprove: "and yet, think how many ingredients (by themselves, like suet, uneatable) may combine into a tooth-aching plum pudding."[76] A yearning to "breed variety"[77] also appeared in the placement of Edward Wadsworth's decorative initials. For this express purpose, every page in Books IV and VII began with one; in others, the pattern varies. The effort to foster the diverse leaves the book without a sense of unity, a sense that William Morris found paramount to good book design. Bruce Rogers, himself inspired by the Kelmscott Press, took leave from Morris's aesthetic on many occasions but still endeavored to maintain a unity of design. While Lawrence did not endeavor to follow Morrisonian principles strictly in designing *Seven Pillars*, the end product would have been more successful if a greater concern had been shown toward creating a "harmonious whole."[78] Thus while the book is in large part visually pleasing, it does possess a significant imperfection.

In order to reach conclusions regarding Lawrence from this evidence, we must first understand what his role in the production was. Despite Lawrence's intimation (*SP*, 19) that Kennington was the guiding force behind the book's artwork, it seems that Kennington only nominally served as the edition's art editor. Rather, his task seems to have been more one of contributing artist and overseer of proofs. Judging from Lawrence's letters to Kennington and Manning Pike, Lawrence more than anyone else was responsible for the ultimate decorative "look" of the edition. It was Lawrence who decided upon an Appendix of illustrations without borders, and Lawrence who chose to publish the "comic drawings," a number of which were simply quick cartoon jests executed by Kennington in his correspondence. And it was Lawrence who, to some extent at least, guided several of the artists by suggesting compositional structures for their chapter tailpieces.[79] Thus, while a thorough understanding of the exact nature of Lawrence's and Kennington's duties regarding the visual design of *Seven Pillars* may never be known, it seems that the more influential "art editor" was Lawrence.

If this is the case, we may now assess Lawrence's artistic abilities. Certainly in a few components of *Seven Pillars*' design Lawrence's pictorial sensibilities appear rather strong. The use of illustrations without margins in the Appendix is effective. Also, Lawrence's suggested compositions for tailpieces—directed primarily to Roberts and Hughes-Stanton—were sound. Compositionally, in fact, Lawrence seems to have possessed a definite talent, as witnessed by his photographs of

Jidda. But these are isolated elements of the book's design, and an evaluation of Lawrence's abilities must be made with regard to the overall impression the volume creates. As Lawrence readily admitted, he never had or acquired the power of expression in a visual form, with the possible exception of his work in photography. He regarded the pictorial arts from the point of view of an "appreciative onlooker." His genius was literary, not pictorial. In approaching the visual problem of creating a decorative format for his book, he attempted to create a visual sophistication to parallel the book's literary complexity. But without the power of a visual technique, multiplicity seems to have replaced complexity as Lawrence looked at a visual problem in literary terms. The resultant diversity would have been very difficult to synthesize into a unified whole; but for Lawrence, who owned a "self-confessed weakness in synthesis,"[80] it would have been nearly impossible. The result embodied in *Seven Pillars* bears this out.

Vyvyan Richards has written that "*Seven Pillars* was a private study [of Lawrence] of the most penetrating intimacy and he could not bear to have it in the hands of any but a chosen few. . . ."[81] Beyond the written confessions *Seven Pillars* contains, the book's visual imperfection may in fact inadvertently reveal one of Lawrence's most intimate and personally disappointing deficiencies. Yet, even in this failure, Lawrence, on the strength of the pure ambition of his book's design, is frequently more interesting than are other book designers in their successes.

N·O·T·E·S

1. *L*, 360.

2. See Vyvyan Richards's article in *T. E. Lawrence by His Friends*, ed. A. W. Lawrence (London: Cape, 1937), 383–92. Hereafter this book will be cited as *Friends*.

3. Philip M. O'Brien, *T. E. Lawrence and Fine Printing* (Buffalo, N.Y.: Hillside Press, 1980), 3.

4. *L*, 295.

5. *Friends*, 263.

6. As Lawrence mentions in his list of illustrations in the 1926 and 1935 editions, he was able to "get to work only some of the artists" he respected, and some of these disappointed him. Stanley Spencer, for example, did not fulfill his commission to

portray Air Marshal Sir Geoffrey Salmond. The greatest disappointment to Lawrence, however, was in the failure of Wyndham Lewis, an artist whom he greatly admired. Lawrence's correspondence with Kennington in the University of Texas Humanities Research Center (hereafter HRC) is rife with questionings over Lewis's "silence." The disappointment later turned to bitterness. (See *T. E. Lawrence to His Biographers Robert Graves and Liddell Hart* [Garden City, N.Y.: Doubleday, 1963] 1:166.) Lewis's account of the incident is recorded in his *Blasting and Bombardiering* (Berkeley and Los Angeles: University of California Press, 1967), 244.

7. T. E. Lawrence, Letter to Paul Nash, 3 August 1922, Dartmouth College Library.

8. T. E. Lawrence, *Letters from T. E. Shaw to Bruce Rogers* (privately printed, 1933), "To Bruce Rogers," 24 May 1929.

9. *T. E. Lawrence to His Biographers*, 1:76.

10. *L*, 408.

11. John Mack, *A Prince of Our Disorder* (Boston: Little, Brown, 1976), 335. Quote from Paul Nash to Gordon Bottomley, 12 September 1922; quoted in Anthony Bertram, *Paul Nash* (London: Faber and Faber, 1955), 112.

12. Robert Wohl, *The Generation of 1914* (Cambridge, Mass.: Harvard University Press, 1979), 208.

13. Ibid., 119.

14. Ibid., 210.

15. John Rothenstein, *Summer's Lease* (New York: Holt, Rinehart and Winston, 1965), 65.

16. Vyvyan Richards, *Portrait of T. E. Lawrence* (London: Cape, 1936), 190.

17. As examples: the dadaists, constructivists, surrealists, and the Bauhaus group.

18. William C. Wees, *Vorticism and the English Avant-Garde* (Toronto: University of Toronto Press, 1972), 212.

19. Dennis Farr, *English Art 1870–1940* (Oxford: Clarendon Press, 1978), 249.

20. *SP*, 19. When the 1926 text is referred to, it will be called either the Subscribers' Edition or *Seven Pillars*, 1926. *SP* will refer to the 1935 Cape edition.

21. The illustrations are listed in the Subscribers' Edition between pages xix and xxii. There are several aberrations in the list. One, the misidentification of Roberts as the artist of Kennington's "Gad-fly," was corrected by Lawrence. Others, however, remain: two drawings by Paul Nash, "The Prophet's Tomb" (pp. 92, 644) and "A Garden" (pp. 208, 607), are listed as appearing twice. Both appear but once, on the later pages listed. The only drawing that appears twice is Roberts's "As-hab"—on pp. 460 and 591. Also, the Kennington drawing "Prickly Pear," which is placed near the beginning of the Appendix, is not listed.

22. T. E. Lawrence, Letter to Eric Kennington, 20 July 1926, HRC.

23. T. E. Lawrence, Letter to Eric Kennington, n.d., HRC.

24. *Letters from T. E. Shaw to Bruce Rogers*, "To Bruce Rogers," 10 October 1928.

25. *T. E. Lawrence to His Biographers*, 1:56.

26. T. E. Lawrence, Letter to Eric Kennington, n.d., HRC. The "buffer" drawings were, first, Roberts's "Night Bombing," and, second, Clark's "At Akaba." The drawings in essence segregated the English and Arab portraits. Within these segregated

units the plates were variously arranged for the different copies to make each unique. It must be stressed, however, that I can only confirm that the scheme holds true for the copies examined in preparing this essay—namely, those at the Huntington Library and Houghton Library. It is suspected, however, that these observations are valid for other copies of the edition as well.

27. Jeffrey Meyers, *The Wounded Spirit* (London: Martin Brian and O'Keefe, 1973), 74.

28. *SP*, 5.

29. These photographs, and the one of Damascus, are the only visual images of Lawrence's making in the book. Significantly, they represent perhaps the only visual medium and subject matter in which Lawrence showed a facility of expression. The architect Herbert Baker, in whose Barton Street rooms much of the book was written, found that "The artist in [Lawrence] is shown in that book in the composition of the photographic views of the street-scenes in Jidda" (*Friends*, 251). An architect's prejudice for architectural images perhaps, but Lawrence too found a significance in the photographs, and of a more literary nature: "My views [in *Seven Pillars*] are like my photographs of Jidda: the edges, even of the sharpest, are just modulated off, so that you can't put a pin point on them. Drawn, not in line, but in tone. Atmospheric." (T. E. Lawrence, Letter to Charlotte Shaw, 10 June 1927; excerpt quoted in Thomas J. O'Donnell, *The Confessions of T. E. Lawrence* [Athens: Ohio University Press, 1979], 79.)

30. T. E. Lawrence, Letter to Eric Kennington, 31 August 1926, HRC.

31. Susan Otis Thompson, *American Book Design and William Morris* (New York: R. R. Bowker, 1977), 228. (Quoted from May Morris, *William Morris: Artist, Writer, Socialist*, vol. 1 [New York: Russell and Russell, 1966], "The Woodcuts of Gothic Books," 318–38.)

32. Ibid., 229.

33. O'Donnell, *The Confessions of T. E. Lawrence*, 43.

34. *Friends*, 250–51.

35. For a literally specific image of "sentient puppets," see *The Woodcut: An Annual*, 1927. The fourth plate in the appendix of "15 Contemporary Woodcuts" is a Hughes-Stanton print executed for *Seven Pillars*, which, for unknown reasons, was not included in the published edition (plate 3).

36. *L*, 372.

37. *L*, 775.

38. *SP*, 19.

39. *SP*, 32.

40. Meyers, *The Wounded Spirit*, 85.

41. Stephen E. Tabachnick, *T. E. Lawrence* (Boston: Twayne, 1978), 35.

42. Ibid., 105.

43. *L*, 469.

44. *L*, 373.

45. *Friends*, 266.

46. *Friends*, 266.

47. *L*, 366.

48. *L*, 554.

49. Quoted in O'Donnell, 87. Italics mine.

50. T. E. Lawrence, Letter to Manning Pike, n.d., private collection.

51. *SP*, 550.

52. *L*, 372.

53. O'Donnell, *The Confessions of T. E. Lawrence*, 161.

54. *SP*, 551.

55. Anthony Nutting, *Lawrence of Arabia* (New York: Clarkson N. Potter, 1961), 243–44.

56. Ironically the drawing that replaced it on p. 416 was "A Jolly Evening."

57. To Charlotte Shaw, 31 December 1928, excerpt quoted in O'Donnell, *The Confessions of T. E. Lawrence*, 16.

58. *Friends*, 534.

59. Meyers, *The Wounded Spirit*, 72.

60. *L*, 372.

61. *SP*, 508. Considering that "there was nothing female in the Arab movement, but the camels," Roberts's tailpieces seem to contain too many women. In addition to "The Flashing Sword," women appear in, among others, "Male and Female" (p. 119), "The Little Less" (p. 372), and "Dhaif Allah" (p. 212) of the Subscribers' Edition.

62. O'Donnell, *The Confessions of T. E. Lawrence*, 99.

63. Tabachnick, *T. E. Lawrence*, 83.

64. *SP*, 276.

65. T. E. Lawrence, Letter to Eric Kennington, n.d., HRC.

66. O'Donnell, *The Confessions of T. E. Lawrence*, 102.

67. Wees, *Vorticism and the English Avant-Garde*, 84; reprinted from Ezra Pound's *Catholic Anthology, 1914–1915* (London: Elkin Mathews, 1915).

68. William Gaunt, *A Concise History of English Painting* (London: Thames and Hudson, 1964), 224. Roberts's approach to such drawings seems to have been to concentrate on building rhythms and then to fill out the mechanical forms. Many preparatory sketches for *Seven Pillars'* drawings (as well as most of the drawings themselves) are housed in the Houghton Library. They are executed in charcoal or conte and clearly show the structural approach Roberts used.

69. Wees, *Vorticism and the English Avant-Garde*, 203; reprinted from Wyndham Lewis, "A Review of Contemporary Art," *Blast*, no. 2 (July 1915): 44.

70. *Friends*, 250.

71. *L*, 371.

72. Farr, *English Art 1870–1940*, 248.

73. Gaunt, *A Concise History of English Painting*, 207.

74. T. E. Lawrence, Letter to Eric Kennington, 7 March 1925, HRC.

75. *L*, 469.

76. T. E. Lawrence, Letter to Eric Kennington, 23 January 1924, HRC.

77. T. E. Lawrence, Letter to Manning Pike, 21 October 1925, private collection.

78. Thompson, *American Book Design and William Morris*, 228.
79. T. E. Lawrence, Letter to Eric Kennington, 1 April 1926, HRC.
80. *T. E. Lawrence to His Biographers*, 2:172.
81. Richards, *Portrait of T. E. Lawrence*, 191.

T. E. Lawrence: Strategist

KONRAD MORSEY

*Translated by Linda Gration
and Stephen E. Tabachnick*

In the critical examination of T. E. Lawrence's career, his importance as a strategist is particularly disputed. Controversial opinions range from that of the military author B. H. Liddell Hart, who ranks Lawrence with the great generals,[1] through the attitude of the political scientist Walter Laqueur, who regards Lawrence's military successes largely as the product of his literary ability,[2] to the debunking of Richard Aldington, who dismisses Lawrence's conduct of the Arab war as plain "banditry."[3] The discovery of the truth about this issue is important because it is precisely his actions in the Arab Revolt of 1916–18 that have given Lawrence the title and fame of Lawrence of Arabia.[4] Does he justly bear this title of honor, or is it the result of an exaggerated legend?

So long as the documents of World War I were kept sealed in the London Public Record Office, we were forced to rely to a great extent on Lawrence's own description of his strategic principles as elucidated above all in the much-quoted thirty-third chapter of *Seven Pillars of Wisdom*. But because Lawrence wrote his book after the successful conclusion of the uprising, when his fame was already established, it is difficult for the historian to decide where Lawrence refers to contemporary sources and where he made judgments after the event.[5] And the problem of the evaluation of Lawrence's military career is further complicated by the autobiographical nature of *Seven Pillars*, which makes no claim whatsoever to be an official account of the war. Indeed, the book was conceived by Lawrence as a literary work of art in which the author wanted to explore his talent as a writer.[6] In the introductory chapter Lawrence expressly stresses his partiality and even admits to changing the names of some of the "characters."

Lawrence consciously structured the work in order to make clear the inevitable triumph of the rebellion, as the book's subtitle and introductory statements make clear.[7] Lawrence based his feeling of the inevitability of this triumph on a theory of guerrilla warfare that he tells us he devised in March 1917 during a several-day period of illness in Wadi Ais. On reviewing the ideas of great military thinkers from Saxe through Clausewitz, Lawrence concluded that their strategic-tactical concepts did not apply to the revolt in Arabia because war and revolution are fundamentally different things. The orthodox schools of war had taught that the deciding factor in battle was the destruction of the enemy forces. But to fight modern battles with the poor armament and primitive skills of Beduin warriors would have been suicidal. Lawrence therefore chose another starting point. He no longer took conventional strategy and tactics seriously into account: "They seemed only points of view from which to ponder the elements of war, the Algebraical element of things, a Biological element of lives and the Psychological element of ideas" (SP, 192).

The most important deductions from Lawrence's thoughts can be concisely summarized as follows: (1) No target should be offered the enemy. His attacks should be like stabs in the dark. This goal could be achieved by distributing the Arab forces over the whole countryside. The key idea here is attack-in-depth on the most extensive plane possible. (2) Since the enemy's weakest point is supply, it is not important to kill as many soldiers as possible but, rather, to destroy all accessible war materiel of the enemy while avoiding casualties on the Arab side as far as possible. (3) The Arabs fight with conviction for the ideal of freedom. They are individual fighters, not soldiers of the line. Therefore they must be morally well armed. Not only the active fighting Beduin should be considered in this respect. The entire civilian population must be included in the propaganda effort so that they become at least passively sympathetic to the rebel cause. To the same degree, the enemy army must be influenced by propaganda in order to weaken its morale. To sum up, the trump card of the Arab irregulars is mobility and speed. Surprise attacks on the weakest links of the enemy defense chain of bases must be effected; the Arabs should under no circumstances become involved in a regular battle. "Tip and run; not pushes but strokes!" should be the motto of the intangible specter of the Arab forces.[8]

When Lawrence crystallized these ideas in the early part of 1917, the uprising was already ten months old, but he had been present on the scene of the war for only six months. In October 1916 he had gone to Jidda, commissioned by the military intelligence service in Cairo and its newly founded Arab Bureau there. He went in order to collect reliable information about the complicated state of the revolt along with exact military-topographical reconnaissance data, and not on holiday as he claims in *Seven Pillars*;[9] and he confronted the following military situation. After an initially successful but hastily organized and, for the British, sudden beginning—which saw Sherif Hussein expel the Turks from Mecca in June 1916—the revolt was frustrated by an abortive attempt to capture Medina and actually became threatened by premature failure owing to a Turkish counterattack.

The English found themselves faced with the awkward alternatives of either saving the badly organized revolt (which they had desired and encouraged for two years) by sending a brigade of British troops to Rabegh or of having to suffer the loss of prestige that would follow the defeat of the allied Arabs. As a result of his mission, which included reconnaissance and detailed analysis, Lawrence solved this Rabegh crisis to the satisfaction of British Commander in Chief Archibald Murray and High Commissioner Sir Henry McMahon. Lawrence inveighed against sending British soldiers, and instead offered the more comfortable alternative of indirectly supporting the revolt with instructors, auxiliary technical equipment, and arms shipments. As an unintentional consequence of his suggestions, he was sent back to Arabia as liaison officer to the Emir Feisal, who of all the four sons of the Sherif bore the greatest burden of the fighting against the Turks.

Lawrence had scarcely returned to the Arabs when he experienced the successful climax of the crisis. The Turks retreated without a fight from Yenbo, and the initiative was recovered by the Arabs with the capture of the seaport Wejh in January 1917. As a result of this action, Medina—although the Arabs could not capture it—became until and even after the end of the war an isolated stronghold, connected to the front in Syria only by the umbilical cord of the Hejaz railway.[10] The

Hejaz war was brought to a successful conclusion with the unexpected (by both Turks and British) capture of the port of Akaba from the land side (summer 1917); this capture was the fruit of an arduous 600-kilometer Arab march through the desert, in which Lawrence had taken part.[11]

To a certain degree, with this success the Arabs had made their unorthodox desert campaign respectable in the eyes of British headquarters. Almost simultaneously there occurred a change in British command when General Murray was succeeded by General Edmund Allenby, who was to prove of great use to the Arab revolutionaries. Allenby recognized and utilized the advantages of the capture of Akaba for his military planning. According to the official British account of the war, "He at once realised that it would alter the conditions of the desert war."[12] The new task that devolved upon the Arabs as a result of this thinking was flank protection during the intended English breakthrough into Palestine. This task demanded the coordination of both theaters of operations, and in November 1917 a Hejaz Operations Staff called "Hedgehog" was formed in British headquarters. This new organization resulted in Feisal's troops having to transfer themselves from King Hussein's jurisdiction to that of Allenby.

The chief command over the remaining operations in the Hejaz, where Medina and isolated railroad posts continued to remain in the hands of the Turks, stayed with the former Sirdar and new High Commissioner, Wingate. Yet, from the British angle, this area was in future to be granted only subordinate importance, first because of the geographical perspective ("its capital and government were as far from the scene of projected operations as London from Petrograd"[13]) and second, as a result of the strategic and tactical situation. From then on, the Turks here found themselves completely on the defensive.

Because of its completely different geographical and cultural quality, the Syrian theater of operations demanded a new strategy. The underlying reason for "the problem which faced us" in Syria that Lawrence stresses is the cultural difference between nomads of the desert and the urbanized dwellers of the Levant: the problem was "one of character—the learning to become civil" (SP, 328).

In addition to this new sociocultural adaptation, the British realized that a change in the method of fighting would be necessary in Syria. The military effectiveness of the Arabs had been increased as a result of augmented materiel and technical support from the British and the seconding of actual British and French detachments. The Arabs were now called upon to perform systematically coordinated operations, but, according to Lawrence, the nomadic Beduin were not suited for this. The consequence was the extensive renunciation of the irregular tribal warriors in favor of Feisal's regular army, which in the course of the war in Wejh was made up mainly of Turkish army deserters of Arab extraction.[14] However, Lawrence continued to use some raiding detachments made up of various, even rival, tribes. To prevent dissension, warring tribes were variously divided and mixed and appointed according to district.

Lawrence compared the maneuver war that he now conducted with naval operations: "Camel raiding parties, self-contained like ships, might cruise confidently along the enemy's cultivation-frontier, sure of an unhindered retreat into their desert-element which the Turks could not explore" (*SP*, 337). Its tactical principle was defined by the formula "tip and run: not pushes, but strokes. . . . We should use the smallest force in the quickest time at the farthest place" (*SP*, 337). As a result of this principle, not the mass of fighters but the individual man determines the unit's power of attack: "Our ideal should be to make our battle a series of single combats, our ranks a happy alliance of agile commanders-in-chief" (*SP*, 340).[15]

The Arabs achieved striking military successes with the aid of this new strategy—above all, the capture of Tafileh, the encirclement of Deraa, and the defeat of the Turkish Fourth Army during its retreat. The greatest victory of course was the eventual seizure of Damascus. After the revolt was successfully concluded in this way, Lawrence left the Middle East and a short time later became, owing to the lectures of the American journalist Lowell Thomas, a hero of the desert surrounded by legends: Lawrence of Arabia.

While writing his lectures in the early postwar years, Thomas could not suspect the evolution of the "uncrowned king of the desert" into the simple soldier Ross/Shaw, a development that, however, did not impair the fascination of Lawrence's personality. As far as Thomas was concerned, Lawrence had earned his title of honor with his achievements during the Arab Revolt. But subsequent critics have called Lawrence a swindler who "gives an account, in the first person and as supposed victor, of battles in the First World War which were fought by other generals and at which Lawrence was not even a spectator."[16] In attacking Lawrence, critics frequently make the mistake of assessing his personal military ability in terms of the debatable value of the Arab uprising to the British Palestine campaign. Aldington, for instance, writes that "you will see . . . how exaggerated are the claims that the 'Arab Revolt' and Lawrence's military activities (whatever they may have been) had a decisive or even considerable effect on the war."[17] Apart from the fact that there are many authoritative descriptions of the revolt as definitely valuable to the general English victory over the Turks, a just assessment should not measure Lawrence's achievement with reference to the wider war.[18] Instead, we should find out how important and skillful his role was in the "side-show of a side-show" (as Lawrence himself called the Arabian theater of operations) in which he found himself. Lawrence himself wanted his contribution to be understood and evaluated in this way.[19]

Robert Asprey sees the whole situation correctly when he writes that "Lawrence and his Arabs were fighting a separate war, a carefully defined war of insurrection that, although dependent on British arms and finances, helped Allenby enormously."[20] We can check Lawrence's military achievements definitively by means of the official documents that became available with the opening of British archives in the late 1960s. And the War Office documents, "Cabinet Papers," and the Foreign Office war documents—among which the "Arab Bureau Papers" are of particular importance—verify unequivocally that Lawrence's positive description of the Arab Revolt and his part in it in *Seven Pillars of Wisdom* is to a great extent historically correct.

Among the many British advisers in Arabia, Lawrence occupied an outstanding position. The capture of Akaba, which made the Arabs important to the British Palestine Army as flank protection, marks the beginning of his important role. As a result of this victory, Lawrence came into the foreground, since as liaison officer he alone had the difficult task of coordinating the joint strategy of Allenby's headquarters and Feisal's northern army. Even before the post-Akaba period, Clayton, the head of British intelligence in Cairo, had judged that "The value of Lawrence, in the position *which he has made for himself with Feisal* is enormous, and it is fully realised that if we could find suitable men to act in the same way with Ali and Abdulla it would be invaluable."[21] And even one of Lawrence's contemporary critics, Vickery, recognized without envy that "Lawrence with Feisal is of inestimable value."[22] In fact, Lawrence's role after the capture of Akaba and after his secret excursion into Syria became so decisive that British plans of attack in Palestine were changed in favor of Lawrence's plan of action.[23] General Allenby himself was convinced that "The advantages offered by Arab co-operation on lines proposed by Captain Lawrence are, in my opinion, of such importance that no effort should be spared to reap full benefit therefrom."[24]

More detailed illustration of these assessments is given in Mark Sykes's commentary to the War Cabinet. Sykes describes Lawrence's secret excursion as marking an epoch in the Arab Revolt:

> The exploit of Captain Lawrence gains in importance. This officer's extraordinary performance shows signs of having set alight the Arab movement in Syria, and so giving the Turks anxiety in regard to the communications on which their forces depend for supplies. This is an important change in situation. Hitherto our operations in Sinai and near Gaza have added to the safety of the King of Hejaz; his followers and sympathisers, under the stimulus of Captain Lawrence's personality are giving now a material contribution to the operations of the Egyptian forces.[25]

Clayton comments on Sykes's statement by writing, "Lawrence is of course essential and unique."[26]

During the subsequent course of the uprising, Lawrence's star rose even higher. The eyewitness A. S. Kirkbride remembers his first meeting with Lawrence:

> The senior British officer was a Lieutenant Colonel P. Joyce but another member of staff, Major (later Colonel) T. E. Lawrence, was stealing the limelight and acting as though he was independent of local control. Apparently, Lawrence's original role had been to act as liaison officer. . . . But, owing to the distinguished part he had played in the capture of Aqabah, he had obtained direct access to the Commander in Chief and had thereby established a position in which he was able to exercise great influence.[27]

On the Arab side, Nouri Al Said, one of the central figures in the Arab Revolt and later defense minister in Iraq, has testified that "It was possible for Lawrence to understand at first instance the Arabs better than any other Briton who worked for the Arab cause."[28] C. S. Jarvis, who lived among the Arabs for eighteen years, illuminates further Lawrence's success with them: "The fact of the matter is that Lawrence's many-sided activities were forced upon him, not because he was deficient of capable British assistants—as an actual fact he had many—but because the Arab, being a man of one idea, had no faith in anybody but the queer forceful character that had caught their fancy— 'El Aurens.' "[29]

Lawrence's preeminent position is perhaps documented best in his self-confident letter of 27 August 1917 to his superior, Clayton: "However I take it that no modification of the policy agreed upon in Cairo will be decided upon, without my being given an opportunity of putting forward my views in detail."[30] Furthermore, it is striking that suddenly many different people stress that a given suggestion was put forward only after consultation with Major Lawrence. Finally, in the last phase of the revolt, the War Cabinet concerned itself repeatedly with Lawrence's merits and considered how it could best honor his "valuable services."[31]

Lawrence's special place vis-à-vis the Arabs is highlighted by a comparison with the complaints about the difficulties of leading Arabs contained in Hejaz-Operations-Staff colleagues' reports. We find a repeated complaint about conditions of work and the shortcomings of the Arabs in military terms. As Major Vickery wrote in a postwar article, the British felt that the Arabs were suited for plundering rather than for fighting.[32] "Bimbashi" Garland, another colleague of Lawrence's, and the Arabs' instructor in explosives, summarizes the reproaches of the Arabs' British advisers in a letter of August 1917 to Colonel Wilson. Garland writes that under no circumstances should one imagine being able to exercise any form of control over the Arabs or being generally welcome among them. He says that he was treated in many cases by Sherif Nasir as one of his slaves. If one levels criticism, one comes up against a silent wall of defensiveness and makes oneself unpopular. The only practicable way to handle the Arabs, concludes Garland, is therefore to praise all their work on principle whether it be well or badly carried out. Perhaps hinting at Lawrence, he continues: "It is not given to every British officer to be able to sink his identity or to see the Arabs always through rosy glasses, and those of us who cannot help but draw attention to waste, neglect and disobedience, must not expect to remain long popular with the rank and file."[33] Captain Ormsby-Gore, a co-worker of Lawrence's for a time in the Arab Bureau in Cairo, therefore sees the problem correctly when he states in an early postwar article that the British had difficulties in finding people such as Lawrence who were "particularly gifted" in getting along with the Arabs and who "have got the feeling of the Middle East in their blood."[34]

In retrospect, how can we explain Lawrence's success without resorting to generalities about his exceptional position and his special talents? The main reason for this success resides in the fact that Lawrence understood the Arab Revolt not as a military campaign in the sense of a usual war but as a national movement,[35] which he successfully pursued with the aid of a strategy of guerrilla warfare. Because of this unconventional approach, he almost insured himself a lack of understanding on the part of regular army officers because, as G. B. Shaw later commented ironically, the camels of Lawrence's men were not even fed according to regulations.[36]

As has already been mentioned, Lawrence claims to have conceived this theory of guerrilla warfare during his illness in Wadi Ais and to have hurriedly written it down (SP, 196). Proof of this assertion cannot be produced to this day. Direct reference to the gestation of Lawrence's strategy can be found neither in the documents of the Public Record Office nor in the manuscripts in the British Library. Lawrence's strategic conception appears for the first time and in polished form in his October 1920 essay "The Evolution of a Revolt," which was written with a clear propagandistic intent.[37] Lawrence's critics therefore attribute no importance to these notes for the time of the Arab Revolt, "because they amount to no more than ink on paper, but also because they were written down five full years after the date of his stay at Wadi Ais."[38] However, this criticism is not convincing. When Lawrence transferred this strategic theory to *Seven Pillars*, he merely systematized and generalized it, as he himself admits in a footnote: "the argument has been compressed into an abstract form," and in this literary retrospection he, in his own words, generalized strategic problems which he originally thought of "mainly in terms of Hejaz" (SP, 196).

The fact that Lawrence did develop his theory not retrospectively but before and during the revolt itself can be proved—if generally rather than precisely—from the contemporary sources. Lawrence had already written in a much-quoted letter of March 1915 to D. G. Hogarth that he wanted to "roll up Syria by way of the Hejaz in the name of the Sherif . . . and rush right up to Damascus."[39] The revolt of the protector of the holy cities of Mecca and Medina, the Hashemite Sherif Hussein, provided him with the opportunity to test these premises a year later. After the beginning of the rebellion, however, it became clear to Lawrence (as his first report from the Arabian theater of operations shows) that the only method of fighting suitable for the Arabs was guerrilla warfare. After returning from his first meeting with Feisal, he wrote in his military notes that he had been unable to convince the Emir of the necessity of small raiding parties for use against the railway line. Feisal wanted, instead, to lead large attacks, a method to which Lawrence did not concede any prospects of success whatsoever. Lawrence then explains and substantiates his views in detail:

> The value of the tribes is defensive only and their real sphere is guerrilla warfare. They are intelligent, and very lively, almost reckless, but too individualistic to endure commands, or fight in line, or to help each other. It would, I think, be possible to make an organised force out of them. . . . The Hejaz war is one of dervishes against regular troops—and we are on the side of the dervishes. Our text-books do not apply to its conditions at all.[40]

Later, on the occasion of the advance on Wejh, Lawrence completed these thoughts:

> As a mass they are not formidable, since they have no corporate spirit of discipline, or mutual confidence. Man by man they are good: I would suggest that the smaller the unit that is acting, the better will be its performance. A thousand of them in a mob would be ineffective against one fourth their number of trained troops: but three or four of them, in their own valleys and hills would account for a dozen Turkish soldiers. When they sit still they get nervous, and anxious to return home. . . . When, however, they have plenty to do and are riding about in small parties tapping the Turks here and there, retiring always when the Turks advance, to appear in another direction immediately after, then they are in their element, and must cause the enemy not only anxiety, but bewilderment.[41]

These quotations show unequivocally that Lawrence had in fact already planned his guerrilla war at the time of the beginning of the uprising, although testimony from Lawrence's colleagues verifies how unusual this method of conducting a war was to them. They felt, as one of them appropriately wrote, responsible "for keeping our movements at least quasi-military."[42]

In opposition to this conventional view, Lawrence recommended a brilliantly unconventional course of action in a catalog of "Twenty-seven Articles" of conduct.[43] The substance of these rules of conduct, intended for British military advisers of the Arabs, is the maxim of avoiding at all costs English military regulations when leading the Arabs. "Never give orders to anyone at all" warns Lawrence expressly (Article 3). Lawrence sees the ideal circumstances for an English adviser in a situation "when you are present and not noticed" (Article 8). Also, "Wave a Sherif in front of you like a banner, and hide your own mind and person" (Article 11). Lawrence was totally aware that it is difficult for a European "to keep quiet when everything is being done wrong, but the less you lose your temper the greater your advantage." He emphasizes again and again his basic perception: "Do not try to trade on what you know of fighting. The Hejaz confounds ordinary tactics. Learn the Bedu principles of war as thoroughly and as quickly as you can" (Article 22).

Lawrence then comments on the utilization of the Beduins' mobility and scouting skills and their familiarity with the local terrain, but he also refers to their fear of surprises and their unsuitability for defensive and trench warfare. This interesting wartime document, written in early August 1917, shows clearly once again the development and use of Lawrence's theory of guerrilla war during the Arab Revolt, and also explains why Lawrence enjoyed greater success than most of his colleagues. In accordance with his own catalog of conduct, he skillfully kept himself in the background. The importance of this achievement can be best judged if we consider Michael Foss's dictum that "Arabia was not only the physical frontier of Europe, it was also the frontier of the western mind."[44] Robert Asprey therefore correctly sees Lawrence's prime attainment in the fact that he followed his own advice, and uses this fact to explain Lawrence's positive results: "Lawrence's most amazing feat was assimilating himself to his environment, or, to put it another way, the ability to respect the Arabs as individuals leading their own way of life. Many of Lawrence's achievements stemmed from this relatively simple outlook."[45]

The practical relevance of Lawrence's basic guerrilla theory during the time of the Arab Revolt can be proved from the quoted sources, although the problem of Medina must be seen separately. In spite of all their attempts, the Arabs were simply not in a position to take the Holy City. But if Lawrence's claims in *Seven Pillars* are to be believed, capturing this city would not have been at all advantageous to the Arab side. Lawrence justifies this surprising thesis with the following words:

> We must not take Medina. The Turk was harmless there. In prison in Egypt he would cost us food and guards. We wanted him to stay in Medina, and every other distant place, in the largest numbers. Our ideal was to keep his railway just working, but only just, with the maximum of loss and discomfort. . . . If he tended to evacuate too soon, as a step to concentrating in the small area which his numbers could dominate effectually, then we should have to restore his confidence by reducing our enterprises against him. (*SP*, 225)

In fact, the risk of voluntarily allowing an enemy bastion to remain behind one's own lines sounds ingenious, but it was first formulated by Lawrence only in his postwar essay "The Evolution of a Revolt" for propagandistic reasons after the supposed "experiment" of leaving Medina alone had succeeded.[46] During the war, at exactly the same time when he is supposed to have outlined this theory, Lawrence wrote instead: "the fall of Medina is now merely a question of when the Arabs would like to put an end to the affair."[47]

The description of the Medina situation that appeared in February 1919—in *A Brief Record of the Advance of the Egyptian Expeditionary Force*, a forerunner of the official history of the war—is therefore more nearly correct. And the author possibly was Lawrence himself![48]

> It had become clear that owing to their inexperience in modern siege warfare the Arabs could not expect to reduce Medina. The only operation likely to be fruitful would be systematic attack on the 800 miles of the single track of the Hejaz railway which connects Medina with Damascus. . . . The raiding carried out during the following six months, with British and French help, lowered the strength and spirit of the Turkish forces in Medina. . . . But it did not cut off Medina. The permanent way proved harder to wreck irretrievably, and the enemy better prepared to make interruptions good, than had been expected. The alternative scheme, that of blowing up trains, was

evolved, and under the direction of Lieut-Colonel T. E. Lawrence, this form of military activity began to rank almost as a national sport.[49]

In treating the Medina situation, authors of the official British account of the war come to the conclusion that "To allow the railway just, but only just, to remain working and never to frighten the enemy so seriously as to induce him to evacuate Medina was for the time being the best policy from the British point of view. That in 1917 they ever consciously acted upon that principle is improbable; at least it is not put forward in any contemporary appreciation."[50]

Apart from his retrospective Medina theory, Lawrence's achievements are appropriately honored in the words of the official history prepared for the Foreign Office archives:

> In all the long drawn operations . . . the influence of Captain Lawrence is always apparent. He kept the vision of the Arab military leaders fixed upon essentials; instructed them in the canons of modern warfare; and harmonised the loose and disorderly fighting methods of the Arab camelry and horsemen with the ordered operations of the great British Army in the advance through Palestine and Syria.[51]

All these proofs of the contemporary gestation and validity of his theory of guerrilla warfare and the confirmation of Lawrence's leading role in the Arab Revolt constitute a belated justification for his premature assertion of 1927, when he rebuffed criticism of his achievements with the words: "All the documents of the Arab Revolt are in the archives of the Foreign Office, and will soon be available to students, who will be able to cross-check my yarns. I expect them to find small errors, and to agree generally with the main current of my narrative."[52]

But the timeless importance of Lawrence's guerrilla theory is perhaps even more striking than proof of the contemporary validity of his actual irregular warfare strategy, since guerrilla fighting has become increasingly prominent in the twentieth century. Lawrence in fact developed a theory containing the essential elements of modern guerrilla warfare. When we compare Lawrence's World War I perceptions with the results of the small-war investigations of the Münster military historian Werner Hahlweg in his 1968 essay "Aspekte und Erscheinungsformen des Kleinkrieges in Geschichte und Gegenwart" ("Aspects and Outward Appearance of the Small War in History and in the Present"), the amazing topicality of Lawrence's thoughts becomes conspicuous.[53]

Hahlweg attempts a critical evaluation of small war, considering, among other aspects, the following fundamental elements characteristic of this method of fighting: (1) The partisan war is the natural recourse of those who, in the beginning, are on the weaker side. Therefore, the first, conspiratorial phase of small war is the most delicate stage, the stage during which this kind of war can most easily be terminated by the opponent. (2) The different character of each small war depends on the particular political, socioeconomic, historical, and geographical conditions of the country concerned. Thus it is the civilian sector that becomes of central importance for the guerrilla war, for this is the basis from which the partisan action draws its power and strength. The success or failure of the small war ultimately depends on the intensity of support given the guerrillas by the vast majority of the people. This is the reason that there exists no model of small war which can unadaptably be transferred as an "export item" to other countries. Instead, it is always necessary to consider—in each individual case—the relevant situation, which is never identical in any two places or times. (3) In order to achieve maximum effect, the small-war fighters need the cooperation of regular forces. A strong allied power must back the guerrilla fighters if they are to succeed fully. The final aim of small-war forces is to transform themselves into regular and larger military units. (4) The guerrilla fighter acts as an independent, thinking personality.

All of these aspects can easily be traced in Lawrence's thoughts on guerrilla war. The most important point, however, is that Lawrence had stressed the priority of the civilian sector over the military one. This explains, on the one hand, why the regular army was constantly irritated by the amateur soldier Lawrence, and, on the other, his disrespectful attitude toward professional soldiers. C. A. Johnson has correctly pointed out that of Lawrence's three basic elements of war two were political and only one was military.[54]

Lawrence's small-war concept was very effective in practice as well as in theory. Baljit Singh and Ko-Wang Mei point out that Lawrence's ideas have been imitated enthusiastically in later decades. The guerrilla wars in France, the Balkans, Russia, and Southeast Asia during

World War II were wars of Lawrence's type.[55] Colonel James L. Mrazek even goes so far as to describe Mao Tse-tung's work merely as the piracy of Lawrence's conceptions.[56] And Geoffrey Fairbairn points out that "To an astonishing degree Lawrence's doctrine and practice anticipate many of the features to be found in the military guerrilla campaigns in China and, on a very much smaller scale, in Indo-China. . . . The parallels go down even to the smallest of things."[57] Hillman Dickinson stresses another component of Lawrence's significance: "His emphasis on the importance of psychological factors was a major innovation in modern military practice. . . . Today's psychological warfare doctrine has closely followed this pattern."[58] Dickinson judges Lawrence's "Twenty-seven Articles" permanently valid when he recommends that "They are well worth study even today and far excel in general usefulness and detail Mao's later but more widely known 'Eight Points.'"[59] In 1975 Robert Asprey repeated earlier praise of Lawrence's guidelines: "These could be studied with profit by today's Western advisors to foreign armies."[60] And, in fact, this has been done. During the course of instruction at the American Partisan War School at Fort Bragg, North Carolina, the students are required to demonstrate in multiple-choice examinations repeated proof of their understanding of Lawrence's theory of guerrilla war. Above all, the catalog of conduct with its twenty-seven articles is greatly respected in the school as "the ideal control which Special Forces Teams should seek in their relations with native guerrillas."[61]

We can conclude by confirming Werner Hahlweg's estimate of Lawrence's importance:

> The guerrilla led by Lawrence against the Turkish lines of communication was, in outward appearance, in organization, in method of fighting as in its kind of political-strategic objectives, trend-setting—at least in the region of the Western world. . . . Lawrence, a creative outsider of the military profession thus inscribed himself in the history of the military art.[62]

Laqueur's view that "Lawrence's theories gained their generally wide currency and appeal because he was a romantic figure and had little, if any, competition,"[63] cannot be sustained. Lawrence's romantic personality may undoubtedly have helped increase his attractiveness, but this fact does not impair the basic validity of his theory and achievement any more than his literary talent does. As a strategist, "Lawrence of Arabia" deserves his ornament of honor.

N·O·T·E·S

1. B. H. Liddell Hart, *"T. E. Lawrence": In Arabia and After* (Berlin: Vorhut Verlag Otto Schlegel, 1935), 272–73 (in German).

2. "It was neither the first nor the last time in the history of guerrilla warfare that the measure of attention paid to a particular campaign depended less on its military importance than on the accident that a gifted writer wrote about it." Walter Laqueur, *Guerrilla: A Historical and Critical Study* (London: Weidenfeld and Nicolson, 1977), 155. Indirectly, Linda J. Tarver also levels this reproach: "Other British liaison officers enjoyed similar freedom, but they did not . . . write *Seven Pillars of Wisdom*." See her article "In Wisdom's House: T. E. Lawrence in the Near East," *Journal of Contemporary History* 13 (July 1978): 591.

3. Richard Aldington, *Lawrence of Arabia: A Biographical Enquiry* (London: Collins, 1969), 210–11. For the history of the origin and publication of this book, see Phillip Knightley, "Aldington's Enquiry Concerning T. E. Lawrence," *Texas Quarterly* 16 (Winter 1973): 98–105. See also Aldington's illuminating correspondence with Alan Bird, *A Passionate Prodigality: Letters to Alan Bird from Richard Aldington, 1949–1962*, ed. Miriam Benkovitz (New York: New York Public Library, 1975). For the synonymous use of the terms *guerrilla, small war, guerrillero, partisan,* and *bandits*, see Baljit Singh and Ko-Wang Mei, *Theory and Practice of Modern Guerrilla Warfare* (London: Asia Publishing House, 1971), 2.

4. Cf. also Elie Kedourie: "For it is these [his military activities] which became the foundation of his renown, not to say his legend." "The Real T. E. Lawrence," *Commentary* 64 (July 1977): 54.

5. Paul Zweig is therefore of the opinion that "We will never know how much of Lawrence's theorizing was done in the midst of the action, as he claims it was, and how much during the early 1920s, when he wrote three versions of his book, against the never-mentioned background of his immense fame." *The Adventurer* (London: Dent, 1974), 230.

6. See Richard Meinertzhagen, *Middle East Diary, 1917–1956* (London: Cresset, 1959), 38. For Lawrence as author, see Stanley and Rodelle Weintraub, *Lawrence of Arabia: The Literary Impulse* (Baton Rouge: Louisiana State University Press, 1975), and Stephen E. Tabachnick, *T. E. Lawrence* (Boston: Twayne, 1978). Re the source value of Lawrence's writing, see my historical study, *T. E. Lawrence and the Arab Uprising 1916–1918*, Studies in Military History, Military Science and Conflict Research, vol. 7 (Osnabrück: Biblio, 1976), 12–20 (in German).

7. See the introductory chapter in *Seven Pillars of Wisdom* (Harmondsworth: Penguin, 1969), 21. All other references are to the 1935 Cape edition and will be designated by *SP* in the text.

8. Liddell Hart, 119, 173.

9. Concerning this, see also Morsey, *T. E. Lawrence*, 109–27. The reconnaissance missions are complemented by the photos in the Lawrence Collection in the Imperial War Museum in London, which contain exact details of the position of the views of the terrain, for instance "looking 87°E from a mound in the Wadi Yenbo . . . " Numerical W.W. 1, Q. 58735.

10. For this, see Elie Kedourie, "The Surrender of Medina," *Middle Eastern Studies* 13 (January 1977): 124–43.

11. The help afforded by the Royal Navy in the Hejaz campaign, which has been too little taken into consideration, must also be stressed. See the pioneering article by Charles L. Parnell, "Lawrence of Arabia's Debt to Seapower," *United States Naval Institute Proceedings* 105 (August 1979): 75–83.

12. George MacMunn and Cyril Falls, eds., *Military Operations, Egypt and Palestine* (London: H.M.S.O., 1930), 2:395.

13. Ibid., 397.

14. In a precursor of the official account of the war, the origin of Feisal's troops is indicated: "He had collected, from one source or another, some thousands of partly trained troops, besides contingents from Bedouin tribes of higher quality than the Hejazis. Also he was much better equipped with guns, small arms and auxiliary services than any Arab army had been heretofore." H. Pirie-Gordon, ed., *A Brief Record of the Advance of the Egyptian Expeditionary Force under the Command of General Sir Edmund H. H. Allenby, July 1917 to October 1918* (London: H.M.S.O., 1919), facing plate 53.

15. W. Laqueur generalizes too broadly when he writes that "Military actions after the capture of Aqaba were no longer along unorthodox lines." Laqueur, *Guerrilla*, 156.

16. So Harold Vocke, in a criticism of the German edition of Desmond Stewart's biography *T. E. Lawrence, Frankfurter Allgemeine Zeitung* 69 (21 March 1980): 27 (in German).

17. *Lawrence of Arabia*, 208.

18. In addition to the famous contemporary statements made by Allenby, Wavell, Lloyd George, and Djemal Pasha, the historian Uriel Dann has recently come to the conclusion that "A balanced appraisal weighing as carefully as possible the colossal amount of evidence that has accumulated over the years, must conclude that the 'Arab Revolt' as a whole, and the Transjordanian operations since the encounter of Tafileh (January 1918) in particular, did cause the German-Ottoman command growing worry, and ultimately deflected a considerable portion of their forces to where they were least harmful to Allenby." "Lawrence 'of Arabia'—One More Appraisal," *Middle Eastern Studies* 15 (May 1979): 156.

19. Lawrence writes in his essay "The Evolution of a Revolt": "We believed we would prove irregular war or rebellion to be an exact science, and an inevitable

success, granted certain factors and if pursued along certain lines. We did not prove it, because the war stopped." *The Essential T. E. Lawrence,* ed. David Garnett (New York: Viking, 1964), 220.

20. *War in the Shadows* (Garden City, N.Y.: Doubleday, 1975), 288.

21. F.O. 882/6, 2.3.1917, pp. 203–4.

22. F.O. 882/6, p. 196.

23. F.O. 882/16, pp. 248–49, 252 (map); W.O. 158/634, pt. 1, 16.7.1917. For this, see Morsey, *T. E. Lawrence,* 178–83, 466–67.

24. W.O. 158/634, pt. 1, 19.7.1917.

25. Quoted in Robin L. Bidwell, "Queries for Biographers of T. E. Lawrence," *Arabian Studies III* (London: Hurst, 1976), 21.

26. Ibid.

27. *An Awakening: The Arab Campaign 1917–1918* (London: Tavistock, 1971), 6.

28. "Revolt in the Desert," a review of the Arabic version of the book, in *The Near East and India* (28 April 1927): 497.

29. "Lawrence and the Arab Revolt," *Three Deserts* (London: John Murray, 1936), 296.

30. F.O. 882/7, p. 89.

31. CAB 23/7, no. 475 (3), 20.9. 1918; no. 477 (6), 25.9.1918; a further instance is in Bidwell, "Queries," 23 (29.10.1918).

32. "Arabia and the Hedjaz," *Journal of the Royal Central Asian Society* 10 (1923): 51–52.

33. F.O. 882/4, 14.8.1917, pp. 50–52.

34. "The Organization of British Responsibilities in the Middle East," *Journal of the Central Asian Society* 6, nos. 3–4 (1919): 96.

35. In the previously quoted letter of 27 August 1917 to General Clayton, Lawrence writes: "I don't think that any appreciation of the Arab situation will be of any use to you, unless its author can see for himself the difference between a national rising and a campaign." F.O. 882/7, p. 92.

36. *T. E. Lawrence by His Friends,* ed. A. W. Lawrence (Leipzig: Paul List, 1938), 132–33 (in German). Capt. H. Dinning, who was occasionally Lawrence's pilot during the closing phases of the war, asks, "What are you to do with an army in which every soldier considers himself a sort of a brigadier?" "Working with Lawrence," *Nile to Aleppo* (London: George Allen and Unwin, 1920), 231.

37. See Erik Lönnroth, *Lawrence of Arabia: An Historical Appreciation* (London: Vallentine, Mitchell, 1956), 31.

38. Suleiman Mousa, *T. E. Lawrence: An Arab View* (London: Oxford University Press, 1966), 56. In stating "five full years," which refers to the Oxford edition of *Seven Pillars* (1922), Mousa overlooks the fact that Lawrence had published his theory two years before in his 1920 essay "The Evolution of a Revolt."

39. Quoted from Richard P. Graves, *Lawrence of Arabia and His World* (London: Thames and Hudson, 1976), 24.

40. T. E. Lawrence, *Secret Despatches from Arabia* (London: Golden Cockerel, 1939), 33, 35.

41. Ibid., 65.

42. Hubert Young, *The Independent Arab* (London: John Murray, 1933), 243.

43. Manuscript preserved in F.O. 882/7, pp. 93–97.

44. "Dangerous Guides: English Writers and the Desert," *New Middle East* 9 (June 1969): 41.

45. Asprey, *War in the Shadows*, 291.

46. See n. 37, above.

47. *Secret Despatches*, 111.

48. See Stanley and Rodelle Weintraub, *Lawrence of Arabia: The Literary Impulse*, 163. In the register of contributors to the history, Lawrence's name does not appear.

49. Pirie-Gordon, *A Brief Record*, 52.

50. MacMunn and Falls, *Military Operations*, 2:396.

51. Quoted by Bidwell, "Queries," 22.

52. *T. E. Lawrence to His Biographers Robert Graves and Liddell Hart* (London: Cassell, 1963), 1:117.

53. For this in detail, see W. Hahlweg, "Aspects and Outward Appearance of the Small War in History and in the Present," *Allgemeine Schweizerische Militärzeitschrift* 9 (1968): 501–8 (in German); and Morsey, *T. E. Lawrence*, 274–79.

54. "What is significant is that he thought of only a third of war as a military, or technical, problem. Because the political two-thirds of guerrilla warfare has been ignored or misinterpreted by many recent commentators, a major confusion has entered into much thinking about guerrilla struggles." "Civilian Loyalties and Guerrilla Conflict," *World Politics* 14 (October 1961): 646–47.

55. See Singh and Mei, *Theory and Practice*, 4. Cf. also Richard Clutterbuck, *Guerrillas and Terrorists* (London: Faber, 1977), 30: "Many of the lessons learned from Lawrence were applied in the resistance movements against German and Japanese occupation in the Second World War."

56. "What Mao Tse Tung plagiarized so profitably from Lawrence has been fashioned recently into an elaborate programme for world conquest." "The Philosophy of the Guerrilla Fighter," *Army Quarterly and Defence Journal* 96 (April 1968): 72.

57. *Revolutionary Warfare and Communist Strategy: The Threat to South-East Asia* (London: Faber and Faber, 1968), 152.

58. "Master Guerrilla of Araby's Desert," *Army* (August 1967): 70.

59. Ibid., 77. Already in 1954, Major O. B. Patton had recommended the study of Lawrence, because it "provides numerous principles of operation for the present-day American political and intelligence officer." "Colonel Lawrence of Arabia," *Military Review* 34 (October 1954): 18.

60. Asprey, *War in the Shadows*, 292 (n. 27).

61. Quoted by Werner Hahlweg, *Teachers of the Small War: From Clausewitz to Mao Tse-Tung and (Che) Guevara*, Contributions to Defense Research, vol. 18/19 (Darmstadt: Wehr und Wissen, 1968), 202 (in German).

62. *Guerrilla: War without Fronts* (Stuttgart: Kohlhammer, 1968), 105 (in German).

63. Laqueur, *Guerrilla*, 171.

T. E. Lawrence:
Intelligence Officer

GIDEON GERA

In order to appreciate T. E. Lawrence's achievements as an intelligence officer—a role that came to an end in 1918, when he involved himself more and more in the politics of the Arab Revolt and its aftermath—we must first understand what intelligence is. "Intelligence is an activity which consists essentially of three functions. Information has to be acquired; it has to be analyzed and interpreted; and it has to be put into the hands of those who can use it."[1] The word can also refer to the knowledge acquired itself and to the organization necessary for acquiring it. The frameworks, methods, and means employed to gather information are termed collection, while those used to analyze and interpret it are termed production or evaluation, the ultimate goal of which is prediction of events to come. Positive intelligence is the acquiring of information about foreign countries, while counterintelligence means the foiling of attempts to gain access to one's own information. To these various facets we can add covert operations.

From the beginning of this century, the increasingly complex character of modern warfare has brought about many advances in the craft of intelligence. As military commanders and political leaders have confronted one another in an ever-denser fog of war, more and more intelligence has been required to penetrate the uncertain and unknown, both in space and in time; and World War I greatly accelerated the development of intelligence work.

The secrecy in which intelligence organizations are shrouded by their very nature has been the main difficulty in writing this paper. More than most, the British seem to be sensitive to the need for secrecy of their intelligence services, even from historical distance and after many Cabinet records have been opened to public view. When some exploits of British intelligence during World War I were published, general restraint was practiced. Thus, the mere existence of a special intelligence agency in the eastern Mediterranean was revealed only by the chance appearance of an unexplained abbreviation in a book published in 1925, and only in 1971 could one find its meaning in the memoirs of a former member.[2] There is no mention or reference at all in any official history. No wonder, then, that Lawrence, who was very eloquent about his Arabian adventures, actually told little about his secret intelligence work.

· PRELUDE AND INITIATION ·

Lawrence joined the British Museum archaeological expedition to the great mound at Carchemish in March 1911 and worked there for more than three years. This was his second stay in the Near East. The first was his summer 1909 journey across today's Lebanon, Syria, and Israel, when he gathered material for his Oxford thesis on Crusader castles, gained firsthand impressions of land and peoples, and began practicing Arabic. He showed an early grasp of the military implications of terrain.[3]

During his years at the dig, on the frontier between Arabs, Turks, and Kurds, Lawrence continued his cross-country travels, sometimes in local garb. He deepened his geographical and anthropological knowledge of the area, and learned its politics and government, by "simple penetration and assimilation, by impressions as well as by study."[4] His detailed diary reminds one of some of his later descriptive reports from Arabia.[5]

Undoubtedly these years were an excellent preparation for Lawrence's future intelligence activities.[6] Already at the beginning of 1914, while still on the Carchemish team, he participated in a secret survey of Sinai undertaken by British military intelligence. Thus the involvement of Lawrence in intelligence must have begun during the Carchemish episode. A major connecting link was David George Hogarth,

Oxford don, Keeper of the Ashmolean Museum, archaeologist, orientalist, sometime journalist and intelligence officer, and mentor, guide, and patron of T. E. Lawrence; it was Hogarth who personally introduced him to the site.[7]

Hogarth organized and supervised the British Museum archaeological expedition to Carchemish (1911–14). Recently the dig has been depicted as a cover operation, designed for close observation of German activities along the Baghdad Railway.[8] The authorities of the museum have angrily rejected these allegations.[9] However, the dig was at least partly financed by Walter Morrison, a wealthy Oxford benefactor and Unionist M.P., who was also one of the founders of the Palestine Exploration Fund (which definitely did supply cover for the Sinai survey). Moreover, his contribution was kept confidential at the time, for some reason.[10] The cover thesis seems unproven so far, but any political, military, and geographical observations made during the dig were probably welcome to British authorities dealing with the area.

The second link connecting Lawrence to intelligence was his close relations with British consulates in the area, mainly those at Aleppo and Beirut. He was supported by them, brought them political information, and once even helped naval officers smuggle arms into the Aleppo consulate.[11] These actions should be considered against the background of increased British intelligence activities in Syria, which was decided upon by the Committee for Imperial Defence in 1909. Not only was the improvement of intelligence on the area recommended but an increase in intelligence capabilities of the consulates in Syria was urged by senior British officials in Egypt.[12] The organizational setup of British intelligence at the time was as follows: from 1910, the Foreign Section of the Secret Service Bureau came under the Admiralty, enhancing the operations of Naval Intelligence—which was very active in the eastern Mediterranean in cooperation with the consulates. Among other projects, emergency intelligence networks were set up by the consulates, to serve during the war as the main assets of the Eastern Mediterranean Special Intelligence Bureau (EMSIB).[13] It seems plausible in this framework to see Lawrence as a "correspondent" of British intelligence in Syria, something of which Hogarth was not unaware.[14]

Thus, when he was suddenly asked by Hogarth, via the Aleppo consulate, to proceed to Beersheba for a survey of Sinai under the command of (then) Captain S. F. Newcombe, Royal Engineers, Lawrence asked no questions.[15] The requirement to complete a secret survey of Sinai was part of British preparations to defend the Suez Canal. No better cover seemed available than an archaeological expedition by the Palestine Exploration Fund—completing a survey interrupted in 1878. The executive of the fund included—among others—Walter Morrison, Hogarth, and Colonel Hedley, head of the Geographical Section, General Staff—Newcombe's superior.[16]

Lawrence and his partner from Carchemish, Leonard Woolley, duly joined Newcombe and his team for six weeks of survey work in January and February 1914. Then Lawrence returned on his own to northern Syria via Akaba and Petra, annoying Ottoman authorities on the way. To placate their anger, Kitchener—patron of the survey—urged the two archaeologists to publish their findings speedily.[17]

The growing involvement of Lawrence in intelligence work after this expedition may be gathered from his reconnaissance with Newcombe of the roads and railway built by the Germans through the Amanus mountains in the summer of 1914.[18] Thus, the importance of the survey of Zin for Lawrence's intelligence career was that for the first time he participated in an organized undercover operation in which he demonstrated his ability, that he came to know the people with whom he was to work closely in the future, and that it gained him access to military intelligence at the outbreak of the war.

· EGYPT ·

With the declaration of war on the Ottoman Empire, British intelligence operations in Egypt were reinforced by some experienced officers: Newcombe was put in charge of military intelligence, and soon his Sinai teammates—Lawrence and Woolley—were sent to join him. Lawrence—who had been commissioned second lieutenant (interpreter) in the Geographical Section—arrived in Egypt in December 1914.[19] This was the hour of the archaeologists, whose intimate knowledge of remote places, people, and languages made them valuable recruits for intelligence work.[20]

Lawrence worked in Egypt for almost two years, coming a long way as General Staff intelligence officer. Officially his appointment was as map officer (a post he held until mid-1916), but practically he took part in the various tasks of his section: collecting information, processing it into intelligence, making strategic evaluations, and producing finished reports. He shared in both positive and counterintelligence work, thus preparing himself for his later activities in the field in Iraq and the Hejaz. And already during this period, Lawrence began to glide from pure intelligence work toward involvement in politico-military disputes.

As map officer Lawrence was responsible for the supply of maps to his headquarters and for the updating of situation maps. These duties put him into close contact with the Survey of Egypt (he also was liaison there for the Navy and Mediterranean Expeditionary Force), which produced the large quantity of maps required by the various forces in the Near Eastern theater of operations, which extended from Gallipoli to the Arabian Peninsula. Up to February 1916 one million copies of six hundred different map sheets were printed, and Lawrence helped create an efficient wartime operation out of a thousand-strong civilian bureaucracy by exercising leadership, coordinating the flow of essential cartographic information, and sometimes even supplying spare parts for various purposes.[21]

Concurrently Lawrence took part (with the other officers of his section) in running agents, thus he was able to stay in touch with his "boy" at Carchemish (Dahoum), at least until early 1916, and in interrogating prisoners of war whose dialect he spoke (many of them were at that time of Syrian or Palestinian origin).[22] Lawrence was also busy analyzing and evaluating incoming information, giving it "good sense," and composing "short geographical essays." His writing talent was soon noticed by his superiors, who made him editor of an intelligence bulletin.[23]

In these manifold ways Lawrence took part in the intelligence preparations for two major operations—the stillborn Alexandretta landing and the Arab Revolt (which was part of the strategic conception advocated by Lord Kitchener).[24] Lawrence had a share in both the analytical and the operational aspects, even enlisting the aid of his friend and mentor Hogarth, before the latter's appointment to Cairo.[25] An outstanding example of Lawrence's work at this time is one of his "short geographical essays," later called "Syria—the Raw Material" (published in the *Arab Bulletin* in March 1917 as "fragmentary notes written in early 1915 but not circulated"). This is a masterly social and political analysis of geographical Syria, probably intended as an introductory brief to the area, but slanted to enlist sympathy for the Sherifian revolt. This emerges clearly from the conclusion:

> Only by the intrusion of a new factor, founded on some outward power or non-Syrian basis, can the dissident tendencies of the sects and peoples of Syria be reined in sufficiently to prevent destructive anarchy. . . . The only imposed government that will find in Moslem Syria any really prepared groundwork or large body of adherents is a Sunni one, speaking Arabic and pretending to revive the Abbassides or Ayubides.[26]

The measure of the quality of the analysis contained in this article is that some of its insights on the region are as valid and pertinent today as they were almost seventy years ago.

When serious negotiations with the Sherif of Mecca were resumed in the summer of 1915, the pace of intelligence preparations in Cairo quickened, culminating in the establishment of a special coordination and support agency—the Arab Bureau. Headed by Hogarth, the bureau was charged with dealing with intelligence, propaganda, and interdepartmental communications (with the Foreign, India, and War Offices, Admiralty, Committee for Imperial Defence, and the government of India) concerning Arab affairs (outside Egypt and the Sudan).[27]

Lawrence was part of these activities—supervising the preparation of maps of Arabia,[28] interrogating deserters and prisoners of war (among others, he questioned and impressed the Syrian nationalist leader Dr. Abd Al-Rahman Shahbander),[29] and composing further essays: notes on North Arabian tribes, camel trade in Arabia (a report that surveyed the potential of animal transport for future operations in Syria and Transjordan),[30] the vulnerabilities of the Baghdad Railway, and "The Conquest of Syria If Complete."[31] He was also involved in the staff work around the negotiations with the Sherif, and analyzed the possible implications of an Arab revolt in a paper entitled "The Politics of Mecca."[32]

Taking part in these political and operational preparations also involved Lawrence in the quarrels and disputes concerning them. One of these was a major controversy on the Ottoman order of battle in the region, in which not only genuine intelligence problems but personal differences of opinion on operations were reflected. Together with some of his colleagues, Lawrence took exception to what they considered a highly inflated estimate of Ottoman strength, forwarded by Colonel Holdich, the new chief of military intelligence in Egypt. Not surprisingly, the relations between Lawrence (a subaltern) and his superiors on the military staff grew tense, as he busied himself with work on Arabia for the Arab Bureau—to which he did not officially belong. The situation was aggravated by the fact that Lawrence stayed behind in Cairo, near the Survey of Egypt, while GHQ moved to the Canal area.[33]

Upon his return from his secret mission in Iraq (March–May 1916), and especially after the revolt in the Hejaz began, Lawrence's relations with military intelligence became impossible. In June he started editing the *Arab Bulletin* for the Arab Bureau. Following his first mission to the Hejaz, his unofficial situation with the bureau was changed into formal membership (in November 1916).[34]

· INTERLUDE: IRAQ ·

The sensitive mission in Mesopotamia with which Lawrence was entrusted in March 1916 (together with Aubrey Herbert, M.P., a long-standing expert on the Ottomans) pertains to an additional aspect of intelligence—covert operations (or intelligence warfare). The mission was twofold: on behalf of the War Office (the idea was Kitchener's)—to try to ransom the besieged British-Indian force at Kut Al-Amara; on behalf of the Arab Bureau—to check on the feasibility of an Arab uprising in Syria. To conceal the very secret nature of his mission, a cover story was circulated to the effect that Lawrence was sent to Iraq to teach British forces there new techniques of mapping from aerial photographs.[35]

The ransom mission failed, as the besieged British commander (General Townshend) had already begun negotiations for his surrender with the Ottoman commander, Khalil Pasha. Lawrence and Herbert crossed the lines and met with Khalil (who was the nephew of the Ottoman minister of war, Enver Pasha), offering unsuccessfully first one and then two million pounds sterling for the release of the British garrison. However, they arranged for the exchange of a thousand wounded for a similar number of Ottoman prisoners of war. These meetings enabled Lawrence not only to observe the workings of the Ottoman headquarters but also to note the ill feeling between Arab (and possibly Kurdish) and Turkish soldiers and the fickle loyalty of the former (Khalil wanted no Arab prisoners in exchange).[36]

As for the secondary mission, some clandestine meetings at Basra with the so-called Pan Arab Party convinced Lawrence that there was not much of a will to revolt and that the party was "about 12 strong. Formerly consisted of Sayid Taleb and some jackals."[37]

· HEJAZ ·

In the framework of British assistance to the Sherifian Revolt, directed by Sir Reginald Wingate, Lawrence served no longer as a staff officer but as a semi-independent political and military adviser; his degree of independence largely varied according to the state of available communications containing orders and instructions. Three main intelligence aspects of his work in Arabia will be discussed here: his mission to assess Feisal's capabilities (October 1916); combat intelligence functions he carried out while adviser to Feisal; his mission in the depth of Ottoman territory (June 1917).

Lawrence's first mission to the Hejaz was to secure a reliable assessment of Feisal's personality and chance of success. Although there were British liaison officers with Feisal's father, Sherif Hussein, and his brothers, the Emirs Ali and Abdullah, there was until Lawrence's appearance no British representative with Feisal. This situation of neglect probably came about because of British distrust of Feisal owing to his unsuccessful activities in Syria in the spring of 1916.[38] Furthermore, an Ottoman counterattack was in the making, things seemed confused to the British authorities, and "nobody knew the real situation at Rabegh [Feisal's camp]."[39]

The extent to which Lawrence accomplished his mission is evident from the variety of information contained in his reports on the terrain (including topography, water resources, population, trafficability for vehicles and artillery), on Feisal's camp (biographical details on the Sherifian family, including the Emir himself, and their standing among the tribes; tribal strength and morale; military potential), and on the enemy (capability and possibility of reinforcement). Lawrence concluded that, although no large-scale Ottoman reinforcements were probable, a small aggressive Turkish force could decide the issue if transport difficulties could be overcome.[40] Thus Lawrence supplied his superiors with a comprehensive assessment as to chances and risks of the revolt seen from Feisal's angle. This report earned him the appreciation of Wingate (who forwarded it to London), appointment to the Arab Bureau, and a posting as liaison to Feisal with promotion to captain.[41]

Lawrence served with Feisal along the northwestern part of Hejaz from November 1916 until May 1917. He regarded himself "as primarily Intelligence officer or Liaison."[42] His intelligence mission was both to contribute to Feisal's success and to keep his superiors informed of the situation of enemy and ally alike; and his reports were very appreciated.[43] Under the circumstances, Lawrence was to a large extent his own combat-intelligence officer, performing the following tasks: *Reconnaissance.* When in the face of the Ottoman advance toward the Red Sea in December 1916 no reliable information was available in Feisal's camp, Lawrence went to look for himself and took two prisoners, through whom he duly ascertained the limited strength of the enemy.[44] *Aerial Reconnaissance.* Supported on and off by a few reconnaissance aircraft, Lawrence arranged for landing strips, briefed the pilots (maps were hopelessly inadequate), and joined them in flights over Ottoman lines west of Medina to assess the enemy's strength.[45] *Interrogation of Prisoners.* Lawrence personally interrogated Ottoman prisoners and deserters, both for Feisal's tactical and the Arab Bureau's strategic and political requirements. Furthermore, valuing this source of information, he endeavored to keep prisoners unhurt and to make this known in the enemy camp.[46] *Running Agents.* Lawrence sat in on Feisal's meetings with his agents (posing as a deserting Syrian officer) and ran at least one agent of his own, an Arab Ottoman captain.[47] *Field Security.* Lawrence faced two main field security problems: countering Ottoman attempts to subvert Feisal's following, and providing for his own personal safety. He solved the latter problem by dressing as an Arab and using the cover of a Syrian officer.[48]

Lawrence summed up his experiences with the Bedu in the famous "Twenty-seven Articles," intended "as stalking horses for beginners."

They deserve an analysis of their own, but from the intelligence point of view the essence of these "articles" lies in the conclusion: "The beginning and ending of the secret of handling Arabs is the unremitting study of them. . . . Bury yourself in Arab circles. . . . your success will be proportioned to the amount of mental effort you devote to it."[49]

Between 4 (or 5) and 16 (or 18) June 1917, Lawrence went deep behind the Ottoman lines into Syria and Lebanon.[50] Accompanied by only two bodyguards, he rode from the fringe of the Hejaz to Palmyra, in order to meet some of his old contacts of the Carchemish period (they did not turn up) as well as a friendly Bedu chief, who supplied him with an escort of thirty-five riders. From there he went into eastern Lebanon, blowing up a small railroad bridge not far from the Ottoman depot at Baalbek, in order to stir up local Shi'i tribes, and then to the outskirts of Damascus, where he met the governor of the city, an acquaintance from Aleppo. His next stop was in the Druse area, where he talked to some of the chiefs, and then back into the desert, where he met one of the paramount Bedu sheikhs, Nuri Sha'alan— known to play both sides but considered to lean toward the Sherifian cause.

On returning to his forward base, Lawrence dispatched one of Feisal's trusted Syrian supporters, Nasib Al-Bakri, who awaited him there, to the Druse area to set up intelligence networks in southern Syria and to gain support in the region for the Arab revolt.

Lawrence's "Syrian trip" gained its notoriety because of his obvious reluctance to elaborate on it and because of the argument advanced by the Jordanian author Suleiman Mousa that it never happened.[51] Today, with many British archives—public and private—open, there can be no doubt that this outstanding feat was actually performed. Even before that, however, sufficient evidence to counter the Mousa thesis was available. The "trip" was mentioned in the official history and Lawrence was commended by Wingate for a high award for his "magnificent achievement," appointed a Companion of the Bath, and congratulated by the War Cabinet.[52]

Obviously the details of the trip were considered highly classified; only a short version of its findings was published in the secret *Arab Bulletin*.[53] The reasons become clear when we analyze the purpose of the operation (and subsequent instructions to Bakri). In order to plan future campaigns up to the line Beirut-Damascus, reliable intelligence was required by GHQ. Lawrence was sent to clarify the attitude of the various elements of the Syrian population (Bedu, townspeople, non-Sunni tribes) toward the Turks, the British, and the Sherifian Revolt and to gauge their eventual readiness to undertake guerrilla actions against the Turkish army. Thus there were several considerations for secrecy. Ascertaining the real extent of Sherifian influence and support for the Arab cause (probably without Feisal's knowledge)[54] was rather delicate. Even more sensitive in the eyes of the British was the fact that the "trip" encroached on the area considered to be under French influence.[55] In addition to the political considerations, there were intelligence reasons for silence. First, the British were concerned about the security of the agents who were alerted and contacted and who possibly were unconnected to the Sherifian camp (and maybe still active after Lawrence's trip). For instance, how could a man who was "east of Ragga"—that is, in western Iraq—be expected to meet Lawrence clandestinely at Palmyra on a certain day without being notified in advance by a go-between? Second, the British were worried during the period of the war itself about Lawrence's own security (there was a price on his head); this reason was mentioned in the War Cabinet.[56]

In sum, the strategic reconnaissance carried out by Lawrence led to changes in British operational planning. For the first time, a combined effort in southern and eastern Syria was considered.[57]

· TRANSJORDAN: FINALE ·

After the occupation of Akaba in July 1917, Feisal's Arab Force became more regularized. It was put under the command of the Egyptian Expeditionary Force (General Allenby), supported by a special British liaison staff, and reinforced with regular British and other troops. In this new setup, Lawrence continued to serve as liaison officer to Feisal and became increasingly occupied with the political and operational aspects of the Arab Revolt. However, he continued some of his intelligence work (for which he was given in August 1917 "a monthly allotment for secret service purposes up to £200").[58] He reconnoitered the whole Transjordan area up to the Hauran by land and by air and ran some agents. However, this part of his activities was curtailed when a special representative of EMSIB was posted to his area to run agents up to Damascus.[59] Still Lawrence continued to contribute occasional assessments to the Arab Bureau—on the battle of Tafileh (considered too sensitive for inclusion in the *Bulletin*), on the inadequacies of existing maps, and on tribes and their politics.[60] With the Ottoman collapse and the occupation of Damascus, Lawrence's intelligence activities in the area came to an end. All his reports, memoranda, assessments, and even articles written after this time cannot be considered proper intelligence work because of their public and political aspects.

· CONCLUSION ·

Years later, World War I long behind him, Lawrence repeatedly stressed the importance of intelligence to political and military action. Thus he wrote B. H. Liddell-Hart in 1933: "When I took a decision . . . it was after studying every relevant—and many an irrelevant—factor. Geography, tribal structure, religion, social custom, languages, appetites, standards—all were at my finger ends. The enemy I knew almost like my own side. I risked myself among them a hundred times, to *learn*" (*L*, 769).

During seven years (1911–18, if one counts all of the Carchemish episode), Lawrence was actively engaged in most aspects of intelligence work all over the Middle East. By turns and often concurrently his activities included: *Reconnaissance*. Traveling by foot, car, camel, or airplane all over the desert and settled land, observing terrain, enemy, scouting, mapping, measuring. *Collection*. Interrogating (sometimes even catching) prisoners of war, deserters, and refugees; running agents, also deep behind enemy lines. *Counterintelligence*. Taking care of the security of his operations, disrupting possible achievements by his Turkish and German opponents. *Covert Operations*. Undertaking highly sensitive missions to Iraq, the Hejaz, Transjordan, and Syria. *Assessment*. Gaining expertise on the Ottoman army and the Arabs, analyzing terrain and enemy separately and together, and combining his findings into well-argued and articulate assessments.

No portrait of Lawrence the intelligence officer would be complete without mention of a serious shortcoming of his, which repeatedly impaired his judgment: a fervent, uncompromising, emotional approach to some objects of his work. Even before the war, he was anti-Ottoman and to some degree a Francophobe.[61] Prejudice colored his relations with Arabs—all things Bedu were "clean," while Lebanese townspeople and Egyptian peasants were contemptible. This attitude drove him toward dispute and political action and away from proper intelligence. However, against these drawbacks, his self-control under physical and mental stress and conditions of strict secrecy seems remarkable.

During World War I, British intelligence chiefs grew aware of the different qualities required from operatives in the field and from those engaged in long-range evaluatory work.[62] Lawrence seems to have been a rare combination of these two distinct sets of qualities. This was probably due to personal ability, suitable training, and political circumstances in which his special talents could be articulated. To my mind, one should see Lawrence as Gertrude Bell did when she met him at Carchemish: "He is going to make a traveller."[63] In other words, Lawrence was one of the last "generalist" intelligence officers in the nineteenth-century tradition. It is doubtful whether people such as Lawrence are around anymore in the highly complex, specialized, and technological world of late twentieth-century intelligence.

N·O·T·E·S

1. F. H. Hinsley, with E. E. Thomas, C. F. G. Ransom, and R. G. Knight, *British Intelligence in the Second World War* (London: H.M.S.O., 1979), 1:4.

2. Alec S. Kirkbride, *An Awakening* (London: Tavistock, 1971); Lewen B. Weldon, *"Hard Lying"* (London: n.p., 1925).

3. *L*, 94–96.

4. *T. E. Lawrence by His Friends*, ed. A. W. Lawrence (London: Cape, 1937), 96, 183, hereafter *Friends*; on wearing local dress, *Friends*, 97; *L*, 149; Hubert Young, *The Independent Arab* (London: John Murray, 1933), 21; B. H. Liddell Hart, *"T. E. Lawrence": In Arabia and After* (London: Cape, 1935), 77; on Arab politics, *Friends*, 83; *HL*, 243; Suleiman Mousa, *T. E. Lawrence: An Arab View* (London: Oxford University Press, 1966), passim; on Ottoman government, *HL*, 179–80, 215, 218, 256–57, 447; Young, p. 20.

5. The diary is reprinted in T. E. Lawrence, *Oriental Assembly* (London: Williams and Northgate, 1939).

6. Cf. his article, "The Evolution of a Revolt" (1920), reprinted in *Oriental Assembly*.

7. On Hogarth, see J. R. H. Weaver, *Dictionary of National Biography 1922–1930* (London: Oxford University Press, 1937), 422–23; C. R. L. Fletcher, "David George Hogarth," *Geographical Journal* 71 (April 1928): 321–44; David G. Hogarth, *The Wandering Scholar* (London: Oxford University Press, 1925); *Friends*, 18, 86.

8. Phillip Knightley and Colin Simpson, *The Secret Lives of Lawrence of Arabia* (London: Panther, 1971), 45, 50–51.

9. R. D. Barnett (Keeper of Western Asiatic Antiquities, British Museum), "Letter to the Editor," *Times Literary Supplement* (16 October 1969), 1210–11.

10. Ibid.; H. W. C. Davis and J. R. H. Weaver, *Dictionary of National Biography 1912–1921* (London: Oxford University Press, 1927), 338–39; *HL*, 210, 291.

11. *HL*, 178–80, 192, 215, 247, 263, 517, 591; *Friends*, 83–84; *L*, 131, 140, 163; *Young*, 4–5, 9–10, 18; James E. Flecker, *Some Letters from Abroad* (London: Heinemann, 1930), 59, 64–66.

12. PRO/CAB 11/M4, pp. vii, 9, 95; CAB 16/12, 21 June 1909.

13. Hinsley et al., 16; Stephen Roskill, *Hankey, Man of Secrets*, vol. I, *1877–1918* (London: Collins, 1970), 81–85; Kirkbride, 18, 21.

14. Jean Béraud-Villars, *Le Colonel Lawrence* (Paris: Albin Michel, 1955), 43.

15. *HL*, 278–79, 494–95; Liddell, Hart, 31.

16. Liddell Hart, 95–96; CAB 16/12—Report and Appendices of an Enquiry by the Standing Committee of the C.I.D. into the responsibility of the Navy and Army for the Defence of the Suez Canal, Appendix 2; *Friends*, 131–32; Weldon, 100; C. Leonard Woolley and T. E. Lawrence, *The Wilderness of Zin* (London: Palestine Exploration Fund, 1915), iv.

17. Woolley and Lawrence, xiii–xv, 10–18, 28, 35, 128–30; *L*, 165–70; *Friends*, 105–7, 133; Knightley and Simpson, 55–57.

18. Knightley and Simpson, 57.

19. *Friends*, 103, 133; *HL*, 300; Liddell Hart, 94–96.

20. *Arab Bulletin* 92 (11 June 1918), 194; C. Leonard Woolley, *Dead Towns and Living Men* (London: Humphrey Milford, 1920), 6.

21. *Friends*, 133–43; *HL*, 309, 314; Weldon, 4.

22. *HL*, 302, 307; *L*, 192, 197; Liddell Hart, 98; Knightley and Simpson, 58–60.

23. *L*, 191; *HL*, 301, 305–6, 308–9.

24. D. G. Hogarth, "The Burden of Syria," *Nineteenth Century and After* 87 (1920): 388–90; Roskill, 224, 226, 234; George MacMunn and Cyril Falls, eds., *Military Operations, Egypt and Palestine* (London: H.M.S.O., 1928), 1:20, 79, 82.

25. *HL*, 304; *L*, 192–200.

26. *Arab Bulletin* 44 (12 March 1917).

27. Relevant documents from British records are quoted in Konrad Morsey, *T. E. Lawrence und der arabische Aufstand 1916/18* (Osnabrück: Biblio, 1976), 82, 329.

28. *HL*, 314.

29. Mousa, 9–10.

30. *HL*, 311–13.

31. Quoted in Knightley and Simpson, 75.

32. Knightley and Simpson, 78. Cf. Jukka Nevakivi, *Britain, France, and the Arab Middle East 1914–1920* (London: Athlone, 1969).

33. MacMunn and Falls, 89, 157–59, 204–5; F. J. Moberly, *The Campaign in Mesopotamia 1914–1918* (London: H.M.S.O., 1924), 2:537; *T. E. Lawrence to His Biographers Robert Graves and Liddell Hart* (London: Cassell, 1963), 2:89, 92; Liddell Hart, 57, 98, 103; *HL*, 332; Morsey, 115, 339.

34. Morsey, 115, 339; *HL*, 327; Liddell Hart, 103–4; *Arab Bulletin* 100 (28 August 1918).

35. W. F. Stirling, *Safety Last* (London: Hollis and Carter, 1953), 67; Moberly, 452–58; *L*, 202; Liddell Hart, 99–100; Knightley and Simpson, 61–67.

36. *L*, 206, 209; Knightley and Simpson, 64–65.

37. Quoted in Knightley and Simpson, 66; Mousa, 6–7.

38. Isaiah Friedman, "The McMahon Correspondence and the Question of Palestine," *Journal of Contemporary History* 5 (1970): 95–97.

39. Morsey, 116, 339.

40. Morsey, 118–22, 340–41; *Arab Bulletin* 31 (18 November 1916) and 32 (26 November 1916).

41. Morsey, 129; Knightley and Simpson, 79.

42. *HL*, 334; Morsey, 122, 345.

43. Morsey, 128–29.

44. *L*, 211, 213, 215–16; *Arab Bulletin* 42 (15 February 1917).

45. *Arab Bulletin* 36 (26 December 1916); *Friends*, 159–60; *L*, 211.

46. *L*, 212, 214; *Arab Bulletin* 59 (12 August 1917).

47. *L*, 211, 214.

48. *L*, 212, 423; Knightley and Simpson, 89–90; Mousa, 57; Young, 156; Kirkbride, 15; Morsey, 183–85, 358–59.

49. *Arab Bulletin* 60 (20 August 1917).

50. Lawrence's report is reprinted in *L*, 225–31. His diary is kept in the British Library. Morsey, 173, 355.

51. Mousa relied on Bakri's allegation that the "trip" never occurred. But this was forty years later, when connections with the British, however old, were embarrassing to Syrian politicians such as Bakri. Mousa, 74–77, 281–82, 287; *T. E. Lawrence to His Biographers*, 1:88–90; Liddell Hart, 194; Knightley and Simpson, 100.

52. Knightley and Simpson, 100–101; MacMunn, 239; Morsey, 172, 178–79, 187–88, 355–57, 359.

53. *Arab Bulletin* 57 (24 July 1917).

54. *T. E. Lawrence to His Biographers*, 1:87–88.

55. French intelligence and political action were directed from the Lebanese and Syrian shore inward, north of Saida, and supported mainly by Maronites and Catholics. The British worked from the south and east, using Sunni and Shi'i Moslems, Druze, and non-Catholic Christians. Nicholas Z. Ajay, Jr., "Political Intrigue and Suppression in Lebanon during World War I," *International Journal of Middle East Studies* 5 (1974): 144–47; Weldon, 140–41; Kirkbride, 20–21; *L*, 198; Morsey, 179, 357.

56. Morsey, 179, 272, 357, 383; Knightley and Simpson, 101.

57. Morsey, 174, 179, 355, 357.

58. Morsey, 190, 361.

59. Kirkbride, 8–36 passim.

60. Morsey, 207, 365–66; *Arab Bulletin* 66 (21 October 1917); *Arab Bulletin* Supplementary Paper no. 5 (24 July 1918).

61. For a full discussion of this point, see Larès's essay in this collection and his *T. E. Lawrence, la France, et les Français* (Paris: Imprimerie Nationale, 1980).

62. Kenneth Strong, *Men of Intelligence* (London: Cassell, 1970), 32–33.

63. Gertrude Bell, *The Letters of Gertrude Bell*, ed. Florence Bell (London: Benn, 1927), 1:305.

T. E. Lawrence and France:
Friends or Foes?

MAURICE LARÈS

*The French conception of their country as a fair woman lent to them
a national spitefulness against those who scorned her charms.*

SEVEN PILLARS OF WISDOM

After the Arabs, the French had the most dealings with T. E.
Lawrence. Hence Franco-Lawrentian misunderstandings have
been the source of an abundant and often repetitive literature.

Relatively unforeseen and short-lived, Lawrence's contacts with the
Arabs had lasting consequences. His connections with France, on
the other hand, were easy to anticipate, were fairly close throughout
the first part of his life, and had no lasting consequences. However,
they continue to be widely and sometimes fiercely debated.

· EARLY EXPERIENCE ·

The contacts Lawrence had with France achieved considerable intensity at times. They started probably in December 1891, when his
family settled at Dinard for financial reasons. Between the ages of three
and five, Lawrence could not actually participate in French life, but
in 1893 he went to the Ecole Sainte-Marie with his brother Bob for
an hour every morning. He also went to a private gymnastic class in

Saint-Malo twice a week. He met few French people apart from his parents' landlords, the Chaignons. These experiences sufficed to teach him French. When he left France, he had "a child's lip-knowledge" of French.[1]

Lawrence could not have formed final impressions about France when he left it at the age of five. But his relations with some French people were maintained. His departure had nothing to do with any unpleasantness suffered in France, and his memories must have been good. Thus, Lawrence was prepared not to feel like a stranger, but his first stay was his longest in France. After this, he visited it briefly on many occasions, once for a few months, and crossed the country many times on his way to the Middle East.

His second sojourn in France was in 1906. Lawrence writes of Mr. Chaignon, who was waiting for him at the Customs: "we recognized each other at the same moment. He has hardly changed at all" (*HL*, 5–6). After twelve years, this implies the maintenance of a rather close relationship and the exchange of many pictures.[2] Lawrence seems to have felt at home. Psychologically, the ground was well prepared. Unlike Montaigne, who "forgot his Latin at school" (learned orally as a child, like Lawrence's French), Lawrence writes: "I have no difficulty at all in understanding what is said, and people have no difficulty in understanding me" (*HL*, 10). He comprehends French people when they talk to one another, but the use of French words in his letters is sometimes rather faulty (*HL*, 4, 5, 11, 14 and passim). The Chaignons' memories of his spoken French are not flattering. Lawrence had retained much of his former spoken French, but he made no great effort to improve it. Thus imperfectly equipped, he met all his former acquaintances.[3] Spiritually, he judges the French in a mildly disapproving manner. He dislikes Dinard,[4] complains of excessive prices,[5] thinks French customs officers lax in the exercise of their duty (*HL*, 6), French antique furniture fake,[6] and, finally, French firemen ineffective: "I never saw such an instance of incapacity" (*HL*, 14–15). The food and the number of courses of a French meal amuse him, but he rarely indulges in such feasts. He even complains, quite unjustly, that "There is great difficulty in getting decent drink in France" (*HL*, 27). No Gallophobia appears, only a foreigner's sometimes slightly irritated reactions, especially when Lawrence plays at straining his powers.

He returned to France the year after, at the age of nineteen, in August 1907. His French was better. "The Chaignons, & the Lamballe people, complimented me on my wonderful French: I have been asked twice since what part of France I came from" (HL, 59). His letters are sprinkled with French words, but with the same inaccuracies and spelling mistakes as before. His contacts with French people do not always show him in a pleasant light. His picture of a family evening at the Chaignons' is more of a caricature than a friendly description, revealing little congeniality on his side. Still he keeps his sense of humor: "They were quite upset at the idea of my going off the next day. Mr. Corbeil [Corbel] . . . collapsed when he heard where I had come from" (HL, 59). No attack against the French appears, but one can feel a slightly more tense atmosphere than in 1906. Lawrence complains about details and behaves like a foreigner.

His third French trip took place from July to September 1908. Lawrence was then twenty and had finished his first year at Jesus College. His French seems unchanged: orally it was perhaps as good as he says, but it was unimpressive and erratic if we judge by his written efforts. Many French words appear in his English letters. He Anglicizes French verbs ("to degust," HL, 70) and Frenchifies English ones ("criticiser," HL, 58). When he writes to the Chaignons, he does so in English. He does not seem to have met many French people. Yet he appreciates what he sees and revels in accurate descriptions[7] that are objective and unbiased.[8] His enthusiasm, often excessive but sincere, appears frequently: "One could stay here for months, painting every day, supposing one escaped fevers or other trifles of that sort" (HL, 72).[9]

The following year, in 1909, Lawrence made his first Middle East trip and completed his B.A. thesis, Crusader Castles.[10] This work reveals important points about the problem of "Lawrence versus France": the knowledge he displays of French castles and related technical literature is extensive. His five-title bibliography includes three standard French books on the topic. Although he staunchly retains his independence with regard to the theories propounded by French authors, he does not grudge his compliments nor does he hesitate to praise French at the expense of British scholars. Finally, the castles he visited or cites (or both) clearly show the importance of his French documentation: of 135 place-names, 54 are in France; in Syria, at least 10 places are French castles or towns.[11]

Lawrence returned to France in 1910, when he was twenty-two. He went in August and September to revisit some places he knew well, and in November he visited the Musée des Beaux-Arts in Rouen, carrying a recommendation from the French philologist and archaeologist Salomon Reinach, which demonstrates his good relations with French scholars. He has not left us much information about these trips, but we have valuable reports from his brothers Frank and Will. Since his B.A. was completed, this return to France, including renewed visits to familiar places, reveals a genuine interest unmixed with research purposes. However, once again, we find no hints of contacts with French people. He uses few French words in his letters, but we find an appreciation of Frank's spoken French: "His speaking of French whatever his writing is no great success: & I don't like trying to correct him, since I am little better myself" (*HL*, 109). This assertion contrasts with what he had written a year before: "I will have such difficulty in becoming English again, here I am an Arab in habits and slip in talking from English to French & Arabic unnoticing: yesterday I was 3 hours with an Orleannais, talking French, & he thought at the end I was a 'compatriot'! How's that?" (*HL*, 105). As usual, Lawrence's own remarks about his French make any assessment rather debatable. Either he has been bragging, or he is hard to please, or he has gone out of practice since 1909! His understanding of written French, though, may have been thorough. He gives his friend Vyvyan Richards a list of the works he has bought: *Petit Jehan de Saintré*, thirteenth-century fabliaux, *Tristan and Yseult*, Corneille, Molière, Racine, Montaigne, Voltaire, and Nerval.

No longer encumbered by an academic need for the information he is collecting, Lawrence gives more frequent vent to his personal reactions. Of the Gisors area, he writes: "If I stayed very long I would take root . . . the view has the same effect on people as a forest or a church: they talk in whispers" (*HL*, 110). The enthusiasm aroused in Lawrence by Reims cathedral appears in a passage that his mother copied and distributed among her friends in a (vain) attempt to demonstrate Lawrence's religious feelings (*L*, 86).

After 1910 Lawrence's student life stopped. Henceforward, his relations with the French took a different turn. In what spirit was he prepared to maintain these relations? He apparently retained a positive attitude: he knew France, probably better than many Frenchmen, although he had no real French friends—he never had any real friend except, perhaps, Dahoum. We find no trace of any real disagreement or even difficulty with any French people yet. His first "French" period does not seem to have given him any prejudice against the French. Conversely, it did not give him any desire to concede anything that France was not entitled to. His acquaintance with France left him a totally virgin mind so far as political agreements and everyday contacts with French people were concerned. And objectivity and total sincerity appear to characterize Lawrence's attitude in the war period as well.

· 1914–1918 ·

Lawrence's position with regard to French policy has often been characterized as hostile by French people in particular and by some English people as well. His reputation in France is easy to define: an Intelligence Service agent, a devoted friend of the Arabs, and, hence, an enemy of France. Few legends have no basis whatever, but this does not mean that the appendices to these legends are gospel truth. An impartial investigation of what Lawrence wrote about the French during the war, and of what French individuals wrote or said about him, may help to elucidate the matter.

One consideration must be kept in mind: the French and the English had competitive ambitions in the Middle East. Difficulties were numerous, even if the Sykes-Picot agreement translated potential animosity into a hopeful distribution of the future spoils of the Turkish Empire, disregarding the fact that this empire included Arab territories that had not the slightest desire of being treated as Turkish spoils. The agreement was subjected to violent criticism in the Middle East as well as during the Paris Conference in 1919. The representatives of France and of one side (only) of British policy were bound to oppose one another. And Lawrence's previous French links did not weigh heavily in his mind when balanced against his national British feeling or his idea of what was best for the Arabs. And this also happened to conflict with British views—hence part of Lawrence's moral tortures, or at least uneasiness—if we admit that he may have overdone his reactions for romance's sake.

The contacts Lawrence had with Frenchmen during the war were not extremely numerous and could not be. There was no real French army in the Middle East, only a detachment whose strength never exceeded 3,086 French soldiers (and this only on 1 November 1918) and 4,292 "natives." At the beginning of the war, the French government had in the area only a Military Mission and the Détachement Français de Palestine (D.F.P.) which, once the corps and its field of operations were enlarged, became the D.F.P.S. ("S" standing for Syria). The French Military Mission was commanded by Colonel (later General) Edouard Brémond, a typical regular officer (who for instance wrote to a friend of his on 11 September 1916: "do not forget that the Boche is to be killed wherever you can find him"[12]). He was not to get along with Lawrence, who had a thorough dislike of this category of men.[13]

For want of space, we cannot describe all of Lawrence's mentions of Brémond in *Seven Pillars* (SP, 111–12, 131–34, 166, 167–69, 197, 213–14, 229, 390, 542). Suffice it to say that the opposition between the two existed at every level: psychological, political, technical, physical. Lawrence was not happy about this clash, but he managed to find a good source of artistic inspiration in it:

> It was a curious interview, that, between an old soldier and a young man in fancy dress; and it left a bad taste in my mouth. The Colonel, like his countrymen, was a realist in love, and war. Even in situations of poetry the French remained incorrigible prose-writers, seeing by the directly-thrown light of reason and understanding, not through the half-closed eye, mistily, by things' essential radiance, in the manner of the imaginative English: so the two races worked ill together on a great undertaking (SP, 132).

We should not attach too much value to this passage, which was probably meant to amuse. Lawrence did not think the British "imaginative,"[14] and he did not think the French only "prose-writers." But the words sound good.

We do not know everything about his relations with the French. Some aspects are still to be investigated: the fact that he was awarded the much-coveted Legion of Honor on 18 March 1916, when he was a practically unknown reserve lieutenant is surprising, and bears witness to services or missions that can scarcely be based on hostile relations. It cannot be denied that he did his best to have Brémond removed from the Oriental scene, and it was probably Lawrence who had the colonel reprimanded by the French G.H.Q. He may have had a part in Brémond's final dismissal at the end of 1917. But there were certainly no personal feelings in this action. The proof that there was no animosity on Lawrence's side appears in the various answers about Brémond that he later gave to Liddell Hart.[15] If we bear in mind the sixty-odd attacks Brémond made on him in Le Hédjaz dans la guerre mondiale,[16] we cannot help thinking that Lawrence was not very vindictive. Unlike Lawrence, Brémond probably mixed personal and political feelings and even stooped to making remarks about Lawrence's physique. Pettiness is not absent from Brémond's manners either: entrusted by the French war minister with the drafting (painful for him) of Lawrence's mention in dispatches (23 November 1917) after his capture of Akaba, Brémond deliberately failed to mention Akaba. (Of course Lawrence is sometimes denied any share in the capture of Akaba.)

Lawrence's relations with the other French officers, n.c.o.'s, and diplomats were far smoother. Captain Pisani was the chief of the detachment of 65-mm mountain guns that came to be regarded as the spearhead of the Arab column sent after the routed Turks for the purpose of occupying Damascus before the arrival of English and Australian troops (who were deliberately kept behind for the required amount of time). Pisani is cited twenty-three times in Seven Pillars[17] and nineteen of these mentions are taken up in Revolt in the Desert,[18] once in Lawrence's article in World's Work,[19] three times in Lawrence to His Biographers,[20] and four times in Secret Despatches.[21] The tone is often humorous, even ironical (Lawrence's usual manner), but always appreciative and laudatory. He presents Pisani as: ". . . first volunteer. He was the experienced commander of the French at Akaba, an active soldier who burned for distinction—and distinctions" (SP, 377). Some French critics reproach Lawrence for his use of the word "distinctions" here. But why not acknowledge "distinctions" as such and be happy that they cost nothing and are none the less appreciated by so many officers and even civilians? Lawrence has been blamed for minimizing the rôle of the French elements in the campaign. But the only actions he witnessed (those undertaken by the Pisani column) he described ungrudgingly.

He had dealings with other Frenchmen: Adjutant Prost, Adjutant Lamotte, Captain Cousse, F. Georges-Picot. Again his remarks are often humorous but never cutting; and they usually express a fair tribute to the individual described. Lawrence was even considerate to these men. When the French criticize him, it is on account of what he did out of his feeling of duty toward the British and the Arabs, primarily toward the British. Corporal Marcel Matte, for instance, took a view similar to Brémond's.[22] He disliked Lawrence's attitudes and, as an Arabic specialist himself, perhaps resented what he may have considered an intrusion into his field. He disparages the soldier, the diplomat, and the technician, but he is honest enough to acknowledge Lawrence's pleasant manners and not infrequent offers of friendly services.

When he went to Cairo, Lawrence frequently visited the French Military Attaché, Lt. Doynel de Saint-Quentin, with whom he was on very good terms. Lawrence must have provided Saint-Quentin with much of the information we find in a secret report about him sent to the French Ministry. Nothing in this report would have ruffled Lawrence's feelings. General Bailloud wrote in a postcard to Saint-Quentin: "Thank your friend Captain Lawrence. I feel sure that when I get to know him I shall find him entirely worthy of the warm feelings you have for him. Indeed, in all honesty, I cannot keep a grudge against him for being English before being French."[23] Compliments are not all on one side. Commandant Cousse writes: "Major Lawrence praised very highly our Hotchkiss platoon, which took part in the Seil-Hesa fight."[24]

For all this, there remained some difficulties. Saint-Quentin could also write "[T. E. Lawrence] is indeed, without any pettiness, but with as much resolution as sincerity, hostile to any French action in Arabia, Syria, and Palestine. . . . His opposition is all the clearer as he sincerely believes he founds it . . . on the superior interests of the Arab race. Incidentally, I think he is too loyal not to comply with the orders of his chiefs if they clearly prescribe a French-British collaboration programme to him."[25]

Such details—and more could be quoted—show that Lawrence could behave in a friendly manner with French officials while revealing his true opinions. Was this a cover for a spy's activity? It is doubtful. In fact there was little secrecy in most of Lawrence's activities and opinions; his basic views can easily be found in his letters, especially in those to Hogarth.

The issue that helped crystallize Lawrence's opinions about French policy was the proposed landing at Alexandretta. This would have been a vast operation, and a junior officer could hardly have implemented it. Lawrence claims to have initiated it but to have been forced to entrust senior officers with its development. The French were against the project, which aimed, as they did, at cutting Turkish armies in two, but which would have brought British armies into Syria, where the French considered themselves to have "historical rights."[26] Lawrence deeply resented what he considered their veto. In fact, the English were as responsible as the French for the plan's abandonment.[27] But what the Alexandretta incident shows is that Lawrence was not against France but against French policy in the Middle East. He continued to maintain good relations with the French authorities on the spot (outside of Brémond), but he did write to Hogarth: "So far as Syria is concerned it is France & not Turkey that is the enemy" (HL, 303). He probably accepted the idea of a French Syria[28] (an important point that many Frenchmen overlook) in spite of undisguised fears: "In the hands of France [Syria] will provide a sure base for naval attacks on Egypt—and remember with her in Syria, & compulsory service there, she will be able to fling 100,000 men against the canal in 12 days from declaration of war. . . . And in any case in the next war, the French will probably be under Russia's finger in Syria" (L, 193). This statement was certainly dictated more by fear or caution than by offensive designs; on 22 March 1915 he wrote to Hogarth: "I think [Alexandretta] is our only chance in face of a French Syria" (L, 195). Here again he seems to consider a "French Syria" as a not unlikely possibility. But his ridiculous prophecies concerning France and Russia may be partly excused on the grounds of what Britain always saw (often rightly) as the Russian threat against her imperial roads. There is no opportunism in Lawrence's statement. It is linked to a general attitude that Glubb Pasha describes well when he explains that for thirty years France and Britain were allies in Europe while at the same time hostility prevailed between them in the Middle East.[29]

Unfortunately, many people who never examined the mass of available documents keep alive the myth that Lawrence was the enemy of France rather than of some French policies, and that he did not give due credit to French military action. For instance, in November 1967, in an article that is not even deliberately intended to debunk Lawrence, Lieutenant-Colonel Yves Jouin writes: "That day [Lawrence] 'admired' the French captain [Pisani], but this feeling did not incite him to bring the French participation into full relief in his book."[30]

If we consider the numerous positive comments Lawrence makes about Pisani, who received the Military Cross from Allenby thanks to Lawrence's praise ("Brilliant behaviour and services rendered in the course of operations undertaken against the Hejaz railway"), what is the basis of Lieutenant-Colonel Jouin's complaint? Jouin's view is further invalidated by the "note" sent by Mr. Maugras (a French civil servant posted in Cairo) to Paris on 16 November 1917 after the attack on Gaza and Ramleh undertaken by troops who were nearly all British: "Extravagant articles seem to attribute to French troops all the merit of the successes obtained. These articles have been censored. . . . It would be highly desirable, in order not to antagonize British military authorities, that our French press should refrain from speaking otherwise than in measured and reasonable terms of our military rôle in Palestine."[31]

It would have been wise to follow this advice. Lawrence suffered from attacks derived from the attitude castigated by Maugras and from the assumption that the French paid the same high price in the Middle East that they did on the European battlefield. Whatever the courage and self-sacrifices displayed by the very few Frenchmen who were sent to the Middle East, this assumption is not true.

· PEACE CONFERENCE ·

Lawrence left Damascus on 4 October 1918, presented the Cabinet with a memorandum on "the reconstruction of Arabia" on 4 November, and escorted Feisal, who reached England in December. Lawrence's purpose was twofold: to consolidate the future of the Arabs as a nation, a project that the French considered to be dangerous "daydreaming" directed against them (Lawrence must have been totally indifferent to French worries on this point); and to implement the Balfour Declaration (2 November 1917). Lawrence had contributed to the beginning of the relations between Weizmann and Feisal, to which the French did not object. Indeed, as Weizmann wrote in February 1919: "We got quite a good press in Frence—except for the *Journal des Débats*. The evening of the hearing, M. Tardieu, French Representative on the Council of Ten, issued an official statement, saying that France would not oppose the placing of Palestine under British trusteeship, and the formation of a Jewish State. The use of the words 'Jewish State' was significant; we ourselves had refrained from using them."[32] Although the word "State" does not appear in the Balfour Declaration, it was in the minds of the British statesmen.

A full study of Lawrence's conversations, contacts, declarations, and writings from January to September 1919 cannot be undertaken here (see Larès, *T. E. Lawrence*, 159–242). But we can summarize the general impression derived from what we know of his life during this period.

He had high ambitions for the Arabs. When he realized that the opposition to his dream of Anglo-Arab rule over Syria would not be overcome (it was the India Office and French government versus the Foreign Office and Lawrence), he came to consider that the Sykes-Picot agreements were, after all, not wholly disadvantageous to the Arabs. They were second best perhaps, but certainly not worse than the pure French annexation that sometimes seemed to threaten. He therefore accepted the idea of a rapprochement between the French and Feisal when he realized that the British government was not willing to jeopardize its friendship with France for the sake of the Arabs. He did consider France the enemy of Great Britain "in those areas," but "in those areas" only.[33]

Although the tension was sometimes great between the two countries, cool-headed Englishmen such as Arthur Balfour and R. Vansittart succeeded in obtaining English abandonment of Feisal's pretensions for the sake of good relations with France. In spite of Clemenceau's and Lloyd George's explosive tempers, an agreement was reached at the price of the complete disregard of President Wilson's Fourteen Points. Lawrence was invited to convince Feisal that the best step under the circumstances was to recognize the fait accompli of 15 September.[34] We have no definite proof that he is the one who convinced Feisal of the merits of the proposition, but Feisal did accept the fait accompli and tried to come to an agreement with France. He could not really do otherwise in any case.[35]

· 1920–1921 ·

On 11 September 1919, Lawrence initiated his press campaign in favor of the Arabs after realizing that there was nothing more to do on their behalf in Paris. His Colonial Office appointment in December

1920 as Churchill's technical adviser was probably the direct consequence of his newspaper articles.

Between 11 September 1919 and October 1920, he published twelve
articles (totaling some eighty pages). The tenor of these articles contributes to the destruction of the legend of Lawrence's hostility to
France.

In the first article, "The Yale Plan" (*The Times*, 11 September 1919),
Lawrence tries to demonstrate that the four main promises made to
the Arabs are not incompatible. Unfortunately, Wickham Steed, chief
editor of *The Times*, cut before publication the sentence where Lawrence "had written that he had been led to believe that the British
Government meant to live up to its promises to the Arabs, and that
it was because of this belief that he had encouraged the Arabs. He
wished to inform the Arabs and the British that he regretted what he
had done because the Government evidently had no intention of living up to the promises it had authorised him to make to the Arabs"
(*L*, 284). It happened that an anonymous article published in *Le Temps*,
"L'accord franco-anglais," six days later, 17 September 1919, made use
of Lawrence's "The Yale Plan." In order to demonstrate that there was
no contradiction between the Hussein-McMahon letters and the Sykes-
Picot agreement, the author used the argument of Lawrence, who was
thus presented as a supporter of the latest agreements. The author was
unaware of Steed's cut. The misunderstandings and possibilities for
misjudgment of Lawrence's position were increasing in France: whereas
Lawrence had actually disassociated himself from British policy in the
Middle East, he was presented in France as its supporter. It is scarcely
surprising that after a few similar errors of comprehension, Lawrence's
image in France should have become so distorted.

In *The Sunday Times* of 30 May 1920, Lawrence wrote against both
English and French policies and against the granting of English subsidies to Feisal, which would be used to fight the French occupation in
Syria and could therefore indirectly bring about Feisal's fall. Lawrence's
advice here is tantamount to telling Feisal to put up with the French
presence in Syria. Is this anti-French?

On 22 July 1920, Lawrence sent to *The Times* a violent attack against
British policy in Mesopotamia: "The Arabs did not risk their lives in
battle to change masters, to become British subjects or French citi-
zens. . . ." Here the English and the French are attacked equally.

On 7 and 17 August, Lawrence published two anonymous articles in *The Times*. They contain complimentary passages about Feisal—"a modern Saladin"—in the wake of his defeat at Meissaloun and his expulsion from Syria. These long articles contain no attacks against the French, although they were the direct agents of Feisal's overthrow.

On 8 August 1920, Lawrence's "France, Britain, and the Arabs" appeared in the *Observer*. It contains more praise of Feisal, whom he thinks poorly rewarded by the French. But his criticism is not limited to the latter:

> Yet we have really no competence in this matter to criticize the French. They have only followed in very humble fashion, in their sphere in Syria, the example we have set in Mesopotamia. It would show a lack of humour if we reproved them for a battle near Damascus, and the blotting out of the Syrian essay in self-government, while we were fighting battles near Baghdad. . . . It is odd that we do not use poison gas on these occasions. . . . By gas attacks the whole population of offending districts could be wiped out neatly; and as a method of government it would be no more immoral than the present system.

On 22 August 1920, in *The Sunday Times*, after another attack on British policy in Mesopotamia, he concludes:

> How long will we permit millions of pounds, thousands of Imperial troops, and tens of thousands of Arabs to be sacrificed on behalf of a form of colonial administration which can benefit nobody but its administrators?

The only document—a private letter—in which Lawrence attacks France, sounds moderate compared to this.

In September 1920, "The Changing East" was published anonymously in the *Round Table*. The theme is the same as in the introductory chapter in *Seven Pillars*:

> When we won it was charged against me that the British petrol royalties in Mesopotamia were become dubious; and French Colonial policy ruined in the Levant. I am afraid I hope so. We pay too much for these things in honour and in innocent lives.[36]

Among his other writings of the same period, we must mention Lawrence's Memorandum to the Foreign Office, no. 129405, dated 15 September 1919, whose tone regarding France is conciliatory, even appeasing:

To satisfy French agitation, we should agree to . . . retire to the "International" area of the Sykes-Picot agreement. We may also be able to stop our subsidies to Feisal. . . . We should secure assurances from the French and the Arabs that they would mutually respect the boundary of the direct French zone of the Sykes-Picot agreement (which Feisal had best initial for the Damascus Government). . . . If the French are wise and neglect the Arabs for about twelve months, they will then be implored by them to help them. If they are impatient now they only unite the Arabs against them (*L*, 288–90).

Does anything in this sound unfriendly to the French?

What was the result of Lawrence's criticism of official British policy? Was he attacked, called anti-British, sued for libel? Scarcely. Lloyd George received and listened to him, and proceeded to detach the Middle East from the Foreign Office (Lord Curzon) and to give it to the Colonial Office (Winston Churchill). And Churchill took Lawrence as his adviser, although Lawrence "had stipulated that the promises made to the Arabs should be redeemed as far as was consistent with a French Syria" (*L*, 323).

I have stressed this short period of Lawrence's life for two reasons. First, in order to show that when Lawrence might have found a sound excuse to attack France, he remained moderate and attacked British policy in Mesopotamia instead. Had he felt any hatred for France, he would not have missed this clear opportunity to express it.

Second, this was the prelude to a period (Cairo Conference of 1921, and stay at Amman as British Resident) that made Lawrence again the target of bitter French criticism. The French were worried when they saw Feisal's protector elevated to an official position and so near the Syrian border. They did not realize (or refused to realize) that, although Lawrence wanted to make up for Feisal's loss in Syria, he did not necessarily want this compensation to come at the expense of the French or as some sort of revenge. But the French considered Feisal's appointment as king of Iraq to be a "subtle" maneuver aimed at "tormenting the French."[37] Although untrue, such an opinion is understandable since all the Syrian refugees, including civil servants overthrown by the French and political opponents, took refuge in Transjordan, where they urged the launching of a campaign to reconquer Syria. Abdullah, second son of King Hussein, entered Transjordan during the Cairo Conference and openly proclaimed his intention of invading Syria in order to give the throne back to his brother Feisal. The British, absolutely opposed to any such action, had posters put up at Amman and Kerak reading: "The British Government has been informed that a small group had arrived from the Hejaz to fight France in Syria, pretending to have British support. The British Government has no connection with this group, and warns people not to join it."[38] The British government did not write this out of love of France. But all its efforts were aimed at calming the Arabs and restraining them when they were most aroused against the presence of the French in Syria.

Transjordan was created on 1 April 1921. France never did believe in Great Britain's innocence and candidness regarding Syria, and was not altogether wrong, since she met with many difficulties in which British agents were not completely uninvolved.[39] As for Abdullah, his situation quickly became so precarious that Lawrence was sent to his rescue. Just before, Lawrence's mission to King Hussein of the Hejaz had also worried the French, who followed his moves closely.[40] A strange example of their interest in him can be found in a letter sent by Captain Depui to Aristide Briand, French prime minister and minister of foreign affairs, on 25 September 1921. Depui was the only French officer who converted to Islam. His letter seems to reveal a genuine hatred of Lawrence:

> Helped on by his self-importance, Lawrence, doubtless accustomed to the sovereign authority conferred on him by his handling of hard cash subsidies, to his long-standing intimacy with Emir Feisal—whom he knew in his Greatness and his Fall—and to his belief that the fate of Arabia lies in his very own hands, comes before the *little Malik* as a Sovereign, without even bowing his head, his hand raised to his chest, as if he were awaiting the King's homage, this accompanied by a fixed mocking smile on his lips, breaking out into a cackle at the slightest opportunity.[41]

Lawrence probably never had a chance to read this letter, but he certainly knew well about the existence of such feelings. It is therefore surprising that he never expressed strong feelings against any French people in particular or ventured to generalize more often about them. Such reports as Depui's unfortunately went far in influencing the judgments of French statesmen. Hence we are not surprised to read the following comments by Aristide Briand, about one month later (October 1921):

> It is believed that Lawrence intends to suggest that Transjordan be completely detached from Palestine. She would belong to the Colonial Office. . . . Colonel Lawrence therefore remains true to his Sherifian plan. . . . The mandate and the alliance still create obligations for the British Government that it cannot overlook, even to satisfy Colonel Lawrence's Arabian and anti-French designs.[42]

According to the French phraseology of the time and even later, although France is supposed to be the friend of the Arabs, for another country to be "pro-Arab" often amounts more or less to its automatically being called "anti-French." General Gouraud, haut-commissaire in Syria, stressed this on 2 November 1921: "Transjordan would be independent and Colonel Lawrence would remain at Amman as a consul. . . . I consider this measure . . . serious."[43]

If Lawrence refrained from openly voicing hostility toward the French in high circles, he did not mince his words privately when he felt he had no choice. On 8 November 1921, six days after Gouraud's telegram previously quoted, he answered his friend Colonel S. F. Newcombe about the French request for the handing over of the suspected would-be assassins of General Gouraud. The general escaped the attempt, and the assassins were thought to be hidden in Jordan, from where it was always supposed they had come. Lawrence wrote:

> We cannot afford to chuck away our hopes of building something to soothe our neighbours' feelings: and the French have made our job here as difficult as possible—if it is possible at all—by their wanton disregard of the common decencies observed between nations.
>
> Please remind them that they shot Arab prisoners after Meisalun and plundered the houses and goods of Feisal and his friends. The dirty dog-work has been fairly shared, & I thank what Gods I have that I'm neither an Arab nor a Frenchman—only the poor brute who has to clean up after them. . . .
>
> If you can, drop over here friendly-fashion some time, & I'll show you the French picture from underneath. Not lovely. à toi. (*L*, 336)

Lawrence, however, recommended the handing over of the terrorists.[44] Things settled down only in 1922, when H. St. John Philby made a half-"state," half-"family" visit to Syria, accompanied by Lieutenant-

Colonel Peake Pasha, the founder of the Arab Legion. The latter's presence meant much since Peake also had had many difficulties with the French. By then, Lawrence was back in England, about to leave the Colonial Office for good (4 July 1922) and enlist in the R.A.F. (30 August 1922). From then on, he was still accused of undertaking secret missions and stirring up tribes against various colonial powers, but these accusations were never substantiated.

We can also learn much about the problem of Lawrence's alleged hatred of France from the literary field, always a central concern of his. For want of space, and because this subject has already been investigated (see Larès, *T. E. Lawrence*, 299–322), I am not going to examine Lawrence's knowledge of French literature. But we should note that a man rarely devotes much of his time and effort to the study of the language and of the literature of a people he hates, unless this is in order to work for its destruction (Eichmann's behavior may be an instance of this), which was clearly not Lawrence's case. Had Lawrence really disliked the French, would he, even for financial reasons, have translated French novels into English? The quality of his translation of *Le Gigantesque* (*The Forest Giant*) reveals not only his conscientiousness as an artist but also a knowledge of French that can scarcely have derived from unfriendly feelings.[45]

In view of all the evidence to the contrary that I have presented, it is time to ask why Lawrence has been so long and so often accused of virulent anti-French prejudices.

The first and, I think, logical temptation is to look for reasons, perhaps proofs, in the archives of the Service Historique de l'Armée (at Vincennes) or of the Ministère des Affaires Etrangères (at the Quai d'Orsay). If there is any basis for the French attacks against Lawrence, it might perhaps be found in the secret reports, confidential messages, or telegrams sent from Syria. These documents contain no mention of Lawrence after 10 October 1918. Some citations can be found again in 1921, but none after (see Larès, *T. E. Lawrence*, 278–83). They do not contain anything like a proof of Lawrence's alleged Francophobia, although they are replete with hints, accusations, suppositions, and assertions. The nature of these documents makes one wonder whether their mere existence does not arise from the fact that the French wanted a scapegoat. After all, the French situation in Syria was far from comfortable, and they may not have seen the future clearly. The spectacle of a Mesopotamia become Iraq and endowed with some sort of self-government, as well as the fear of Syria's being encircled by united Arab countries,[46] can account for the French reaction, which led them, not unnaturally, to focus their doubts on one man. And who was better suited for this rôle than such a famous and well-advertised personality as Lawrence, who concealed his political opinions so little? Perhaps it was also known that he never contradicted assertions concerning him, however farfetched they might be, which added to his value as a scapegoat. This choice could also be a profitable lever in the hands of high French officials in their attempt to show how dangerous the situation was and to try to obtain more help (men and equipment) to be sent to Syria by a government reluctant to take such measures. Gouraud, for one, may have had this in mind.

After a vain inquiry into official papers in an attempt to explain French feelings toward Lawrence, I met some of the few French survivors of this period who had known him. Here too, the result was inconclusive. Sympathizers disclaim any anti-French action of Lawrence's. The others (such as Marcel Matte), who are convinced of Lawrence's hatred of France, simply answer: "Proofs, you won't find any. These are things one can catch a whiff of." And Matte adds: "The Lawrence Bureau is a real mafia meant to put down possible detractors systematically."[47] No witness, not even Matte, could recount any definite hostile gesture of Lawrence against France, but, on the contrary, they did speak of many thoughtful offers of services and kindnesses.[48]

If the fear Lawrence may have engendered in some local spheres is unfounded (as I think it is), it was nonetheless real. And this explains the existence of a plot that, so far as I know, has not been mentioned in any written document. It was revealed to me orally by one of the conspirators, now dead. His death does not release me from the promise of confidentiality I had to make in order to be given some details: in 1921, when it was feared that Lawrence might come back to Syria, all measures were taken so that he should not leave it alive. The executioner was appointed and accepted the rôle. Can such a plot have been inspired by any other feeling than that of hatred or fear? Once more, hatred appears on the French side, not on the English.

If we examine the writings likely to bear out one theory or the other, the same pattern appears again and again. In Lawrence's writings there is no hatred, but merely criticism, sometimes (rarely) violent, and at any rate always local and limited to French policy in Syria. In French writings (ten books, fifteen essays, four hundred newspaper articles), where no proof of Lawrence's supposed hatred of France appears, one rarely discovers marks of real hatred of him. But the widespread legend of his supposed hatred of the French influenced the French themselves, who wrongly took it for granted, without, curiously enough, taking it ill. From Lawrence's opposition to French Oriental policy, they inferred that he hated them, and so followed the prevalent but unformulated theory of the Quai d'Orsay and of some military circles. Francophilia was equated with intelligence, morality, strength (and also, pure origins); Francophobia, with silliness, wickedness, weakness (and also mixed origins).

Many French writers often describe what they take to be Lawrence's hostility to France. (This may well be an instance of the now-understood psychological process of diffusion of ideas usually called intoxication.) But they take it tolerantly, even with good humor. They are interested in Lawrence and accept his supposed hostility, but they do not really hold it against him. They admit he had a right to hate the French, and they think he did use this right. The legend of Lawrence's hatred of France has therefore not damaged his image in the eyes of the French public, which did not really reciprocate it. But it has not yet realized that there is nothing to reciprocate.

Why not limit the origin and the consequences of this almost entirely forged feeling to the field clearly delineated by Leonard Woolley?

> For Syria [Lawrence] had a passion. . . . He liked France and often talked of the pleasant times he had had there, and I think he was even fond of the French people. But especially after a long stay in the Lebanon, he felt a profound jealousy of the part they played or wished to play in Syria. That French politicians should aim at a control of the country he had come to love infuriated him.[49]

T. E. Lawrence and France—friends or foes? Not really friends, certainly not foes.

N·O·T·E·S

1. B. H. Liddell Hart, "T. E. Lawrence": In Arabia and After (London: Cape, 1964), 15.

2. I was shown some copies by Commandant Chaignon, the son of Lawrence's landlord.

3. The Féceliers, parents of Mrs. Chaignon, the Burnels, the Lefévriers, M. Corbel, and Frère Fabel.

4. ". . . it has a misplaced ambition of becoming a watering place like Bournemouth, which it will never perform" (*HL*, 20).

5. "In the morning, the hotel presented a great bill"; "we were robbed shamefully at Tréguier" (*HL*, 15).

6. Its antiquity is "all in the polish!" (*HL*, 20).

7. Cordes (*HL*, 73); Tarn food (*HL*, 70–71).

8. Jean Béraud-Villars, *Le Colonel Lawrence ou la recherche de l'absolu* (Paris: Albin Michel, 1955), 31.

9. With Lawrence, appreciation is generally mixed with irony.

10. As it was called when published posthumously (1936).

11. For a fuller discussion, see my *Lawrence d'Arabie et les Châteaux des Croisés* (Paris: Publications de l'Association des Médiévistes Anglicistes de l'Enseignement Supérieur [AMAES], 1980; available from the U.E.R. d'anglais, Université de Paris I, 1 rue Victor Cousin, 75230 Paris Cedex 05), 122 pp.

12. Service Historique de l'Armée, Vincennes, hereafter cited *S. H. S. H.* Carton 7 N 2139.

13. A dislike that allowed notable exceptions, such as Allenby, Dawnay, Meinertzhagen, Trenchard, and Young, among others.

14. See, for instance: "the unimaginative British" (*SP*, 636).

15. *T. E. Lawrence to His Biographers Robert Graves and Liddell Hart* (London: Cassell, 1963), 2:93, 125, 157.

16. Général Edouard Brémond, *Le Hédjaz dans la guerre mondiale* (Paris: Payot, 1931).

17. *SP*, 377, 379, 520, 542, 577, 578, 586, 593, 594, 595, 596, 599, 605, 606 (lines 11, 22) 608, 617, 620, 623 (lines 17, 36), 630 (lines 2, 30), 658.

18. *Revolt in the Desert* (London: Cape, 1927) 309, 327, 346, 356, 365, 366, 368, 370, 373, 380 (lines 1, 27), 381, 382, 383, 395, 400, 402, 408, 409.

19. *The World's Work* (21 July–21 October 1921), 222.

20. *T. E. Lawrence to His Biographers*, 2:118, 142–43, 158.

21. *Secret Despatches from Arabia by T. E. Lawrence*, published by permission of the Foreign Office (London: Golden Cockerel Press, 1939), 137, 138, 141, 166.

22. In *Les Nouvelles Littéraires*, (14 March 1963): "Un témoin dépose: la vérité sur Lawrence d'Arabie."

23. "Merci à votre ami le capitaine Lawrence. Je suis sûr qu'à l'usage je le trouverai tout à fait digne de la sympathie que vous avez pour lui, ne pouvant équitablement lui tenir rigueur d'être anglais avant d'être français." Dated "12 August." *S. H.* Vincennes, Carton 17 N 499.

24. "Major Lawrence m'a fait vif éloge de notre section Hotchkiss qui a pris part au combat du Seil-Hesa."

25. "T. E. Lawrence est en effet, sans mesquinerie, mais avec autant de résolution que de franchise, hostile à toute action française en Arabie, Syrie et Palestine. . . .

Son opposition est d'autant plus nette qu'il croit sincèrement la fonder . . . sur les intérêts supérieurs de la race arabe. Je le crois d'ailleurs trop loyal pour ne pas déférer aux ordres de ses chefs si ceux-ci lui prescrivent nettement un programme de collaboration franco-anglaise." S. H. Vincennes, Carton 16 N 3200. Dossier 12.3805.

26. A. J. Balfour, in his "Memorandum on Syria, Palestine, & Mesopotamia," dated 11 August 1919, states that the historical basis of French pretensions to Syria seems doubtful to him, but he admits that they have been accepted.

27. See Maurice Larès, *T. E. Lawrence, la France et les Français*, Publications de la Sorbonne (Paris: Imprimerie Nationale, 1980), 122–34. Hereafter *T. E. Lawrence*.

28. "The French insist upon Syria—which we are conceding to them . . . " (*L*, 193). It must be noticed that "we" may mean the English in general, and Lawrence may then be protesting against this concession, but it may also mean that he personally adheres to this concession.

29. Sir John Bagot Glubb, *A Soldier with the Arabs* (London: Hodder and Stoughton, 1957), 415.

30. Lieutenant-Colonel Yves Jouin, "Hedjaz 1916–1918. Les compagnons français de Lawrence," *Revue Historique de l'Armée* 23 (November 1967), 107–21: "Ce jour-là, il 'aima' donc le capitaine français, mais ce sentiment n'est pas allé jusqu'à le déterminer à donner, dans son livre, tout son relief à la participation française."

31. S. H., Carton 16 N 3200 no. 2024, p. 256. "Des articles dithyrambiques paraissant attribuer aux troupes françaises tout le mérite des succès obtenus. Les articles ont été supprimés par la censure . . . Il serait extrêmement souhaitable que, pour ne pas indisposer les autorités militaires anglaises, notre presse en France s'abstienne de parler autrement qu'en termes mesurés et raisonnables de notre rôle militaire en Palestine."

32. Chaim Weizmann, *Trial and Error* (London: Hamish Hamilton, 1949), 306.

33. E. L. Woodward and Rohan Butler, eds., *Documents on British Foreign Policy, 1919–1939*, first series (London: H.M.S.O., 1952), 4:370–71.

34. Including the evacuation of Syria by English troops and their replacement by French ones. Between 13 and 15 September 1919, Lloyd George and Clemenceau came to an agreement on part of the *Aide-Mémoire in Regard to the Occupation of Syria, Palestine, and Mesopotamia pending the Decisions in Regard to Mandates*. President Wilson's Fourteen Points as well as the conclusions of the King-Crane Commission were beautifully ignored. Another point was easily agreed upon: not to wait for Feisal, then on his way to Paris, and to settle at least part of the problem before his arrival. Thus, Feisal could only wage (and lose) a rear-guard battle. See Larès, *T. E. Lawrence*, 224–25, for full details.

35. As for Lawrence, he may have felt that his hand had been forced. But the episode of his sending back his decorations in protest (whereas he had probably already done so on 30 November 1918) can be no more clearly interpreted than the tale of his fixing his Croix de Guerre to the neck of Hogarth's dog.

36. T. E. Lawrence, *Oriental Assembly*, ed. A. W. Lawrence (London: Williams and Norgate, 1939), 143.

37. Henri H. Cumming, *Franco-British Rivalry in the Post-War Near East* (Oxford: Oxford University Press, 1938), 104.

38. King Abdullah of Transjordan, *Memoirs of King Abdullah of Transjordan*, ed. Philip Graves (London: Cape, 1950), 194.

39. See C. J. Jarvis, *Arab Command* (London: Hutchinson, 1943): "The Emir was doing his best to control matters, but, as practically every member of his government hailed from either Syria or the Damascus region and had recently been expelled from their country by the French, their sympathies were openly with the rebels, and there is no doubt that . . . active assistance was given covertly to the bands of rebels" (p. 90). About another incident, the arrest of Fuad Salem, Jarvis writes: "In reality it had been entirely due to the double-dealing of the Trans-Jordan Government in taking advantage of the British Resident's ignorance of the wanted man's identity. Fuad Salem served in the Legion with Peake for another two years and then, joining the rebels in Syria, he was killed in 1926 fighting against the French" (p. 92). Could the French easily believe in the "British Resident's ignorance," in this matter or other similar ones?

40. *S.H.* 4 B 2, Diplomatie 1920–23.

41. Archives des Affaires Etrangères, Paris, E 310, vol. 13, pp. 209–16. "Sa suffisance aidant . . . Lawrence sans doute habitué à l'autorité souveraine que lui conférait le maniement des subventions sonnantes et trébuchantes, à l'intimité familière de l'Emir Feysal qu'il connut dans sa Grandeur et dans sa Déchéance, à sa croyance en la possession personnelle du sort de l'Arabie, se présente au *petit Malik* en Souverain, sans même une inclinaison de tête, la main élevée à hauteur de poitrine, semblant attendre l'hommage du Roi, ceci accompagné d'un sourire moqueur stéréotypé sur ses lèvres, éclatant en crécelle à la moindre occasion."

42. Archives des Affaires Etrangères, Paris, 1418–1420/6. "Lawrence aurait l'intention de proposer que la Transjordanie soit complètement détachée de la Palestine. Elle relèverait uniquement du Colonial Office. . . . le colonel Lawrence reste donc fidèle à son plan chérifien . . . le mandat et l'alliance créent tout de même, il me semble, au Gouvernement anglais des obligations qu'il ne peut négliger, même pour satisfaire les plans arabes et antifrançais du colonel Lawrence."

43. Ibid. Telegram 1524/6. General Gouraud must have felt relieved when Lawrence had himself replaced by H. St. J. Philby on 29 November 1921. "La Transjordanie serait indépendante et le colonel Lawrence resterait à Amman comme consul. . . . je considère la mesure . . . comme grave."

44. H. St. John Philby, *Forty Years in the Wilderness* (London: Robert Hale, 1957), 94.

45. For a detailed study of the circumstances of Lawrence's French translations, see Larès, *T. E. Lawrence*, 323–35. For a thorough examination of the *Forest Giant* translation itself, see Larès, "T. E. Lawrence as a French Translator," *T. E. Lawrence Studies*, no. 2 (forthcoming).

46. A vain fear, as we can see sixty years later and as Lawrence already saw and explained in his "Letter-Preface" to D. G. Pearman's *The Imperial Camel Corps with Colonel Lawrence* (London: Newton, 1928), reprinted in *L*, 576: "When people talk of Arab confederations or empires, they talk fantastically. It will be generations, I expect—unless the vital tempo of the East is much accelerated—before any two Arabic states join voluntarily."

47. Telephone conversation in 1970 between Marcel Matte and Maurice Larès: "Des preuves, vous n'en trouverez pas. Ce sont des choses qu'on sent dans le nez." "Le Bureau-Lawrence est une véritable mafia destinée à matraquer systématiquement les détracteurs éventuels."

48. A desire to help France, and not only individual Frenchmen, was also present in Lawrence. In his letter dated 5 March 1928, to D. G. Pearman, he wrote: "my objects were to save England, *and France too*, from the follies of the imperialists, who would have us, in 1920, repeat the exploits of Clive or Rhodes" (*L*, 578); italics mine.

49. A. W. Lawrence, ed., *T. E. Lawrence by His Friends* (London: Cape, 1937), 93–94.

Lawrence as Bureaucrat

AARON KLIEMAN

Despite sustained interest in T. E. Lawrence's every mood, movement, and motivation, there is one particular phase of his
career that remains under researched and, as a result, un-
appreciated.[1] From February 1921 to July 1922 Lawrence was employed
as political adviser in the Middle East Department of the Colonial Office, with direct access to the secretary of state for the colonies, Winston Churchill. During this eighteen-month bureaucratic tour of duty—
which he would later claim to be the period "of which I'm proudest"[2]—
Lawrence attended the historic Cairo Conference in March 1921, was
instrumental in formulating and then executing Britain's interwar
Sherifian policy of identification with conservative Arab nationalists,
orchestrated plans for securing the Iraqi monarchy, undertook a sensitive diplomatic mission to Arabia, and, in what is proving to be his
most lasting contribution to Middle Eastern history and politics, helped
set in motion the eventual emergence of the Hashemite Kingdom of
Jordan as an independent state separate from Palestine.

These early postwar years, 1921–22, are noteworthy for several reasons. First, they represent a period of transition decisive for Lawrence
personally and for the larger Anglo-Arab relationship with which his
name is still so closely identified. His Colonial Office days mark the
second and final stage of his involvement in the "complex web of war,
politics and diplomacy"[3] spun out over the Middle East region in the
preceding decade. They also can be seen as a brief civilian interlude
bracketing two distinct phases of his military career, after which the
celebrated Colonel T. E. Lawrence (*the* Lawrence of Arabia) abandons
public life and seeks refuge in anonymity as a very private Private

Shaw. Similarly, employment as a British civil servant is hardly consistent with the popular conception of Lawrence as individualist and as heroic figure. The man of action and the man of letters: these are the two molds cast for him by friends and biographers. Lawrence's role as bureaucrat fits neither really; but it does help to place him in Edward Said's dual category of "expert-adventurer-eccentric" and "colonial authority"—*cum* administrator.[4]

On a second level, Lawrence's internship coincides with a determined effort by Great Britain to secure a firm grip over the strategic Middle East. At a time when calls for reductions in expenditure and overseas garrisons were being sounded at home, and in a local situation of political uncertainty that tended to encourage extremism, the objective was formidable: to convert a mix of imperial interests and overlapping wartime pledges into the foundations for a durable peacetime policy toward this region that Lawrence had so recently had a hand in liberating from Turkish rule. Success or failure depended upon providing answers to a range of complex issues that included: a final partitioning, with France, of the Ottoman Empire into spheres of influence; insulating the successor states from the twin outside revolutionary forces of Bolshevism and Kemalism while providing them good government and internal stability under the League of Nations mandate system; defining the nature and geographic extent of Arab independence; and overseeing the establishment of a Jewish national home in Palestine premised upon cooperation between Arab and Zionist. Among the first steps taken by His Majesty's Government early in 1921 to terminate the previous policy of drift and to reassert control over events were a major reorganization, with Middle Eastern responsibility entrusted in the Colonial Office, and the appointment as colonial secretary of Churchill, who, in a customary burst of enthusiasm, then proceeded to surround himself with an able, experienced staff for which Lawrence was especially recruited.

Said claims that "what appealed to Lawrence's imagination was the clarity of the Arab, both as an image and as a supposed philosophy . . . toward life."[5] In 1921, however, he is forced to encounter the Arabs in concrete form as political actors, with ambitions as well as defects of their own. In this sense, when Lawrence as bureaucrat and policymaker confronts the reality of his limitations and those of his Hashemite protégés, the Sherif Hussein of Mecca and his sons, Feisal and Abdullah, he is in fact mirroring those of Great Britain too in contending with the Middle East in an unidealized form. As symbolism, the contrast is striking. The dominant image of Lawrence resplendent in full Arab regalia is supplemented by the later one of him dressed in suit and tie, diminutive and diffident, virtually indistinguishable among the forty other officials posing confidently for a group photograph at Cairo. It is not as Liddell Hart's "Great Captain" that Lawrence left his imprint on history but rather as a gray bureaucrat, dutiful yet determined and purposive.

What prompted Lawrence to join the Colonial Office? How well did he adjust to bureaucratic routine? What kind of relationship did he have with fellow employees and with Churchill? How influential was he really in the making and conduct of policy? Do we find in the Middle East Department's office files and correspondence some clue as to his true feelings toward the Arab cause? Finally, what effect if any did his experiences in government service have on Lawrence's subsequent decision to break with the past?

The end of 1920 found Lawrence in the quiet confines of Oxford, where, through the intervention of friends, a position had been arranged for him in November 1919, once his services were no longer needed as British liaison to the Hejazi delegation during the Paris Peace Conference. Elected to a seven-year research fellowship at All Souls College, Lawrence sought solitude, like thousands of fellow countrymen coming home from the Great War. "Now I'm tired and I want to rest and forget," he confided.[6] Oxford seemed an ideal place for reflection, literary effort, and a return to old, familiar haunts. Three factors combined, however, to upset these plans.

Fame was the first, since it was at this time that Lowell Thomas began to popularize the Lawrence legend in nightly film and lecture shows at the Royal Opera House in Covent Garden. Developments in the Middle East were the second factor, for while the French occupation of Damascus by force in the summer of 1920 may only have discomforted officials in London, a series of escalating tribal uprisings throughout Mesopotamia that autumn in defiance of Britain's authority had an alarming effect, challenging the very premises for her continued presence in the Middle East. Reputation, firsthand knowledge of the Arabs, and obvious writing talents made Lawrence sought after as a commentator on the Middle East, especially as events sug-

gested the validity of his earlier criticism of British callousness toward
former Arab allies.[7] Responding to requests, Lawrence in editorials,
interviews, and letters attacked this failure to honor commitments and
the resultant paralysis of policy in Middle Eastern affairs.[8]

But his own restlessness was the third critical factor that intervened
to end Lawrence's residence at Oxford and that best explains his pre-
disposition to accept the offer by Churchill. In fact it is Churchill who
would later eulogize Lawrence as being "like some prehistoric monster
carried by a tidal wave from ocean depths far inland" after the Armi-
stice, "and left strangely stranded when the waters fell."[9] We know, for
instance, that he spent most of his time away from the college, experienced anxiety in drafting the manuscript for what would eventually
appear as *Seven Pillars of Wisdom*, and was burdened by the lack of
money.[10] Personal dissatisfaction thus compounded the dissonance he
must have felt between Arab estrangement, on the one hand, and the
romanticized version of their liberation being promoted by Thomas,
on the other, leaving Lawrence both angry and depressed, fighting
"between limelight and utter darkness."[11] Whether he was prompted
into becoming a civil servant by financial necessity, by boredom, or by
prospects for redressing injustices is uncertain. But because there is a
strong element of escapism in so much of Lawrence's life—the fantasies and the literary excesses, the later air force enlistment—one cannot help but note that his Colonial Office phase, rather than being
exceptional, actually conforms to this pattern. By entering the ranks
of bureaucracy, he regained not only a sense of importance and an
ability to influence events but also that kind of security which a bureaucratic structure is best at providing, together with freedom from
direct, personal accountability.

Apparently Lawrence's own needs and motives were compatible with
those of his new employer, forming the basis for an effective working
relationship grounded in mutual dependence. Most historians agree it
was Churchill who sought out and personally recruited Lawrence.[12]
Aldington even suggests that, coming fresh to the situation and finding Lawrence installed in public opinion as the authority on Arabia,
Churchill really had no choice but to invite his collaboration.[13] Clearly
the new colonial secretary was in need of legitimacy and expert advice
in undertaking his formidable assignment; enlisting Lawrence was consistent with Churchill's aim of staffing the newly formed Middle East

Department with qualified personnel; if nothing else, co-opting Law-rence would effectively neutralize the government's strongest critic.

To the credit of both men, and considering the skepticism with which the appointment as political adviser was greeted, Lawrence's adaptation to bureaucratic life proved surprisingly smooth. As Ke-dourie points out, alongside his positive attributes of bravery in war and a great capacity for physical endurance, the record also shows him to have been "self-centered, mercurial and violently unstable"[14]—hardly qualifications to be recommended in a bureaucrat. Small wonder that Masterton Smith of the Colonial Office observed, "He is not the kind of man to fit easily into any official machine," adding: "I gather that Col. Lawrence has got used to dealing with Ministers—and Ministers only—and I see trouble ahead if he is allowed too free a hand."[15]

It was perhaps only natural to have anticipated trouble. Friction and rivalry were inherent in the situation. That other members of the department no less qualified than he took a dim view of Lawrence was owing partly to jealousy at his public acclaim, partly to clashes of temperament and personality, and the rest to legitimate differences over substantive policy issues. Working in the same room with him were John Shuckburgh, who headed the Middle East Department, and Hubert Young, who had served with Lawrence in Arabia during the war and who, as a Foreign Office holdover, had greater experience in Arab affairs and Middle Eastern diplomacy. In offering his recollec-tions of Lawrence, Young expresses thinly veiled criticism of the man whom he saw as the "little monkey," pointing out that despite such "small failings" as unscrupulousness, "calculated departures from the strict path of the truth," and complete ignorance of Mesopotamia, Lawrence committed a cardinal sin of organizational politics in trying "to create a picture in the minds of the responsible authorities of him-self as the best possible adviser" on the Middle East.[16] Joining them later in the year was the military adviser, Richard Meinertzhagen, whose friendship with Lawrence did not prevent Meinertzhagen's characterizing him as a "humbug" whose "meek schoolboy expression hides the cunning of a fox and the intriguing spirit of the East."[17]

Had Lawrence been desk-bound or, alternatively, working for some-one else, the likelihood of a blowup would have been great. For, as another contemporary observed, here was "an individual of driving intelligence, with nothing of the administrator."[18] That he lasted eighteen months owes much, as we shall see later, not only to Churchill's skillful use of Lawrence but also to the fact that he spent relatively little time in London handling routine administrative matters. For most of 1921 Lawrence was away from the office and in the field on various special assignments. The following is a calendar of his activities on behalf of the Colonial Office in 1921.

7 February.	Meets Churchill, accepts position as political adviser.
15 February.	Churchill assumes office.
1 March.	Churchill sets off for Egypt.
12–23 March.	Cairo conference of Middle East experts.
25 March.	Proceeds via Gaza, Jerusalem and Amman to escort Abdullah.
28 March.	Attends Churchill-Abdullah meeting in Jerusalem.
10 April.	In Amman.
15 April.	Meets secretly with Feisal in Cairo.
17–19 April.	Accompanies Herbert Samuel to Amman.
20 April.	Final meeting with Feisal who leaves for Baghdad.
May.	Back in England.
14 June.	Churchill presents policy in speech to Commons.
8 July.	Departs for Jidda on Arabian mission.
23 July.	Begins talks with Hussein.
15 August.	Suspends talks, proceeds to Aden.
29 August.	Resumes Jidda negotiations.
22 September.	Breaks off talks, sails to Egypt.
27 September.	By train to Jerusalem.
12 October.	To Amman for final recommendation on Abdullah's future.
8 December.	Concludes Anglo-Hejaz Treaty with Abdullah.
9 December.	Jidda . . . Jerusalem . . . Egypt . . . Paris . . . London.

A suspicious Foreign Secretary Curzon, commenting on Lawrence's pace of activities, confessed, "These movements are beyond me";[19] even Churchill, trying to locate his adviser, at one point admonished, "You should in future keep me fully informed of your movements."[20]

The year actually divides into two parts: preliminary planning for the Cairo Conference, the sessions themselves, and the immediate aftermath; followed by Lawrence's six-month stay in the region, from July through December, with Amman as the centerpiece.

· THE CAIRO CONFERENCE ·

In recalling preparations for Churchill's publicized assembly of Middle Eastern experts, Lawrence boasted: "Talk of leaving things to man on spot—we left nothing."[21] Which was essentially true. Determined to initiate a fresh approach toward the troublesome yet vital Arab regions, and to do something both dramatic and prompt, the new Colonial Secretary resolved to convene a meeting within only a month of taking office in order to consult with all those responsible for handling political, economic, military, legal, technical, and financial matters pertaining to the Middle East. Yet he also felt it was imperative to confront the assembled British authorities with a concrete set of proposals. Toward that end Churchill immediately set his new team in the Middle East Department to work discussing options, drafting position papers, and advocating specific policy guidelines. Throwing himself into the project, Lawrence wrote with satisfaction on 2 March, "We are making a most ambitious design for the Middle East: a new page in the loosening of the Empire tradition; and are working like beavers to end it by Wednesday."[22]

The Cairo agenda and decisions reflect a good deal of Lawrence's own thinking, and it is clear that he significantly helped to shape the policy as finally drafted and approved by Churchill in London. (1) *Iraq.* It was agreed that British interests might be best safeguarded by having a local ruler committed to, and dependent upon, Great Britain. Deemed most qualified for this post was none other than Lawrence's wartime comrade-in-arms Feisal Ibn Hussein. Air power, a subject with which Lawrence was already becoming fascinated, would be introduced in Iraq in place of static defense and conventional ground forces. (2) *Arabia.* The delicate balance between the two local contenders, Ibn Saud and Lawrence's favorite, Hussein, would be preserved along with British interest through a clever system of monthly subsidies to be used as an incentive for good behavior. (3) *Palestine.* The civilian administration under the British High Commissioner Sir Herbert Samuel would stress economic prosperity as a means of facilitating Arab-Jewish understanding and as a substitute for political development. Zionism, meanwhile, could be regarded as useful in serving British ends. (4) *France.* The French, as Lawrence had long argued, were of course allies, but also a potential threat to British interests and an embarrassment. To the extent possible, it was deemed advisable to disengage from French policy toward Syria and if necessary to act unilaterally. (5) *Arab nationalism*. In contrast to the direct rule of France, Britain would henceforth seek an accommodation with Arab nationalists through a policy of indirect rule founded on cooperation with moderate, conservative Arab elements.

These various components came together neatly in London and Cairo to form the so-called Sherifian policy. This policy had at its center the notion that past commitments, current pressing needs, and prospective interests might all be fulfilled through support for the Hashemite dynasty headed by the Sherif Hussein of Mecca. Lawrence took the lead in arguing that with Hussein already positioned in Arabia, simply by installing Feisal at Baghdad it would be possible to coordinate efforts on a region-wide scale through pro-British allies at a cost to prestige and exchequer immeasurably cheaper than stationing troops. This clever stratagem gained added appeal and logic when another son of the Sherif Hussein, Abdullah, suddenly appeared in Transjordan while the Cairo Conference was in session and a *modus operandi* hastily reached with him.

Everything else, however, was thoroughly planned and for the most part went according to schedule. At Cairo, Lawrence participated in the political and military committees where the serious work took place, particularly the timetable for the election and investiture of Feisal as first king of modern Iraq. The minutes of the conference show Lawrence emphatic in promoting Feisal's candidacy, describing him as an "active and inspiring personality" in contrast to the "lazy" Abdullah.[23] This presumptuousness and self-confidence on Lawrence's part doubtless must have offended sensitivities of the Mesopotamian contingent, which may explain the outburst by Gertrude Bell, who at one point turned on him and said: "You little imp!"[24] Aside from this, however, the conference passed smoothly. In a letter to his brother, Lawrence wrote: "Here we live in a marble and bronze hotel: very expensive & luxurious: horrible place." "We have done a lot of work," he continued: "We're a very happy family: agreed upon everything important: and the trifles are laughed at."[25] He even found time to escort the Churchills and Miss Bell on a tour of the Pyramids. The main proposals were endorsed, with the participants dispersing, each to carry out his or her part in successfully implementing the Cairo decisions, while Churchill and Lawrence proceeded next to Jerusalem, in part to deal with the worrisome situation developing across the Jordan River.

The one scenario unanticipated in London was that Transjordan might become a trouble spot. The departmental consensus had provided for a symbolic British presence in what nearly everyone took to be an integral, even if peripheral and undemarcated, part of the Palestine mandate. The arrival of Abdullah at the dusty town of Amman at the head of a ragtag army bent upon liberating Syria from the French suddenly threatened to upset British calculations. The year before, the Foreign Office had advised precautions against permitting French influence south of the Sykes-Picot line, agreed upon in 1916; otherwise, "we shall lose all control and practically bring the French down to the Red Sea."[26]

When news reached Cairo of Abdullah's threatened invasion of Syria, it posed the following likelihood: while there was no danger of Abdullah being strong enough to defeat the French army under General Gouraud, he just might be capable of arousing Arab tribes along the way, cross into Syrian territory, ambush a French patrol, and then retreat southward with the French in full pursuit. Before the British government could react, they would be presented with a fait accompli and a geopolitical setback of the highest magnitude: France, poised in Transjordan, might then be able to endanger Britain's favored position not merely in Palestine and the Arabian peninsula but within striking distance of the Suez Canal. It was clear to Churchill that Abdullah had to be dissuaded from any such foolhardy escapade, and he dispatched Lawrence on ahead of him to arrange a meeting with Feisal's brother in Jerusalem.

According to Abdullah, in discussing the impending meeting Lawrence had already broached the idea of his remaining temporarily in Transjordan. "You are well-known for sacrificing your personal ambitions for your country, so stay here. If you succeed you will achieve the unity of Syria in six months."[27] With the help of Allah, "we will visit you in Damascus to offer our congratulations." Whether or not Abdullah was deluded by Lawrence into believing he might replace his brother as king of Syria with British help, realized the folly of engaging the French army, or, as is more likely, appreciated that Transjordan was the best he could hope for under the existing circumstances, he consented to meet with the colonial secretary.

The meetings took place at Government House on 28 and 29 March, with Lawrence in attendance and evidently serving as translator.[28] Churchill took the opportunity to outline before Abdullah Britain's Sherifian policy of support for the Hashemites, plans for Iraq, and determination to have order and stability in Transjordan. At the close of their first meeting, he also proposed that Abdullah might wish to consider an offer to stay on temporarily in Amman to guarantee quiet until an Arab governor could be appointed. Abdullah asked for time to consider the proposal. When the conversations resumed the following morning, he sought in vain British consent for Arab rule over Transjordan and Palestine—an intimation of his future aspirations—before consenting to the terms: British money, troops, and advisers in return for guaranteeing that there would be no anti-French or anti-Zionist agitation. By mutual consent this arrangement was meant explicitly to last for a period of only six months.

From the standpoint of Lawrence, architect of the Sherifian formula, a potential defeat had now been brilliantly converted into a triumph. In his cabled report to the Cabinet a week before, Churchill had been candid in confessing: "As we cannot contemplate hostilities with Abdullah in any circumstances, there is no alternative to this policy. We must therefore proceed in co-operation and accord with him."[29] Virtue was made of necessity; and this ad hoc agreement would be presented subsequently as "a definite part of general policy of friendship and co-operation with Shereefian influence," harmonizing with plans for Mesopotamia. Churchill ended this message to the prime minister prior to his Jerusalem talks: "fortified by views of Colonel Lawrence, I have no doubt whatever that occupation of Trans-Jordania on basis of an arrangement with Abdullah is right policy for us to adopt." Abdullah in Amman reinforced the whole scheme of working through one family. Still it bears emphasizing that this all came about not because of British desires but through his initiative.

The support of British agents in the field enlisted on behalf of the Sherifian policy, and the Transjordanian crisis defused, Churchill returned to London to prepare for the next challenge of defending his policy at home. He left Lawrence behind, however, to oversee the fulfillment of British wishes. Reporting to Churchill on 10 April, Lawrence cabled: "Today with 4 machines I went over to Amman and saw Abdullah," whose financial position was described as "more difficult than he gave us to expect" since "as he has to entertain all comers, and deputations of 2 or 3 hundred are a daily matter, his living expenses are very great."[30] Nevertheless, Lawrence felt confident that an embryonic administration could be built and that matters would straighten out there. He then proceeded to Cairo for secret meetings with Feisal to brief him thoroughly in preparation for Feisal's impending entry into Iraqi politics. Initial plans called for Lawrence to travel at least part of the way with him, but these plans were canceled because of Foreign Office sensitivities over possible French charges of a British conspiracy with their former enemy.[31] Instead, having helped to bolster Feisal's courage, Lawrence was ordered back to England.

· AMMAN AND JIDDA ·
"Sequels Are Rotten Things"

Some indication of Lawrence's state of mind in mid-1921 can be derived from a letter written in London on 21 May to Robert Graves. Of the recent events relating to the Cairo initiative, he wrote: "Our schemes for the betterment of the Middle East race are doing nicely: thanks." Still, "I wish I hadn't gone out there: the Arabs are like a page I have turned over: and sequels are rotten things."[32] But neither did the security of Whitehall suit him, for he confided to Graves, "I'm back in the Colonial Office and hating it," adding: "I'm locked up here: office every day, and much of it." It was not long, however, before he managed to escape the bureaucratic confines of the Middle East Department, returning on special assignment to the region for what proved to be his final encounter with the Arabs and with Arab politics. Had he known then the toll it would take on him, physically and mentally, Lawrence might have preferred staying at home.

His mission in the latter half of 1921 was twofold. He was to report back to Churchill on conditions in Transjordan as the end of Abdullah's six-month period of grace neared. But he was also asked by the Foreign Office to conclude a formal pact with Hussein recognizing Britain's standing in the area and her policy toward Iraq, Syria, and Palestine. The latter assignment proved to be profoundly exasperating for Lawrence, even though he had been given full plenipotentiary powers in representing His Majesty's Government and arrived in Jidda with a draft treaty already prepared. Lawrence was forced to spend two months in wearisome discussions with an embittered Hussein, at the end of which his diplomatic mission was aborted.

The failure was not really Lawrence's, even though the mutual dislike between him and Hussein together with his habitual restlessness may not have made him the most suited for an assignment that required, above all, patience and tact. That it would almost certainly fail might have been predicted in advance owing to the Arab leader's overweening ambition and justifiable sense of having been betrayed, and to the presumptuousness of both Churchill and Lord Curzon in assuming that Great Britain still could manipulate all aspects and actors of Middle Eastern affairs at will.[33] In effect Lawrence was being sent to persuade the former head of the Arab Revolt and would-be pretender to hegemony over the Arabs to subordinate hopes for independence to British imperial interests.

Excerpts from reports sent back by Lawrence from Jidda help to convey the atmosphere of the negotiations. On 7 August he wired that Hussein had accepted virtually all articles of the proposed treaty save for Article 15, which involved recognition of the British mandates over Mesopotamia and Iraq. The cable ends, "it has been a bad week for both of us."[34] A month later he reported the following: "On my return King Hussein went back on his decision and demanded, firstly, return of all States in Arabia except his own to pre-war boundaries; secondly, cession to him of all areas so vacated; thirdly, right to appoint all kadis and muftis in Arabia, Mesopotamia and Palestine; fourthly, recognition of his supremacy over all rulers everywhere."[35] Lawrence's categorical rejection of these demands made Hussein "send for dagger and swear to abdicate and kill himself"; to which Lawrence replied: "I said we would continue negotiating with his successors."[36] This may have had a sobering effect upon Hussein, because Lawrence concludes this particular description of the exchange on a note of optimism: "Things are now going in most friendly and rational way."

In seeking to press Hussein toward agreement, Lawrence, exercising his own discretion, resorted to a range of tactics from flattery to deception. At various points in the Jidda negotiations, he offered to soften the blow to Hussein's personal ambitions with further gifts of money and a yacht; when this did not work, he threatened an immediate cutoff of subsidies and of British support for him vis-à-vis Ibn Saud. Nor was Lawrence above some court intrigue, enlisting the aid of Hussein's wife and sons, Ali and Zeid, in trying to neutralize the king, whom he regarded as "brave, obstinate, hopelessly out-of-date." Yet to no avail. On 22 September he cabled Curzon a final report. Hussein had approved the treaty and announced publicly his forthcoming signature of it, only to renege. When presented with the text for ratification by his son Ali, Hussein shouted and struck at him, then sent Lawrence eight contradictory sets of prior conditions and stipulations—"all unacceptable."[37] His patience at an end, his services needed elsewhere, after asking the king to return 80,000 rupees paid him in advance of his regular subsidy on the assumption he would sign, Lawrence—"bored stiff: and very tired and a little ill"[38]—must have greeted with undisguised relief instructions from London ordering him to proceed to Transjordan.

At Jidda, Lawrence failed because he was unable to persuade an unbending and unrealistic King Hussein to save himself through a closer relationship with England. In the Emir Abdullah, by contrast, Lawrence found an Arab leader who, unlike his father, came to personify the opposite qualities of realism, a pragmatic approach, open identification with England, and a keen sense of survival. Only by working to help himself that previous March had Abdullah succeeded in acquiring any kind of bargaining position with the British. Now, finding himself with nowhere else really to go at the end of 1921, Abdullah was ready to settle, at least temporarily, for what he himself candidly dismissed as "this wilderness of Trans-Jordania." Since this corresponded essentially with Lawrence's own plans for the area east of the Jordan, he was far more effective in serving British aims at his next station, Amman. In fact, here his role was decisive.

What brought him again to Transjordan was the question that still remained open of what to do now that the six-month temporary arrangement between Churchill and Abdullah was drawing to a close. There did appear to exist something of a consensus among British officials, however. First, Transjordan was to be an integral part of the

Palestine mandate. After all, the colonial secretary himself had pledged to support the formula: "While preserving Arab character of area and administration to treat it as Arab province or adjunct of Palestine."[39] Second, Abdullah's services were no longer needed in Transjordan since, as Foreign Secretary Curzon noted of Churchill's improvisation with some satisfaction, "Abdullah was much too big a cock for so small a dunghill and the experiment was foredoomed to failure."[40] Everyone involved simply assumed Abdullah would be invited to London as a way of bowing out gracefully.

This was certainly the prevailing Colonial Office view too. In Jerusalem, the Palestine Administration officials, headed by the high commissioner himself, Sir Herbert Samuel, since April had been reporting back on Abdullah's inability to govern. In a dispatch on 13 June, Samuel had written: "It now appears that the people are far from content under the new regime, that tax-collecting is subject to much the same difficulties as before, and that public security leaves much to be desired."[41] Of Abdullah, he wrote: "The Emir is preoccupied to some extent with ideas of wider bearing and greater ambition. He does not conceal his opinion that the position in Mesopotamia should have been offered to him and not to his brother. His mind is still much preoccupied by Syria." Even earlier, on 17 April, Samuel had dismissed Abdullah's rule as "more of a picnic than an administration" and urged that he resign—"the sooner the better."[42]

Based on this flow of information, even cautious people in the Middle East Department such as Hubert Young came to appreciate that the Transjordan experiment "had proved a failure" and "we have not the right man" in Abdullah.[43] In July he wrote of Abdullah, "he made an admirable stop-gap, but he would not do as a permanency at all";[44] and in September it was Young who proposed that Lawrence finish up at Jidda and go to Jerusalem to discuss with Samuel what ought to be done "to get rid of Abdullah."[45]

Expressing the departmental view, a junior official minuted: "If we don't invite 'A' to London it is quite possible that he may disappear sulkily down the Hejaz Railway, which if not perhaps the best would be at any rate the cheapest solution."[46] Churchill, however, was far more circumspect. While agreeing with the prevailing sentiment, he preferred to keep the options open, as reflected in a cable to Samuel on 11 July:

As to Trans-Jordania I am not quite happy and we must now consider the nature of the position at the end of the six months for which Abdulla accepted responsibility. . . . Whether Abdulla should return to Trans-Jordania or not [following a visit to London in September] will depend largely on his own wishes and partly on Lawrence's success in effecting a reconciliation between him and his father. While Abdulla is here I might be able to suggest to him that he should go straight from London to Mecca and later to be employed by his father in negotiating with the Imam and Idrisi [Arabian peninsula rulers].[47]

Toward this end of clarifying the situation, Young was ordered to join Samuel and Lawrence in Jerusalem during October.

At this decisive juncture it was Lawrence who swung the pendulum in favor of deferring the union of Transjordan with Palestine and retaining Abdullah on a permanent basis. On 7 October, Young cabled the Colonial Office, "We have exhaustively discussed question of Trans-Jordania during past three days," and promised that concrete proposals would be reaching London "which will probably contemplate immediate removal" of Abdullah and his Syrian entourage.[48] Yet Young must have had serious reservations that he was ready to share in a second cable that same day. Following a conversation with Lawrence, Young described him as "still pretty confident he will be able to get rid of Abdullah or 'Sunny Jim' as he is called locally, and I hope he has not over-estimated his powers of persuasion."[49] After all, he recalled, "one cannot lose sight of the fact that all the plans that were made in Cairo in March about Trans-Jordania were upset when Abdullah himself was consulted"; it is "possible that the same thing may happen again."

And it did. There is one piece of evidence to show that Lawrence all along had diverged from the departmental consensus. On 29 June he had written: "We asked Abdulla only to keep peace with his neighbours, not to run a good administration. His total cost to us is less than a battalion; his regime prejudices us in no way, whatever eventual solution we wish to carry out, provided that it is not too popular and not too efficient!"[50] What he found in Amman upon arriving there in October quickly led him to conclude, contrary to everything the Colonial Office hierarchy was contemplating, that the status quo ought to be preserved and, indeed, institutionalized.

Lawrence's files from Amman are not merely a model of colorful reporting but actually turned the tide in favor of Abdullah's reign over

Transjordan. Inquiries and firsthand observations led him to conclude that the situation was better than indicated by previous reports. Discovering that Abdullah was ready to stay on, he advocated a series of marginal moves aimed at strengthening the infant regime, including removal of certain Syrian troublemakers who insisted Abdullah antagonize the French, using Transjordan as a base; improving Abdullah's financial position with monies to be used for buying tribal support; providing a strong individual to act as permanent British Resident; enhancing local police enforcement capability; easing fears of Zionism through an amendment to the Palestine Mandate explicitly precluding application of its Zionist provisions such as Jewish land ownership or settlement east of the Jordan River.[51] Thus he argued it was futile to expect a strong administration when "in Trans-Jordania every man of military age carries a rifle as a mark of self-respect," whereas Abdullah's so-called military force "is the only unarmed body of men in the country."[52] Should these measures be authorized, Lawrence felt confident "for the future things should go better."

His appraisal was accepted in London, as were the specific recommendations, which involved a minimal outlay and which obviated the unappealing alternative of controlling Transjordan through direct military occupation. Few dared challenge the considered opinion of Lawrence. Sir Herbert Samuel, for one, did take issue, as witnessed by "a note on Colonel Lawrence's Report" prepared in the High Commissioner's Secretariat in November. Giving another view of the situation, it objected to "drifting further and further in the direction of complete political separation between Palestine and Trans-Jordania," which, if achieved, "can hardly have other than a most unfavourable reaction on the economic and possibly on the political situation in Palestine."[53] Second, the note stated the belief of those who—unlike Lawrence—"have had experience of Trans-Jordania during the last six months and who consequently have had opportunities of hearing the views of the inhabitants" that facilitating Transjordan's development can best be brought about "by the elimination of the Emir Abdullah." Meinertzhagen, in the Middle East Department, also looked on Lawrence's report with suspicion; on 18 November he noted: "The political separation of Trans-Jordania from Palestine is no doubt one of Lawrence's ideals and must be combatted."[54] But to no avail. Lawrence had succeeded in effecting a turnabout in policy, at the same time securing a throne for Abdullah with full British backing.

Here we have the opinion of H. St. John Philby, who on 28 November relieved Lawrence as chief British representative in Transjordan, finding himself "in charge of a chaos which was called an office." In his first report, Philby recalled how the situation at the end of September 1921 was "about as bad as it could be." "But the storm cleared with amazing suddenness" on Lawrence's arrival; his "short sojourn at Amman served to dissipate prevalent misconceptions" of British policy and "gave the Amir a new lease of life."[55] Bolstered by British support and Philby's presence, Abdullah's image in London as an "ideal constitutional monarch" improved thereafter, his departure constituting "a serious setback to the progress of the country."[56]

That Lawrence won out over opposition from Jerusalem and London owes, in the first instance, to the compatibility of views between him and Churchill and to his success in gaining the full support of the colonial secretary. Thus on 26 October, upon reading Middle East Department minutes critical of Abdullah, Churchill wrote the following:

> I do not altogether share these views. After all we have put through 6 months without using any troops and at no great expense. I see Col. Lawrence's latest telegram recommends Abdullah carrying on. This is my wish too. I do not mean to throw him over easily. He has an impossible task.[57]

If anything, with time, Churchill's resolve stiffened. By February 1922 he was answering interdepartmental queries emphatically:

> Do we or do we not wish to see Abdulla settle himself firmly in the Trans-Jordanian saddle? [Churchill]: Yes.
> If we allow this to happen, it is certain that he will develop ambitions in the direction of Palestine . . . embarrassing to us. [Churchill]: Not necessarily.[58]

Lest his will or intent be subject to misinterpretation, the colonial secretary added for good measure: "I do not want to change Abdulla or the policy followed during the last 9 months." Of Lawrence and his mission, Churchill later wrote glowingly:

As a last resort I sent him out to Trans-Jordania, where sudden difficulties had arisen. He had plenary powers. He used them with his old
vigour. He removed officers. He used force. He restored complete
tranquility. Everyone was delighted with the success of his mission.[59]

Such unstinting praise, however, was not enough to offer Lawrence
contentment when, his Middle East mission essentially completed, he
returned to the Middle East Department in December. Given to shifting moods while in Jidda and Amman, neither did he find peace of
mind in bureaucratic work. Graves depicts him as being in a very
nervous condition in the winter of 1921–22; while his brother, who
viewed him as "out of harmony with the normal," confirms that in 1922
Lawrence "came as near as anyone could do to a complete breakdown."[60] Whether or not the last months as civil servant governed his
decision to resign, in that they were too uneventful and "normal,"
remains unclear. We do know of his intention to quit from a remark
at the beginning of October: "This life goes on till February 28 next
year."[61] Apparently persuaded by Churchill to stay on a while longer,
nevertheless by the summer he was ready to make the break. In a letter
of resignation to Shuckburgh, dated 4 July 1922, he recalled that his
had been an emergency appointment during an expected stormy period: "Well, that was eighteen months ago"—"So if Mr. Churchill
permits, I shall be very glad to leave so prosperous a ship."[62] A month
later, to borrow from Liddell Hart's description, Lawrence freed himself from government service and enlisted in the Royal Air Force,
leaving a position of high responsibility "to return in a status of irre-
sponsibility."[63]

· LAWRENCE AS BUREAUCRAT ·
An Assessment

Kingmaker or functionary? In much the same way that other facets
and phases of Lawrence's career defy hard-and-fast categories, so too
does his stint in the Colonial Office. On the one hand, he was not a
free agent. There are no historical grounds, consequently, for magni-
fying or exalting his role in the events of 1921, as though he were
individually accountable for the manner in which Great Britain handled

Arab affairs. At times he labored to encourage such a view by gross exaggeration, as in describing the origins of R.A.F. control: "As soon as I was able to have my own way in the Middle East, I approached Trenchard on the point, converted Winston easily, tricked the Cabinet into approving . . . and it has worked very well."[64] Everything Lawrence did took place within an institutional framework.

Yet, on the other hand, neither are we justified in discounting his personal influence. Lawrence was far less intimidated than others by bureaucratic custom or by standard operating procedures. Whenever presented with the opportunity, he did not hesitate to exercise discretionary authority. And he proved especially effective in the decision-making process through the role explicitly assigned him, that of political adviser behind the scenes to Winston Churchill. Lawrence as bureaucrat is thus subject to the three tests for any policymaker, whether principal or proximate: originality, resourcefulness, success.

Originality. In analyzing the Cairo policy we are led to conclude that in truth Lawrence contributed precious little to the internalized debate over a Middle East strategy. Each component originated with others or was already engrained in governmental thinking before Lawrence appears. Thus, for example, the call in 1920 for radical change in the ministerial arrangements of Whitehall was being sounded from various quarters. Similarly, plans were already in motion in the summer of 1920 in the Foreign Office to promote Feisal's candidacy for the throne of Iraq. Support for Hussein had been a longtime commitment. Francophobia espoused by Lawrence is traceable to the ideas of his mentor, Commander D. G. Hogarth, and other members of the Arab Bureau during the war.[65] Abdullah's independent action made him a factor to be contended with. Trenchard and others promoted the utility of air power in commanding vast desert areas. And of course Lawrence's inability throughout to accept the fact of Saudi ascendancy is well documented. In fairness, though, he showed originality in pulling together many of these strands in promoting a comprehensive Sherifian policy designed to meet essential British needs throughout most of the region. Purposive, energetic, he demonstrated greater independence of action than of thought, and in this way was able to influence policy outcomes.

Resourcefulness. Lawrence showed little patience toward administrative matters. To cite merely one example, when asked about debts incurred by Feisal while in exile, he minuted the file on 13 May: "I cannot suggest any means at present. We paid Feisal money in March when he left England; we paid him more in Egypt; we may pay him more next month; and no doubt it will all be charged somewhere sometime. Suppose we add this to those?"[66] Similarly, personality and policy differences did not make for complete collegiality with Young, Shuckburgh, Meinertzhagen, Samuel, Bell, and other officials.

Rather, the key lies in the relationship of trust and complementary support established during 1921 between Churchill and Lawrence. His earlier confidential guide to newcomers from the British Army in the art of handling Arabs could serve equally well as a bureaucrat's manual. Some of the "Twenty-seven Articles"[67] very much apply to his performance in the role of civil servant: "Be shy of too close relations with subordinates"; "The less apparent your interference the more your influence"; "Wave a Sherif in front of you like a banner and hide your own mind and person"; "Your ideal position is when you are present and not noticed," etc. Yet none better explains the reasonable success of Lawrence as a bureaucrat than Article 4: "Win and keep the confidence of your leader."[68]

To start with, Churchill and Lawrence shared several things in common: a mutual dislike for Curzon, his "Grand Design" and deference to the French, his lack of suppleness and subtlety, and his previous mishandling of Middle Eastern affairs; a devotion to the British Empire;[69] confidence in their ability to cut expenditures and reduce garrisons by such instruments as the air force, with which both men were fascinated; and the need for a comprehensive regional formula in place of a piecemeal, ad hoc approach and divided ministerial responsibility.

Strengthening the productive Lawrence-Churchill relationship were the qualities each brought to the task. Churchill provided the authority figure and the source of approval, while Lawrence lent an aura of legitimacy to the entire administration. Much of the credit accrues to the colonial secretary for his careful handling of Gertrude Bell's "little imp." He permitted Lawrence access to him, and knew how to channel Lawrence's energies. The political adviser, in turn, was loyal but also understood how to exploit his employer's weaknesses in order to press his own personal preferences. Churchill, to be sure, was painfully ignorant of the region he had been called upon to administer; hence his deference to Lawrence's expertise.[70] When preparing his speech on the Cairo policy for presentation in the Commons, for example, Churchill urgently requested: "Let me have a note in about three lines as to Feisal's religious character. Is he a Sunni with Shaih [sic] sympathies, or a Shaih with Sunni sympathies, or how does he square it? What is Hussein? Which is the aristocratic high church and which is the low church? What are the religious people at Kerbela? I always get mixed up between these two."[71] In him, Lawrence found a leader open to ideas, one both willing to act and sensitive to the moral as well as political need to meet the commitment to the Arabs without damaging British interests. In a personal letter late in 1922 Lawrence confided to his former mentor, "I've had lots of chiefs in my time, but never one before who really was my chief," emphasizing for us the special quality of this relationship going beyond the normal bounds of employer-employee ties. In an extraordinarily revealing passage, he then added, "it doubles the good of a subordinate to feel that his chief is better than himself."[72] In short, Lawrence synthesized the ideas of others, added his dream of Hashemite supremacy and sold this package to Churchill, who then rammed it through despite Arab, French, Zionist, and internal opposition.

Success. Success is the third test for policy and policymaker alike. Certainly at the moment T. E. Lawrence took final leave of Arab affairs and the Colonial Office, to be followed shortly by Churchill, their Sherifian policy seemed the model for sound, pragmatic, and even liberal management of relations with the Middle East. Stabilization of the region had been achieved through a blending of British privilege and responsibility with a gradualist approach toward Arab—and some thought possibly even Jewish—self-government. Yet we know their work ended in ruins. Why?

The answer lies perhaps in the realization that neither side of the Anglo-Arab alliance was well served by the other. Who more than Lawrence entrusted British hopes to the Hashemites, even though he had never held Hussein, Feisal, or Abdullah in particularly high esteem? Just as during the war, he was prepared to use them despite their individual failings; but then there could have been no room for surprise or disappointment in London when each in his own way contributed to undermining the premises of the 1921 Cairo Conference. Hussein's exposed position and diplomatic isolation led to his fall from power in 1924 at the hands of the rival Saudi dynasty, thereby sealing not only his own fate but that of the elaborate Sherifian formula. In the years to come, the Saudis would use their enhanced position in the Arabian peninsula to challenge the authority of the surviving Iraqi and Jordanian branches of the Hashemites. Thrown on the defensive, Feisal found contentment in Iraq and, for all intents and purposes, abandoned the larger goal of Arab independence and Arab unity. Abdullah, on the other hand, never ceased to pursue designs aimed at expanding both his prestige and realm. This reputation, however, together with a relationship of almost total dependency upon, as well as identification with, Great Britain, disqualified him for leadership of the Arab movement. If the individual Hashemites were flawed in character, so the ideology that they represented of conservative nationalism and mutuality of Anglo-Arab interests soon became discredited in the eyes of the succeeding generation of Arab leaders. The Sherifian alliance, in short, was nullified by altered circumstances and hence no longer practicable already in the late 1920s.

Seen in this light, the frustration experienced by Lawrence during 1921 became a microcosm of Britain's larger difficulties in relating to the Middle East in the critical interwar period. Arab historians are neither right nor fair in claiming, as Antonius does, that "in Arabia he had encouraged, because he genuinely shared, the Arab hopes; in Whitehall, the boom of imperial interests silenced all other sounds."[73] Lawrence clearly sympathized with Arab aspirations and was ahead of his time in sensing the potential vigor of the Arab awakening. It is no less inaccurate, however, to present Lawrence as, in Churchill's words, "the truest champion of Arab rights whom modern times have known."[74]

Lawrence genuinely sought independence for the Arabs as a means of righting earlier wrongs. But he functioned as a servant of Great Britain and of British interests, particularly when in the employ of Churchill and the Colonial Office's Middle East Department. Moreover, in performing his responsibilities, like any other member of the policymaking establishment, he was asked to respond not to an idealized situation but to an imperfect reality.

The experience could only have been disillusioning for Great Britain and for Lawrence. They came to realize the limits of their own power and those of their Arab partners. Under these conditions, Lawrence erred only in accepting the inherent logic as well as political feasibility of Anglo-Arab interdependence or mutual dependence, best symbolized by Transjordan, the creation of his own hand. In seeking to assist both causes—British and Arab—he grossly exaggerated their compatibility. Whether owing to an obsession or to necessity, he—and Churchill—backed the wrong horsemen. Regardless of whether one chooses to view modern Jordan as a vindication of T. E. Lawrence's original conception or testimony of its bankruptcy, the Hashemite Kingdom remains as the solitary memorial to a lost cause.

N·O·T·E·S

1. Unlike other chapters of his life, Lawrence's Colonial Office service can be fully documented. Yet largely it has been neglected. Mack, however, devotes a full chapter to this phase, but Kedourie has questioned his historical judgment. See notes 2 and 3 below. Lawrence figures only marginally in Martin Gilbert's treatment of the 1921–22 period in Churchill's career. See note 12 below. See also Uriel Dann, "T. E. Lawrence in Amman, 1921," *Abr Nahrein* (Leiden) 13 (1972): 33–41.

2. John E. Mack, *A Prince of Our Disorder* (London: Weidenfeld and Nicolson, 1976), 297. Lawrence wrote, "The work I did constructively in 1921 and 1922 seems to me, in retrospect, the best I ever did. It somewhat redresses to my mind the immoral and unwarrantable risks I took with others' lives and happiness in 1917–1918" *T. E. Lawrence to His Biographers Robert Graves and Liddell Hart* (London: Cassell, 1963), 1:113.

3. Elie Kedourie, "The Real T. E. Lawrence," *Commentary* 64 (July 1977): 52.

4. Said places Lawrence in the company of such "British agent-Orientalists" as Gertrude Bell, D. G. Hogarth, Ronald Storrs, and H. St. John Philby, who during and after the First World War combined both roles, taking up positions in support of indigenous rulers: Lawrence with the Hashemites, Philby with the Saudis. Edward W. Said, *Orientalism* (New York: Vantage, 1979), 246.

5. Said, *Orientalism*, 229.

6. A. W. Lawrence, ed., *T. E. Lawrence by His Friends* (London: Cape, 1954), 255; hereafter cited as *Friends*.

7. See Stanley and Rodelle Weintraub, eds., *Evolution of a Revolt* (University Park: Pennsylvania State University Press, 1968), 66–77.

8. See, for example, a solicited editorial by ex–Lt. Col. T. E. Lawrence in the *Sunday Times* (22 August 1920) in which he charged the Lloyd George government with "losing men, money and supplies" by a "willfully wrong policy"; see also an interview with a special correspondent from the *Daily News* on 25 August.

9. Churchill, in *Friends*, 163.

10. Phillip Knightley and Colin Simpson, *The Secret Lives of Lawrence of Arabia* (London: Nicholls, 1971), 160; Richard Aldington, *Lawrence of Arabia* (London:

Collins, 1969), 297; Liddell Hart, *"T. E. Lawrence": In Arabia and After* (London: Cape, 1934), 407–8.

11. Richard Meinertzhagen, *Middle East Diary 1917–1956* (London: Cresset, 1959), 32.

12. Gilbert maintains that the two men met on 8 January and that Lawrence accepted the offer immediately; whereas Lawrence later insisted he consented only after Churchill's third appeal. Martin Gilbert, *Winston S. Churchill 1919–1922* (London: Heinemann, 1975), 510, and *T. E. Lawrence to His Biographers*, 1:10.

13. Aldington, *Lawrence of Arabia*, 303.

14. Kedourie, "The Real T. E. Lawrence," 56.

15. Gilbert, *Churchill*, 527–28.

16. *Friends*, 106–7.

17. Meinertzhagen, *Middle East Diary*, 34–35.

18. *Friends*, 147.

19. F.O. 371/6352, file E8122 of 16 or 17 July.

20. F.O. 406/46, file E4700/4531/93, Churchill–T.E.L. (secret cable), 19 April 1921.

21. *T. E. Lawrence to His Biographers*, 2:143. For the significance of the Cairo Conference, see Aaron S. Klieman, *Foundations of British Policy in the Arab World* (Baltimore: Johns Hopkins University Press, 1970).

22. *T. E. Lawrence to His Biographers*, 1:12.

23. F.O. 371/6343, p. 40.

24. See Sir Reader Bullard, *The Camels Must Go* (London: Faber and Faber, 1961), 121.

25. Gilbert, *Churchill*, 557.

26. F.O. 371/5245, file E9032, minuted by Eyre Crowe on 29 July 1920.

27. Suleiman Mousa, *T. E. Lawrence: An Arab View* (London: Oxford University Press, 1966), 239.

28. Minutes of the conversations are in F.O. 371/6343, appendix 19, pp. 107–14.

29. Churchill to Lloyd George (secret and personal), 18 March 1921. F.O. 371/6343.

30. C.O. 733/2, file 17941.

31. F.O. 406/46, E4035/4035/91, Foreign Office to Colonial Office, 6 April 1921, p. 126; C.O. 732/4, file 18519.

32. Mack, *A Prince of Our Disorder*, 304–5.

33. On 25 July, Curzon explained Lawrence's mission to the British ambassador to Paris: before actually granting Hussein a subsidy, His Majesty's Government "desire to secure [his] assent to the issue of some form of public declaration whereby he would recognize the mandatory principle and, in particular, the mandatory status of Great Britain in Palestine and Mesopotamia and of France in Syria." F.O. 406/47, file E8424/4/91.

34. F.O. 406/47, E9070/4/91, Lawrence to Curzon, 7 August 1921.

35. F.O. 406/47, E10152/4/91, Lawrence to Curzon, 6 September 1921.

36. Ibid. Incidentally, the filed report confirms the validity of this story, which

later circulated and which Liddell Hart, for example, dismissed as untrue. Liddell Hart, "T. E. Lawrence," 413.

37. F.O. 407/47, E10623/4/91, Lawrence to Curzon, 22 September 1921.

38. Mack, *A Prince of Our Disorder*, 307.

39. F.O. 371/6342, file E3919/533/65 (C.P. 2770). Paraphrase of telegram from Churchill to Prime Minister Lloyd George.

40. F.O. 371/6373, file E10397, minuted in mid-September.

41. C.O. 733/3, file 31760.

42. F.O. 406/46, E4700/5431/93.

43. C.O. 733/4, file 36252, minuted in July.

44. C.O. 733/13, Young to Deedes, 18 July 1921.

45. C.O. 733/11, file 44664, dated 7 September 1921.

46. C.O. 733/11, file 47205.

47. C.O. 733/3, file 31760, of 11 July 1921.

48. C.O. 733/6, file 50764, Young to Shuckburgh, 7 October 1921.

49. C.O. 733/17B, file 56585, Young to Shuckburgh, 7 October 1921.

50. C.O. 733/17A, file 32297.

51. Recommendations and analysis in C.O. 733/7, files 53454 (report on 24 October) and 57016 of 4 November.

52. C.O. 733/7. Secret dispatch in file 57016 relayed to Colonial Office on 4 November. Lawrence gained the support of Young, who, in a separate letter to Shuckburgh on 15 October, urged: "Whatever the cause may have been it is clearly necessary for Lawrence to take the whole thing in hand at once" (file 53454).

53. C.O. 733/7, file 57016.

54. Ibid.

55. C.O. 733/21, dispatch on 18 April 1922.

56. Ibid.

57. C.O. 733/6, file 52088.

58. C.O. 733/8, C.O. 261, Shuckburgh to J. Masterton Smith, 31 January 1922, annotated by Churchill on 2 February.

59. Churchill, in *Friends*, 126.

60. Mack, *A Prince of Our Disorder*, 310; see also *Friends*, 127, and Liddell Hart, "T. E. Lawrence," 417.

61. Mack, *A Prince of Our Disorder*, 307.

62. Letter of resignation reprinted in *L*, 344. In *Seven Pillars of Wisdom*, Lawrence inserted the following footnote about Churchill: "at his conference in Cairo, he made straight all the tangle, finding solutions fulfilling (I think) our promises in letter and spirit (where humanly possible) without sacrificing any interest . . . of the peoples concerned. So we were quit of the war-time Eastern adventure, with clean hands, but three years too late to earn the gratitude which peoples, if not states, can pay" (*SP*, 276).

63. Liddell Hart, "T. E. Lawrence," 414.

64. Lawrence's correction of Liddell Hart's draft of "T. E. Lawrence": *In Arabia and After*, quoted in *T. E. Lawrence to His Biographers*, 2:112.

65. See Linda J. Tarver, "In Wisdom's House: T. E. Lawrence in the Near East,"

Journal of Contemporary History 13 (July 1978): 593; see also Weintraub and Weintraub, *Evolution of a Revolt*, 92, citing Lawrence's comment in the *Observer*, 8 August 1920: "England controls nine parts out of ten in the Arab world, and inevitably calls the tune to which the French must dance." For a full discussion of this issue, see M. Larès, *T. E. Lawrence, la France et les Français* (Paris: Imprimerie Nationale, 1980).

66. C.O. 733/2, file 22537.

67. Reprinted in Mack, *A Prince of Our Disorder*, 463–67.

68. The article, telling in its application to Churchill, continues: "Win and keep the confidence of your leader. Strengthen his prestige at your expense before others if you can. Never refuse or quash schemes he may put forward. . . . Always approve them, and after praise modify them insensibly, causing the suggestions to come from him, until they are in accord with your own opinion."

69. Lawrence wrote: "Mr. Churchill was determined to find ways and means of avoiding so complete a reversal of the traditional British attitude. I was at one with him in this attitude: indeed I fancy I went beyond him, in my desire to see as many 'brown' dominions in the British Empire as there are 'white.' It will be a sorry day when our estate stops growing" *T. E. Lawrence to His Biographers*, 1:111.

70. Meinertzhagen's diary entry for 24 December 1921 relates a luncheon session following Lawrence's return from the Middle East. He was "struck by the attitude of Winston toward Lawrence, which almost amounted to hero-worship." Lawrence is described as "interlarding his remarks with a suitable amount of flattery." "Winston revelled in it, but to Shuckburgh and me it was nothing but nauseating." Meinertzhagen, *Middle East Diary*, 33.

71. C.O. 732/5, file 29674.

72. Written on 18 November 1922 and quoted in Martin Gilbert's *Winston S. Churchill, Companion Volume IV* (London: Heinemann, 1978), pt. 3, p. 2125. A second assessment offered by Lawrence is equally revealing. "I take to myself credit for some of Mr. Churchill's pacification of the Middle East for while he was carrying it out he had the help of such knowledge and energy as I possess. His was the imagination and courage to take a fresh departure and enough skilled knowledge of political procedure to put his political revolution into operation in the Middle East, and in London, peacefully" *T. E. Lawrence to His Biographers*, 1:112.

73. George Antonious, *The Arab Awakening* (Philadelphia: Lippincott, 1939), 324. See also Mousa, *T. E. Lawrence*, 252.

74. Quoted in Mack, *A Prince of Our Disorder*, 313.

Lawrence of Arabia:
The Portraits from Imagination,
1922–1979

STANLEY WEINTRAUB

While T. E. Lawrence was proceeding to help biographers manufacture his own myth, he was already turning up in works in which the intention was not even biographical—in fiction, poetry, and theater. As early as 1922, a young Irish archaeologist possessed of some Arabic appears in Maurice Barrès's Crusader castle story *Un Jardin sur l'Oronte* (Paris: Plon-Nourrit). Because the character is unnamed and there are some ambiguities about dates, we cannot be sure that T. E. Lawrence was intended; but no one else fits Barrès's description.[1]

Like all portraits, the imaginative images of Lawrence reflect their creators' personalities, needs, and times at least as much as they do Lawrence himself. It may be that Lawrence felt he was fixed in, and could never escape, his personality and past, as Texas professor William Burford wrote of him in his sonnet "Lawrence/Ross/Shaw" of 1962: "Unlike the lizard, that could shed its skin, / Wherever he fled, still it went with him."[2] But because of his ambiguous remarks and writings, Lawrence's personality and career have proven endlessly adaptable to the spiritual, literary, and commercial concerns of two generations of writers. In the 1920s and 1930s, writers moved by the problem of heroism in World War I, and still reacting to the influence of the Lowell Thomas myth, found it possible to use Lawrence for left- and right-wing visions of the ideal or failed hero. After World War II, under the influence of a second great and profoundly dislocating conflict and Richard Aldington's complementary debunking of the Thomas vision of Lawrence as perfect hero, artistic commentators began taking a far more complex view of Lawrence's psychology and motivation than had been the case in most of the early writings on him, dwelling on the themes of homosexuality, masochism and sadism, and self-division. And, beginning in the late 1960s, Lawrence became the focus for Western anxieties about a Middle East that had begun to dominate the West economically, reversing the situation in Lawrence's own time.

· II ·

In all the works on Lawrence in the period between the wars, we see a constant concern with the problem of heroism. He early proves a tempting subject for treatment in superficial mysteries and thrillers, while in highbrow poems, plays, and novels, writers on the left and right (particularly in the 1930s) try to define their own ideas of heroism using Lawrence as a basis for their investigations. This is not surprising, for as Christopher Isherwood commented at the time, "Like Shelley and Baudelaire, it may be said of [Lawrence] that he suffered, in his own person, the neurotic ills of an entire generation." (And he added later that Lawrence "was the myth-hero of the 'thirties.") That Lawrence is sometimes found wanting as a hero is as frequently a function of the various writers' perceptions as of any real failure on Lawrence's part. In these early works we also find the first, if undeveloped, traces of the more complex, inner view of Lawrence that was to take hold after World War II.

In 1929 T.E.'s old service friend John Buchan decided to make Lawrence the obvious hero of his thriller *The Courts of the Morning* (London: Hodder and Stoughton). Originally titled in manuscript "Far Arabia," the novel features the guerrilla-style exploits of Sandy Arbuthnot, "an ageing child of forty" who "can't grow up" because he is "crazed by the spell of far Arabia." Arbuthnot (Scottish rather than Irish, following Buchan's own ancestry) wishes he had been born an Englishman, and confesses to never having had "any sense of a continuing city," echoing Lawrence's identity problems. Arbuthnot's ideas of strategy and tactics seem right out of Lawrence's "Evolution of a Revolt" essay, which Buchan had read while working on his novel. "I hate war, except my own sort," says Sandy, and another character confirms that Sandy has no use for fighting "unless it was war on his special plan, an audacious assault upon the enemy's nerves." Buchan's biographer, Janet Adam Smith, observes that Arbuthnot, a hero of earlier novels where he is distinctly unlike Lawrence, in the new book becomes "very like him. A 'tallish' man in *Greenmantle*, he has shrunk to 'a head shorter' than Castor, which would bring him down to T. E. Lawrence's five feet four inches, and he is saddled with T. E. Lawrence's 'finical conscience.'"[3] Despite some eccentricities, Lawrence comes off in Buchan's vision very much like a traditional hero in the Lowell Thomas vein.

C. Day Lewis, whom Lawrence had encouraged as a poet, exploited a similarly traditional heroic Lawrence figure in his early mystery novel *Shell of Death* (New York: Harper, 1936), written under the nom de plume Nicholas Blake. A Lawrence figure called Fergus O'Brien is "something out of the ordinary run of 'heroes,'" having made his name surviving air crashes, taking enemy forts single-handedly, and flouting military authority. Now retired, O'Brien leads an ascetic existence—which, however, includes a library of books inscribed to him by their authors, including a fine *Travels in Arabia Deserta*—as he avoids a publicity-hungry press. The novel is overly literary and full of improbabilities, and it is unfortunate that Lewis never attempted a deeper treatment of Lawrence's personality; but he does achieve flashes of insight transcending a young writer's hungry treatment of a sensational subject. "He told me," one character confides, "a lot of Munchausen sort of stories about his adventures in the war and after; at least if anyone else had told them they would have been pure Munchausen, but I had heard enough about him to know that they were probably true. Founded on fact, anyway—you know how an Irishman will garnish a true story with any number of picturesque falsehoods just to make it more appetising. Fergus was a true artist in that."

Robert Graves and W. B. Yeats also presented heroic visions of Lawrence, but in a more highbrow vein. As a postwar student at Oxford, Graves had met Lawrence, who became both benefactor and literary sponsor. To his new friend, by then "T. E. Shaw," Graves dedicated "The Clipped Stater," which he published in *Poems (1914–1926)*

(Garden City, N.Y.: Doubleday, 1929). Ostensibly the poem is about Alexander, who after his death as god-king takes "the soldier's trade" and "glories in its limitations." But much like the T. E. Shaw or J. H. Ross of *The Mint*, he stoically endures the life of the ranks and suffers masochistic humiliation.

> Stripes and bastinadoes, famine and thirst
> All these he suffers, never in resolution
> Wavering, nor in his heart enquiring whether
> God can be by his own confines accursed.
> As he grows grey and eats his frugal rice;
> Endures his watch on the fort's icy ramparts,
> Staring across the uncouth wildernesses,
> And cleans his leather and steel; and shakes the dice.
> He will not dream Olympicly, nor stir
> To enlarge himself with comforts or promotion. . . .

W. B. Yeats's "Stories of Michael Robartes and His Friends" appeared in *A Vision* (Dublin: Cuala Press, 1931) and probably dates to 1930. In one of the stories, Robartes, Yeats's alter ego, confides how he joined a tribe of Arabs and "accepted its dress, customs, morality, politics, that I might win its trust and its knowledge. I have fought in its wars and risen to authority. Your young Colonel Lawrence never suspected the nationality of the old Arab fighting at his side."

But just as Lawrence's heroic myth as related by Lowell Thomas inspired easy imitation and embellishment, so it early excited negative reactions. D. H. Lawrence, who may have been competitively irritated by the great publicity surrounding the publication of the limited edition of *Seven Pillars of Wisdom* in 1926, attacked Lawrence in *Lady Chatterley's Lover* (1928). Every schoolgirl of sixteen should read Lawrence's book, Bernard Shaw told South African leader Jan Christian Smuts, whose morals were as fundamentalist as his Dutch Reformed religion. Assuming Shaw was referring to *Seven Pillars of Wisdom*, Smuts politely agreed. But Shaw had *Lady Chatterley's Lover* in mind. Shaw enjoyed upsetting Smuts's moral notions by recommending a sexually explicit book, but he may also have been fascinated by the aspersion upon his good friend, T.E., in this book. Connie Chatterley describes Mellors, her gamekeeper lover who had been an officer in India, as "like Colonel C. E. Florence, who preferred to become a private soldier again." But Mellors rejects the comparison: as the narrator tells us, he "had no sympathy with the unsatisfactory mysticism of the famous C. E. Florence. He saw too much advertisement behind all the humility. It looked just the sort of conceit the knight most loathed, the conceit of self-abasement." As much as T.E. admired D.H. as a writer, D.H. could not fit T.E. into his conception of the ideal sexual hero, as the name C. E. Florence itself implies, hinting at homosexuality or effeminacy.

In the 1930s, following the drift of the times, the Lawrence figure in literature becomes a political expression. The portrait of Lawrence in G. B. Shaw's *Too True to Be Good* (1931) as Private Napoleon Alexander Trotsky Meek, who combines self-abasement and a penchant for command and runs his own show from the ranks—as Lawrence sometimes did in the R.A.F.—is largely affectionate caricature. But the style of the play is serious farce, with Shaw trying to mirror the chaos of the years that followed World War I in part through the apparent chaos of the play's structural lines. What more logical thing for Shaw to do, when planning a play to expose the absurdities of postwar civilization, than to use as obvious hero the man with the most absurd postwar career of all England's wartime heroes? And Shaw's portrait of Lawrence is far more serious than appears in the cheeky Private Meek alone.

When Lawrence was invited to Ayot so that Shaw could read an act of the new play to him, T.E. listened partly with anxiety and partly with relief, not knowing how he would come out of it. Soon he realized that Meek was a thorough but affectionate parody of himself. The genuine suspense he felt as he listened had left him unable to discuss many of the points of the play with Shaw right away, but after he returned to duty he mailed Shaw some notes and suggestions. Some were taken literatim into the play, others substantially adopted, as Shaw tried to marry farce to military reality. The letter itself called the second act "priceless." Then T.E. added, "I'm afraid, only, that [Cedric] Hardwicke will let my conception of Aubrey frantically down. He will never understand what he represents." The implication is that Lawrence did: although it was always an open secret that Private Meek, complete to the long head adorned with Wellingtonian nose, was a portrait of Private T. E. Shaw, it is seldom realized that Aubrey Bagot, ex-R.A.F. combat officer, represents another side of the same complex man—the "Colonel Lawrence of Arabia" side. Here is the young officer thrust into the horrors of military necessity so graphically described in *Seven Pillars*, from the murder of prisoners to the massacre of civilians in mined railroad cars. Aubrey, who had left behind his university education to join a combat service, is warped by his wartime experience to such an extent that he cannot resume his life at the point war interrupted it, and lapses into irrational behavior. "I was hardly more than a boy," Aubrey recalls, "when I first dropped a bomb on a sleeping village. I cried all night after doing that. Later on I swooped into a street and sent machine gun bullets into a crowd of civilians: women, children, and all. I was past crying by that time." Like Lawrence, he questions the "very poorly designed silver medal" he receives for doing such deeds. Lawrence's war experience has obviously strongly influenced Shaw's serious political criticism in this play, as Aubrey calls himself "a soldier who has lost his nerve" with "no Bible, no creed: the war has shot both out of my hands."

The final portrait of Meek appears in the second proof, entitled *Too True to Be Good: A Collection of Stage Sermons by a Fellow of the Royal Society of Literature*, and the 1932 published version, subtitled more briefly *A Political Extravaganza*. Here appear definitive details of Colonel Lawrence/Aircraftman Shaw: his appearance, insignificant and authentic in physical particulars; his pseudo-meek quick-wittedness, combined with modest omniscience; his voluntary shifting down the ladder of rank from colonel to private; his knowledge of dialects and tribal psychology; his charismatic leadership qualities; his technical facility with explosives; and his ear-shattering motorcycle. Lawrence liked the play and Walter Hudd's portrayal of Meek ("I only wish nature had let me look half as smart and efficient as yourself," he wrote him), but under all the play's farce and caricature he understood its serious message about society.

As befits a satirist with a play rather than a polemic in mind, Shaw's political criticism is general rather than particular. But the 1930s saw Lawrences in books with rightist politics and Lawrences in books with leftist politics. From the right came Henry Williamson's *The Gold Falcon* (London: Faber and Faber, 1933), with its poet-aviator of Great War fame, Major Manfred Fiennes-Carew-Manfred, V.C., D.S.O., M.C., who establishes his credibility as a writer-hero by regular allusions to his great and good friend T. E. Lawrence. Williamson, a writer on the right who saw the future as belonging to Nazi Germany and attempted to encourage similar views in Lawrence—T.E. was arranging to meet him to talk politics on the last day of his life—had been in the trenches in France. His Manfred (the Byronic allusion is not accidental) is a wish-fulfillment fantasy version of his own career as well as of his association with Lawrence.

Major Manfred thinks often about Lawrence, refers regularly and impressively to their friendship, and makes Lawrence the benchmark for almost all qualitative judgments:

> The trouble with the War-generation is that we can't get away from our blooming selves, T. E. Lawrence had recently written to Manfred . . . *if I did the wonders they ascribe to me, then it was wholly by accident, for in normal times I'm plumb ordinary. I don't believe the yarns they tell. Only it seems conceited to refuse to accept public opinion about oneself.*

Manfred's own book is finished in the manner of the obsessive legendary completion of *Seven Pillars*:

> He saw in the viewless darkness beyond the thread of his life the sudden flash which was the fusing point of his poetic emotion: the mental flash that was inspiration, beyond the personal self. Or was it nerve-weakness: lack of food, sleeplessness, the quietness of himself working under the black motionless avalanche of despair. Fifteen thousand words in forty-eight hours; and the book was finished. He had kept his word to himself. . . .

Manfred dies in a suicidal air crash, and the novel closes, in William Golding's later *Pincher Martin* fashion, with the drowning hero hallucinating his return home in his last millisecond. The violent end anticipates Lawrence's death as other elements in the novel reflect his life and impact. For the spiritually tormented hero Manfred, unable to exorcise the ghosts of war, invoking an association with the still-living Lawrence establishes the appropriate credentials. One is asked to accept Manfred's near-T.E. "great man" status, bordering on fascism, as well as his Lawrentian spiritual malaise. But it is unlikely that Lawrence ever accepted this view of himself. He wrote to Williamson cautiously after reading *The Gold Falcon* (13 February 1933): "Are my letters real extracts, or have you polished? . . . I can't say how I really regard the book" (L, 761–62).

On the left are the Lawrence-inspired writings of W. H. Auden.

Although Auden years afterward cited his *The Orators* (London: Faber, 1932) as an example of "the fair notion fatally injured"—a reference to its obscurity—one of its clearest elements is its indebtedness to Lawrence, who often crops up in Auden's work of the early 1930s. In August 1931, Auden had written to a friend that, in Book II, he was attempting a sort of memorial to Lawrence in the sense of what he had been, and that its theme was "the failure of the romantic conception of personality."[4] Part of the first book of this blend of poetry and prose concerns the search for a hero, a redeemer, a savior, an important theme in the depression-ridden 1930s. In its second book, "Journal of an Airman," appears such a hero, who had in him (besides Auden's then-obligatory cryptic and Marxist elements) something of Aircraftman Shaw. His sense of guilt and isolation are extreme, and there is a suggestion of homosexuality (perhaps reflecting Auden's own concerns) as well as of permanent adolescence. On the positive side, he preaches man's commitment to the new element, air, overthrowing his bonds of land and water. Here the symbolic point is revolution, but the literal love of air travel is close to Lawrence's public views during his R.A.F. years.

Auden also wrote about Lawrence in publisher Jonathan Cape's house publication *Now and Then* in the spring of 1934, two years after *The Orators*, quoting with reference to T.E.'s life style a passage from Lenin, who had written that one must "go hungry, work illegally and be anonymous. . . . The self must learn to be indifferent." In "A Happy New Year" (a reference to a dismal 1933), Auden's satirical dream-vision described Lawrence as an airman passing derisive judgment on the tawdry political representatives of contemporary England below. Flying overhead in a Bristol fighter, he throws down a note announcing, "I've a devil. . . . I'm ordered elsewhere. / God what a crew! But your best are there."[5] In the 1934 sonnet "Who's Who"—beginning with "A shilling life will give you all the facts"—Auden wrote of a Lawrence equivalent who became "the greatest figure of the day" as a man of action, yet was mysteriously uneasy about his fame and his position above the masses.

> With all his honours on, he sighed for one
> Who, say astonished critics, lived at home;
> Did little jobs about the house with skill
> And nothing else; could whistle; would sit still

> Or potter round the garden; answered some
> Of his long marvellous letters but kept none.[6]

The lines, depending upon how one reads them, suggest a domestic love interest (perhaps to deflect identification from the living T.E.L.) or the subject's desire for the proletarian life of the common man. They foreshadow graphically the post-retirement Lawrence, however little he subscribed to Auden's political or sexual tendencies.

We see in the later 1930s a more complex view of Lawrence—transcending the merely political—suggested in Auden and Isherwood's play *The Ascent of F.6* and Archibald MacLeish's poem "Speech to the Detractors" of 1936. In *The Ascent of F.6* (London: Faber, 1937), Auden and Isherwood base their hero Ransom partly on Lawrence, as Isherwood wrote to E. M. Forster: "Please don't expect our play to cast a dazzling light on the subject. I only say the play's about him for shorthand-descriptive purposes. . . . It's only about Lawrence in so far as the problem of personal ambition versus the contemplative life is concerned."[7] The play's discussion of Lawrence's personality, however, goes beyond Isherwood's restrictions, and is perhaps the most complex view of Lawrence presented in this period. Ransom is a hero of exceptional courage and tenacity, driven by the "deep cleavage" in his own nature to undertake impossible quests. Another character in the play, Stagmantle, asks Ransom, "You're a scholar, I believe? Well, now, that intrigues me. Scholar and man of action: an unusual mixture, eh?" What is even more unusual is the addition of a sickly conscience. "There was a choice once," Ransom says, having committed himself to the ascent of the F.6 mountain, "I made it wrong." Now he needs to be saved "from the destructive element of our will, for all we do is evil." The dead in the expedition he mounts are victims, he confides, to his pride. "My minor place in history is with the aberrant group of Caesars: the dullard murderers who hale the gentle from their beds of love and . . . escort them to the drowning ditch and death in the desert." Ransom's body will eventually be found too on the summit of F.6 (Auden's "Who's Who" hero had "fought, fished, hunted, worked all night, / Though giddy, climbed new mountains."), but not before Ransom asks, into a gale on the crag,

> Is Death so busy
> That we must fidget in a draughty world

> That's stale and tasteless; must we still kick our heels
> And wait for his obsequious secretaries
> To page Mankind at last and lead him
> To the distinguished Presence?

The play, it is apparent, was written soon after Lawrence's violent end. As another member of the Auden group, Louis MacNeice, put it, Auden, "being so interested in the phenomenon of the man of action (for example, in Colonel Lawrence), many of the lyrics contain in condensed form what is worked out at length in the play, F.6—the tragedy of the man who gets his own way."[8] Auden's literary executor Edward Mendelson, quoting the 1934 *Now and Then* essay to suggest that Lawrence's life for Auden first had been "an allegory of the transformation of the Truly Weak Man into the Truly Strong Man," finds in F.6 evidence that Auden had now discovered that the assumed Lawrentian synthesis had never happened. "The climber-hero of the 1936 play . . . is a partial portrait of Lawrence as the Truly Weak Man to the end, his spectacular heroic acts prompted by childhood neurosis, indentured to the private realm and exploited by the public one. Lawrence gave only the illusion of reconciling the divided worlds."[9] If so, Auden's apparent epiphany explains why he never again utilized Lawrence as a subject. However what seems at least as likely is that Auden, recognizing his own weaknesses and secret aspirations in Lawrence, had exploited T.E.L. as far as he could. As far as Auden knew, Lawrence's hidden life had died with him, and the poet had his own life to live, and his own inner life to exploit.

During this period, there are forgettable book-length poems by the half-Irish physician Ernest Altounyan (*Ornament of Honour*, 1937) and by the American Selden Rodman, who strove for authenticity in his *Lawrence: The Last Crusade* (New York: Viking, 1937) by freely versifying the memoir-writings about Lawrence, including T.E.'s own. It ends with his elongating Lawrence's last moments in a rigid soliloquy influenced, perhaps, by poetic futurism:

> "Hold! Jam the brakes!
> What's here? A little boy? Whose son is this
> That rides a bicycle across the path
> Of my triumphant destiny? Whose life
> Intrudes that I should save it? Down, press down

Into the brake-drums: danger: not too hard. . . .
And if it slides, what then? Which way to turn?
Better decide unpoisoned, grown mature—
Than one confirmed by twenty perilous years
Of force and speed and dynamite—
                              "Hsss. . . .
"And so the wheels locked! Locked. And still the air
About my face and body . . . the tender air! . . .
The hills that press: O heavy diorite,
O tamarisk and rimth and native fern! . . .
Too late . . . too late. . . ."

Rodman's book uses as an epigraph—and perhaps as a spring-board—lines from a poem by Archibald MacLeish (from *Public Speech*, New York: Farrar and Rinehart, 1936), "Speech to the Detractors." In it men are asked to "love excellence . . . / Whether the hare's leap or the heart's recklessness." The recognition of achievement, MacLeish urges, ennobles the bestower as well as the recipient of praise. A negative example, he regrets, had occurred in the blind and ignorant dispraise of Lawrence after his death:

Why then must this time of ours be envious?
Why must the great man now,
Sealed from the mouths of worms, be sucked by men's mouths?
Refusing ribbons that the rest have clowned for,
Dying and wishing peace,
The best are eaten by the envy round them.
When Lawrence died the hate was at his bier.
Fearing there might have lived
A man really noble, really superior,
Fearing that worth had lived and had been modest,
Men of envious minds
Ate with venom his new buried body.
We cheat ourselves in cheating worth of wonder.
Not the unwitting dead
But we who leave the praise unsaid are plundered.

The wheel has come full circle: Lawrence begins this period as a hero on an epic scale, suitable for use in thrillers, and ends it—as MacLeish laments—with his reputation already somewhat clouded, at least in part because of the way writers had used his persona to reflect their own concerns.

· III ·

After World War II, a more self-conscious, complex vision of Lawrence's personality and career emerges, even before the impact of Richard Aldington's debunking. The spectacle of a second great war, encompassing even greater horrors than the first, profoundly affected writers as well as the humanistic ideal itself; and Aldington's savage attack on Lawrence seems to mirror this dislocation, as an attempt to destroy once and for all the very image of military heroism. Writers of the new era appropriated Lawrence to their own uses, as had their predecessors, and the emphasis is upon personal psychology and aberrations rather than, as before, on Lawrence's heroism or cynicism. Thus Terence Rattigan's *Ross* explores the theme of homosexuality and a divided will, and even David Lean's and Robert Bolt's film spectacular features a deeply uncertain and hesitant hero who flirts with sadism and masochism. The conventionally heroic Lawrence appears gone forever, apparently, as a novel such as Anthony West's *David Rees among Others* parallels Aldington's ferocious view of Lawrence's personality, while Alan Bennett's lighter play *Forty Years On* mocks and parodies the entire Lawrence myth and the controversy surrounding it. We have moved into a more psychological age, profoundly affected by the fact of Western moral failure, although the needs of the box office also seem a factor in writers' treatments of Lawrence.

André Malraux, who had written sensitively about T.E. as man and writer, and whose own career was perhaps more parallel to Lawrence's than anyone else's, put Lawrence into *The Walnut Trees of Altenburg* (London: J. Lehmann, 1952). Vincent Berger "could perhaps have found some means of destroying the mythical person he was growing into, had he been compelled. But he had no wish to do so. His reputation was flattering. What was more important, he enjoyed it." Berger actually likes war, particularly "the masculine companionship, the irrevocable commitments that courage imposes." The novel opens and closes with an autobiographical section about the 1939–45 war, but within this framework are three longer episodes, each describing ex-

periences of the narrator's father. What becomes clear through them
is that Malraux has given Lawrence a son—himself. Vincent Berger
is Lawrence and Malraux, with all their complexities as intellectuals
and men of action, in equal proportions.

James Aldridge's *Heroes of the Empty View* (New York: Knopf, 1954),
as its title implies, also presents a deeper view of Lawrence than the
conventionally heroic. The phrase "empty view" actually comes from
the beginning of chapter 40 of *Seven Pillars*, indicating that Lawrence
is invoked in the guise of the hero "Gordon or Gordion," a desert
leader. Deliberate references to Lawrence of Arabia as someone else
fail to deflect the suspicion that Aldridge is furnishing a relatively
accurate rather than glorified portrait of Lawrence:

> He was small (of height and shape), and automatically he was lithe-
> some and perky in all his body, yet long and solid in the face, with a
> head that was too big for the rest of him. Even in sleep he was not
> at rest, but taut with weariness and overloaded with nerve. If he could
> have stood off and seen his body asleep, as he often wished he could,
> he would have pictured himself as a cunning mimicry of a desert lord—
> perfect outwardly, but so perfect that it became an obvious role: a false
> and exacting role for a self-conscious man of thirty whose whole ele-
> ment of life was self-command. This was his innate antithesis to the
> extrovert naturalness of the tribal leader he was creating of himself . . .
> much of this contradiction was apparent in the mark of his face. It
> was a torn mixture of self-dependency, of sensitive response, of intel-
> lectual height and width, and of sensual disorder kept under control.

This is a Lawrence transplanted to a later postwar generation, his
contradictions highlighted, but still the antiquarian who says, "Progress be damned! In progress the Tribes will lose their very nature and
nobility, their strength, their courage, their bold poetry," and now
leads the Beduin against the oil fields which threaten the old ways.
But he cannot restore the past, and in the end the reincarnated Lawrence will lose his quest and his life.

Although more complicated psychologically than earlier Lawrences
in fiction, Malraux's and Aldridge's Lawrence figures treat the problem
of heroism in a more or less standard manner. After Aldington's attack
in 1955, which presented Lawrence as a liar and neurotic, imaginative
treatments of Lawrence tended to become internalized. E. M. Forster
had long been fascinated by his friend T.E. Like Forster, Lawrence had

a secret life (in his case, flagellation repeated at long intervals) to conceal, and exchanged private peeks at self-suppressed manuscripts (although T.E. prudently rejected the opportunity to read *Maurice*). There was, however, Lawrence assured Forster in 1927, "a strange cleansing beauty" about the homosexual story "Dr. Woolacott," although "indecent people" might describe it instead as "passionate."[10] Only in 1957–58, however, did Forster apparently put his own intimations about Lawrence obliquely into "The Other Boat," posthumously published in *The Life to Come* (London: Edward Arnold, 1972). In the story, a British officer with wartime Near Eastern fighting experience and a habit of writing often to his mother in England, is posted to India, as was Lawrence. Shipboard, Captain March is seduced by a dusky and "supple" native boy, who asks him, as they lie together, whether he has ever shed blood. "Vividly and unexpectedly the desert surged up, and he saw it as a cameo, from outside. The central figure—a grotesque one—was himself going berserk."

The episode suggests a reading of the Tafas episode (117) of *Seven Pillars*, although what follows are Forster's own intimations. Lionel March soon finds that he is trapped by the native into further caresses. When he refuses, there is a scuffle; March is bitten, and when blood comes, "He was back in the desert fighting savages. One of them asked for mercy, stumbled, and found none." The boy is strangled, and March commits suicide by diving into the shark-infested sea. ("It was part of a curve that had long been declining, and had nothing to do with death.") The affair is covered up as best as can be done.

In subsequent works in this period, we see the same concern with homosexuality and sadomasochism as in Forster's story. Long attracted by homosexual themes because of his own painful private life, Terence Rattigan had been seeking a subject that might expose the dilemma sympathetically. In *Ross* (London: H. Hamilton, 1960), Rattigan indulges in the dramatic speculation, based upon Lawrence's own ambiguous account, that when T.E. was whipped and abused at Deraa, his will was broken by the traumatic awakening he experienced: that he had recognized himself as a latent homosexual. Further, Rattigan suggests, the Turkish commander ordered the torture not primarily because he fancied his prisoner himself and was refused, as Lawrence suggests in *Seven Pillars*, but to break the will of the self-styled Circassian who the Turk realized was his disguised enemy Lawrence. The play's theory—a very appealing one—is that all of Lawrence's life thereafter constituted a series of attempts on his part to achieve personal triumphs of the will—a will the Turks assumed had been destroyed. It implies, however, that the Turkish general knew who Lawrence was and feared him as an enemy, but believed that the best way to destroy the Arab Revolt would be to return its inciting spirit to the Arabs broken in mind and body rather than to kill him. However, would a general indulge in the hazard of returning the enemy's field commander when he could do away with him? Rattigan's treatment of Lawrence—like many other such treatments—may have more of the author's own conflicts in it than Lawrence's.[11]

Sadomasochism again provides the sensation in the film *Lawrence of Arabia*, released in 1962/63 and successfully reissued since. Here the box office was obviously an important influence in developing a vision of Lawrence. The film rewrites rather than merely dramatizes Lawrence's Arabian experience. For instance, the opening scene, in which Lawrence is shown allowing a match to burn his fingertips in order to demonstrate his ability to withstand pain, is Robert Bolt's invention.[12] And Lawrence—in a clear violation of *Seven Pillars*—confesses during his first meeting with General Allenby that he once led an Arab servant to his death in quicksand (a fabrication of Bolt's) and executed another Arab with a pistol, and "didn't like" his discovery that he had actually "enjoyed it." The execution of Hamed the Moor in *Seven Pillars* (31) may be construed in this manner, but the text itself offers no suggestion that Lawrence was conscious of "enjoying" killing Hamed, and in such fashion the film indulges in invention and exaggeration, while making the possibly implicit, explicit and obvious. These are the things from which successful film drama, at least in the freer postwar period, are made. But however shaky the film is as accurate biography, it is a visual classic with vivid acting by Peter O'Toole, and will be remembered.[13]

Sadomasochism would emerge again, nourished further by the Knightley and Simpson flagellation revelations in *The Secret Lives of Lawrence of Arabia* (New York: McGraw-Hill, 1970), in Spanish émigré writer Juan Goytisolo's *Juan the Landless* (New York: Viking, 1977, trans. Helen R. Lane), a vivid novel that in inspiration is a throwback to Jean Genet. The shimmering heat of a summer day in Paris evokes a *Seven Pillars* vision in Juan, the timeless and landless exile. As laborers, very likely of Arab origin, work at excavating a sandy sewer trench, he imagines himself as Lawrence, "master of the air, the winds, the light, the vast desert expanses, the enormous emptiness." The sweaty workmen conjure in Juan the "radiance of sons of the desert," and the chatter of their pneumatic drill triggers the illusion of machine-gun fire. With the "trackless sand" suggestively underfoot, the narrator, a perverse Walter Mitty, discovers a raid on an Ottoman train exploding in his brain. Assuming Arab coloration "like a chameleon," he leads the imaginary slaughter, carrying it out "with the implacable precision of a ceremonial rite," and leaving enemy soldiers and passengers stripped to await the vultures.

Climbing atop the boxcars, standing on planks resembling those of the walkway across the sewer ditch, Juan fantasizes in the second person, "you will begin to execute a nimble dance step, watching out of the corner of your eye your own moving silhouette, as in a Chinese shadow play: elegant gestures surrounded by a halo of tutelary messianism that will inflame the passions of your legion." With a bold flourish of his revolver, the Beduin-clad narrator leaps from one boxcar roof to another "in the full regalia of your disguise, clad in white from head to foot, concealed beneath the billowing tulle veil of a bride at the altar." Spurring on the faithful, he dances back and forth across the boards "with the air of a prima donna, a pontifex, and a transvestite: the derailments follow one upon the other with a stepped-up rhythm, and the treacherous gunshot wound inflicted upon you by a straggler in the rear guard of the enemy will confer upon you a spectacular blood-baptism: the bright red stains will sully the immaculate whiteness of your garments with their impure viscosity."

Finally, Goytisolo writes, further echoing the brothel fantasy of Genet's *The Balcony*, the narrator's eyes "glisten roguishly beneath the thin black veil, the thick makeup dissolves and runs down the corner of your lips in ridiculous trickles. . . . Far from the cruel and captious plains of Jordan: in the heat of a summer day in Paris that beams its burning rays down, . . . having recovered from your optical illusions . . . you continue onward . . . along the deserted streets of the city: like El-Orens before his secret mission in Deraa, with a snow-white turban atop his head, floating along."

Both Rattigan and Bolt had interpreted Lawrence's life along lines opened up by Aldington's "biographical enquiry," and Goytisolo's novel suggests an awareness of Bolt's film script. However, the apparent malice of the Aldington exposé seems to emerge, later, only in Anthony West's novel *David Rees among Others* (New York: Random House, 1970). It is difficult to find much fictional justification for the inclusion in this novel of a lengthy, acidulous chapter dominated by a character identified openly as T. E. Lawrence. Rees, the autobiographical narrator, is very much like Anthony West, son of H. G. Wells and Rebecca West. His mother, the concert pianist Gwendolyn Rees, is only a slight remove from Dame Rebecca; Gwendolyn is not married to the hero's absent and uncaring father. David's mother masquerades as "Aunt Gwen," but the boy accidentally discovers his bastardy. Isolated from his own masculinity in a household of women, he must painfully learn how to break free from innocence.

Unfortunately for David, men are disappointments, distortions of the ideal—even the famous hero Lawrence of Arabia, whom he has read about in Lowell Thomas's book. Invited by a friend, the great man turns up on his Brough Superior but proves to be "such a little man"—moreover, one who smugly pretends to be a common, bashful soldier. West's Lawrence, whose dialogue is grotesquely unbelievable, is small in other ways as well. He snubs David's worshipful governess, Miss Foster, and continuously drops names, while saying absolutely nothing of interest or importance. His comeuppance finally occurs when he turns up, unannounced as usual, to find only David and Sally McGuire, the pretty and unsophisticated farm girl who is the temporary cook. West's Lawrence tries to charm her with the same "curiously brittle triviality" as had magnetized other women, but it does not work. For someone "that's had his name in the papers and talked man to man with kings and princes and the great ones of the earth," she observes, "you're terribly like a little fellow I used to know [who] . . . had the gift of the gab too, and I swear he could have talked a bird out of the bush. . . . The only trouble was that it was all play-acting with him."

Lawrence looks "blindly out of a pinched masklike face," then scoops up his uniform cap and gloves and is gone. When Aunt Gwen returns, Sally McGuire reports that the "queer little fellow . . . that used to be Colonel Lawrence" had come and gone, and was unlikely to be back. The news sends Miss Foster into irreversible decline, while from the dismaying experience young David Rees learns something about the futility of doglike devotion, the superficiality of heroes when separated from their pedestals, and the uselessness of hero worship. But West's bitchy caricature also suggests the writer's own disappointed ambitions. The child of two major novelists but recognized only as a readable literary critic, West at fifty-six was witnessing the unpredictability of heredity. *David Rees* was his fifth forgettable novel, most of them variations on the story of his parentage. Striking out at Lawrence— the only "real" character in his fiction—he was denigrating someone else whose parents had not been married, yet also one who had overcompensated for his embarrassments and had, unlike West, driven himself to fame.

Alan Bennett's *Forty Years On* (London: Faber, 1969) is an unpretentious work for theater that, unlike West's novel, demonstrates in good-natured fashion the unending permutations of which the Lawrence figure is capable. In the course of this wry, irreverent sendup of public-school life, the befuddled old headmaster of Albion House, in his fiftieth and last term, delivers a rambling farewell address that splits off into past and present, and includes the headmaster's pièce de résistance—his slide-lecture on Lawrence of Arabia. It contains all the Lawrence clichés, a snicker at the newest flagellation revelations, and a few original additions to the legend by the headmaster, who has sent thousands of young Englishmen into alleged maturity with his picture of T.E. intact:

> HEADMASTER (*Slide 1. Portrait of T. E. Lawrence*): T. E. Lawrence, the man and the myth. Which is man and which is myth? Is this fact or is it lies? What is truth and what is fable? Where is Ruth and where is Mabel? To some of these questions I hope to be able to provide the answer. No one who knew T. E. Lawrence as I did, scarcely at all, could fail but to be deeply impressed by him. It is given to few men to become as he did, a legend in his own lifetime, and it was in pursuit of that legend that I first sought him out in June of 1933 at his cottage at Clouds Hill in Dorset.
>
> (*Slide 2. Picture of Clouds Hill.*)
> It was a simple cottage but I thought I detected Lawrence's hand in the rough white-washed wall, the stout paved doorstep and the rough oak door, upon which I knocked, lightly. It was opened by a small, rather unprepossessing figure slight of frame, fair-haired and with the ruddy gleam face of a schoolboy. It was a schoolboy. I had come to the wrong house. . . .

(Slide 4. Picture of an Eastern person.)
It was at this time he was taken for a Circassian eunuch by the infamous Sheikh Hans and subjected to unspeakable privations, the mark of which he bore for the rest of his life, and which bored everyone else thereafter.

(Slide 5. T. E. Lawrence in Arab dress.)
Shaw, or Ross as Lawrence then called himself, returned from the East in 1919. Shyness had always been a disease with him, and it was shyness and a longing for anonymity that made him disguise himself. Clad in the magnificent white silk robes of an Arab prince, with in his belt the short-curved, gold sword of the Ashraf descendants of the Prophet he hoped to pass unnoticed through London. Alas, he was mistaken. . . .

(Slide 6. T. E. Lawrence at All Souls in Oxford.)
Here he could mix on equal terms with some of the greatest men of his age, but, as Robert Graves has noted, he could not bear to be touched, so that even to rub shoulders with the great filled him with deep loathing.

(Slide 7. A smiling picture of T. E. Lawrence.)
One hesitates to talk of Lawrence and his body, though the two were inseparable. He feared his body as a savage fears the night. His body was a wild beast to be tamed and cowed into submission, and when I first knew him it had been beaten and tanned to the texture of an old whip. . . .
But can one ever forget him, those china blue eyes, that boyish, almost girlish figure and that silly, silly giggle. The boys at his school had called him Tee Hee Lawrence, and always at the back of his hand or the back of his mind there was that ready snigger. When I became headmaster the first boy I ever expelled was for reading the works of Lawrence. This morning I received in my post a letter from the Oxford and Cambridge Matriculation Board telling me that the works of Lawrence are next year's set texts. I just can't keep up.

FRANKLIN: D.H. not T.E.

HEADMASTER: Oh, these literary fellows, they're all the same.

Bennett's play mocks all aspects of the Lawrence controversy, particularly the sexual elements that have aroused so much interest in the postwar period. He reveals how encrusted the Lawrence myth had grown by the end of the 1960s, after a full fifty years of manipulation by writers and commentators.

· IV ·

In the late 1960s and 1970s, political and economic tensions reminiscent of the 1930s again assert themselves in the form of Middle East instability and petro-politics, and Lawrence becomes not a tortured "inner" being but an ideal focus for thrillers. But in place of the omnipotent hero of the twenties, the Lawrence figure becomes an expression of Western fears; he does not palliate our worries and vanquish our enemies but himself becomes victim or unscrupulous exploiter.

Lawrence plays a minor role, including some dialogue to add credibility and interest, in *Behold the Fire* (New York: New American Library, 1965), Michael Blankfort's novel about Jewish intelligence operatives working in Palestine for the British during World War I. But Matthew Eden's *The Murder of Lawrence of Arabia* (New York: Crowell, 1979) is wholly dedicated to Lawrence's role in Middle Eastern affairs, rewriting history with a blend of real and fictional characters. The novel begins with the premise that Lawrence's fatal crash in 1935 was no accident, a theory also put forth in Desmond Stewart's 1977 biography. In an author's note Eden explains, "The events and characters in this novel are historically accurate, except where the demands of fiction are stronger than those of history. Where one truth ends and another begins is, as always, for the individual to decide." Lawrence scholars will have no difficulty separating fact from fancy, yet the fancy includes elements thought plausible in the 1930s—that the recently retired aircraftman had been teased with dreams of fascist glory, as Britain's counterpart to Hitler, by Mosleyite novelist Henry Williamson. Williamson made such suggestions—that part is on record. Whether Lawrence would have accepted them is more than doubtful, but Eden guesses that he might have, had not another offer intervened—an invented invitation from King Abdullah of Transjordan to lead a rebellion against the British mandatory government in Palestine that would prevent further Jewish immigration and erosion of the Arab position.

Lawrence's opening description is based upon the familiar photograph of him cycling into civilian life from his final R.A.F. station. After that, the novel alternates the forward narrative with melodramatic flashbacks into Lawrence's wartime and postwar past—the massacre at Tafas, the capture and sexual defilement, the hired floggings, and other predictable episodes, building to the hypothesis that he might have been tempted to take the Arab side again to atone for French and British duplicity in wartime dealings with the Arabs. The implication is that Lawrence knew more about that during the war than is provable or probable. The double postwar burden of guilt given the fictional Lawrence is that after Deraa, and the reliving of the episode in its many rewritings and partial concealments, he could achieve sexual release only when flogged by another man; and that however used by British politicians himself when working to further Arab independence, he was culpable if only by being part of the colonial system.

Abdullah's emissary is the fictional Selim Shaalan, who brings Lawrence a lengthy appeal to assist the Arabs against the Jews. "I fear their ambition," he writes. "The Zionists plan to absorb the land of all of us. . . . Are the Arabs in Palestine to be victimized because of the misdeeds of the Germans, who persecute the Jews in their land and force them to look for refuge among us?" Lawrence is increasingly persuaded as Shaalan waits in London for his response. Finally he furnishes a reply that would repay the Arabs for his earlier failure to win for them at Versailles what they thought they had been promised. But it is less than the violent guerrilla operation for which he is invited. He offers his leadership on condition that there be no killing— of Jews or of British. Instead, he proposes "a campaign of economic and social dislocation. You would blow up railway lines, factories, warehouses, destroy Jewish crops. Do everything to make Palestine inhospitable to the Jews. But there must be no killing. . . . Believe me, Selim, it would be the most effective way, as I describe it. Wage a bloodless war and you will have sympathy and respect from many quarters in your struggle. Kill Jews and you will be accused of savagery against a weaker people, and the world will be against you."

The message goes to Abdullah. He confers with other conspirators, who collectively decide to use Lawrence by pretending to go along with his strategy until they have him in Palestine fronting for them and trapped by events. But the Zionist underground army, the Irgun, has followed Shaalan to Britain, Eden devising a plot of cross-purposes in which the Jews see the Arab designs of Lawrence as a covert British plan, while British intelligence, which has penetrated the operation, visualizes only a bloody civil war if Lawrence is allowed to leave England for the Middle East.

While the Irgun agents wound, but fail to kill, Shaalan, the British, despite the ineptitude of the prematurely senile Prime Minister Ramsay MacDonald, manage to head off Lawrence by arranging to force his motorcycle off a lonely country road—a murder without a weapon; and Selim Shaalan is then run down by a sports car operated by British intelligence agents.

The Irgun agents are cardboard figures and the MI-5 operatives watered-down Le Carré, but the Arab characters have more life. As for Lawrence, the political views attributed to him are pure speculation, and one must accept a tremendous megalomaniacal pressure pent up in the prematurely aged forty-six-year-old, who confessed in reality that he felt like a leaf fallen from a tree. On the facts leading up to page one, however, Matthew Eden has done his homework.

If Lawrence is victim in Eden's book, he becomes exploiter in Anthony Burgess's satiric look beyond Orwell, *1985* (Boston: Little, Brown, 1978), which portrays an Arab-dominated Britain. The colonizer Lawrence has become the colonized as he works for the Arabs by keeping British laborers in line while harboring fascistic ambitions of his own. In London the Arabs own "Al-Dorchester, Al-Klaridges, Al-Browns, various Al-Hiltons and Al-Idayinns, with soft drinks in the bars and no bacon for breakfast. They owned things that people did not even know they owned. . . . And, in Great Smith Street, soon would stand the symbol of their strength—the Masjid-ul-Haram or Great Mosque of London."

One day Colonel Lawrence appears, discharged from the army and now an alcoholic. The narrator soon discovers that Lawrence has gone into the Arab service:

> "Look, Colonel, sir. What exactly are you after? A free Britain or an Islamic Britain? I have to know. You've appointed me as your provisional mouthpiece."
>
> "The only way out of Britain's troubles, Mr. Jones, is a return to responsibility, loyalty, religion. A return to God. And who will show us God now? The Christians? Christianity was abolished by the Second Vatican Council. The Jews? They worship a bloody tribal deity. I was slow in coming to Islam, Mr. Jones. Twenty years as one of His Majesty of Saudi Arabia's military advisors, and all the time I kept, as was my right, to my father's Presbyterianism. Then I saw how Islam contained everything and yet was simple and sharp and bright as a sword. I had dreamt of no Islamic revolution in Britain but rather of a slow conver-

sion, helped by an Islamic infiltration expressed in terms of Islamic wealth and moral influence. Slow, slow."

Lawrence carries a riding crop, here a symbol of sadistic power, and eventually the narrator, Jones, discovers that Lawrence (echoing allegations in the 1930s) has Mosleyite aspirations to become an English Hitler and is secretly using his opportunities by forming the "Free British Army," a fascist force. In Burgess's Lawrence we see—despite the satirical nature of the book—very real Western fears finding expression. Instead of the 1920s hero who controlled the tribes and led them to victory as an expression of British power, Burgess portrays a morally decadent Lawrence controlled by the Arabs and restlessly seeking his own personal opportunity, all in the atmosphere of a dangerously economically depressed England.

Burgess's reincarnated Colonel Lawrence suggests that the personality of T. E. Lawrence continues to have almost unlimited possibilities for the imaginative writer. Who knows what future Lawrences—the products and mirrors of their own times and creators—are yet to appear? Even when he is not invoked for his own story's sake, the suggestion of Lawrence of Arabia in a poem, novel, or play has been appropriated by writers as a guarantee of an added dimension of interest. If he had not existed, authors would have had to invent him. Thriller hero, tormented warrior, fascist, redeemer, sadomasochist, whodunit villain, victim—he has appeared in more guises than he wore in life. Yet in reinventing him, in expanding the myth, writers have neither deciphered it nor improved upon it. The reason why the attempts to imitate Lawrence in literature appear so unsuccessful—or, at best, modest achievements—is that his own self-portrait is so rich in its resonances. In its narrative power, ambiguity of characterization, vivid prose, and epical sweep, Lawrence's writing, particularly in *Seven Pillars of Wisdom*, overwhelms the challenges it evokes.

N·O·T·E·S

1. The central story of the book dates back as far as 1905, long before Lawrence's appearance on the scene; but the prologue in which Lawrence seems to be indicated was written in 1921–22. The original draft of the prologue identifies the young ar-

chaeologist as English rather than Irish—Barrès apparently had not been sure about Lawrence, who may have presented himself (with some accuracy) as an Irishman. This information is contained in a letter (4 October 1980) from Paris-based Lawrence researcher Jonathan Mandelbaum to me; Mandelbaum arranged to have the Barrès MS. at the Bibliothèque Nationale examined in order to determine the date of composition of the prologue.

2. William Burford, "Lawrence/Ross/Shaw," *Texas Quarterly* 5 (Autumn 1962): 33.

3. Janet Adam Smith, *John Buchan* (Boston: Little, Brown, 1965), 262.

4. Quoted in Charles Osborne, *W. H. Auden* (New York: Harcourt Brace Jovanovich, 1979; London: Faber and Faber, 1979), 91.

5. In Michael Roberts, ed., *New Country* (London: L. & V. Woolf, 1933).

6. "Who's Who," in W. H. Auden, *Collected Shorter Poems 1927–1957* (New York: Random House, 1966), 78.

7. Quoted by Christopher Isherwood, review of A. W. Lawrence, ed., *T. E. Lawrence by His Friends*, in *The Listener*, 1937; reprinted in C. Isherwood, *Exhumations* (New York: Simon and Schuster, 1966), 24.

8. Ibid.

9. Edward Mendelson, *Early Auden* (New York: Viking, 1981), 181–82.

10. Quoted by Oliver Stallybrass in his introduction to Forster's *The Life to Come* (New York: W. W. Norton, 1972), xv.

11. For more details of Rattigan's version of Lawrence's story, see Stanley and Rodelle Weintraub, *Lawrence of Arabia: The Literary Impulse* (Baton Rouge: Louisiana State University Press, 1975), 140–44.

12. A poem by English writer Paul West in the doggerel meter of a children's song, "Homage to the Circuits," in his *The Snow Leopard* (New York: Harcourt, Brace, 1965), satirizes the sadomasochism in the filmic Lawrence, raising him in rank in each episode. Thus in one stanza the narrator announces,

> My name is Major Lawrence,
> I stroke the burning match;
> It animates my cuticle
> And proves the flesh won't catch.

13. For more on the film's distortions of *Seven Pillars*, see Weintraub and Weintraub, *Lawrence of Arabia: The Literary Impulse*, 145–49.

Collecting T. E. Lawrence Materials

PHILIP O'BRIEN

The two major problems facing the Lawrence collector (and indeed all collectors) are the difficulty of obtaining desired material and bibliographic control (the enumeration and classification of the material). These two problems remain constant whether the collector is a major library, such as the Bodleian Library, British Library, University of Texas Humanities Research Center, or Harvard's Houghton Library (the primary Lawrence repositories), or an individual. However, since there are between two and three hundred Lawrence collectors worldwide, and I have known personally no more than three of these, my detailed comments carry only the weight of my own experience.

The greatest obstacle to the acquisition of worthwhile material is of course financial. There is no substitute for a ready supply of money, and this has always been true for Lawrence's works. The prices asked for the limited 1926 edition of *Seven Pillars of Wisdom*,[1] variously known as the Subscribers' Edition or Cranwell Edition, astonished the public when the book first appeared. It was published at 30 guineas, and within a few months a copy was offered for sale at £570.[2] Herbert Read noted the "topical interest" in Lawrence's book, and went on to say that "The heartless neglect which descends on all modern books, whatever their scale or quality, after their brief day will descend on this book, and the meditative reader will wonder if, after all, it was a good book."[3] But *Seven Pillars* has sustained its early reputation as a great work of literature, and its various editions continue to excite interest among collectors. The prices asked for this first edition have continued to be among the highest of any twentieth-century British book, reaching twelve thousand dollars or more in recent days, and most of Lawrence's other editions and volumes have also steadily increased in value. The Corvinus Press *Diary of T. E. Lawrence MXMXI*[4] sold in 1967 for £48 and in 1979 brought £560; copies of *Letters from T. E. Shaw to Bruce Rogers* and *More Letters . . .* [5] were sold together for $200 in 1967 and by 1978 brought $600. Any number of additional examples can be found in the auction records and dealers' catalogs. Much of the Lawrence canon was issued in private limited editions, often by fine presses, such as the last two examples cited. This reflects Lawrence's own interest in fine printing[6] and increases the value of his books even more.

At first, interest in Lawrence was fed mainly by the spotlight focused on him by Lowell Thomas, but soon it was recognized that the Subscribers' Edition, for instance, met the test of quality recognized by collectors: here was a finely printed and illustrated book of very limited availability, with a high literary reputation. Only a few of the 207 copies were available at any one time until the recent surge in prices commanded by each copy. Between 1975 and 1980 seventeen copies were auctioned at an average price of £2020 compared to eleven copies that appeared between 1965 and 1974 averaging £1137 per copy.[7] There are finer-published books (Lawrence's own Bruce Rogers/Emory Walker produced translation of the *Odyssey*[8] included) and scarcer books, but none has been able to compete for interest.

Recent speculation in all types of collectibles owing to inflation has had the adverse effect of driving the prices of the scarcer items beyond the means of the average collector. These prices may benefit collectors by increasing the value of what they own, but collectors are now often prevented from acquiring important missing items. Dealers will refer choice selections directly to customers who they know have adequate resources; and today only those with money or unbelievable luck can hope to acquire all they desire. However, a satisfying collection can be assembled without these expensive items even if a true collector will always nourish the hope of someday, somehow, affording them. If I could relive the life of collecting I have enjoyed, I would invest all my resources in the high-priced items of today at 1960s prices. I would contrive to purchase a Subscribers' Edition if I could locate one for sale. I would seek out as many of the Corvinus Press works as I could. I would make myself known to the major dealers who then had a Lawrence stock: Duschnes, Rota, Herbert West, Sawyer, and Maggs among them. Perhaps if I were to attempt to begin collecting today, I might decide against the whole idea because much is now out of my reach, but I somehow doubt this would deter me.

Every collector must set limits for himself if he wishes to collect with discrimination and to keep himself reasonably satisfied. For my own peace of mind, I have restricted myself to printed materials, deliberately avoiding holograph items and memorabilia unless they literally come as a gift; and, on the strength of three years' residence in Western Europe, I consciously decided to attempt collecting as much of the non-English material as possible both in the original and in translation. When I began collecting Lawrence seriously in the early 1960s, the major collections known to me stressed English-language works almost exclusively, in one case being limited to works published in Britain. Most have broadened their scope in recent years. One item I am proud of is the 1940 edition of Nakano's book on Lawrence, an original work in Japanese. The 1941 edition of Léon Boussard's *Le Secret du Colonel Lawrence* is another.[9]

The higher prices caused by the boom of the past ten years also have their advantage. Scarcer items are now floating to the surface more often. As noted earlier, more copies of the Subscribers' Edition have come up for sale in 1975–1980 than in the ten years before. Three copies of *An Essay on Flecker* have been auctioned since 1977, while only one was auctioned between 1965 and 1977. Those eager to speculate devote less attention to the more ordinary titles and editions, in effect leaving these to the dedicated collectors. The number of collectors, however, has increased since the appearance of the Robert Bolt–David Lean film, making for greater competition and higher prices than in the pre-1962 period; my own involvement dates from this film. Besides high prices, the collector faces the tendency of some dealers to pigeonhole collectors in order to isolate them from one another; this prevents collectors from possible exchanges that would eliminate the dealer. One individual long interested in Lawrence material used to let it be known that he had numerous collectors for customers but carefully avoided letting any one of them know who the others were. Until very recently the major collectors seldom made contact with one another. With the advent of *T. E. Lawrence Studies*,[10] there was a move toward the breaking down of barriers between collectors and between collectors and researchers. Most of us became aware of others with the same interest for the first time through this publication. An essay collection such as the present volume also helps bring together many of those actively involved in collecting as well as in Lawrence research.

I learned long ago that the unattainable item eventually turns up if one is patient enough—and prepared to grab it when it does. Given the patience and investment of time spent in dusty bookstores, the alert collector will be rewarded in many small ways; good-willed friends are also an invaluable asset. My own copy of the 1940 Nakano was found for me by a Whittier College student on a trip to Japan. I had heard he was going and asked if he would watch for any Japanese-language works on Lawrence. He returned and with diffidence regretfully reported that he had only been able to find one small item. I wish I could repay him in some meaningful way for the single slim volume he delivered for the majestic sum of one dollar. Such finds are often more rewarding than the acquisition of an expensive cornerstone item.

So much for the basic problem of acquiring Lawrence materials. The second major problem is accurate bibliographic control, both descriptive and enumerative, of the canon and the myriad associated material. Some progress has been made in this direction, but not enough. Books and articles written by Lawrence present no classification problem, for they are automatically part of the canon, but no definitive listing yet exists. Under one heading in the bibliography would be the books written or translated by him or for which he wrote prefaces. Other bibliographical categories include his magazine and newspaper articles and ephemeral materials in leaflet and pamphlet form. The total list of his works is not long, but the enumeration of all the various editions and states, both English and American, to say nothing of the myriad translations of his works, soon becomes remarkably extensive.

Books in which he is treated or mentioned may be of value or not, depending on the parameters of the individual collection. But here again they are many and elusive, and a bibliography of them is needed badly. Also, there are many other associated materials, such as books from Lawrence's Clouds Hill library, holograph letters, photographs, memorabilia, and official or unofficial documents in which he had a part. Recent personal examples of the lack of bibliographic control of published Lawrence materials are the two French-language articles[11] that I found on the shelves of the Whittier College library, but of which I had no knowledge because they were listed in no bibliography until the recent publication of Maurice Larès's book.[12] This discovery of items unknown to me points up the problem of non-English-language Lawrence publications in general. Lawrence is now so widely published and translated that no one collection contains more than a small portion of all such works. The best, though not the sole, means of obtaining them is to haunt the antiquarian book shops in many countries, an almost impossible task. On the positive side, there is more serious interest in Lawrence than ever before; this, combined with the high prices rare items bring, means that these expensive items and, to some extent, the more moderately priced items increasingly in demand are less likely to be overlooked by collectors, researchers, and book dealers.

There seems to be no apparent limit to the number of materials relating to Lawrence. This is owing to the fact that he attained distinction in so many fields, to the film, to his friendships with so many people of all social levels, and to the attempts of those such as Aldington and, more recently, Desmond Stewart[13] to debunk Lawrence, and to the consequent counterefforts of his defenders. While trying to put the Lawrence legend to rest, Aldington and other detractors have only sparked interest in him among a wider public than might otherwise have been interested.

Books and articles about Lawrence fall into the following categories: biographies, full-length studies of specialized aspects of his career, juvenile biographies, journal and periodical articles, newspaper items, bibliographies, and prospectuses (printed statements advertising forthcoming works and collections for sale). I will analyze each of these categories in the course of this article.

In addition to the works of Aldington and Stewart, I count more than thirty full-length biographies and studies[14] plus more than fifteen juvenile biographies.[15] The recent upswing in academic and popular attention will lead to even more such publications. This is an impressive display of interest in a man who died only forty-five years ago. A gauge of his continued popularity can be found by comparing him to his American contemporary Charles Lindbergh, whose sudden fame, concern for privacy, and personal tragedy kept him in the public eye much like Lawrence. But the number of Lawrence biographies far exceeds the number of Lindbergh biographies. Perhaps the reason is that in spite of all the detailed information we have on Lawrence, we still seem to know less about him than we do about others.

Two of the English-language works difficult to obtain (though they are not really expensive) are Vyvyan Richards, *Portrait of T. E. Lawrence* (1936) and Erik Lönnroth, *Lawrence of Arabia*, translated from the Swedish. Lönnroth's slim volume is a perceptive analysis of Lawrence staying well within the limits of its subject. Richards tries to establish an intimacy with the workings of Lawrence's mind which cannot be sustained merely on the basis of their friendship, but his work is valuable as a memoir. Edward Robinson's *Lawrence the Rebel* is an unjustly neglected biography whose reputation was damaged by a sensationally publicized charge of dishonesty leveled against its author ("Lawrence manuscript sold to pay blackmailer," *Evening Standard*, 16 January 1937), who is accused of having sold Lawrence material loaned him by A. W. Lawrence.

The biographical and specialized studies in some cases contain bibliographical lists. They have been useful first sources for most Lawrence researchers in the absence of a much-needed comprehensive bibliography. But outside of Edmonds's work of 1935, which contains a fairly good bibliographical note considering its publication date, and the bibliography in Richards's second book (1939), we find few or no reasonable bibliographies in these works until the 1950s. Aldington's book contains a massive bibliographical section, and the other works of the decade also contain similar listings, if not as extensive. Roger Stéphane, in his *T. E. Lawrence* of 1960, provides a good, detailed listing; so does Jacques Benoist-Méchin. Later in the sixties, Suleiman Mousa made a smaller but significant contribution by adding some Arabic works. In the 1970s, Morsey and Larès made significant contributions to the non-English portion of the bibliography by adding German and French sources, respectively. The bibliographies in these two writers' works are excellent, but still fall far short of the complete bibliography that is needed.

Of all the Lawrence biographies, none are more elusive than the juvenile works. The cost of these books is relatively low, but the problems of location of copies and bibliographical control are difficult. How many collections boast a copy of Gorman, *With Lawrence to Damas-*

cus?[16] How many copies of Fritz Steuben's *Emir Dynamit* are extant?[17] These and items such as *American Boy Adventure Stories*,[18] which exists in two editions, are not easily located. Stookie Allen's *Men of Daring Deeds*[19] is yet another of these difficult finds, and I am convinced that there exist more "boy's adventure" books on Lawrence that are unknown to collectors and that reveal an important aspect of his contemporary (and later) fame. Before closing this section on monographs about Lawrence, I would call attention to two important tools for locating material, *Essay and General Literature Index* and *Dissertation Abstracts*, which identify items in collections and dissertations that cannot readily be located elsewhere.

Periodical and journal articles range from the worst pulp magazine sensationalism[20] to some of the most considered criticism of Lawrence and his work, such as H. S. Canby's excellent piece[21] and important academic essays. Although for most periodical articles, photocopies are possible, one has difficulty locating original copies. Dealers rarely want to spend time on periodical items, and back-issue dealers who will search for single issues are hard to find. They are understandably reluctant to seek out long lists of single issues for collectors, whose volume of business is too low to justify such an expenditure of time; and such dealers can expect little return business. With persistence, many if not most of the items can be obtained. The majority of the back-issue periodical dealers are located in large metropolitan areas and can be found in their respective local directories. Bibliographic control here is about the same as with monograph materials. In America, there has been a continuing effort to bring periodical materials into some order, but by no means can all articles on Lawrence be located through periodical indexes. *Arts and Humanities/Social Sciences Citation Index*, *Reader's Guide to Periodical Literature*, and *International Index to Periodicals* (now divided into *Social Sciences Index* and *Humanities Index*) are the most useful; *Art Index* provides coverage of those articles relating to portraits and drawings of Lawrence. The German *Internationale Bibliographie der Zeitschriftliteratur* is also useful.

In terms of descending order of availability and efforts at bibliographic control, newspaper articles comprise the bottom layer of printed materials. Outside the *New York Times Index*, the *London Times Index*, and a handful of others, we lack any means of ever approaching a complete listing of newspaper items about Lawrence. One's best hope in this respect comes in the form of Lawrence collections that contain clippings among their holdings. However, in my experience, collection listings of newspaper articles are redundant and incomplete at best. With the exception of Stanley and Rodelle Weintraub's *Evolution of a Revolt*,[22] little has been done to organize and make available newspaper sources on Lawrence, even though some of his earliest writing is to be found in this form. Items not identified in any of these indexes include a series of articles from the *Pasadena Star News* of 1931 based on interviews with Lawrence, and a single article that appeared in the *New York Sun* in 1913 describing a visit to Carchemish.[23]

In addition to these various print formats, there are nonprint vistas for the energetic collector. The film has sparked a minor industry of a variety of materials, which adds a new dimension to the many forms in which likenesses of Lawrence appear. We have also the many representations of him painted during his lifetime and after. Many are gathered in the fine *Portraits of T. E. Lawrence* by Charles Grosvenor.[24] The fortunate few can purchase the originals of some of the items listed there.[25] There are also bas-reliefs, busts, portraits, photos, cigarette cards, and prints galore. Today slides, recordings, documentary films, postcards, and video tapes must be added to this list.[26] Such items are not hard to obtain if one learns of them soon enough; they are also relatively inexpensive. Once they become unavailable through retail channels, however, they are very difficult to locate. As with printed material, there are inadequate listings of this sort of item.

Association items, ranging from a pocket knife Lawrence carried to books from his library, also interest collectors because they are one of a kind. In this category, the most difficult to obtain because they are the most expensive are the holograph items. Letters continue to bring high prices at auction, while manuscripts are virtually unobtainable. Groups of letters to or about him are also part of a few rich collections. Here the only value set is what the market will bear, since in recent years most of this kind of material has been auctioned. Subscription to catalogs of the major auction houses in England and America proves worthwhile for those able to compete, but here too there is no complete listing.

It should now be clear that Jack Paar's 1962 television show claim that he had read everything written on Lawrence must be considered quite an achievement, if not actually impossible to attain. Paar's boast brings us to the problem of how we can be sure what exists, much less to have read it all. As I have tried to show, one of the Lawrence collector's or researcher's maddening concerns is finding complete and accurate bibliographical information. Despite a dozen bibliographic efforts in the Lawrence field, a recent academic author[27] justly laments the difficulty of finding one really complete bibliography. The existing bibliographies will be examined in some detail in the final part of this essay in order to show what is lacking in them and what work must yet be done. Some of the general problems of compiling a Lawrence bibliography must be discussed first.

In spite of a prevalent feeling that there is some intuitive means of identifying a first edition, that there is a divining rod that can be pushed into the past of a book, the only certain way to identify a first edition is to consult an authority who has taken the time to examine the book in question. Lacking the guidance of such authorities—that is, bibliographers—the collector has a formidable task before him. If, however, the work has been done well, bibliographies often can tell one even more than one wants to know. How important is it that the plates in one state of the 1936 reprint of *The Wilderness of Zin*[28] precede the appendices? Perhaps not at all, except to the ardent collector, and to him or her it will be of considerable interest. Basically, though, when confronted with an unknown book or citation, the collector needs to know the following: author, title, publisher, place of publication, date, and the status of the volume in question within the canon as a whole. Usually these bits of information can easily be located, except for the last. Occasionally, however, one or more of them may be difficult to establish or, even worse, incorrectly given. Bibliographic ghosts—that is, citations for books that do not exist or citations that contain major errors, making identical books appear to be separate items—are among the world's most maddening errors. Some statements in bibliographies can be accepted only with caution. The term "edition" is far too often used interchangeably with "impression" and "issue."[29] There are cases of false statements in the publications themselves, for instance in Roseler, *Lawrence, Prince of Mecca*:[30] the "second edition" of this book is nothing more than the first issue with a canceled title page—simply a reissue of the original sheets and binding with a new title page glued to the stub left when the original title page was cut out. The apparent intention was to imply to the would-be purchaser that the book was so well received that the first edition was sold out and demand had caused a second impression to be printed. There are also a number of undated books. These tend to be cheaper reprints issued without dates because the sheets are intended to be sold over a period of years without advertising themselves as old stock. Edition bindings and marks of ownership are useful in dating some of these. In the absence of trustworthy bibliographic control, we have at the very least difficulty in identification of materials and in some rare cases even this becomes impossible. These problems are frequent obstacles for the serious researcher and a constant concern of the collector.

I have indicated that the Lawrence canon is fairly well established, and in most cases this information has been made available through general publication. Yet how many have seen or have access to the Viking edition of the suppressed chapter of *Seven Pillars of Wisdom* and are able to compare its text with that of the Oxford edition of *Seven Pillars*, *Oriental Assembly*, the current edition of *Seven Pillars*, or the recently privately printed text of the chapter?[31]

Aside from the ongoing bibliographic sources that reward examination as each issue appears (MLA *Bibliography*, *The Year's Work in English Studies*, *Annual Bibliography of English Studies*, and the aforementioned *Citation Index*, for example), there are many separate bibliographies on T. E. Lawrence. Unfortunately, only a small number of them are of much value. Some, because of omissions or errors, are to be used only with caution. Particularly noteworthy for their excellence are those compiled by Elizabeth Duval and J. M. Wilson. But there are many items not described even in these otherwise fine listings. Duval is hopelessly out of date, and our best chance is that Wilson will complete his projected work on the canon and then move on to describing the biographical and incidental materials. Failing the continuation of his work, it will remain for another serious and competent bibliographer to devote himself to Lawrence; much needs to be done. A brief summary of Lawrence bibliographies follows. Some are general volumes that are primarily short title checklists; others are full-dress descriptive bibliographies.

Elizabeth Duval's *T. E. Lawrence: A Bibliography* was long out of print, but it has been reissued recently.[32] The original edition is much sought after, and this work remains one of the most reliable volumes for the period it covers. It was published in 1938, and therefore is quite limited in chronological scope. In fact the *Times Literary Supplement* reviewer of 1938 regrets that Duval did not delay a short time and include the *Letters* and other works that appeared soon after the bibliography was published.[33] Except for this early cut-off date and some omissions such as the American copyright edition of the *Diary of 1911*,[34] there has been no single work to date that surpasses it.

Very unlike the detailed work of Duval is the much more up-to-date compilation by Meyers, *T. E. Lawrence: A Bibliography*.[35] Where Duval limited herself to Lawrence's own work, with only brief mention of other materials, Meyers attempts to be universal. He proposes to cover all relevant material by and about Lawrence in whatever form it may appear. In addition to the main work, a supplement has been published in the *Bulletin of Bibliography*.[36] Its major value is that it is as current as any listing of Lawrence material. But unfortunately, despite the title, this is merely a checklist. One glaring fault of this work is that for monograph material the names of the publishers are omitted, which makes accurate identification difficult. How this important category of information could have been left out is hard to imagine. A confusing list of symbols for varying types and evaluation of materials is employed. All the articles and studies of the author of the bibliography that are included in the work are designated as "significant works," which in a number of cases is less than accurate, while valuable studies by other authors sometimes fail to be so designated. Another problem is Meyers's alphabetical arrangement of Lawrence's works rather than a chronological listing separating the book, periodical, and other forms. Even those with considerable knowledge of the materials can find these defects quite frustrating despite their discovery of new information in this work. Although his checklist suffers from major defects, Meyers has contributed in *PMLA*[37] a very fine bibliographic essay on the composition of *Seven Pillars*, which in its thorough treatment of the subject is the best to date.

Unfortunately there is nothing, at least to the present, that improves upon the Duval and Meyers works by combining the detailed descriptive bibliographical treatment of Duval with the current broad scope of Meyers, and since 1938 the need for precise description has grown ever more acute. Most early bibliographic attempts are now sought primarily as collectors' items rather than as tools for the re-

searcher. Three early slim volumes testify to an almost immediate contemporary interest in the physical description of Lawrence's works.
These volumes are all limited in numbers issued and were produced
with an eye for quality of printing as well as utility.

The *Bibliophile's Almanack for 1928* contains an article on *Seven Pillars* by Herbert Read[38] which is a negative reaction to the popularity
of the book with some description of it. Read's article was followed
almost immediately by T. German-Reed's *Bibliographical Notes on T. E.
Lawrence's "Seven Pillars of Wisdom" and "Revolt in the Desert,"* a title
almost as long as the work is. This volume was originally issued in an
edition of 375 numbered copies and has been reprinted by Folcroft
Library Editions.[39] It contains nothing more than a bibliographic essay
on the two works mentioned in the title. There are errors, especially
concerning American editions. No indication is given, for instance,
of the limited American edition of *Revolt in the Desert*.[40] As early as
the work is, its information is generally accurate and useful. German-
Reed's was the single attempt at serious bibliographic treatment of
Lawrence's works until 1935, when Terence Armstrong, alias John
Gawsworth, alias G., published *Annotations on Some Minor Writings of
"T. E. Lawrence."*[41] Described by the author himself as "provisional,"
this volume misses some bets but still provides annotations and substantially accurate descriptions. It includes an interesting list of extracts from letters published in dealers' catalogs and newspapers. All
in all, the information found here is useful, if incomplete, and can be
a reliable starting point. The author in the prefatory note makes the
prescient comment that a future bibliographer will need access to private sources to complete his work.[42] This is still true nearly half a
century later.

In recent years a number of guides have appeared that treat both
the canon and books about Lawrence. They must all be used with
caution. The first of these, Guyla Houston's *Thomas Edward Lawrence
(1888–1935): A Checklist of Lawrenciana 1915–1965*[43] is the most accurately labeled of all these works. It does not attempt to be a descriptive bibliography, and as a checklist lacks many details outside of basic
imprint information. In this respect, however, it is much more useful
than Meyers. Its main fault, aside from typographical errors, is that no
apparent effort has been made to edit out quite obvious mistakes. Items
318 and 331, for example, are exact duplications of entries 319 and

332, a fact that careful examination of the works cited would have revealed. One must read Houston's list with awareness of the fact that the citations are simply gleanings of Lawrence entries from the *National Union Catalog*, *Cumulative Book Index*, and other published catalogs. This method provides a real service but also makes it easy to duplicate entries, as I have shown. The method of arrangement could have been profitably utilized by Meyers, dividing as it does both the canon and auxiliary materials into various subdivisions, including type of publication. In the main, Houston's work is useful and will repay attention if the user is aware that he cannot rely on the accuracy of each entry; it is especially rich in identification of foreign titles in translation.

T. E. Lawrence of Arabia: A Collector's Booklist by David Disbury[44] contains no bibliographic data; the contents are merely checklists. I have counted many errors. On page 1 alone, items 3 and 6 are identical to items 4 and 7, and the slightest check would have verified this fact. There are serious omissions, the most important being that no pagination for newspaper or magazine articles is included. In fact, the skeleton information given in this work tends to create confusion rather than the order intended by the author. As a listing that must be used with extreme caution, it is suitable only for the experienced Lawrencian who will be familiar with the details of the books being described.

The last of the separate attempts to date to provide a complete listing of works by and about Lawrence is Clements, *T. E. Lawrence: A Reader's Guide*.[45] This work offers the first attempt since Duval to give a descriptive bibliography including annotations. However, striking omissions mar it considerably. No mention is made of the American copyright editions of *Crusader Castles* or the *Diary of 1911*, which should have appeared as items 2 and 4 in the present arrangement. Their omission is even more noticeable, as the copyright edition of *An Essay on Flecker* is included.[46] Clements and Disbury might have benefited from collaboration. Disbury at least had most of the issues but none of Clements's description and annotation. In Clements, the information for those items that are covered is accurate and useful both in the full bibliographic citations and in the annotations. It would seem that Clements's work is based on an incomplete knowledge of the canon; it may reflect the contents of one collection. As such it is an inadequate guide for those needing to learn the extent of the canon.

The work of J. M. Wilson is, unfortunately, not yet completed, and appears in fragmentary form in two sources: "T. E. Lawrence: Notes for Collectors," in *Antiquarian Book Monthly Review*; and "Catalogue Raisonné of Books by, about, and relating to T. E. Lawrence," in *T. E. Lawrence Studies*.[47] While incomplete, Wilson's work is meticulous in detail and totally accurate. The work is the best to date in scope, arrangement, and detailed knowledge of the materials. He also has had access to virtually all of the material, in most cases in the copies that are essential to good bibliography. This should be the authoritative work when and if it is completed, needing only supplements from time to time for new materials that are published or come to light.

In addition to work on published material, there has also developed quite an industry in materials that add to the effect of bibliography but are technically unpublished. The most important of such materials are the dealers' prospectuses, catalogs, and lists. No attempt can be made here to provide a complete compilation of these. Herbert West in 1956 issued a list of a Lawrence collection he was offering for sale for $6,500. The collection included a Subscribers' Edition of *Seven Pillars* along with other scarce items. West's forty-page list is a catalog of some of the scarce items, but verification is needed for the claims made in the annotations. If nothing else, the list provides a reflection of the knowledge of one dealer who long dealt with Lawrence material.

James Hebden of Lymington, England, issued two catalogs (1971, 1973), both of which contain annotations by J. M. Wilson. Although directed to the collector, these annotations are contributions in their own right, containing much of use to researchers. Dawson's of Los Angeles, Roy Bleiweis of Los Angeles, Blackwell's of Oxford, and Maggs of London have all issued catalogs of Lawrence materials over the years.[48]

Other segments of bibliographic listings are those generated by collectors and researchers. These unpublished lists of various collections are cited from time to time, such as that of Theodora Duncan, acknowledged by Meyers in the prefatory note in his bibliography. Dr. Frank Baxter of the University of Southern California also compiled a checklist of his collection which is cited occasionally. This is the work of a man who knew his books and had read them intelligently. However, one serious error[49] is his identification of the "gift" edition of the

American *Revolt in the Desert*[50] as the first American impression. Also, many items are omitted. In addition to these lists, there is a series of mimeo lists generated by the Imperial War Museum, London, and numerous lists of other collections, such as the Herberger collection and J. M. Wilson's collection.

Given this far-from-complete description of attempts to enumerate and in some cases to describe the Lawrence canon and related works, what will be needed once the bibliographic record is complete? The following projects come to mind. An important measure of Lawrence's impact on his and later generations can be found in the literature of non-English-speaking societies. Some of the sanest, most balanced critical thinking on the Aldington-sparked controversy, for instance, can be found in the German reviews of Aldington.[51] Brémond[52] and Nakano, Morsey and Larès, like other non-English writers, deserve translation and evaluation. I have heard that Mao had a Chinese edition of *Seven Pillars*. If true, it would be interesting to know how it influenced his thought.[53] A collation of Lawrence's own texts would be productive, as would the publication of a more complete edition of his letters, which is now being considered. We need an active clearinghouse for Lawrence studies, along the lines of the Shaw, Emerson, and Whittier newsletters. This can be provided through *T. E. Lawrence Studies*, which began so well and deserves to be continued more regularly.

I am not qualified to expound the problems of textual transmission, but I am a bibliophile with a serious interest in T. E. Lawrence. As such, I feel a serious lack in the record that now exists—or rather, does not exist. Although there are few bibliographic vagaries or obstructions in the canon today, there remains a vast field of material treating Lawrence that must be enumerated and described. Future study of Lawrence will benefit greatly from the ongoing work of the bibliographer.

N·O·T·E·S

1. T. E. Lawrence, *Seven Pillars of Wisdom* (n.p.: privately printed, 1926).

2. T. German-Reed, *Bibliographical Notes on T. E. Lawrence's "Seven Pillars of Wisdom" and "Revolt in the Desert"* (London: Foyle, 1928), 2.

3. Herbert Read, "The Seven Pillars of Wisdom," in *The Bibliophile's Almanack for 1928* (London: Fleuron, 1928), 35.

4. T. E. Lawrence, *The Diary of T. E. Lawrence MCMXI* (n.p.: Corvinus Press, 1937).

5. [T. E. Lawrence], *Letters from T. E. Shaw to Bruce Rogers* (n.p.: privately printed, 1933); *More Letters from T. E. Shaw to Bruce Rogers* (n.p.: privately printed, 1936).

6. See Philip O'Brien, *T. E. Lawrence and Fine Printing* (Buffalo, N.Y.: Hillside Press, 1980).

7. *American Book Prices Current.*

8. [T. E. Lawrence], trans., *The Odyssey of Homer* (London: privately printed, 1932). Limited to 530 copies.

9. Yoshio Nakano, *Lawrence of Arabia* (Tokyo: Iwanami-Shinsho, 1940); Léon Boussard, *Le Secret du Colonel Lawrence* (Paris: Editions Mont-Louis, 1941).

10. *T. E. Lawrence Studies* 1 (1976). 5/75 West Hill, London SW15 2UL.

11. André Rousseux, "La Mystique de T. E. Lawrence," in *Littérature du Vingtième Siècle*, vol. 4 (Paris: Albin Michel, 1955), 53–62; André Rousseux, "La Fin de T. E. Lawrence ou Prométhée Embourbé," in *Littérature du Vingtième Siècle*, vol. 6 (Paris: Albin Michel, 1958), 234–43. These articles were first published under different titles in 1949 and 1955, respectively.

12. *T. E. Lawrence, la France et les Français* (Paris: Imprimerie Nationale, 1980). This appeared as a much longer dissertation in 1978.

13. *T. E. Lawrence* (London: Hamish Hamilton, 1977).

14. In order of date of publication through 1968; for 1969 on, see the bibliography that concludes this collection. Lowell Thomas, *With Lawrence in Arabia* (New York: Century, 1924); Robert Graves, *Lawrence and the Arabs* (London: Cape, 1927); B. H. Liddell Hart, *"T. E. Lawrence": In Arabia and After* (London: Cape, 1934); Edward Robinson, *Lawrence* (London: Oxford University Press, 1935); Charles Edmonds, *T. E. Lawrence* (London: Davies, 1935); Vyvyan Richards, *A Portrait of T. E. Lawrence* (London: Cape, 1936); Georg Sejersted, *Lawrence og Hans Arabere* (Oslo: Aschehoug, 1936); Vyvyan Richards, *T. E. Lawrence* (London: Duckworth, 1939); Yoshio Nakano, *Lawrence of Arabia* (Tokyo: Iwanami-Shinsho, 1940); Clair Sydney Smith, *The Golden Reign* (London: Cassell, 1940); Léon Boussard, *Le Secret du Colonel Lawrence* (Paris: Mont-Louis, 1941); Edward Robinson, *Lawrence the Rebel* (London: Lincolns-Praeger, 1946); Rolf Schröers, *T. E. Lawrence: Schicksal und Gestalt* (Bremerhaven: Dorn, 1949); Roger Stéphane [Roger Worms], *Portrait de l'Aventurier* (Paris: Le Sagittaire, 1950); Richard Aldington, *Lawrence of Arabia* (London: Collins, 1955); Flora Armitage, *The Desert and the Stars* (New York: Holt, 1955); Jean Beraud Villars, *T. E. Lawrence* (London: Sidgwick and Jackson, 1958); Erik Lönnroth, *Lawrence of Arabia* (London: Valentine, 1960); Roger Stéphane, *T. E. Lawrence* (Paris: Gallimard, 1960); Jacques Benoist-Méchin, *Lawrence d'Arabie* (Lausanne: Claire-Fontaine, 1961); Anthony Nutting, *Lawrence of Arabia* (London: Hollis and Carter, 1961); Robert Payne, *Lawrence of Arabia* (New York: Pyramid, 1962); Victoria Ocampo, *338171 T. E. (Lawrence of Arabia)* (London: Gollancz, 1963); Stanley Weintraub, *Private Shaw and Public Shaw* (New York: Braziller, 1963); Suleiman Mousa, *T. E. Lawrence: An Arab View* (London: Oxford University Press, 1966).

15. In order of date of publication: David Roseler, *Lawrence, Prince of Mecca* (Sydney: Cornstalk, 1927); Lowell Thomas, *Boys' Life of Colonel Lawrence* (New York: Century, 1927); R. H. Kiernan, *Lawrence of Arabia* (London: Harrap, 1935); Harry Irving Shumway, *Lawrence, the Arabian Knight* (Boston: Page, 1936); John Thomas, *Lawrence of Arabia* (London: Muller, 1953); John Kennett, *Prince Dynamite* (London: Blackie, 1958); Geoffrey Bond, *The Lawrence of Arabia Story* (London: Arco, 1960); James Cadell, *The Young Lawrence of Arabia* (New York: Roy, 1960); Alistair Mac-Lean, *Lawrence of Arabia* (New York: Random, 1962); James Barbary, *Lawrence and His Desert Raiders* (London: Parrish, 1965); Phillip Knightley, *Lawrence of Arabia* (London: Sidgwick and Jackson, 1976); August K. Stöger, *Wüste in Flammen* (Dusseldorf: Hoch, 1977); Paxton Davis, *Ned* (New York: Atheneum, 1978). See also nn. 16–19 below.

16. James Gorman, *With Lawrence to Damascus* (London: Oxford University Press, 1940).

17. Fritz Steuben, *Emir Dynamit* (Stuttgart: Kosmos, 1931).

18. Benge Atlee, "The Bridge at Tel-El-Dhebab," in *American Boy Adventure Stories* (Garden City, N.Y.: Doubleday, Doran, 1928; Dial, 1928).

19. Stookie Allen, *Men of Daring Deeds* (New York: Cupples and Leon, 1933).

20. Ray Lunt, "Lawrence of Arabia: Soldier of Fortune Who Became a Desert Legend," *Men* 9 (July 1960): 26–29, 43–44, 86–87.

21. Henry Seidel Canby, "The Last Great Puritan," *Saturday Review of Literature* 12 (28 September 1935): 3–4, 14.

22. T. E. Lawrence, *Evolution of a Revolt*, ed. Stanley and Rodelle Weintraub (University Park: Pennsylvania State University Press, 1968).

23. Henry T. Russell, four-part series on Lawrence in *Pasadena Star News* (1931); and Maynard Owen Williams, "Unearthing Greatest Hittite Inscription World Has Seen for Three Thousand Years," *New York Sun*, 21 September 1913.

24. Charles Grosvenor, *The Portraits of T. E. Lawrence* (Hillsdale, N.J.: Otterden, 1975).

25. In 1964 Lew David Feldman listed one of the Kennington busts for $1,750. See *Sixty Four* (New York: House of El Dieff), item 36. Barry Scott in his *Catalogue Nine* lists an original Kennington drawing for *Seven Pillars* at $3,000.

26. For instance, Jeremy M. Wilson, *T. E. Lawrence* (Oxford: Ashmolean Museum, 1976), which comprises a booklet with six slides.

27. Konrad Morsey, *T. E. Lawrence und der arabische Aufstand 1916/18* (Osnabrück: Biblio, 1976), 4.

28. C. Leonard Woolley and T. E. Lawrence, *The Wilderness of Zin* (London: Cape, 1936).

29. Edition: copies of books printed at any time (or times) from substantially the same setting of type and includes all the various impressions, issues, and states. Impression: all copies of an edition printed at any one time. Issue: all copies of that part of an edition that is identifiable as a consciously planned unit distinct from the basic form of the ideal copy.

30. David Roseler, *Lawrence, Prince of Mecca* (Sydney: Cornstalk, 1927).

31. T. E. Lawrence, *Cancelled First Chapter of "Seven Pillars of Wisdom" and Letters*

(New York: Viking, 1937); *Seven Pillars of Wisdom* (Oxford: privately printed, 1922); *Oriental Assembly*, ed. A. W. Lawrence (London: Williams and Norgate, 1939); *Seven Pillars of Wisdom* (London: Cape, 1965); *Suppressed Introductory Chapter* (Totnes, England: privately printed, 1977).

32. Elizabeth Duval, *T. E. Lawrence: A Bibliography* (New York: Arrow, 1938; reprint, New York: Haskell House, 1972).

33. "First Editions of T. E. Lawrence," *Times Literary Supplement* (24 December 1938), 820.

34. T. E. Lawrence, *The Diary of T. E. Lawrence* (Garden City, N.Y.: Doubleday, Doran, 1937).

35. Jeffrey Meyers, *T. E. Lawrence: A Bibliography* (New York: Garland, 1974). Substantially the same as his "T. E. Lawrence," *Bulletin of Bibliography* 29 (January–March, 1972): 25–36.

36. Jeffrey Meyers, "T. E. Lawrence: A Supplement," *Bulletin of Bibliography* 35 (April–June, 1978): 84–87.

37. Jeffrey Meyers, "The Revisions of *Seven Pillars of Wisdom*," *PMLA* 88 (October 1973): 1066–82.

38. See n. 3.

39. See n. 2 (reprint, Folcroft, Pa.: Folcroft, 1976).

40. T. E. Lawrence, *Revolt in the Desert* (New York: Doran, 1927). Large paper issue of 250 copies.

41. G. [Terence Armstrong], *Annotations on Some Minor Writings of "T. E. Lawrence"* (London: Eric Partridge, 1935). Limited to 500 numbered copies.

42. Ibid., vii.

43. Guyla Bond Houston, *Thomas Edward Lawrence (1888–1935): A Checklist of Lawrenciana 1915–1965* (Stillwater, Okla.: privately printed, 1967); supplements 1971, 1975, 1978.

44. David G. Disbury, *T. E. Lawrence of Arabia: A Collector's Booklist* (Thorpe Kea, Egham, Surrey: privately printed, 1972).

45. Frank Clements, *T. E. Lawrence: A Reader's Guide* (Newton Abbot, Devon.: David and Charles, 1972; American edition, Hamden, Conn.: Archon, 1973).

46. T. E. Lawrence, *Crusader Castles, The Diary of T. E. Lawrence, An Essay on Flecker* (Garden City, N.Y.: Doubleday, Doran, 1937).

47. Jeremy M. Wilson, "Notes for Collectors," *Antiquarian Book Monthly Review* 1 (April–May 1974): 1–4, 3–6; also *T. E. Lawrence Studies* 1 (Spring 1976): 44–53.

48. Dawson's Bookshop, Los Angeles, *T. E. Lawrence* (1972), listing 62 items; Roy Bleiweiss, Los Angeles, *List L: Lawrence of Arabia* (1975), 57 items; Blackwell's, Oxford, *A Collection of Books by T. E. Lawrence*, catalog 1018, 45 items; Maggs Bros., London, *Colonel Lawrence of Arabia* (1936), 14 lots of mainly MS. material (especially Robert Graves–T.E.L. items). These represent just a few of the catalogs containing Lawrence materials.

49. Frank Baxter, *An Annotated Checklist of a Collection of Writings by and about T. E. Lawrence* (Los Angeles: privately printed, 1968), 13.

50. T. E. Lawrence, *Revolt in the Desert* (New York: Doran, 1927). This edition is taller in format than the first American trade printing, is bound in brown buckram,

and has illustrated endpapers and extra text illustrations not present in the first American printing. It was issued as a later impression and priced at $5.00 as compared to the $3.00 price of the first American impression.

51. "Lawrence—Held oder Hochstapler?," *Der Tagespiegel* (9 January 1955), 6; Hans Bütow, "Lawrence von Arabien. Zu Richard Aldingtons kritischer Untersuchung," *Die Gegenwart* 10 (12 March 1955): 173–75; Peter Stadelmayer, "Die Aufzeichnungen von 352087 A/c Ross und die Enthüllungen des Richard Aldington," *Frankfurter Hefte* 10 (1955): 371–73; Roland Hill, "Arabiens 'Ungekrönter König'?" *Wort und Wahrheit* 10 (1955): 334–39; Paul Herre, "Der Fall T. E. Lawrence," *Historische Zeitschrift* 183 (1957): 636–38; Herbert Tauber, "Geheimnisse um T. E. Lawrence" *Der Monat* 7 (April 1955): 72–79.

52. Edouard Brémond, *Le Hédjaz dans la Guerre Mondiale* (Paris: Payot, 1931).

53. See n. 56 of Morsey's essay in this collection for an answer to this question.

The T. E. Lawrence Revival, 1969–1983: A Selected Bibliography

Bibliographies

Clements, Frank. *T. E. Lawrence: A Reader's Guide*. Newton Abbot: David and Charles, 1972.

———. *The Emergence of Arab Nationalism from the Nineteenth Century to 1921: A Bibliography*. London: Diploma Press, 1976.

Hebden, James [J. M. Wilson]. *James Hebden. Lawrence of Arabia: Books by, about, and relating to T. E. Lawrence, Together with a Selection of Interesting Background Material*. Lymington, Hants., 1971.

———. *James Hebden. Catalogue Two*. Lymington, Hants., 1973.

Houston, Guyla Bond. *T. E. Lawrence: A Checklist. First Supplement: Books about Lawrence*. Stillwater, Okla., 1970.

———. *T. E. Lawrence: A Checklist. Second Supplement: Articles about Lawrence*. Stillwater, Okla., 1975.

———. *T. E. Lawrence: A Checklist. Third Supplement*. Stillwater, Okla., 1978.

Meyers, Jeffrey. *T. E. Lawrence: A Bibliography*. New York: Garland, 1974.

———. "T. E. Lawrence: A Supplement." *Bulletin of Bibliography and Magazine Notes* 35 (April–June 1978): 84–87.

Wilson, J. M. "Notes for Collectors." *Antiquarian Book Monthly Review* 1 (April–May 1974): 1–4, 3–6.

———. *T. E. Lawrence: Books from the "London Reference Collection" of J. M. Wilson*. Oxford: Antiquarian Book Monthly Review, 1975.

———, ed. *T. E. Lawrence Studies* 1 (Spring 1976): 1–85.

———, ed. *T. E. Lawrence Studies Newsletter* 1, no. 1 (1981): 1–16.

Books and Dissertations on Lawrence

Allen, M. D. "The Medievalism of T. E. Lawrence ('of Arabia')." Ph.D. dissertation, Pennsylvania State University, 1983.

Benoist-Méchin, Jacques. *Lawrence d'Arabie, ou Le Rêve Fracassé*. Rev. Ed. Paris: Librarie Académique Perrin, 1979.

Boccazzi, Cino. *Lawrence d'Arabia: un avventuriero dell'assouto*. Milan: Rusconi, 1980.

Brent, Peter. *T. E. Lawrence*. London: Weidenfeld and Nicolson, 1975.

Friedman, John S. "The Challenge of Destiny: A Comparison of T. E. Lawrence's and André Malraux's Adventure Tales." Ph.D. dissertation, New York University, 1974.

Graves, Richard Perceval. *Lawrence of Arabia and His World*. London: Thames and Hudson, 1976.

Grosvenor, Charles. *The Portraits of T. E. Lawrence*. Hillsdale, N.J.: Otterden Press, 1975.

Knightley, Phillip, and Colin Simpson. *The Secret Lives of Lawrence of Arabia*. London: Nelson, 1969.

Larès, Maurice. *T. E. Lawrence, la France et les Français*. 2 vols. Doctorat d'etat dissertation, Sorbonne, 1976. Lille: University of Lille Reproduction Service, 1978.

———. *Lawrence d'Arabie et les Chateaux des Croises*. Paris: Asso. des Médiévists Anglicistes, 1980.

———. *T. E. Lawrence, la France et les Français*. Paris: Imprimerie Nationale, 1980.

Mack, John. *A Prince of Our Disorder: The Life of T. E. Lawrence*. London: Weidenfeld and Nicolson, 1976.

Marriot, Paul J. *Oxford's Legendary Son: The Young Lawrence of Arabia, 1888–1910*. Oxford: privately printed, 1977.

Meyers, Jeffrey. *The Wounded Spirit: A Study of "Seven Pillars of Wisdom."* London: Martin Brian and O'Keeffe, 1973.

Montgomery-Hyde, H. *Solitary in the Ranks: Lawrence of Arabia as Airman and Private Soldier*. London: Constable, 1977.

Morsey, Konrad. *T. E. Lawrence und der arabische Aufstand 1916/18*. Osnabrück: Biblio, 1976.

O'Brien, Philip. *T. E. Lawrence and Fine Printing*. Buffalo, N.Y.: Hillside Press, 1980.

O'Donnell, Thomas J. *The Confessions of T. E. Lawrence.* Athens: Ohio University Press, 1979.

Orgill, Douglas. *Lawrence.* New York: Ballantine, 1973.

Scheyer, Amram. *Lawrence: The Revolt in the Desert and Afterward* (in Hebrew). Tel Aviv: Workers' Library, 1972.

Stewart, Desmond. *T. E. Lawrence.* London: Hamish Hamilton, 1977.

Tabachnick, Stephen E. *T. E. Lawrence.* Boston: Twayne, 1978.

Umari, Subhi al. *Lawrence as I Knew Him* (in Arabic). Beirut: Dar Al Nahar, 1969.

Weintraub, Stanley, and Rodelle Weintraub. *Lawrence of Arabia: The Literary Impulse.* Baton Rouge: Louisiana State University Press, 1975.

Articles on Lawrence, and Articles, Books, and Dissertations Containing References to Lawrence

Adelson, Roger. *Mark Sykes: Portrait of an Amateur.* London: Cape, 1975.

Aldington, Richard. *A Passionate Prodigality: Letters to Alan Bird from Richard Aldington, 1949–1962.* Edited by Miriam Benkovitz. New York: New York Public Library, 1975.

Allen, Louis. "French Intellectuals and T. E. Lawrence." *Durham University Journal* 69 (December 1976): 52–66.

Anderegg, Michael. "Lawrence of Arabia: The Man, the Myth, the Movie." *Michigan Quarterly Review* 21 (Spring 1982): 281–300.

Asprey, Robert. *War in the Shadows: The Guerrilla in History.* London: Macdonald and Jane's, 1976.

Baker, Randall. *King Husain and the Kingdom of Hejaz.* Cambridge: Oleander Press, 1979.

Bidwell, Robin L. "Queries for Biographers of T. E. Lawrence." *Arabian Studies* 3 (1977): 13–28.

Bidwell, S. "A Military View of T. E. Lawrence." *Army Quarterly* 100 (1970): 71–73.

Braybrooke, Neville. "Charles de Foucauld y Lawrence de Arabie: Dos héroes del desierto," *Arbor* 306 (1971): 21–25.

Brent, Peter. *Far Arabia.* London: Weidenfeld and Nicolson, 1978.

Busch, Briton Cooper. *Britain, India, and the Arabs, 1914–1921.* Berkeley and Los Angeles: University of California Press, 1971.

Capellán, Angel. Review of J. Mack and D. Stewart biographies. *Arbor* 422 (February 1981): 89–95.

Carrington, C. E. "T. E. Lawrence." *Contemporary Review* 215 (1969): 281–87.

Clayton, Sir Gilbert. *Arabian Diary.* Edited by R. O. Collins. Berkeley and Los Angeles: University of California Press, 1969.

Clutterbuck, Richard. *Guerrillas and Terrorists.* London: Faber, 1977.

Dann, Uriel. "T. E. Lawrence in Amman, 1921." *Abr Nahrein* 13 (1972): 33–41.

———. "Lawrence 'of Arabia'—One More Appraisal." *Middle Eastern Studies* 15 (May 1979): 154–62.

Dawn, C. Ernest. *From Ottomanism to Arabism.* Urbana: University of Illinois Press, 1973.

Dilleman, L. "Shedding Some Light on Shady Aspects of the T. E. Lawrence Myth." *Revue Française d'Histoire du Outre Mer* 64 (1979), 225–31.

Foss, Michael. "Dangerous Guides: English Writers and the Desert." *The New Middle East* 9 (June 1969): 38–42.

Friedman, Isaiah. "The McMahon-Hussein Correspondence and the Question of Palestine." *Journal of Contemporary History* 5, no. 2 (1970): 83–122; 5, no. 4 (1970): 185–200.

Friedman, John S. "Lawrence of Arabia and Zionism." *Jewish Spectator* 40 (1975): 43–46.

Garnett, David. *Great Friends: Portraits of Seventeen Writers.* London: Macmillan, 1979.

Gilbert, Martin. *Winston S. Churchill: Volume IV, 1916–1922.* London: Heinemann, 1974.

———. *Winston S. Churchill: Volume V, 1922–1939.* London: Heinemann, 1976.

———. *Winston S. Churchill: Companion Volume IV.* 3 parts. London: Heinemann, 1978.

Greenlee, James. "Malraux, History, and Autobiography: *Seven Pillars of Wisdom* Revisited." *Malraux Miscellany* 7 (1975): 18–35.

———. *Malraux's Heroes and History.* DeKalb: Northern Illinois University Press, 1975.

Helbich, W. J. "Lawrence of Arabia." In R. Suhnel, and D. Riesner, eds. *Englische Dichter der Moderne.* Berlin: Schmidt, 1971. Pp. 373–84.

Hourani, Albert. Review of Maurice Larès' *T. E. Lawrence, la France et les Français*. *Times Literary Supplement*, 29 May 1981, 609.

Howard, Michael S. *Jonathan Cape, Publisher*. London: Cape, 1971.

Hull, Keith. "T. E. Lawrence's Perilous Parodies." *Texas Quarterly* 2 (Summer 1972): 56–61.

———. "Lawrence of *The Mint*, Ross of the RAF." *South Atlantic Quarterly* 74 (Summer 1975): 340–48.

———. "Creed, History, Prophets, and Geography in *Seven Pillars of Wisdom*." *Texas Quarterly* 18 (Autumn 1975): 15–28.

Kedourie, Elie. *The Chatham House Version*. London: Weidenfeld and Nicolson, 1970.

———. *In the Anglo-Arab Labyrinth: The McMahon-Husayn Correspondence and Its Interpretations, 1914–1939*. Cambridge: Cambridge University Press, 1976.

———. "The Surrender of Medina, January 1919." *Middle Eastern Studies* 13 (January 1977): 124–43.

———. "The Real T. E. Lawrence." *Commentary* 64 (July 1977): 49–56; (October 1977): 10–18.

King, Stephen H. "The British Successor States in the Post-War Middle East." Ph.D. dissertation, Claremont Graduate School, 1978.

Kirkbride, Alec. *An Awakening: The Arab Campaign, 1917–1918*. London: Tavistock, 1971.

Klieman, Aaron. *Foundations of British Policy in the Arab World: The Cairo Conference of 1921*. Baltimore: Johns Hopkins University Press, 1970.

Knight, G. Wilson. *Neglected Powers*. London: Routledge and Kegan Paul, 1971.

Knightley, Phillip. "Aldington's Enquiry Concerning T. E. Lawrence." *Texas Quarterly* 16 (Winter 1973): 98–105.

Lacoutre, Jean. *André Malraux*. London: A. Deutsch, 1975.

Larès, Maurice. "Le Colonel Lawrence, le Moyen-Orient et la France." *Le Guru* 3 (March 1977): 17–20.

———. "L'image de la France et des Français pour T. E. Lawrence." *Relations Internationales* 14 (1978): 159–70.

———. "Deux Anti-Colonialistes, T. E. Lawrence et H. St. J. B. Philby." *Le Guru* 4 (March 1978): 32–38.

———. "La Science et l'art Militaires de T. E. Lawrence." *Etudes de Litterature Étrangère et Comparée* 77 (1979): 143–55.

Lord, John. *Duty, Honor, Empire: The Life and Times of Colonel Richard Meinertzhagen*. New York: Random House, 1970.

Lug, Sieglinde. Review of John Mack's *A Prince of Our Disorder*. In *Journal of the American Oriental Society* 100, no. 1 (1980): 29–30.

Mack, John. "T. E. Lawrence: A Study in Heroism and Conflict." *American Journal of Psychiatry* 125 (February 1969): 1083–92; "Correspondence" (May 1969), 1604–9.

———. "Psychology and Historical Biography." *Journal of the American Psychoanalytic Association* 19 (January 1971): 143–79.

———. "T. E. Lawrence and the Uses of Psychology in the Biography of Historical Figures." In *Psychological Dimensions of Near Eastern Studies*, edited by Leon Brown and Norman Itkowitz. Princeton: Princeton University Press. Pp. 27–59.

———. "Lawrence and the Armenians." *Ararat* 21 (Summer 1980): 2–8.

MacNiven, I. A., and Harry T. Moore, eds. *Literary Lifelines: The Richard Aldington–Lawrence Durrell Correspondence*. New York: Viking, 1981.

Martin, B. K. "Ezra Pound and T. E. Lawrence." *Paideuma* 6 (Fall 1977): 167–73.

Merry, Bruce. "Thomas Hardy and T. E. Lawrence: Two English Sources for Beppe Fenoglio." *Romance Notes* 14 (1972): 230.

Meyers, Jeffrey. "E. M. Forster and T. E. Lawrence: A Friendship." *South Atlantic Quarterly* 69 (Spring 1970): 205–16.

———. "Nietzsche and T. E. Lawrence." *Midway* 40 (Summer 1970): 77–85.

———. Review of Knightley and Simpson's *The Secret Lives of Lawrence of Arabia*. *Commonweal* 93 (23 October 1970): 100–104.

———. "The Revisions of *Seven Pillars of Wisdom*." *PMLA* 88 (October 1973): 1066–82.

———. *A Fever at the Core: The Idealist in Politics*. London: London Magazine Editions, 1976.

———. Review of S. and R. Weintraub's *Lawrence of Arabia*. *Sewanee Review* 84 (Summer 1976): lxxxvii–xc.

———. Review of J. Mack's *A Prince of Our Disorder*. *Virginia Quarterly Review* 53 (Autumn 1976): 717–23.

———. "Xenophon and *Seven Pillars of Wisdom*." *Classical Journal* 72 (December–January 1976–77): 141–43.

————. *Homosexuality and Literature, 1890–1930*. London: Athlone Press, 1977.

————. Review of Richard Graves's *T. E. Lawrence and His World*. *Virginia Quarterly Review* 53 (Spring 1977): 50.

————. Review of E. Said's *Orientalism*. *Sewanee Review* 88 (Spring 1980): xlv–xlviii.

————. Review of H. Montgomery Hyde's *Solitary in the Ranks*. *Southern Review* 16 (Spring 1980): 505–8.

Monroe, Elizabeth. "The Round Table and the Middle Eastern Peace Settlement, 1917–1922." *Round Table* 60 (November 1970): 479–90.

————. *Philby of Arabia*. London: Faber and Faber, 1973.

————. *Britain's Moment in the Middle East, 1914–1971*. Baltimore: Johns Hopkins University Press, 1981.

Moorey, P. R. S. *Cemeteries of the First Millenium B.C. at Deve-Huyuk, near Charchemish, Salvaged by Lawrence, T. E., and Woolley, C. L., in 1913*. Oxford: British Archaeological Reports, 1981.

Mousa, Suleiman. "Lawrence et le Rêve arabe." *L'histoire* 39 (November 1981): 25–35.

Nasir, Sari J. *The Arabs and the English*. London: Longmans, 1976.

O'Donnell, Thomas J. "T. E. Lawrence and the Confessional Tradition: Either Angel or Beast." *Genre* 9 (1976): 135–51.

————. "The Confessions of T. E. Lawrence—Sadomasochistic Hero." *American Imago* 34, no. 2 (1978): 115–37.

Olson, Robert. Review of K. Morsey's *T. E. Lawrence und der arabische Aufstand*. *American Historical Review* 82, no. 5 (1977): 1302.

O'Reilly, Timothy. "From Concept to Fable: The Evolution of Frank Herbert's *Dune*." In *Critical Encounters*, ed. Dick Riley, New York: Ungar, 1978, pp. 41–55.

Parnell, Capt. Charles. "Lawrence of Arabia's Debt to Seapower." *United States Naval Institute Proceedings* 105 (August 1979): 75–83.

Payne, Robert. "On the Prose of T. E. Lawrence." *Prose* 4 (1972): 91–108.

Possin, Hans-Joachim. "T. E. Lawrence's *Seven Pillars of Wisdom*: A Reconsideration." *Mitteilungen der Technischen Universität Carolo-Wilhelmina zu Braunschweig* 14, nos. 1–2 (1979): 14–22.

Pritchett, V. S. *The Tale Bearers*. London: Chatto and Windus, 1980.

Rejwan, Nissim. "A Portrait of Elie Kedourie: The Debunker as a Student of Politics." *Forum* 35 (Spring/Summer 1979): 91–110.

Rutherford, Andrew. *The Literature of War: Five Studies in Heroic Virtue.* New York: Barnes and Noble, 1978.

Saccone, Eduardo. "La questione dell' *Un Partigiano Johnny.*" *Belfagor* 36 (30 September 1981): 569–91.

Said, Edward. *Orientalism.* New York: Pantheon, 1978.

Singh, Baljit, and Ko-Wang Mei. *Theory and Practice of Modern Guerrilla Warfare.* London: Asia, 1971.

Tabachnick, Stephen E. "Two 'Arabian' Romantics: Charles Doughty and T. E. Lawrence." *English Literature in Transition: 1880–1920* 16, no. 1 (1973): 11–25.

———. "The Two Veils of T. E. Lawrence." *Studies in the Twentieth Century* 16 (Fall 1975): 89–110.

———. "T. E. Lawrence and *Moby Dick.*" *Research Studies* 44 (March 1976): 1–12.

———. "The T. E. Lawrence Revival in English Studies." *Research Studies* 44 (September 1976): 190–98.

———. *Charles Doughty.* Boston: Twayne, 1981.

———. Review of T. O'Donnell's *Confessions of T. E. Lawrence. Clio* 11, no. 1 (1981): 106–7.

Tarver, Linda. "In Wisdom's House: T. E. Lawrence in the Near East." *Journal of Contemporary History* 13 (July 1978): 585–608.

Thesiger, Wilfred. *Desert, Marsh, and Mountain.* London: Collins, 1979.

Thomas, Lowell. "Letter to the Editor." *Michigan Quarterly Review* 21 (Spring 1982): 301–2.

Tibawi, A. L. *A Modern History of Syria, Including Lebanon and Palestine.* London: Macmillan, 1969.

———. *Arabic and Islamic Themes.* London: Luzac, 1976.

Tidrick, Kathryn. *Heart-Beguiling Araby.* Cambridge: Cambridge University Press, 1981.

Troeller, Gary. "Ibn Saud and Sherif Hussein: A Comparison in Importance in the Early Years of the First World War." *Historical Journal* 14 (September 1971): 627–33.

Weintraub, Stanley. Review of Knightley and Simpson's *The Secret Lives of Lawrence of Arabia. New York Times Book Review,* 22 March 1970, 8, 27.

———. Review of D. Stewart's *T. E. Lawrence* and Montgomery-Hyde's

Solitary in the Ranks. Times Literary Supplement, 13 January 1978, 29.

———, and Rodelle Weintraub. "Chapman's Homer." *Classical World* 67 (1973): 16–24.

Wilcox, D. A. "Lawrence of Arabia: Guerrilla Warrior." *Combat Illustrated* 4 (Summer 1979): 67–75.

Wilson, J. M. Introduction and Notes in T. E. Lawrence, *Minorities*. London: Cape, 1971.

———. Preface in T. E. Lawrence, *The Mint*. Harmondsworth: Penguin, 1978.

Winstone, H. V. F. *Captain Shakespear*. London: Cape, 1976.

———. *Gertrude Bell*. London: Cape, 1978.

———. *The Illicit Adventure*. London: Cape, 1982.

Woodcock, George. "Arabia Infelix." *Queen's Quarterly* 81 (Winter 1974): 605–10.

Zweig, Paul. *The Adventurer*. London: J. M. Dent, 1974.

Contributors

M. D. ALLEN has completed a doctoral dissertation on Lawrence's medievalism at Pennsylvania State University. He has contributed to the *Gissing Newsletter* and the *Dictionary of Literary Biography* and lives in London.

GIDEON GERA received a Ph.D. in the history of the modern Middle East at Tel Aviv University in 1979 and is currently a senior research associate in the Shiloah Center at the university.

CHARLES GROSVENOR works as a layout artist and designer in the animation industry in Hollywood. His 1974 B.A. honors thesis at Bates College was entitled "The Aesthetic T. E. Lawrence." He is the author of *The Portraits of T. E. Lawrence* and *The Fall of the Alamo*.

KEITH N. HULL is associate professor of English at the University of Wyoming, Laramie. He has published several essays on T. E. Lawrence and J. M. Synge and is coeditor of *Teaching Shakespeare*.

AARON KLIEMAN is associate professor and chairman of the Political Science Department at Tel Aviv University. He is the author of *Foundations of British Policy in the Arab World* and *Soviet Russia and the Middle East*.

MAURICE J.-M. LARÈS completed his thèse d'etat on Lawrence at the Sorbonne in 1976 after twelve years' work. *T. E. Lawrence, la France et les Français* was published in book form in 1980. He has been with the Centre National d'Enseignement par Correspondance from 1961 and is director of the Victor Lyon Foundation of the University of Paris.

JEFFREY MEYERS, professor of English at the University of Colorado at Boulder, is the author of sixteen books on modern literature, including four devoted in whole or part to T. E. Lawrence: *The Wounded Spirit*,

T. E. Lawrence: A Bibliography, *A Fever at the Core*, and *Homosexuality and Literature*.

KONRAD MORSEY received his Ph. D. in 1975 at the Westfälischen Wilhelms-Universität in Münster. His thesis is available in book form as *T. E. Lawrence und der arabische Aufstand 1916/18*. He lives and teaches in Münster.

PHILIP O'BRIEN is college librarian and cross-country coach at Whittier College, Los Angeles. He is an avid collector of T. E. Lawrence and children's books, and author of the mini-book *T. E. Lawrence and Fine Printing*.

THOMAS J. O'DONNELL, author of *The Confessions of T. E. Lawrence* and articles on confessional literature and contemporary poetry, is an associate professor of English at the University of Kansas, Lawrence.

STEPHEN E. TABACHNICK is an associate professor of English at the Ben-Gurion University of the Negev, Beersheva, Israel. He is the coauthor of *Harold Pinter* and author of *T. E. Lawrence and Charles Doughty*.

RODELLE WEINTRAUB, coeditor of *Evolution of a Revolt: Early Postwar Writings of T. E. Lawrence* and coauthor of *Lawrence of Arabia: The Literary Impulse*, is a communications consultant specializing in technical writing, which she taught at the university level for fourteen years. She has also edited, among other works, G. B. Shaw's *Captain Brassbound's Conversion*.

STANLEY WEINTRAUB is research professor and director of the Institute for the Arts and Humanistic Studies at the Pennsylvania State University. Of the thirty-three books he has written or edited, three concern T. E. Lawrence: *Private Shaw and Public Shaw*, and, with Rodelle Weintraub, *Evolution of a Revolt* and *Lawrence of Arabia: The Literary Impulse*.

Index

Détachement Français de Palestine/Syria, 225
Dickinson, Hillman, 199
Dinard, 220; TEL's view of, 221
Dinning, Captain H., 202 (n. 36)
Diocletian, Emperor, 119, 121
Disbury, David, 305; *T. E. Lawrence of Arabia: A Collector's Booklist*, 305
Dissertation Abstracts, 299
Djibouti, 6
Dobson, Frank, 160, 162
Dostoyevsky, Fyodor, 11; *The Brothers Karamazov*, 16, 71, 100, 137, 159; *The House of the Dead*, 125
Doubleday, Frank N., 98, 99
Doughty, Charles M., 10; *Travels in Arabia Deserta*, 10, 100, 101, 271; compared and contrasted with TEL, 65, 71, 100, 101, 114 (n. 10); *Dawn in Britain*, 101
Douglas Credit Scheme, 154
Druse, 59, 213
Duncan, Theodora, 306
Duschnes, Philip (TEL materials dealer), 295
Duval, Elizabeth, 302–3; *T. E. Lawrence: A Bibliography*, 302–3

East Africa (German colony), 4
Eastern Mediterranean Special Intelligence Bureau (British), 206, 215
Eden, Matthew, 288–90; *The Murder of Lawrence of Arabia* (TEL figure in), 288–90
Edmonds, Charles, 298
Egyptian Expeditionary Force (British), 214
Eichmann, Adolf, 236
Eliot, T. S.: and Bradley, 19, 20; compared to TEL, 20, 42, 113, 115–23 *passim*; and Aldington, 26; *The Waste Land*, 42, 112, 115, 119, 121
Emerson, Ralph Waldo, 307
EMSIB. *See* Eastern Mediterranean Special Intelligence Bureau
England, 8, 11, 55, 144, 229, 236, 253, 255, 273, 276, 289, 291; castles of, 142. *See also* Great Britain
Enver Pasha, 210
Epictetus: and *SP*, 91–92 (n. 9)
Essay and General Literature Index, 299

Fairbairn, Geoffrey, 199
Fakri Pasha, 60
Farnborough (R.A.F. School of

Photography), 129. *See also* TEL: in Royal Air Force
Farr, Dennis, 162, 177
Fedden, Robin, 57, 58
Feisal, Emir (son of Sherif Hussein), 2, 8, 9, 59, 109, 190, 191, 213, 234, 244, 248, 251, 261; expelled from Damascus, 3, 38, 232; made king of Iraq, 10, 249; character of, 12; TEL's lack of respect for, 12, 263; as character in *SP*, 14, 120; L. Thomas's image of, 24; main fighting son of Sherif Hussein, 32, 187; allegedly glorified in *SP*, 36; and C. Weizmann, 37; TEL's loyalty to, 39; best choice for British, 40; chivalry of, 60; as prophet of Arab Revolt, 108; A. John's portrait of, 163; under Allenby's command, 188; wants large attacks, 194; TEL's assessment of his position, 211–12; TEL secretly assesses support for, 214; at Versailles Conference, 229–30; made to try agreement with France, 230; TEL opposes British subsidies to, 231, 233; TEL praises, 232; defeated at Meissaloun, 232; and French view of his rule of Iraq, 233; TEL argues for versus Abdullah, 250; TEL bolsters courage of, 253; debts of, 262; abandons Arab nationalism, 264
Feldman, Lew David (TEL materials dealer), 309 (n. 25)
ffoulkes, Charles J., 54
Folcroft Library Editions, 304
Ford, Ford Madox, 125
Foreign Office, 209, 232, 247; sides with TEL against France and India Office, 8, 230, 251; chooses Hussein family, 39, 261; war documents of, 190, 197; M.E. moved from jurisdiction of, 233; sends TEL to conclude pact with Sherif Hussein, 253
Forster, E. M., 100, 133, 277; friendship with TEL, 4, 129; high opinion of TEL as writer, 33; criticism of *SP*, 96, 97; *Abinger Harvest*, 97; literary use of TEL figure, 281–82; *Maurice*, 282; "Dr. Woolacott," 282; "The Other Boat" (about TEL) in *The Life to Come*, 282
Foss, Michael, 195
Fougères, 141
Fourteen Points, 230
France, 275; French military detachments in Arab war, 2, 189, 196, 225; French